THE ARDEN SHAKESPEARE

THIRD SERIES

General Editors: Richard Proudfoot, Ann Thompson, David Scott Kastan
and H.R. Woudhuysen

A MIDSUMMER
NIGHT'S DREAM

THE ARDEN SHAKESPEARE

ALL'S WELL THAT ENDS WELL	edited by G.K. Hunter*
ANTONY AND CLEOPATRA	edited by John Wilders
AS YOU LIKE IT	edited by Juliet Dusinberre
THE COMEDY OF ERRORS	edited by Kent Cartwright
CORIOLANUS	edited by Peter Holland
CYMBELINE	edited by Valerie Wayne
DOUBLE FALSEHOOD	edited by Brean Hammond
HAMLET, Revised	edited by Ann Thompson and Neil Taylor
JULIUS CAESAR	edited by David Daniell
KING HENRY IV PART 1	edited by David Scott Kastan
KING HENRY IV PART 2	edited by James C. Bulman
KING HENRY V	edited by T.W. Craik
KING HENRY VI PART 1	edited by Edward Burns
KING HENRY VI PART 2	edited by Ronald Knowles
KING HENRY VI PART 3	edited by John D. Cox and Eric Rasmussen
KING HENRY VIII	edited by Gordon McMullan
KING JOHN	edited by E.A.J. Honigmann*
KING LEAR	edited by R.A. Foakes
KING RICHARD II	edited by Charles Forker
KING RICHARD III	edited by James R. Siemon
LOVE'S LABOUR'S LOST	edited by H.R. Woudhuysen
MACBETH	edited by Sandra Clark and Pamela Mason
MEASURE FOR MEASURE	edited by J.W. Lever*
THE MERCHANT OF VENICE	edited by John Drakakis
THE MERRY WIVES OF WINDSOR	edited by Giorgio Melchiori
A MIDSUMMER NIGHT'S DREAM	edited by Sukanta Chaudhuri
MUCH ADO ABOUT NOTHING, Revised	edited by Claire McEachern
OTHELLO, Revised	edited by E.A.J. Honigmann, with an Introduction by Ayanna Thompson
PERICLES	edited by Suzanne Gossett
ROMEO AND JULIET	edited by René Weis
SHAKESPEARE'S POEMS	edited by Katherine Duncan-Jones and H.R. Woudhuysen
SHAKESPEARE'S SONNETS, Revised	edited by Katherine Duncan-Jones
THE TAMING OF THE SHREW	edited by Barbara Hodgdon
THE TEMPEST, Revised	edited by Virginia Mason Vaughan and Alden T. Vaughan
TIMON OF ATHENS	edited by Anthony B. Dawson and Gretchen E. Minton
TITUS ANDRONICUS	edited by Jonathan Bate
TROILUS AND CRESSIDA, Revised	edited by David Bevington
TWELFTH NIGHT	edited by Keir Elam
THE TWO GENTLEMEN OF VERONA	edited by William C. Carroll
THE TWO NOBLE KINSMEN, Revised	edited by Lois Potter
THE WINTER'S TALE	edited by John Pitcher

* Second series

THE ARDEN SHAKESPEARE

A MIDSUMMER NIGHT'S DREAM

Edited by
SUKANTA CHAUDHURI

THE ARDEN SHAKESPEARE
LONDON · NEW YORK · OXFORD · NEW DELHI · SYDNEY

THE ARDEN SHAKESPEARE
Bloomsbury Publishing Plc
50 Bedford Square, London, WC1B 3DP, UK

BLOOMSBURY, THE ARDEN SHAKESPEARE and the Arden Shakespeare logo are
trademarks of Bloomsbury Publishing Plc

First published 2017
Reprinted 2018, 2019

The General Editors of the Arden Shakespeare have been
W.J. Craig and R.H. Case (first series 1899–1944)
Una Ellis-Fermor, Harold F. Brooks, Harold Jenkins and
Brian Morris (second series 1946–82)

Present General Editors (third series)
Richard Proudfoot, Ann Thompson, David Scott Kastan and H.R. Woudhuysen

Cover design by Adriana Brioso
Cover image © htu/Getty Images

A catalogue record for this book is available from the British Library.

ISBN: HB: 978-1-4081-3350-7
        PB: 978-1-4081-3349-1
        ePDF: 978-1-4081-4276-9
        eBook: 978-1-4081-4277-6

A catalog record for this book is available from the Library of Congress.

Series: Arden Shakespeare Third Series

Typeset by RefineCatch Limited, Bungay, Suffolk
Printed and bound in India

To find out more about our authors and books visit www.bloomsbury.com and
sign up for our newsletters.

The Editor

Sukanta Chaudhuri is Professor Emeritus at Jadavpur University, Kolkata. His publications include *Infirm Glory: Shakespeare and the Renaissance Image of Man* (Oxford, 1981), *Renaissance Pastoral and Its English Developments* (Oxford, 1989) and *The Metaphysics of Text* (Cambridge, 2010). He has edited the two-volume *Pastoral Poetry of the English Renaissance* (Manchester, 2016) besides other early modern texts and collections of essays. He was chief co-ordinator of Bichitra, the online variorum of the works of Rabindranath Tagore, and has translated widely from Bengali to English.

CONTENTS

LIST OF
ILLUSTRATIONS

GENERAL EDITORS' PREFACE

The earliest volume in the first Arden series, Edward Dowden's *Hamlet*, was published in 1899. Since then the Arden Shakespeare has been widely acknowledged as the pre-eminent Shakespeare edition, valued by scholars, students, actors and 'the great variety of readers' alike for its clearly presented and reliable texts, its full annotation and its richly informative introductions.

In the third Arden series we seek to maintain these well-established qualities and general characteristics, preserving our predecessors' commitment to presenting the play as it has been shaped in history. Each volume necessarily has its own particular emphasis which reflects the unique possibilities and problems posed by the work in question, and the series as a whole seeks to maintain the highest standards of scholarship, combined with attractive and accessible presentation.

Newly edited from the original documents, texts are presented in fully modernized form, with a textual apparatus that records all substantial divergences from those early printings. The notes and introductions focus on the conditions and possibilities of meaning that editors, critics and performers (onstage and screen) have discovered in the play. While building upon the rich history of scholarly activity that has long shaped our understanding of Shakespeare's works, this third series of the Arden Shakespeare is enlivened by a new generation's encounter with Shakespeare.

THE TEXT

On each page of the play itself, readers will find a passage of text supported by commentary and textual notes. Act and scene divisions (seldom present in the early editions and often the product of eighteenth-century or later scholarship) have been retained for ease of reference, but have been given less prominence than in previous series. Editorial indications of location of the action have been removed to the textual notes or commentary.

In the text itself, elided forms in the early texts are spelt out in full in verse lines wherever they indicate a usual late twentieth-century pronunciation that requires no special indication and wherever they occur in prose (except where they indicate non-standard pronunciation). In verse speeches, marks of elision are retained where they are necessary guides to the scansion and pronunciation of the line. Final -ed in past tense and participial forms of verbs is always printed as -ed, without accent, never as -'d, but wherever the required pronunciation diverges from modern usage a note in the commentary draws attention to the fact. Where the final -ed should be given syllabic value contrary to modern usage, e.g.

> Doth Silvia know that I am banished?
>
> *(TGV* 3.1.214)

the note will take the form

> 214 **banished** banishèd

Conventional lineation of divided verse lines shared by two or more speakers has been reconsidered and sometimes rearranged. Except for the familiar *Exit* and *Exeunt*, Latin forms in stage directions and speech prefixes have been translated into English and the original Latin forms recorded in the textual notes.

COMMENTARY AND TEXTUAL NOTES

Notes in the commentary, for which a major source will be the *Oxford English Dictionary*, offer glossarial and other explication of verbal difficulties; they may also include discussion of points of interpretation and, in relevant cases, substantial extracts from Shakespeare's source material. Editors will not usually offer glossarial notes for words adequately defined in the latest edition of *The Concise Oxford Dictionary* or *Merriam-Webster's Collegiate Dictionary*, but in cases of doubt they will include notes. Attention, however, will be drawn to places where more than one likely interpretation can be proposed and to significant verbal and syntactic complexity. Notes preceded by * discuss editorial emendations or variant readings.

Headnotes to acts or scenes discuss, where appropriate, questions of scene location, the play's treatment of source materials, and major difficulties of staging. The list of roles (so headed to emphasize the play's status as a text for performance) is also considered in the commentary notes. These may include comment on plausible patterns of casting with the resources of an Elizabethan or Jacobean acting company and also on any variation in the description of roles in their speech prefixes in the early editions.

The textual notes are designed to let readers know when the edited text diverges from the early edition(s) or manuscript sources on which it is based. Wherever this happens the note will record the rejected reading of the early edition(s) or manuscript, in original spelling, and the source of the reading adopted in this edition. Other forms from the early edition(s) or manuscript recorded in these notes will include some spellings of particular interest or significance and original forms of translated stage directions. Where two or more early editions are involved, for instance with *Othello*, the notes also record all important differences between them. The textual notes take a form that has been in use since the nineteenth century. This comprises, first: line reference, reading adopted in the text and closing square bracket; then: abbreviated reference, in italic, to the earliest edition to adopt the accepted reading, italic semicolon and noteworthy alternative reading(s), each with abbreviated italic reference to its source.

Conventions used in these textual notes include the following. The solidus / is used, in notes quoting verse or discussing verse lining, to indicate line endings. Distinctive spellings of the base text follow the square bracket without indication of source and are enclosed in italic brackets. Names enclosed in italic brackets indicate originators of conjectural emendations when these did not originate in an edition of the text, or when the named edition records a conjecture not accepted into its text. Stage directions (SDs) are referred to by the number of the line within or immediately after which they are placed. Line numbers with a decimal point relate to centred entry SDs not falling within a verse line and to SDs more than one line long, with the number after the point indicating the line within the SD: e.g. 78.4 refers to the fourth line of the SD following line 78. Lines of SDs at the start of a scene are numbered 0.1, 0.2, etc. Where only a line number precedes a square bracket, e.g. 128], the note relates to the whole line; where SD is added to the number, it relates to the whole of a SD within or immediately following the line. Speech prefixes (SPs) follow similar conventions, 203 SP] referring to the speaker's name for line 203. Where a SP reference takes the form, e.g. 38+ SP, it relates to all subsequent speeches assigned to that speaker in the scene in question.

Where, as with *King Henry V*, one of the early editions is a so-called 'bad quarto' (that is, a text either heavily adapted, or reconstructed from memory, or both), the divergences from the present edition are too great to be recorded in full in the notes. In these cases, with the exception of *Hamlet*, which prints an edited text of the Quarto of 1603, the editions will include a reduced photographic facsimile of the 'bad quarto' in an appendix.

INTRODUCTION

Both the introduction and the commentary are designed to present the plays as texts for performance, and make appropriate reference to stage, film and television versions, as well as introducing the reader to the range of critical approaches to the plays. They discuss the history of the reception of the texts within the theatre and scholarship and beyond, investigating the interdependency of the literary text and the surrounding 'cultural text' both at the time of the original production of Shakespeare's works and during their long and rich afterlife.

PREFACE

The challenges of editing *A Midsummer Night's Dream* are as much cultural as textual. The knotty textual issues are largely confined to a handful of cruces, though the broad agreement between the three versions of the play makes for few obvious points of vantage in tracing the genetics of the text and the printing history. The theatrical record, on the other hand, is exceptionally wide and varied. A selective survey of notable productions would not reflect this variety; it seemed necessary to present the full range of productions across the world, even if most of them could only find brief mention. The play's afterlife in music, film and opera as well as the visual arts also called for the kind of overview it has not received in any edition so far.

On a possible wedding-night performance, I have tried to be cautious but not totally dismissive. I have not disturbed the bones of old speculations buried from sight in the New Variorum edition, but I felt I should record a few suggestive historical pointers and the hints one might draw from the play's form and ambience. In the commentary, I have made full use of the *OED* to note the elusive nuances (often multiple nuances) of a great many words. I hope their combined impact brings out the consistently subtle texture of the dramatic verse. Other kinds of nuances also called for more attention than they commonly receive: a perceptible charge of sexuality in some passages, for instance, or side-glances at Shakespeare's contemporary theatre. Some special practices followed in the textual notes are explained at the end of this preface.

It is fitting, though superfluous, to state my debt to earlier editors; it is documented *in extenso* in the textual notes and commentary. I should make special mention of Harold Brooks's Second Arden edition. I have benefited not only from specific items in its exceptionally rich and wide-ranging introduction and commentary, but from the overall editorial model it

xvi

afforded. Its one major lacuna, the absence of any account of the play's theatrical history, I have tried to make good as indicated above. I am indebted no less to the host of critics and interpreters of the play. It was daunting, and sometimes exhausting, to find my way through the maze, but there was never a lack of rewarding insights to garner.

My other debts are innumerable. I am grateful to All Souls College, Oxford, for a year's visiting fellowship that offered intellectual stimulation and collegiate hospitality in equal measure. Thanks to the staff of the libraries and archives who attended so ungrudgingly to my needs, often beyond the call of duty: the Bodleian Library and English Faculty Library, Oxford; the Shakespeare Institute and the Shakespeare Centre, Stratford-upon-Avon; the Folger Shakespeare Library; the British Library; the Cambridge University Library; the Widener Library, Harvard; the Shakespeare's Globe archives; the Indian National Library; the Natya Shodh Sansthan, Kolkata; the Jadavpur University Library. Thanks also to the institutions and individuals who supplied the illustrations and granted permission to use them.

I owe so many debts to individual scholars and friends that I can only hope I have not left out any name, and apologize in advance if I have. I am grateful for the information, advice and practical help received from Nikhilesh Bhattacharya, Moinak Biswas, Robin Briggs, Colin Burrow, Helen Cooper, Amlan Das Gupta, Peter Holland, Lee Hyon-u, David Norbrook, Martin Procházka, Richard Proudfoot, Michaela Sidenberg, Subrata Sinha, Tiffany Stern, Paul Taylor, Martin West and Yong Li-Lan. Debapriya Basu provided a crucial first-level check of the text, commentary and citations. Thanks no less to the friends whose warm hospitality made several library visits possible: Francesca Orsini and Peter Kornicki; Shampa and Anil Srivastava; Kate and Bryan Ward-Perkins; Eliza Hilton and Pablo Mukherjee; Nandini Das and Gary Barnes; Susan Powell; Subha Mukherji.

Henry Woudhuysen, my General Editor, was an immense source of strength with his wise advice and awesome attention to detail. The edition is appreciably better for his care. I also owe a debt to Ann Thompson for her support and extensive advice at one stage of my work. With such mentors, I can blame no-one but myself for the errors and lacunae that might remain. Margaret Bartley oversaw the making of the edition with an admirable mixture of patience, tact and sagacity, with just a glint of steel from time to time. Emily Hockley and Susan Furber dealt expertly with the tricky task of acquiring the illustrations and, even more, the permissions, while Lydia Wanstall carried out the intricate copy-editing with the same assured skill. My thanks to them all.

My wife Supriya and my daughter Aparna offered informed support as sharers in the family trade, and my son Siddhartha no less vital aid with computers. They also bore with fortitude (or could it be thankfulness?) my prolonged withdrawals in spirit from our home in Kolkata to a wood near Athens.

The following practices in the textual notes supplement, though they never contravene, the series guidelines laid out in the General Editors' preface. An unascribed reading in a lemma (i.e. a reading adopted in the text) is from the control text Q1, with Q2 and F in substantive agreement unless indicated to the contrary. Elsewhere (usually for readings not adopted in the text), QF indicates the substantive agreement of Q1, Q2 and F; Q, the substantive agreement of Q1 and Q2. In all readings cited, the spelling, fount and punctuation follow the earliest occurrence; later variants are not recorded unless of special significance. The presence or absence of hyphens in compound words has not been noted. Where the source of a reading is a work other than an edition of the play, a page reference follows the siglum or short title. Earliest *OED* citations are noted unless clearly antedated by examples in the *Early English Books Online (TCP)* and *Lexicons of Early Modern English* databases.

Sukanta Chaudhuri

INTRODUCTION

When Wole Soyinka won the Nobel Prize in 1986, the citation described his play *A Dance of the Forests* as 'a kind of African "Midsummer Night's Dream", with dryads, ghosts, spirits, and gods or demi-gods'.[1] In fact, the two plays have little in common beyond a forest setting with supernatural creatures (of very different types). But the comparison is striking testimony to the classic, almost mythic status *A Midsummer Night's Dream* has acquired in world literature and drama.

The play has marked some telling points of history. It appears to have been acted at a makeshift theatre in the 'model' Nazi concentration camp at Terezin in today's Czechia. A twelve-year-old boy, Štěpán Pollak, recorded two scenes in drawings that survived though Štěpán died in Auschwitz in 1943.[2] In 1972, Peter Brook's production drew a half-hour's standing applause from the audience in totalitarian Hungary.[3] It was a moment's draught of liberty, smuggled in under the aesthetic cover of theatre. In 1990, violence-torn Lebanon saw a dance version in a cedar forest outside Beirut, sharply projecting the mortals as 'playthings for the djinn' of uncontrollable external forces (Caracalla, 10). And past enmities stood suspended when Vietnamese and American actors joined in a bilingual production in 2000, as shown in the documentary film *A Dream in Hanoi* (2002).

A Midsummer Night's Dream may be the Shakespeare play most widely circulated across the globe: not only in direct

1 Presentation speech by Lars Gyllensten (translated from Swedish): Nobel Prize website, http://www.nobelprize.org/nobel_prizes/literature/laureates/1986/presentation-speech.html, accessed 26 August 2016.
2 *Dream* was also acted by conscientious objectors in Dartmoor prison after the First World War, and by British prisoners of war in the German prison camp Rotenberg during the Second (Dobson, *Amateur*, 135, 142).
3 Schandl, 101–2. Brook reported that 'The best performances [of his production] lay between Budapest and Moscow' (*Foreign*, 11).

1 Sketch by Štěpán Pollak of a performance of *A Midsummer Night's Dream*
at Terezin ghetto

translations (of which other plays may have more) but in
cultural translation into many social contexts and theatrical
idioms. Its varied, segmented and open-ended structure has
made it richly meaningful for utterly different nations and
cultures. A particular adaptation might foreground one or other
component, or explore the interaction of two or more, according
to the myths, values and practices of the host culture. The plot
might be tilted in one or other direction for ideological or
simply theatrical reasons. *Dream* has equally enthused Western
and non-Western, dominant and subaltern cultures, across
nations and within them. Its productions and interpretations
have taken diverse, imaginative, sometimes bizarre forms.
Postmodern Shakespeare is a socially complex and multicultural
construction. *Dream* has amply met its demands.

Hence the stage history of *Dream* across the world might be
the best means of entry to its themes and structure. The assorted
productions and adaptations bring out the relations between the

groups of characters; the play's status as pastoral; its treatment of the fairy world and of classical history; and the way its plot reflects the wider politics of the theatre, in Shakespeare's day and our own. All these matters are discussed later in this Introduction. But the account must begin with the play as performed in its own time.

STAGE, SCREEN, ART

The play in its time: staging and casting

There is evidence to suggest that *Dream* was reasonably popular during and soon after the dramatist's lifetime, though there are no reports of the earliest performances. It was acted 'publickely' (Q1 title-page), first no doubt at London's earliest public playhouse, the Theatre, and then its successor the Globe; and in due course, by fair conjecture, to a more exclusive audience at the 'private' Blackfriars theatre, by Shakespeare's company the Lord Chamberlain's Men (later the King's Men).[1] There are at least three datable references to the play before the Civil War. The 'play of Robin goode-fellow' performed at court in January 1604[2] was probably the King's Men's Yuletide offering to their new patron from their lead dramatist's repertoire. There was a performance at Hampton Court on 17 October 1630, the only Shakespeare play in a repertoire of sixteen (Bentley, 1.27, 96, 129); and on 27 September 1631, a scandalous sabbath performance before the Bishop of Lincoln, for which the Bishop was censured and 'M[aste]r Wilson', the chief producer (who also played Bottom), put in the stocks wearing his ass's head.[3]

---

1 Grote (28–30) suggests it was first played at the Cross Keys Inn. The Lord Chamberlain had requested permission in October 1594 for his company to use the inn, but it is doubtful whether this was granted (Gurr, 'Letter', 64).
2 Letter from Dudley Carleton to John Chamberlain: Chambers, *Shakespeare*, 2.329.
3 It has sometimes been doubted whether this play is *Dream*: see *Allusion-Book*, 1.352–3n.; Wiggins, 3.302.

General references abound, chiefly to the play-within-the-play. There was an inspired stage convention of Thisbe dispatching herself with the scabbard of Pyramus' sword, mentioned in Edward Sharpham's 1607 play *The Fleer* (Act 2, sig. E1ᵛ).[1] The opening lines of Quince's prologue (5.1.108–10) were misquoted with suitably wrong punctuation in John Taylor's *Sir Gregory Nonsense* (1622; sig. A4ᵛ). Moonshine became a familiar figure, as in Ben Jonson's masque *News from the New World* (1620; 105–18), and more explicitly in John Gee's satire on Jesuits, *New Shreds of the Old Snare* (1624): 'the Comedie of *Piramus* and *Thisbe*, where one comes in with a Lanthorne and Acts *Mooneshine*' (20, sig. D3ᵛ).[2] Somewhat later (1673), Marvell cites Bottom's propensity to corner all roles: 'Had he Acted Pyramus he would have been Moon-shine too, and the Hole in the Wall' (*The Rehearsal Transpros'd: The Second Part*, Marvell, 1.224). Security in Nahum Tate's *Cuckold's-Haven* (1685) has also acted as the Lion, Wall and Moonshine, and repeats the doggerel from Bottom's 'audition' (1.2.27–34) with a few other lines (16, sig. C4ᵛ).

The play-within-the-play, in rehearsal and final performance, may offer clues to actual stage design and practice; but there are differences as well as affinities. As Stern (*Rehearsal*, 30) observes, following Holland, 'The mechanicals as a performing group are a fictional idea'. They resemble country players rather than a professional city troupe. It seems too much even to call them 'subprofessional', as Stern does, since they have never acted before (5.1.72–5); they are rank amateurs putting on a show in honour of their overlords.[3] There is little or no

---

1 For nineteenth-century parallels see *Allusion-Book*, 1.174.
2 For other seventeenth-century echoes and allusions see Halliwell-Phillipps, *Memoranda*, 9–11, 35–6.
3 See Stern, *Rehearsal*, 28–34; Pettitt. Greenfield ('Delight') suggests that a nobleman's tenants might have performed publicly at his behest from time to time, bridging the gap between amateur community efforts and professional companies. But Quince's crew has not advanced so far.

evidence of such performers acting classical themes. But Shakespeare seems to have liked the idea: witness the pageant of the Nine Worthies staged by assorted locals in *Love's Labour's Lost* 5.2.

Analogies between Quince's production and Elizabethan practice extend not only to the makeshift stage in a nobleman's hall, where the artisans played as the Chamberlain's Men would have done on tour (or at a wedding revel: see pp. 283–6), but to the formal public stage. This lends an extra piquancy to Quince's instructions: 'This green plot shall be our stage, this hawthorn brake our tiring-house' (3.1.3–4). His 'tiring-house' is a thicket represented by the actual tiring-house ('attiring-house' or dressing-room, the chief scene of backstage activities) at the Theatre or Globe. The stage representing a forest clearing reverts to being a stage by a double dose of imagination, like a boy actor playing a woman disguised as a man. Like the actual actors and their audience, Quince and his band move back and forth between illusion and reality without coming to rest in either. 'The best in this kind are but shadows' (5.1.210).

As in the public playhouses of Shakespeare's day, Quince's imagined 'stage' is an apron stage, extending outwards with the audience on three sides. That is where the artisans rehearse, and Bottom retreats into the 'hawthorn brake' representing the tiring-house, to re-emerge with his ass's head. Where does Robin wait when he eavesdrops on the scene? The early texts give no clue. He may be on the upper stage, looking down at the actors. Or he may lurk at the back of the stage, 'invisibly' spying on the action downstage as he and Oberon do in later scenes. The two stand 'close' (hidden) at 3.2.41 and 'aside' at 3.2.116 to observe the lovers, presumably advancing downstage to speak when the latter are absent or asleep. At the start of 4.1, in a stage direction in both Quarto (Q) and Folio (F), Oberon enters 'behind' (and unknown to) Titania, Bottom and the attendant fairies. This fairy play has surprisingly few pointers to the upper stage, considering how much use modern directors have made of it.[1] Perhaps that is where, at the Theatre or Globe, Robin disappeared to fetch the magic flower, or from where he confused the artisans in 3.1 or Demetrius and Lysander in 3.2. At the end of the play, the fairies no doubt went upstairs as they coursed through the house scattering their blessings.

The back of the stage served several major functions. Robin and a fairy enter through separate doors (2.1.0), as later do Oberon and Titania with their trains (2.1.59.1). These must have been doors at the back of the stage, probably leading out from the tiring-house as in Johannes De Witt's well-known 1596 drawing of the Swan Theatre. Bradley (29) brings out the controlling function of these doors, the entries and exits the 'systole and diastole' of the theatrical pulse. This interpretation may seem excessive, but the action of *Dream*, especially the lovers' musical chairs in 2.2 and 3.2, is channelled through the repeated entries and exits. Again, during the play-within-the-play, the courtly audience may have sat at the back of the stage, like privileged spectators in Elizabethan theatres (hence next to those actually watching *Dream* at the Theatre or the Globe). The actors in the play-within-the-play presumably performed on the projecting apron stage, oriented to the actual theatre audience rather than the court audience within the play. Needless to say, only that main stage would provide space enough for the final dance. The theatre audience would be involved at two levels: as real-life viewers outside the play's fiction, but also akin to the viewers within that fiction. Quince's audience mingled with Shakespeare's, each authenticating the other's role. By their very function as spectators, Shakespeare's audience would become part of the play.

Though scholars now dismiss the idea of an inner stage, the action of many plays calls for a recess or 'discovery space',

---

1   This suits Grote's theory (29) of a first performance using the limited facilities of the Cross Keys Inn; but there probably never was such a performance (see p. 3, n.1).

2 *Works of Shakespeare*, cd. Nicholas Rowe (1709), vol. 2: frontispiece to *A Midsummer Night's Dream*, reflecting eighteenth-century stage sets

occupied by sleeping characters among others. This may have been set within the tiring-house façade – that is, the wall backing the stage – or extended in front of it, with or without doors or a curtain; or the actual tiring-house doors might have been opened and the space behind them (perhaps faced with curtains) used for the purpose.[1] Titania's bower would be placed there, perhaps as a decorated couch or similar prop, like the two 'moss banks' belonging to the Admiral's Men (see 2.1.249n.). She may have lain asleep behind the curtain, to emerge on hearing Bottom sing and withdraw again in his company.[2] The two are seen again at the start of 4.1, presumably still within the 'bower', where Bottom remains after Oberon and Titania's reconciliation and departure (4.1.101), emerging only at 4.1.199. The continuous action in the wood from 2.1 to 4.1 can be aptly visualized as alternating between the main stage and an inner recess. The upper stage might have been used at times, though there is no clear hint of this.

Who first acted *Dream* on the Elizabethan stage? Will Kemp, the company's chief comic actor at the time, no doubt played Bottom. The abnormally thin John Sincklo would play Starveling (see 'List of Roles' 15n.). The other adult male roles can only be conjectured. John Heminges and Henry Condell, the future Folio editors, presumably took part, perhaps as Demetrius and Lysander. Richard Burbage, the predominantly tragic actor, would have suited Theseus. The modern practice of doubling Theseus with Oberon and Hippolyta with Titania is generally thought to be incompatible with Elizabethan stage convention.[3] And what of Shakespeare himself? If we credit the legend that he played minor elderly parts, Egeus seems the best fit, perhaps doubling as Quince.

---

1 See Gurr, *Stage*, 183, 185; Hosley, 'Discovery'.

2 This suits Beckerman's (78) view of beds being 'discovered' in later Globe plays.

3 Bradley (18–19) supports Ringler (120–1, 133) in this view, though Meagher (193–4, 200) and Smith ('Dream', 1) disagree, as does Booth (106–8) on aesthetic grounds.

The women, of course, were played by adolescent boys: Helena and Hermia – one tall, the other short; one blonde, the other brunette – presumably by the same contrasting pair that played Portia and Jessica in *The Merchant of Venice*, Rosalind and Celia in *As You Like It*, and Beatrice and Hero in *Much Ado about Nothing*. Were the fairies played by adult men or by boys? Ringler (133) thinks adult actors doubled as fairies and artisans. Bradley (19), too, finds the casting of adults as fairies 'amusing' but 'true', though King (83–4, 180–2) thinks child actors played the fairies exclusively in both Q and F versions. In modern productions, adults often act as fairies, as often doubling roles to do so (most commonly with the artisans). But in Elizabethan times, at least on the private stage, boys from the children's companies played fairies in Lyly's plays, which afford the closest formal precedents to *Dream*.[1] If Shakespeare had wanted an effect of 'bulky grotesquerie' (Ringler, 134), he would not have gone out of his way to stress the diminutive size of his fairies, flouting the general belief of the age. Regular child actors would be confined to their own companies, but a little later, in *The Merry Wives of Windsor*, Shakespeare shows a group of boys, untrained but able to sing and dance, being used precisely to act as fairies.[2] We even see how they are recruited and given a rudimentary training. The few words uttered by Cobweb, Peaseblossom, Mote and Mustardseed would not be beyond the powers of such casual child players. There would be no anomaly in an adult playing Robin: however agile, he is of a different hulking build, the 'lob of spirits' (2.1.16).

A tentative casting based on the above assumptions, with twelve adults and eight boys, is offered in Appendix 1, along with the names of some possible actors.

1   In Greene's *James IV* (written for the public stage), the description of fairies as 'puppits' (persons of small stature: Induction 13, 80) may indicate they were played by boys; cf. *puppet*, *Dream* 3.2.288.
2   The 2016 RSC production on tour had local children at each venue playing the fairies.

British productions: Restoration to nineteenth century

Even conjectures fail for the play's stage history after the Restoration of 1660. On 29 September 1662, Samuel Pepys found it 'the most insipid ridiculous play that ever I saw in my life', redeemed only by 'some good dancing and some handsome women' (Pepys, 3.208). This unflattering account may refer to a performance broadly adhering to Shakespeare's text. If so, there was no other such production till Lucia Vestris's in 1840. Prompt-books survive for two abortive attempts in the 1670s, an abridgement for the 'Nursery' or junior troupe of Thomas Killigrew's King's Company and a fuller one for Dublin's Smock Alley Theatre. But the authentic play virtually disappears from the stage for the next 150 years. Instead, separate strands of the plot, chiefly those relating to the artisans and the fairies, emerge as detached points of focus. The artisans provide the staple for stand-alone comic plays and 'drolls'. *The Merry Conceited Humours of Bottom the Weaver*, printed in 1661, was apparently acted by strolling players even in 1698 (*Allusion-Book*, 2.420). The comic portions of *Dream*, in original or adapted form, may also have been a common school entertainment, anticipating the play's later popularity in school productions. In Nahum Tate's *Cuckold's-Haven* (1685), Security played in *Pyramus* 'at School' (see p. 4), as Edmund Gayton 'acted *Pyramus* and *Thisbe*, the Lion and the Moon-shine' at home in 1662 (*Allusion-Book*, 2.127).

Richard Leveridge's *A Comic Masque of Pyramus and Thisbe* (1716) and John Frederick Lampe's *Pyramus and Thisbe: A Mock Opera* (1745) aimed at a more elite audience, with a large infusion of songs and music. Shakespeare's text of the play-within-the-play was more closely preserved as an entertainment embedded in Charles Johnson's *Love in a Forest*, a 1723 adaptation of *As You Like It*. But most high-end adaptations focused on the fairy world: exotic, fantastic, lending itself to music and spectacle. *Dream* was good material for 'English' opera mingling spoken dialogue with music, against the fully sung Italian model. (The contrast is discussed in Leveridge's and Lampe's plays.) A *Dream* 'transformed into an opera' was performed in Lincoln's Inn Fields sometime between 1682 and 1695 (Malone, 2.280). But it was *The Fairy Queen* (Queen's Theatre, London, 1692), with Henry Purcell as composer, that firmly established *Dream* as material for opera.[1] Music and spectacle were the twin props of the production, which drastically reduced Shakespeare's text. Hippolyta disappeared altogether, and *Pyramus and Thisbe* was presented only in rehearsal. There were sumptuous spectacles to compensate: magic landscapes, a 'Masque of Night' (replacing Titania's lullaby), and a final *chinoiserie* with Chinese lovers and an antimasque of monkeys. Purcell's music embellished these additions rather than Shakespeare's text. Moreover, the music was soon lost, to be recovered only in 1900 and performed in 1946.

Even in adaptation, *Dream* seldom reached the eighteenth-century stage, except in three ventures by David Garrick at Drury Lane, London. Despite its title, *The Fairies* (1755) gives the lovers more space than usual, allotting them fourteen of its twenty-eight songs, set by Handel's pupil John Christopher Smith. What disappears are the workmen: Titania's love is briefly dismissed, and *Pyramus and Thisbe* omitted. (It is probably a coincidence that Charles and Mary Lamb's *Tales from Shakespeare* (1807) similarly neglects the artisans.) *The Fairies* was revised for a single disastrous night in 1763 as a pronouncedly courtly play ending with a grand musical procession. To salvage something from the failure, Garrick's associate George Colman the Elder devised a two-act afterpiece, *A Fairy Tale*, with music by Michael Arne. Music and spectacle

---

1   The libretto is variously attributed to Elkanah Settle, John Dryden and Thomas Betterton.

combined in Frederick Reynolds's production for John Kemble (Theatre Royal, London, 1816), with still less of Shakespeare's text. It improbably voiced a patriotic and colonial discourse, with a final triumphal procession where Theseus' conquests stood for Britain's. Hazlitt's comment was devastating: 'The spirit was evaporated, the genius was fled; but the spectacle was fine.'[1] A modified version supplied the first American production of *Dream* in 1826.

Soon after, the play's identity was redefined in musical terms by Felix Mendelssohn. In 1826, when only seventeen, Mendelssohn composed a free-standing concert overture (Opus 21) inspired by *Dream* (which he had seen in Berlin and read in A.W. Schlegel's translation). It was first used onstage by Alfred Bunn (London, 1833), and merged with the suite of incidental music (Opus 61) commissioned from Mendelssohn for Ludwig Tieck's 1843 production at Potsdam, including the famous Wedding March preceding Act 5. Mendelssohn's music remained almost obligatory in productions for over a century, though continually adapted and rearranged. (Gooch and Thatcher list 241 adaptations.) The afterlife of *Dream* owes almost as much to Mendelssohn as to Shakespeare, shaped by Romantic concepts of nature, the supernatural and the imagination. The 'true Shakespearian wood', remarks Angela Carter (46–7), is not 'the wood of Shakespeare's time' but 'Mendelssohn's wood'. Even the music that supplanted Mendelssohn was often reacting to him or somehow taking him on board, as in Max Reinhardt's and Michael Hoffman's films. Brook's stage production relocated the Wedding March ironically as the fairies carried Bottom to Titania's bower.

Lucia Vestris's production of 1840 (Theatre Royal, London) contained many innovations. It was conventional in staging and music, but substantially restored Shakespeare's text. The songs all belonged to the original play, but Vestris added a sufficiency

1   *The Examiner*, 21 January 1816 (Griffiths, 18).

of dance, and mechanical and scenic effects including a diorama. The diorama became almost a requisite for such spectacular productions, being used by Samuel Phelps (Sadler's Wells, 1853) and Charles Kean (Princess's Theatre, London, 1856). Phelps, and still more Kean, also made a fetish of classical decor and costume, setting the play in Periclean Athens, long after Theseus' time. But Kean cut Shakespeare's text drastically while Phelps preserved it, above all for Bottom whom Phelps famously played. Both provided elaborate music and spectacle: Kean's finale featured ninety fairies. (Vestris had fifty-five,

3 Playbill: 1870 production at Queen's Theatre, with John Ryder as director and Samuel Phelps as Bottom

4 Bijou Fernandez as Robin: Daly's Theatre, New York, 31 January 1888

Phelps forty-two.) But the most striking novelty of this period was Vestris playing Oberon. Female Oberons became customary through the nineteenth century, like female Robins, introduced by Kemble in 1816. In fact, Harley Granville-Barker in 1914 first cast an adult male as Robin. Casting Robin as a woman, and still more as a child (like the young Ellen Terry in Kean's production, or the Mowgli-like figure in Reinhardt's film), makes him a sentimentalized fairy-tale character rather than a homely rustic presence. The shift to male actors gives more body to the role – perhaps malicious, perhaps philosophic as in Hoffman's film. Alternatively, new meanings can be drawn today from the ambiguous figure of a female Robin, all the way down to the RSC and Folger productions of 2016.

Edward Saker (Liverpool, 1880) enhanced the musical element further, and set up the popular practice of having children as fairies, anticipated by Garrick and by Charles Calvert in Manchester in 1865. In this he was followed by Frank Robert Benson and subsequent Stratford productions influenced by him. Music and spectacle remained major elements in Benson's productions as in Herbert Beerbohm Tree's; the latter brought live rabbits and mechanical songbirds into a lavishly recreated wood (Her Majesty's Theatre, London, 1900, 1911). A genuine tradition of open-air Shakespeare performance had meanwhile been started in 1886 by Ben Greet, with *Dream*, expectedly, a mainstay of the repertoire. In 1932, an open-air theatre was founded in Regent's Park, London, with Quince's words for a motto: 'This green plot shall be our stage' (3.1.3–4). *Dream* was again a favourite. The 1946 production provided the first full televised broadcast of the play. On quite another plane, *Dream* became a staple of school Shakespeare productions. Obvious reasons include the large cast (with small children to serve as fairies), the scope for music and dance, and the modern view of fairies as juvenile fare.

Many of these productions moved away from Shakespeare's text, but they help us to understand it. They show how its strands can be variously extended or reduced to yield very different renderings, perhaps drastically altering the lines of the original play. We also see how *Dream* acquires a strongly musical identity, in harmony with its poetic texture. Shakespeare holds all these elements in suspension, as I will indicate in my later critical account. Producers choose those components that accord with their purpose.

British productions: the twentieth century and after

A new direction in Shakespeare production, of *Dream* (Savoy Theatre, London, 1914) as of other plays, was afforded by Granville-Barker. He dispensed with spectacle, and the proscenium stage that accommodated it. Instead, he restored the general form and effect of Shakespeare's apron stage, though not its precise design or bare sets. The woodland setting, like most of the other scenes, was created entirely through draperies. Mendelssohn was replaced by English folk music scored by Cecil Sharp, and the dances were based on English folk dances. Somewhat contrarily, the fairies (mostly adult actors) were painted gold and moved slowly and artificially. Granville-Barker's approach invited controversy; but in the last analysis, he was a traditionalist, breaking with the conventions of his time to reinstate what he saw as the true Shakespearean dramaturgy. Above all, he was intent on restoring Shakespeare's verse. His cuts were trifling, his sole addition the opening song from *The Two Noble Kinsmen*, now made the fairies' song at the close. 'Poetry, poetry: everything to serve and nothing to compete with it!' he wrote later with reference to *Dream* (1924: 115). This contrasts with the purpose of many later directors for whom Shakespeare's text is merely the starting-point for their own exploration of the play.

A certain 'cultural fatigue' (Williams, *Revels*, 195) touches the productions of the next few decades, with qualified returns to Victorian lyricism and spectacle alongside new attempts at an Elizabethan flavour. The scholar Nevill Coghill (Haymarket,

5 Oberon (Dennis Neilson-Terry) and Titania (Christine Silver) in Granville-Barker's production, Savoy Theatre, 1914

London, 1945) sought a new authenticity through sets and costumes adapted from Inigo Jones's Jacobean designs for fairy spectacles. This mildly anticipated Peter Hall's setting (Stratford, 1959)[1] of an Elizabethan wedding play in the great hall of a country house. The fairies wore Elizabethan masquing costumes. Titania was costumed like Elizabeth, as again in Hall's last production at the Rose Theatre, Kingston-upon-Thames (2010), where the Queen implicitly *played* Titania. But in between, in Hall's 1968 film of the play, the fairies had been wild, near-naked creatures in a primitive, sinister wood. The

1 There were notably different versions at Stratford (1962) and the Aldwych Theatre, London (1963).

6 Titania (Judi Dench) with Bottom (Paul Rogers) in Peter Hall's film, 1968

subsidiary fairies were bedraggled child actors; the artisans authentic, almost contemporary rustics. They contrasted with the sedate courtly milieu of an actual Warwickshire country house. It was a notable blending of the traditional with the innovative.

Soon after, a new production revolutionized the play's staging and indeed its interpretation. Peter Brook (Stratford, 1970) repeated or extended earlier innovations, doubling not only Theseus/Oberon and Hippolyta/Titania – following the Shakespearewrights (New York, 1956) and Hancock (San Francisco, 1966) – but Robin/Philostrate. Richard Peaselee's music worked Mendelssohn into the score alongside the actors'

7 Titania (Judi Dench) with Bottom (Oliver Chris) in Peter Hall's production
   for the Rose Theatre, Kingston-upon-Thames, 2010

extempore efforts triggered by Brook (Brook, *Acting*, 70). But
the biggest innovation was Sally Jacobs's set: an undefined
white-walled space with ladders, trapezes and catwalks that
reflected colour and freed actors' movements. Titania's bower
was a huge suspended coloured feather. The set virtually called
for acrobatics: Brook drew inspiration from Chinese acrobats,
and rehearsals began with gymnastics and 'circus tricks'
(Brook, *Threads*, 149). This was one of many means whereby
he unleashed the sheer theatrical energy of the play, which he
saw as 'a celebration of the theme of theatre' (*Acting*, 24). He
succeeded in projecting this theatricality not as artifice but as
spontaneous expression. Hence his production inspired a host
of later directors. Few of them escaped Brook's influence, if
only to react against it or to adopt his dramaturgy to very
different ends, replacing his unifying theatrical spirit with
deliberate violence and disharmony. The outstanding instance

8 Titania (Sara Kestelman), Bottom (David Waller) and fairies in Peter
Brook's production for the Royal Shakespeare Company, 1970

of the latter trend was Robert Lepage's so-called 'Mudsummer'
(Olivier Theatre, London, 1992) played around a slushy pool,
with a blind Theseus, Indian Hippolyta, black Oberon, white
Titania, a very American Bottom and a female contortionist
playing Robin. Lepage targeted the ruptures and dissonances in
Dream, dispelling Shakespeare's iconic aura and the play's
own romantic mystique, while also rejecting the alternative
theatrical model set up by Brook. Hodgdon ('Looking')
suggests this may account for the largely adverse reviews of a
production whose power the critics could not deny.

Nor could the British theatrical establishment travel down
this road. Stratford directors after Brook, from John Barton
(1977) to Erica Whyman (2016), have wisely refrained from
emulating him. Bill Bryden (National Theatre, London, 1982)
presented the fairies as hoary creatures from an older world,
more benevolent than usual, working hard to correct the

9 Lysander (Rupert Graves), Demetrius (Simon Coates), Hermia (Indra Ové) and Helena (Rudi Davies) in the forest: Robert Lepage's production, Olivier Theatre, London, National Theatre Company, 1992

disorder arising from their quarrel. Adrian Noble's Stratford production (1994) also generated a film. Noble's stage production doubled not only Theseus/Oberon, Hippolyta/Titania and Philostrate/Robin, but the artisans and fairies *en masse* – a dramaturgic *tour de force*, remarkably integrating the three worlds of the play.

All these doublings and more appeared the same year in Barry Rutter's Northern Broadsides production. Here the fairy choreography adapted the morris dance, linking up with folk tradition and realistic workmen. Shortly after, Shakespeare's plays returned to their first home on London's Bankside at the new Globe Theatre. Its 'Prologue Season' featured Rutter's *Dream* in a new guise, with casual contemporary costumes in the first half only. Since then there have been seven *Dream*s at the Globe, including a Korean version (see p. 36). In Mike Alfreds's production (2002), other characters became fairies simply by turning on lights sewn into their costumes. But multi-casting reached its arithmetical limit in the Globe on Tour productions of 2009 and 2010, where each actor played two if not three roles. Some artisans were women, like all except Bottom in Emma Rice's 2016 production, where they were workers at the Globe itself. Rice also doubled Robin with Egeus, inserted much new dialogue and song and, most controversially, turned Helena into a man.

Both Rutter's and Noble's productions were lauded for the attention paid to the verse (Holland, *English*, 185, 189), replacing an earlier trend (most criticized in Lepage) of underplaying or virtually resisting the substance of the text. The compulsions of the text are obviously less binding on narrative or mythic appropriations that adopt only the play's general structure, perhaps in another language. Like all true classics, Shakespeare's plays operate not only in their original form and cultural context (which also change with time) but as versatile myths, the substance of endless cultural compounds. They diverge from their core textual identity to activate this greater potential. This is spectacularly true of a handful of plays including *Dream*.

Europe

The stage history of *Dream* goes back centuries in Europe, America and even India. Germany has the longest and most intensive engagement with Shakespeare of all Europe, with *Dream* occupying a special place. The history starts with a *Thisbe and Pyramus* acted by touring English players as early as 1604 (Wiggins, no. 1249). The popularity of such plays culminated in the 'Absurda Comica' of *Peter Squentz* (printed 1658, probably composed *c.*1648) by Andreas Greif (Gryphius). Powell (Gryphius, xliii) cites Dutch as well as German performances with local modifications of the name 'Bully Bottom'. The full Shakespearean play was performed at the theatre of the Weimar Republic while Goethe was in charge; a sketch survives of his plan for the stage sets. A Berlin production triggered Mendelssohn's enduring engagement with the play (see p. 12). *Dream* was the first effort of both the early translators, Christoph Wieland and A.W. Schlegel. Ludwig Tieck used it to develop his theory of Shakespeare's dramatic illusion. No less than Mendelssohn, Tieck was attached to the play from boyhood, and at sixteen produced *The Summer Night* (*Die Sommernacht*), a fairy story dreamt by the boy Shakespeare, lost in the woods. In 1843, Tieck produced *Dream* at Potsdam and then Berlin in a vague recreation of Elizabethan stage design, though modified by painted scenery, elaborate dance and spectacle, with the first use of Mendelssohn's full suite of music for the play. All this ensured a run of 169 shows in Germany and Austria.

This was the tradition that Max Reinhardt challenged in a thirty-year tryst with *Dream*, started at Berlin in 1905 with Schlegel's translation. Robin was still a woman, the music Mendelssohn, but Shakespeare's play had emerged from beneath the overlay of stage tradition. The first sets achieved a new lightness of fantasy. They altered variously as the production moved across many venues on two continents. The last avatar, played in the Hollywood Bowl before audiences of 15,000, ended in a grand spectacle complete with torchlight procession. This paved the way for Reinhardt and William Dieterle's star-cast film of *Dream* (1935), the second talkie of a Shakespeare play. Shakespeare and Mendelssohn were worked into the fabric of a Hollywood extravaganza, using cinematic resources to create a new level of fantasy and spectacle. Chaplin reportedly considered a role (Gehring, 124), one might guess as Bottom or Robin. Angela Carter's novel *Wise Children* evokes the phantasmagoria of Reinhardt's Hollywood *Dream*.

A different reaction to earlier German stage tradition marked Otto Falckenberg's three increasingly sombre productions in Munich between 1920 and 1940. Here Schlegel gave way to a later translation by Rudolf Schröder, and Mendelssohn to Carl

10 Oberon (Victor Jory) and Titania (Anita Louise) with fairies and the
Indian boy in Max Reinhardt and William Dieterle's film, 1935

Orff. (For different reasons, the Jewish Mendelssohn's work
was suppressed during Nazi rule.) Notable too was Heinrich
George's open-air production (Friedrichshagen, 1937), with
George himself as an awesome Pan-like Oberon dominating
the play. There was a similar if less overwhelming Oberon in
Gustav Rudolf Sellner's austere production (Darmstadt, 1952),
for which Carl Orff wrote another of his six scores for *Dream*.

When Germany was divided after the Second World War, the
socialist regime in the East favoured public and political
theatre; *Dream* fell out of sight. But it made no less than
seventeen comebacks between 1969 and 1978, exposing the
shadows and ruptures within the state as well as the play. In
1969, Fritz Bennewitz in Weimar could still depict the workers
as the most vigorous presence in the play; but in Berlin in 1980,
Alexander Lang eschewed ideology to present 'manipulation

and loss of identity . . . people helplessly entangled in a mesh of uncontrollable internal and external forces'. The description is Maik Hamburger's (58), whose translation underlay some of these productions. And in 1992, in reunified Germany, another Weimar production by Alexander Haussmann featured an elegant self-absorbed elite divorced from the proletariat. The play changed guise with the political order.

Meanwhile in West Germany, Dieter Dorn (Munich, 1978) presented sets clearly inspired by Brook. In a gripping start, a mummified shape arose to put on a reversible gown as Hippolyta/ Titania. She then dominated the play, even speaking the epilogue. As Hippolyta, she also recognized her asinine lover from another life in the actor playing Pyramus. The Italian-born Roberto Ciulli (Mülheim, 1983) had a single actress playing Robin, Philostrate and Quince, controllers of the three strands in the play's 'revels'. His Titania changed in course of the play from an aged figure on crutches to an attractive young woman, so that her love for Bottom became a magically uplifting force. After reunification, Karin Beier (Düsseldorf, 1995) staged a version in nine European languages, with actors doubling and even 'trebling' roles. Beier was thought to be probing the rationale of the then new European Union. Did this assert Shakespeare's cross cultural presence or reduce it to Babel? A multilingual production would be unintelligible to an audience unfamiliar with the original. Its very possibility proves the presence of Shakespeare across cultures.

The most remarkable French production of *Dream* never took place. In 1915, the dramatist Jean Cocteau, the artist André Lhote and the composer Erik Satie planned to stage the play at the Cirque Médrano, a circus arena, with its popular clowns the Fratellini Brothers as Bottom, Flute and Starveling. There was talk of Picasso designing the sets and costumes. The plan fell through, perhaps because of the ongoing war. Its only output was Satie's *Cinq grimaces*, five short musical pieces for the clowns. Had it taken place, this production might have anticipated Peter Brook's in some respects. That happened, with other innovations like an infusion of Indian kathakali dance, in an avant-garde rendering directed by Ariane Mnouchkine (Paris, 1968) set in a circus ring. Mnouchkine's interpretation, unlike Brook's, was sombre: she found this 'the most violent and savage play anyone could ever dream' (Roose-Evans, 88). Its run was interrupted by political turmoil in Paris. Jan Kott's Shakespeare (see p. 105) was asserting his presence in countries farther west: in Mnouchkine, primarily in psychological and psychoanalytic rather than political terms. Jean Gillibert (Ollioules, 1971) also probed the subconscious, exploring in particular the actor's function as brought out by the artisan-players. Petrika Ionesco (Nanterre, 1977) presented the conscious and the subconscious in two spaces, theatre and nature, side by side onstage. Later, Stanislas Nordey (Nanterre, 1995) made intricate use of theatrical space to present the actors as fictional rather than psychologically defined entities. Nordey's was one of an astonishing forty-five new French productions of *Dream* between 1981 and 1997 (Fayard, 142–3). It is obviously impossible to generalize about them.

Spain has seen several productions since 1980 in various languages of the peninsula. Miguel Narros (Madrid, 1986) replaced the forest with a 'huge black, neutral environment that was changed by lighting effects and mechanical devices' (Portillo and Gómez-Lara, 216).[1] Again we see the impact of Peter Brook. Calixto Bieito's Catalan production (Barcelona, 1991) challenged tradition by infusing the play with pop culture in several popular dance styles, as Charles Charras's French adaptation (Paris, 1965) had done earlier. Helena Pimenta's Basque version (Madrid, 1992) brought acrobatic actors onto a bare stage: again a reflection of Brook with a tinge of Karin Beier, for the artisans came from various parts of Spain and

---

1   Jonathan Munby's production (London Globe, 2008) opened with totally black sets and costumes.

included a Pole. There was also a curious Galician reworking by Manuel Guede and Eduardo Alonso (Centro Dramático Galego, 1992) bringing Lewis Carroll's Alice onstage: first as a spectator who dreams the action, but gradually entering it and undergoing changes of shape. No doubt coincidentally, a Japanese production the same year also had an Alice motif (see p. 36).

It is a far cry from this postmodern world to the Dutch village of Diever. In 1946, the village doctor organized a local production of *Dream* in the surrounding woods. This started a line of Shakespeare productions including several *Dream*s. The village now has a permanent theatre, and a statue of Bottom and Titania.

The Soviet bloc had little use for *Dream*. (The special case of East Germany is noted above.) Even the proletarian identity of the artisans went virtually untapped. In fact, this fairy play acquired an unsuspected charge of political dissent, through off-centre productions doomed to neglect or official censure. At Kiev in 1927, the Ukrainian director Hnat Yura had to withdraw an operatic, expressionist *Dream* inspired by Reinhardt for its 'lack of connection to Soviet reality' (Makaryk, 176). The Czech dissident director Jan Kačer produced a *Dream* in the mining town of Ostrava in 1976. He replaced the Indian boy with a girl, and presented Robin as a near-blind 'aging hobgoblin' (Leiter, 489). Remarkably, there were six Czech *Dream*s in 1977–8. In Poland – Jan Kott's country, but predating his work – Lidia Zamkow (Krakow, 1963) presented the lovers as contemporary students in an aggressively sexual culture. Konrad Swinarski's post-Kott production (Krakow, 1970) had two secret policemen silently observing a series of intense sexual encounters. Clearly, *Dream* was providing an alternative mode of dissent through sexuality rather than direct political protest. After perestroika, the Canadian director Guy Sprung was invited in 1990 to stage *Dream* in Moscow's celebrated Pushkin Theatre. In his account of the visit, Sprung describes a fraught though creative experience: his determinedly theatrical

11 Bottom and Titania: statue at Diever, Netherlands, by Arie Teeuwisse, 1971

and aesthetic orientation might have carried its own political charge.

During and after the disintegration of the Soviet bloc, many productions reflected a regimen of tyranny and surveillance, not entirely confined to the past. Romania saw six *Dream*s in the 1990s. The best known, Alexandru Darie's (1990), was rehearsed during major unrest in Bucharest, like Mikhail Tumanishvili's Georgian version while civil war raged in Tbilisi in 1994. There were more secret policemen in Darie's production than in Swinarski's; and in a sinister parallel to Ciulli's German production, the same actor played Theseus, Oberon and Quince – a figure of total control. The following year, the persecuted Romanian director Liviu Ciulei returned home from America, to adapt his 1985 Minneapolis production to the prevailing situation in Bucharest. In the post-Soviet era, these subversive and fragmenting tendencies connected with Western postmodernism, partly through shared influences like Kott and Brook.

However novel in presentation, European productions almost always remain within visible distance of Shakespeare's play and follow the course of its text. This is largely true of US productions as well, but less so in Australia or Canada. And when we move beyond the anglophone world, the remoter possibilities of *Dream* become strikingly apparent. More often than not, the play is taken apart and a varying number of elements reassembled in accord with the compulsions of local culture. Nothing brings out better the exceptional range of material constituting *Dream*, answering to diverse elements of human life and imagination.

Beyond Europe

Dream reached America rather late at Park Theatre, New York in 1826, in an operatic version deriving from Kemble. Also at the Park, Edmund Simpson in 1841 introduced a female Oberon and Robin, probably following Vestris in London. In 1854,

William Burton and Thomas Barry put on rival shows at the Chambers Street and Broadway Theatres. The fiercest competition was in historical authenticity, but Burton triumphed by his celebrated rendering of Bottom, like Phelps in London around the same time. Burton also preserved Shakespeare's text in unusual measure, perhaps on Vestris's model. Vestris's legacy was directly imported when her protégée Laura Keene moved to New York in 1852, and even took her *Dream* in 1854 to San Francisco, then truly the Wild West. Like Vestris, Keene played Oberon (or Robin, casting another woman in the other role). Later, the actor-manager Augustin Daly staged sumptuous *Dream*s in New York (1873, 1888), also with female Oberons and Robins. There was much music (Mendelssohn), much magic, much play with lights including a diorama. Theseus and his company were conveyed from forest to palace in a barge. Daly was vying with the touring British troupes who overshadowed Shakespeare performance in America for over a century.

An indigenous line· developed at last in the mid-twentieth century, in good part through Shakespeare festivals around the US aimed at students and the general community rather than the urban elite. The earliest success was a *Dream* at Stratford, Connecticut, which then toured widely to great popular response. Alex Reeve (1958) set a production by Howard Payne College, Texas on a Texas ranch to surprisingly good effect. The fairies, like Hippolyta, were Native Americans, opening up a new multicultural front. In New York, Joseph Papp's mobile theatre had its usual popular success with a 1964 *Dream*. Its open-air performance in Central Park was made into a television film in 1982.

Very different was John Hancock's disturbing version (San Francisco, 1966), set in a plague-infested Athens under a harsh regime. The rainbow motif in the pop artist Jim Dine's designs was broken by the drab clothes of the artisans – who, at the end, were driven out by guards when they demanded payment. The fairies were equally disorienting, with a headless Oberon, and the lovers' relations destabilized by a Helena in drag. Alvin Epstein, who played Oberon, produced his own sinister, deeply sexual *Dream* for the Yale Repertory Theater in 1975, with ironic adaptation of Purcell's music. These productions reflected the counter-culture that had arisen in response to the Vietnam War. Yet at Minneapolis in 1985, the Romanian Liviu Ciulei, a fugitive from communist rule, offered a differently dark *Dream* fraught with race and gender issues: a black Hippolyta tyrannized by a white Theseus, a white Titania by a black Oberon fleetingly identified with Bottom. The lovers' pairings remained uncertain to the end, and the courtiers left before the Bergomask concluding the play-within-the-play. But the tide was already turning towards elegant neo-Romantic productions in period settings: Napoleonic for Martin Platt (Alabama, 1981), Edwardian for James Lapine (New York, 1982), Victorian for Richard Sewall (Maine, 1982). Aaron Posner (Folger Theater, Washington, 2016) swung back to a fantasy setting with modern lighting and rap lyrics, Theseus and Hippolyta still doubling as Oberon and Titania, and Robin and Bottom played by women – Bottom a drama teacher whose girls, unprecedentedly, played *Pyramus* as serious romantic tragedy.

Australia has staged many *Dreams*. The play featured in the repertoire of Allan Wilkie's Shakespeare Company, founded in 1920. Played with an English edge, Wilkie's production best realized itself in the colonial subtext of an open-air production in 1921 at the Government House in Perth. Wilkie's legacy was upheld by John Alden's Victorian-style *Dream* (Sydney, 1959). Productions have attained a new sophistication since then. In Jim Sharman's version (Adelaide, 1982), not only were Theseus/Oberon and Hippolyta/Titania doubled in contrasting styles, but the artisans 'turned into fairies by sprouting silver wings at the pull of a string' (Brissenden, 156). Also memorable was Noel Tovey's all-Aboriginal *Dream* at Sydney's 'Festival of the Dreaming' (1997). Tovey mingled Elizabethan fairy lore and Aboriginal 'Dreamtime', with the mortals in white Elizabethan costume alongside supernatural forest dwellers from indigenous myth. There was also a strong Aboriginal infusion in a 2003 production at the 'Walking with Spirits' festival of the Northern Territory.

Dream has had other incarnations in Australia, including several dance versions. But Canada enjoys a rare continuity afforded by the annual Shakespeare Festival at Stratford, Ontario. There have been thirteen productions of *Dream* since 1960, including a full and a 'chamber' version in 2014. Robin Phillips (1976) not only doubled parts but presented Hippolyta/ Titania as aspects of Queen Elizabeth, setting the action in her palace as her own dream. The historical allusion was also contemporary: it marked Elizabeth II's Silver Jubilee visit to Canada. By contrast, John Dowling's 1993 version was set to punk and rap in a recreation of African-American street culture. Off-centre Canadian productions include Jillian Keilly's in an abandoned Newfoundland mine-shaft (1998), using its blackness to create a supernatural setting peopled by fluorescent beings. Chris Earle (Toronto, 2000) presented two simultaneous Robins, both female. A French adaptation by Oleg Kisseliov (Québec, 1998) recast the play around the artisans, with Quince the dramatist as the author-dreamer of Shakespeare's dreamplay. Metatheatrical in a different way was *To Thine Own Self Be True* (Winnipeg, 1999) by the First Nations company Shakespeare in the Red: they used the artisans' rehearsal scene to link excerpts from many Shakespeare plays, concluding with *Pyramus and Thisbe.*

Perhaps no society offered more traumatic dissensions than South Africa in the apartheid era. At the University of Witwatersrand in 1984, David Horner and Sarah Roberts dared apartheid laws by casting a mixed-race actress as Robin, and challenged the sexual rigidity of their society by fairly explicit eroticism. (A 1981 production had a mixed-race actor as the Indian boy.) The protest was even starker in Francois Swart's

1985 production at Rhodes University, which started with a crowd of beggars being chased away from Theseus' palace gates. The forest trees were black, as were the fairy costumes, creating 'a reversal of the usual South African racial power dynamic' (Quince, 118). Snout as Wall symbolized racial as well as sexual segregation. This was at a time when the black townships were torn by anti-apartheid protests.

There are divisions other than those imposed by apartheid. India has had the longest encounter with Shakespeare of any country outside the West. *Dream* became a cultural recourse of the Raj: perhaps through expatriate nostalgia for the British countryside, perhaps by its fitness for amateur productions. C.J. Sisson (*India*, 22) disparages 'bits from *A Midsummer Night's Dream*, with goblin dances' at viceregal functions. A performance near Delhi by the British armed forces in 1945 featured 'two milk-white steeds' lent by the Viceroy (Clayton, *Hole*, 6), who might, like a latter-day Elizabeth, have attended the show. Later anglophone directors have made insouciant use of Indian settings: Baz Luhrmann (Sydney, 1993) placed Benjamin Britten's operatic *Dream* in Raj-period India, with Theseus and Hippolyta as Indian gods finally presiding over their liberated country.

Authentic Indian productions began in the nineteenth century, often drawing on indigenous lines of theatre, dance and opera like the Marathi *sangeet natak* and Bengali *jatra*. *Dream* featured less prominently than one would expect. Later, in assertive contrast, the Marxist Utpal Dutt took a fairly straight Bengali rendering (1964) across the countryside. But the outstanding Indian *Dream*, proletarian in content as well as spirit, was Habib Tanvir's, whose Hindi title translates as *The Love-God's Own, a Springtime Dream* (Bhopal, 1993): a cumbersome label for a spare and lively adaptation, casting tribal people from central India as the artisans and arranging the action around them. In India's changing society, with shifting equations between urban and tribal communities, the

विलियम शेक्सपियर

कामदेव का अपना वसंत ऋतु का सपना

नाट्य रूपांतर व निर्देशन

हबीब तनवीर

12 Cover of the playbook of a Hindi version of *Dream* directed by Habib
Tanvir for Naya Theatre, Bhopal, India, 1993

folk-operatic form of *nautanki* carried a serious social subtext. So did Chetan Datar's Marathi *Jungal mein Mangal* (*Happiness in the Forest*: Mumbai, 2004),[1] cast as a *tamasha* or folk sketch with systematic cross-dressing in all roles, male and female. Men playing women were conventional in Indian as in Elizabethan theatre, the opposite a controversial novelty. Novel in a different way was the most widely travelled Indian production, launched at Delhi (2006) with a British director, Tim Supple, and a cast speaking eight Indian languages plus English. This recalled Karin Beier's multilingual European production (see p. 25), while Supple's set with a rope climbing-wall seemed inspired by Brook. Unlike Beier, Supple did not thematize the babel of tongues; nor did the Indian element pass beyond the ornamental.[2] What sustained the production was its theatrical energy, comic ebullience and physical vigour – a happy tribute to Brook's legacy.

Japan has had a notable line of *Dream*s, with lyrical Mendelssohnian versions yielding to innovative fusions of indigenous and Western practice. The pre-eminent Japanese Shakespeare directors have been Tadashi Suzuki and Yukio Ninagawa. Suzuki's *Dream* (Mito, 1991) was a modest production, but Ninagawa's (Tokyo, 1994) a major effort. With a set depicting the Buddhist stone garden in Kyoto symbolizing the cosmos, it employed avant-garde fusion techniques: sumo wrestling and conventions of the Japanese Noh play alongside pronouncedly Western music and an acrobatic actor from the Beijing Opera as Robin, recalling Brook and Lepage. Alongside these productions, Izumi Motohide (Tokyo, 1991) adopted the spare design of kyogen theatre, with only three characters representing Titania, Oberon and Bottom. Shimodate Kasumi's adaptation (Sendai, 1996) in the Tohoku dialect was set on the

---

1 Not to be confused with a Bollywood film of the same name.
2 See Trivedi. Lal (69–77), Supple's dramaturge, defends the production against these charges.

north Japan coast with Oberon and Titania as sea gods, Robin as a local goblin and Bottom as a fisherman. In a more contemporary and sinister redaction, Hideki Noda (Tokyo, 1992) brought Mephistopheles into the plot, manipulating Oberon and Robin to evil ends. Athens became a restaurant, the woods an amusement park below Mount Fuji. Noda also introduced a startling Carrollian parallel to a Galician production the same year: repeated mentions of an Alice, and a looking-glass dividing the two worlds of the play (see p. 27). Norio Deguchi (Tokyo, 1994) presented three consecutive, contrasting versions: one set in a bar, another in a school, the third virtually in the round with no sets. Across the waters in Korea, Yang Jung-Ung returned to folk culture in a remarkable adaptation (Seoul, 2003) inverting the gender-pattern. Oberon became a comic consort of the ruling Titania-figure, and the object of his affections a

13 Kwon Young-ho as Gabi (Oberon) and Park So-young as Ajumi (Bottom) in a production directed by Yang Jung-Ung for Yohangza Theatre Company, at the Haneul Theatre, Seoul, The National Theatre of Korea, 2003

herb-gathering woman with a pig's head. The fairies, more expectedly, were Korean forest sprites. This was the *Dream* featured in the London 'Globe to Globe' festival of 2012.

The Chinese record is relatively sparse. Once the restrictions of the Cultural Revolution were relaxed, *Dream* was staged at the first Chinese Shakespeare Festival (Beijing, 1986). Xiong Yuanwei's set of suspended ropes recalled Brook, whether or not by design: it has been linked to the Taoist notion of life as a dream. Daniel Yang's version (Hong Kong, 1997) was very different. A veteran of the Colorado Shakespeare festival, Yang applied a Western stage idiom, with vertical neon lights that changed colour and costumes approaching Western garb. A 2000 revision pushed the action back to the remote past, and adjusted the text accordingly.

I end with Brazil: used, like India, as both authentic setting and exotic locale, or something between the two. The American A.J. Antoon produced *Dream* for the Brazilian carnival at the New York Shakespeare Festival of 1988. The Brazilian Cacá Rosset's ebullient version (1991), acrobatic and intensely physical, also opened in New York. In one of his rare stage productions, the German film director Werner Herzog set the play in the Amazon rain forest (Rio de Janeiro, 1992).

This account shows the sea-change in global cultural politics since the mid-twentieth century, and the importance within it of Shakespeare in general and *Dream* in particular. The play's intricate structure, with contrasting groups of characters, can reflect the web of human relations with its entanglements of class, race, gender and power politics, or focus on a particular aspect of the whole. The play also allows a transhuman, supernatural perspective. Moreover, it permits a sustained discourse on art and imagination, music and performance. Hence, however *outré* many productions may seem, they cannot be dismissed as un-Shakespearean. They all take off from Shakespeare's play and bring out some promise latent in it or, at very least, compatible with it. Equally, they show how

Shakespeare's material can suit a seemingly endless range of social and cultural situations. The performance history of *Dream* is inseparable from its political and cultural reception.

Other media: cinema, music, art

The formal and thematic versatility of the play shows even more tellingly, if possible, when it is translated into other media. The Vitagraph company made a silent film of *Dream* in 1909. It was praised for its natural scenic effects and skilful story-telling, though it curiously replaced Oberon with a female 'Penelope', extending the convention of women playing the fairy king. 'Shakespeare is a dramatist for the moving picture screen as well as for the ordinary stage', observed a journalist after viewing the film (Ball, 52). Yet some major cinematic versions of *Dream* have been made by stage directors – Reinhardt, Hall, Papp, Noble – sometimes with relatively little change, sometimes presenting the play's inbuilt themes of performance and illusion in a new key. Max Reinhardt made the first talkie of *Dream* in 1935. Surprisingly, there was no other (except for Jiří Trnka's Czech puppet version in 1959) till another stage director, Peter Hall, took on the task in 1968. (Reinhardt's and Hall's films are noted above alongside their stage productions.)

Notably innovative was Adrian Noble's screen version (1996). Here the action became the dream of a boy in the mansion around which the play was located. Titania was a puppet in his toy theatre, and the fairies arrived in the bubbles he blew. Such effects, already present in Noble's stage version, could be magnified on the screen: doors opened into nowhere or into a forest of light bulbs. Film and theatre mingled in the continuum of a dream. In Michael Hoffman's film (1999), set in nineteenth-century Tuscany, the dream was Bottom's. He became a seriocomic 'Walter Mitty figure' (Rothwell, 25), seeking escape from a domineering wife in a fantasy encounter with Titania,

14 Stanley Tucci as Robin in Michael Hoffman's film, 1999

while the bicycle-riding Robin was a wry elderly philosopher with a satyr's (or devil's?) horns. There have also been many television versions, including seven from the BBC. Elijah Moshinsky's production (1981), placed in a seventeenth-century Cavalier setting, was adjudged a predictably conservative, even 'domesticating' version (Williams, *Revels*, 250). But David Kerr (2016) used a disorienting adaptation by Russell T. Davies where Theseus died, Hippolyta and Titania met and exchanged kisses, and Demetrius and Lysander were in love for a time.

Needless to say, the musical history of *Dream* is much older, but the films mesh more readily with radical reworkings closer to our times. The Beatles made a television special of *Pyramus and Thisbe* for Shakespeare's 400th anniversary (*Around the Beatles*, 1964), as the comedy troupe Crazy Gang had done earlier (*The Music Box*, 1957). A musical-comedy version of the whole play had been staged in 1939 in New York: Gilbert Seldes and Erik Charell's *Swingin' the Dream*, with two jazz bands, a pit orchestra and even a jazz retake of Mendelssohn's Wedding March. Duke Ellington and Billy Strayhorn's album *Such Sweet Thunder* (1957) borrowed its title and a song from *Dream*, while Steve Hackett (1997) based a whole suite of progressive rock on sections of the play.

In more formal music and dance, *Dream* has figured extensively since the seventeenth century. No music for the play survives from Shakespeare's own time. The play has only one indubitable song, the fairy lullaby (2.2.9–28), but composers have seized on the overall aura of musicality. Mendelssohn (see p. 12) is the pre-eminent but by no means the only presence. Gooch and Thatcher list 1,723 musical items (including some cross-references) inspired by *Dream*. Most of them were produced for particular stage productions, or as disjunct compositions perhaps intended as chamber music. Passages of dialogue have often been set to music, and works of other composers borrowed and inserted – above all other Elizabethan songs. Here too, *Dream* is the site of far-reaching cultural transactions. The *New Grove Dictionary of Opera* cites thirty-nine operas till 1992 based on *Dream* in whole or part, starting with Purcell's *The Fairy Queen* (see p. 11).[1] Only *The Tempest* has more operatic versions. Outside England, the biggest number is from Germany, beginning with Georg Christoph Grosheim's *Titania* (1798); but there are several from France and Italy, and examples from various European countries.[2]

The outstanding opera is Benjamin Britten's, presented at the Aldeburgh Festival in 1960 and then, with a fuller score, at Covent Garden. It closely follows Shakespeare's text, adding only one new line,[3] but shifting and omitting a good deal: the co-librettist Peter Pears worked closely with the composer. The opera opens with the fairies. The lovers appear after them, the artisans still later, and Theseus and Hippolyta only in the last scene. Tytania's (so spelt) engagement with Bottom occupies a

---

1 Hotaling (421–3) cites forty-five, not all complete works.
2 Ambroise Thomas's French opera *Le Songe d'une nuit d'été* is not a version of *Dream*. Here Shakespeare encounters Elizabeth in Richmond Park as Bottom did Titania.
3 'Compelling thee to marry with Demetrius', after 1.1.162. For a detailed comparison with Shakespeare's play, see Godsalve, ch. 2.

single sequence near the middle. The work revolves around the wood and the fairies, and to some extent the lovers, both structurally and musically. The fairy music (though Robin *speaks* his lines) sets off the contrasting, controlled music of the court, Bottom's comic tones and the parodic score of *Pyramus and Thisbe*, poking fun at Verdi and Donizetti. As this multifold musical design indicates, Britten's work remains Shakespearean in tone and structure while fulfilling its own role as opera. Britten made a concert version of Purcell's setting as well. He seems to have inspired rather than discouraged further ventures: seventeen of the thirty-nine operas in Grove appeared after Britten's.

Ballet enters into many productions in whole or part. As Sanders (63) points out, to use ballet in specific sequences (usually involving the fairies) is formally almost contrary to casting the entire action in the mode. The first full ballet version was Marius Petipa's at the Hermitage Theatre, St Petersburg (1876); the most celebrated George Balanchine's (1962), followed in 1964 by Frederick Ashton's. The latest, directed by Youri Vámos, premiered in Budapest in 2013. Ballet *Dreams* use Mendelssohn to this day: Balanchine called it his prime inspiration. Like Britten, Balanchine (who had earlier choreographed a stage production) began his ballet with the fairies. The first half, in the forest, provoked and disoriented, the second harmonized, replacing *Pyramus and Thisbe* with a series of ballet numbers as the wedding entertainment, but ending in the forest with the concord of Oberon and Titania. Ashton too foregrounded Oberon and Titania, ending with their dance of love and harmony. Theseus and Hippolyta did not feature at all.

The play has had its afterlife in the visual arts as well. Illustrated versions of the plays, starting with frontispiece engravings from Rowe's edition onwards, led to albums of illustrations alone, and separately sold plates to embellish 'extra-illustrated' editions. They often reflected theatrical practice: in the case of *Dream*, emulating the elaborate architecture of the court scenes and the lavish landscapes with choreographed fairies. The exercise reached heroic proportions in William Boydell's project for a Shakespeare Gallery. His agenda encouraged artists to present their own imaginative engagement with Shakespeare. Joshua Reynolds (1789) showed Robin as somewhat like the infant Hercules he had painted a little earlier. Henry Fuseli's long involvement with Shakespeare produced four large canvases of *Dream* scenes besides smaller works. Sillars (234–5) finds no fewer than five Robins of varying, even sinister intent in Fuseli's *Titania's Awakening* (1785–9; Kunstmuseum, Winterthur). William Blake, too, seems to have bid for the Boydell Gallery, with a lyrically vigorous rendering of the reconciliation of Oberon and Titania

15 *Titania's Awakening*, Henry Fuseli, oil on canvas, 1785–90, Kunstmuseum Winterthur, 1946

42

(*c*.1786; Tate Britain, London). He made two smaller paintings as well, one (for his poem *The Song of Los*) showing two figures, apparently Oberon and Titania, in repose inside a flower. Blake's Oberon is grave and majestic, like a biblical prophet, beside a Titania mollient in both dance and repose, and an enigmatic, epicene but radiant Robin. Blake has charged Shakespeare's work with the rarest expression of Romantic fairy lore.

Other painters – Richard Dadd, Francis Danby, David Scott – drew memorably on *Dream*. Dadd's lapidary yet sombre painting of Oberon and Titania's quarrel is called *Contradiction* (1854–8). It reflects not only the fairies' quarrel but the artist's clinically disturbed mind. A very different, more diffuse romanticism appears in Joseph Noel Paton's crowded canvases of *The Quarrel* (1849) and *The Reconciliation* (1847) *of Oberon and Titania* (both in the Scottish National Gallery, Edinburgh), pushing the theatrical imagination of the Victorian age beyond the limits of stage enactment. Lewis Carroll counted 165 fairies in *The Quarrel*; in real life, Lucia Vestris stopped at fifty-five and still went bankrupt (see pp. 12–13). Such elaborate works in conventional academic style catered to a sentimental valorizing both of Shakespeare and of a mythic English countryside, twin offshoots of a cultural patriotism infusing Boydell's Gallery no less than the Regency or Victorian stage. But the same conventions appear in America too: the popular Chicago painter James Farrington Gookins included a *Titania's Court* (1869) and *The Valour of Master Puck* (1871) in his extensive repertoire of fairy paintings. The former extends beyond *Dream* to include a host of other fairies, not to mention Don Quixote and Sancho Panza.

The painting of Shakespearean subjects virtually died out in the twentieth century, but some American artists continued the line in unexpected veins. Hannah Tompkins's large Shakespeare repertoire includes a *Puck* very like the conventional Shakespearean fool. In 1908, Pinckney Marcius-Simons covered the pages of a copy of Paul Maurice's French translation (now in the Folger Shakespeare Library) with striking fancies in watercolour, like a latter-day Blake. Most curiously of all, the early Dadaist Man Ray has a series of *Shakespearean Equations* (1948), largely abstract mathematical figures with a realistic admixture at times: for *Dream*, two butterflies appear against a background diagonally divided between dark and light zones that may be night and day, or sea and land.

SOURCES AND ANALOGUES: FAIRIES AND MORTALS

Fairies and fairy lore

Dream is Shakespeare's first play involving forces beyond the human. The best point of entry to its complex supernaturalism is through its most celebrated figure. Robin Goodfellow or Puck[1] is compounded of many items of English fairy mythology, of both Celtic and Teutonic origin. He can change shape like the puck or pouka; mislead travellers, again like the puck but also the hobgoblin and will-o'-the-wisp; perform domestic tasks like the brownie but, unlike that creature, without being tied to a household; and work mischievous tricks like the hobgoblin, hob or lob, but unlike the truly evil goblin. The overlap of roles is partly traditional; in part, it seems to be of Shakespeare's own making to yield dramatic capital.[2]

There is a traditional figure actually named Robin Goodfellow, a creature of many roles and guises. His closest links are with the brownie performing household chores and the hobgoblin spinning illusions and knaveries and leading travellers astray. He is mischievous rather than malicious,

---

1   His name is Robin, with 'Goodfellow' as a sobriquet. 'Puck' is the generic name for the type of supernatural being he most resembles.
2   The fullest survey of sources, precedents and later treatments of Robin Goodfellow may still be Latham, ch. 6.

though often associated with the devil or even presented as one. He is a satirical mouthpiece both in Jonson's court masque *Love Restor'd* (1612) and in popular tracts like *Tell-Troth's New-Year's Gift* (1593) and *The Midnight's Watch, or Robin Good-Fellow his Serious Observation* (1643). But his career as a supernatural prankster is most fully recounted in the 1628 chapbook *Robin Good-Fellow, His Mad Pranks, and Merry Jests*. There he is Oberon's son by a country girl, rural and popular in affinity, volatile but basically good-natured. There is also a broadside ballad, *The Mad Merry Pranks of Robin Goodfellow*, ascribed to Ben Jonson though the earliest surviving copy seems post-1660. (It echoes *Dream* much more closely than Jonson would ever have allowed.) In the anonymous play *Grim the Collier of Croydon* (published in 1662 but probably pre-*Dream*) Robin is a minor devil from hell, though his role is mischievously beneficial. The scene where he first comes to the countryside, at the opening of Act 4 (51–2, sig. I2^{r-v}) prefigures the setting of *Dream*. His role is more sordid in *Wily Beguiled* (1606), where he helps a mercenary lover. There he appears to be human, merely putting on a ghostly disguise to frighten his victim. But in *The Sad Shepherd*, Jonson aligns Robin (alias Puck-Hairy) with evil, as the 'hine' or servant (also minder and protector) of the witch Maudlin.

Reginald Scot in *The Discovery of Witchcraft* (1584) is inconsistent in his approach towards all such creatures and their actions. He describes an entirely material means to 'set an horsse or an asses head vpon a mans shoulders' (13.19; Scot, 315, sig. 2B6^r), yet finds genuine witchcraft in Jean Bodin's account of a man fully transformed into an ass but restored to human shape (5.3; Scot, 95, sig. H8^r), alternatively an 'asseheaded man' (5.5; Scot, 99, sig. I2^r). As Steevens (Var 1803, 408) first noted, *The History of Doctor John Faustus* (1592) describes how Faustus magically put ass-heads on an entire company at a feast (ch. 43, sig. Ir^r). In *Demonology*, James I unequivocally calls fairies creations of the devil if not devils themselves (James I, 3.5; sig. L1ʳ). Robert Burton (*The Anatomy of Melancholy*, 1.2.1.2; 1.186) places them (including '*Hobgoblins*, and *Robin Goodfellowes*'[1]) among 'Terrestriall Divels'. Burton cites Paracelsus yet ignores the radically different position of the latter, and of Henry Cornelius Agrippa. Agrippa's *Occult Philosophy* and Paracelsus' *Of Nymphs, Sylphs* [*etc.*] specify a major class of spirits who are neither angels nor devils but *sui generis*, like humans but on a different plane of being. Paracelsus (2nd Tractatus, 231) specifies four types of such spirits, for the four elements of water, earth, air and fire. His description approaches traditional accounts of fairies, and Agrippa's passes well into it:

> . . . some inhabit Woods and Parks, some dwell about fountains and meadows. So the Fairies, and hobgoblins inhabit Champian fields; . . . the *Dryades* and *Hamadryades* the Woods, which also *Satyrs* and *Sylvani* inhabit, the same also take delight in trees and brakes, as do the *Naptae*, and *Agaptae* in flowers: the *Dodonae* in Acorns; the *Paleae* and *Feniliae* in fodder and the Country.
>
> (Agrippa 3.32, sig. 2G1ᵛ)

Empson ('Spirits', 179–87) gives detailed attention to these and other learned authorities. But all in all, they could have had little impact compared to popular belief, especially as shaped by Puritan influence. Milton's *Comus* (1634) marks the imaginative height of that influence, stirring mythic roots in old Teutonic legend. George Peele's *The Old Wives' Tale* (?1594; printed 1595), the most notable play of rustic supernaturalism before Shakespeare, belongs however distantly to this line. Shakespeare does not go so far: his wood near Athens is

---

1 'Hob', cognate with 'Rob(in)', is a conventional rustic name. In *Tarlton's News out of Purgatory* (1590), 'Hob Thrust, Robin Goodfellow' are 'rather pleasantly disposed then indued with any hurtfull influence' (2, sig. B1ᵛ).

sometimes disquieting, but not evil like Milton's 'tangled wood' (*Comus*, 180). Bottom's seduction by the Fairy Queen parodies and diffuses the awesome legacy of medieval legend. There, the Queen herself entraps victims like Tannhäuser and Thomas the Rhymer (Thomas of Erceldoune) by her spells and holds them captive for long periods, or even sacrifices them to the devil, as in the ballad of Tam Lin.

Dream evokes elements of supernatural lore from many periods and brings philosophical traditions to bear on the popular belief of its time. The early modern period also produces an unprecedented literature of unthreatening, aestheticized fairies, sometimes of very small size. Violence, conflict and mischief are scaled down and neutralized in their world. The chapbook *Robin Good-Fellow* talks of 'many harmelesse Spirits called Fayries' (sig. A4ᵛ). The fairies in *Dream* show a strong urge to mischief but not to evil. They are carefully segregated from witches, though the two were often associated, as by Scot and James I.[1] They cause damage and confusion by error, compounded in Robin by love of the 'preposterous' and in Oberon by vicious petulance against his wife; but they finally strive to undo the damage. And as Harris ('Puck', 357) points out, this Robin Goodfellow is innocent of the sexual misadventures commonly ascribed to him elsewhere.

In Purkiss's phrase (174, 180), the fairies in *Dream* have been 'tamed'. They do not lack power. They are potential fates operating behind the action, manipulating human lives without directly engaging with them except in the case of Bottom; but they have been downscaled and exonerated of either will or capacity to work serious harm. Mythological elements from many cultures are placed in a reassuring compound, divested of their original awe and fear. The process reaches a climax in Fletcher's *The Faithful Shepherdess* (?1608; printed ?1610),

---

1   See the extensive evidence in Murray's Appendix 1.

merging classical satyr and native fairy in an entirely benevolent Satyr. He too uses false fire – but only to guide lost travellers back to the right path. Briggs (*Fairies*, 109–10) reports the traditionally inoffensive nature of Warwickshire and Midland fairies; but the extent of the new development argues a distinct literary impetus modifying popular belief.[1] In *Dream*, Shakespeare orients fairy lore to a new sector of the imagination, merged with other elements from very different sources, engaging a different public to different ends.

Two leading writers in the new vein hail from Warwickshire: Shakespeare and Michael Drayton. Others are their direct imitators (as William Browne is of Drayton) or emulators, like the unknown author of *The Maid's Metamorphosis*, printed in 1600 and probably composed shortly before. The elegant fantasies of John Lyly must have influenced this new line, including *Dream*, which becomes an influence in its turn. Lyly's plays have much delicate mythic content but only one fairy scene (*Endimion* 4.3.26–41), prefiguring the fairy episode in *Merry Wives* rather than *Dream*.[2] In *The Maid's Metamorphosis*, the single fairy scene (2.2.52–116) recalls Lyly but shows the clear influence of *Dream*. The resemblance is less marked in *The Wisdom of Doctor Dodypoll*, figuring fairies and an enchanter. Published in 1600 but probably composed before *Dream*, it may underlie a detail in 2.1.15 (see n.). Shakespeare himself affords another high point of fairy lore in the same years: Mercutio's memorable vignette of Queen Mab, unexpectedly set in an urban party-crashing interlude in *Romeo and Juliet* (1.4.53–103). The next century sees many diminutive fairies, often borrowed from or at least inspired by *Dream*. They feature in Drayton's *Nimphidia* and the Eighth Nimphal of *The Muses' Elizium*; Robert Herrick's fairy poems like 'Oberon's Feast' and 'Oberon's Palace'; and the unpublished

---

1 Cf. Latham, 176; Thomas, *Magic*, 726; Wall, 73–4.
2 Scragg proposes more extensive parallels between Lyly's *Gallathea* and *Dream*.

Book 3 of William Browne's *Britannia's Pastorals*. At a more popular level, the 1630 chapbook *Tom Thumb, His Life and Death* links Tom to the fairies at his birth and after his death.

Diminutive fairies are not new to the age: they belong to an established vein of fairy lore, and can be associated with evil or mischief.[1] Small, truly harmless flower fairies, resembling the Scandinavian light elves, feature in English lore.[2] By maximizing their small size, so to speak, the fairies are made more amenable to fanciful control. But the fairies of *Dream* are not uniformly small. For Marina Warner (325), their 'unsettling capacity' to change size and shape makes them more not less perturbing. We may also be perturbed by their miniaturized but graphic cruelty, clipping butterflies' wings and attacking honey-bees' thighs – practices with sexual overtones. But in any such tension between large and small, cruel and gentle, the latter element is as important as the first, and Shakespeare stresses it beyond ready precedent. He may not have foreseen his role in generating diminutive 'children's' fairies, but he certainly anticipates this vein of imagination. His notion of the fairies' size has a practical bearing on how they might have been represented onstage in his time, whether by adults or children (see p. 9). In neither case, of course, could they literally creep into acorns. But child actors would point a contrast with the adults in other roles, including Oberon and probably Robin; also with Titania, who could have been as 'adult' as any other female character played by an older child or adolescent.

Shakespeare also assimilates a traditionally solitary, self-contained creature like the puck or Robin Goodfellow into the body of trooping fairies. Robin's opening encounter with Titania's dew-scattering attendant marks a meeting of two worlds, Robin's the cruder and more rustic: 'Farewell, thou lob

---

1 Briggs, *Anatomy*, 45, *Vanishing*, 28–30 (citing Reidar Christiansen), 210.
2 Briggs, *Anatomy*, 45–6, *Vanishing*, 67. Latham (185–6) notes the *Dream* fairies' 'extravagant attachment for flowers'.

of spirits' (2.1.16). Socialized fairy life is projected through its most conventional activity, singing and dancing, and through the caring and foraging tasks of Titania's retinue. This endows the fairy world with a certain feminine identity, underpinned by Titania's womanly bonding with her dead companion, even if her attendants are male. (How much irony should we read into Bottom's addressing them as bucks and gallants in 4.1.8–23?) Oberon's retinue, by contrast, is virtually absent except for Robin; and Robin, though full of his own wiles and tricks, shows no trace of the rebellious spirit of Ariel in *The Tempest*.

The mixed sources of Shakespeare's fairy world are also reflected in the origins of Oberon. He is small in size but to be ranked among Briggs's 'heroic fairies' (*Dictionary*, 221), perhaps deriving from Alberich, a formidable dwarf in the *Nibelungenlied*. Oberon enters fiction through the thirteenth-century French courtly romance of *Huon of Bordeaux*. There, he is a dwarfish but handsome and mighty potentate, whose supernatural powers support a sumptuous lifestyle and far-flung influence. He guides and aids the hero Sir Huon through his arduous adventures, and finally leaves him his kingdom. That Shakespeare knew the romance (probably through Berners's translation, perhaps *c.* 1530) appears from an unnoted detail. The quarrel of Oberon and Titania is said to have cast nature into profound turmoil (2.1.88–117). There is no other evidence of this; lovers, artisans and fairies all traverse the woods untroubled by even a light shower. This may be one of Shakespeare's characteristic inconsistencies. But equally, he could have read in Berners (*Huon* 1.64; ch. 21) how Oberon's anger conjured up storms and floods with no compelling effect: humans could ignore them if they wished.

Oberon appears in a line of later romances and plays as a figure of varying purport: 'friendly or fearsome', dispensing 'fearful threats mixed with harmless illusions' (Aydelotte, 3). This mixed legacy descends to Shakespeare's fairy king. There were several medieval sequels to *Huon*, one with 'Auberon' as protagonist. Fairies appear also in Renaissance poets like Boiardo and Ariosto, treating the story of Orlando from the same Charlemagne cycle as *Huon*. Greene's play *James IV* (?1590) makes Oberon 'king / Of quiet, pleasure, profit, and content, / Of wealth, of honour, and of all the world' (1 Chorus 1.4–6). Henslowe's diary (20) records a lost play of 'hewen of burdoche', acted by the 'earle of susex his men' on 28 December 1593 and twice more that season.[1] More crucially, Oberon can be a figure of direct political allegory. In Spenser's *The Faerie Queene* 2.10.75–6 (1590), he is the greatest king of the Faerie race, descended from a man created by Prometheus and a 'Fay' in the Garden of Adonis. But Faerie land is also Britain and Oberon clearly Henry VIII, as later in Dekker's *The Whore of Babylon*, where his daughter Elizabeth is Titania (1.2.34–5). This anticipates the allegorical vein of Jonson's masque *Oberon the Fairy Prince* (1611), with Henry Prince of Wales in the title role. Swann (459–69) also finds court satire in the burlesque treatment of miniaturized Oberons in Drayton, Herrick and Browne: their minute size subverts the trappings of grandeur and authority. Most of these examples are later in date than *Dream*, but the source-allegory in Spenser was there for Shakespeare to use. He chose not to do so, indeed to play down the equation of Elizabeth with the Fairy Queen as far as was possible in that age (see pp. 96–7). This accords with his general restraint in drawing out the challenges implicit in the play's themes. I shall have much more to say about this trait.

In Chaucer's *Canterbury Tales*, fairy royals operate in unheroic proximity with humans in *The Merchant's Tale*: the King and Queen of Fairies (conflated with the Graeco-Roman Pluto and Proserpina) wrangle in open gender-conflict in a manner prefiguring Oberon and Titania. (There is also a passing allusion to Pyramus and Thisbe.) In the *Tale of Sir Thopas*,

---

1   A play about Guy of Warwick featuring Oberon, published in 1661, is thought by Cooper ('Guy', 189–90) to date from the early 1590s.

Chaucer's burlesque hero enters a wood and is overcome with sudden love-longing for an elf-queen, prefiguring Bottom's predicament in reverse. Yet *The Wife of Bath's Tale* opens by remarking on the declining belief in fairies. The *Tale*'s context of Arthurian romance is thus culturally distanced from the rustic lore of elves and fairies even while drawing on the latter. Shakespeare, too, evokes the chivalric hierarchy of medieval romance by making Robin, hitherto a homely self-contained figure, serve as Oberon's 'henchman' as the Indian boy may do one day. Never before in fairy history had Robin played such a role (Latham, 254–5). One province of fairyland, the courtly and romantic as represented by Oberon, has acquired hegemony over another, the homely and rural, as represented by Robin.

Ovid: the classics and the fairies

The varied origins and no less varied functions of Shakespeare's fairy world appear in its links with Graeco-Roman mythology, as derived from Ovid's *Metamorphoses* above all. Ovid enters deeply into *Dream*. The grammar-schooled Shakespeare would have known the original Latin as well as Arthur Golding's translation, and at times clearly follows one or the other. The most evident derivation is the burlesqued story of Pyramus and Thisbe; but there is more serious Ovidian substance as well, much of it pertaining to the fairies. A notable example is the name Titania, literally a female descendant of a Titan.[1] It is applied by Ovid to four characters: Pyrrha (*Met.* 1.395), Diana (3.173), Latona (6.185) and Circe (13.968). By virtue of such a name, Titania is raised (like Oberon by other means) above the fairy queen of English rustic lore: she is unlike Mercutio's Queen Mab or 'the mistris-Faerie, / That doth nightly rob the dayrie' in Jonson's 1603 entertainment for the Queen-consort Anne at Althorp (53–4). The link with Diana is most commonly

---

1   When Golding translates the name at all, it is as 'Titan's daughter', so Shakespeare's use of *Titania* argues his recollecting the original Latin (Bate, 136).

cited. Yet Titania is not Diana, and her only stated 'votaress' is a mother, not a virgin like Diana's followers. What is important is the contrast behind the parallel, projecting an alternative, life-enhancing bonding – between women, between lovers, even between supernaturals and mortals. This Titania does not turn a man into an animal and destroy him for seeing her exposed, as Diana did to Actaeon; instead, she takes a man already transformed and opens herself to him in her private bower. Ovid himself is metamorphosed.

There are three other Titanias in Ovid. One, Circe, turns men to animals for a different reason – frustrated love. She features in two separate tales, of Glaucus (*Met.* 13.968–14.74; Golding, 13.1128–14.79) and Picus (*Met.* 14.320–96; Golding, 14.368–452). Circe woos both, as Titania woos Bottom; but unlike Bottom, both Glaucus and Picus spurn her. She has herbs to induce love; they avail her nothing, and she uses other magic to undo the objects of her longing. The hunter Picus is drawn to his doom by an illusory boar while she darkens the heavens and raises fogs (*Met.* 14.367–71; Golding, 14.416–20), as perhaps reflected in *Dream* 3.2.355. Here then is a female of supernatural powers, with influence over the elements, in a wood impregnated with magic. Yet she is the victim of love, her might set against her vulnerability. In Titania, the opposite auras of Diana and Circe mingle to suggest an awesome and complex figure, more than balancing Oberon's enhanced fairyhood, although finally curbed and diminished by her consort as Hippolyta is by Theseus.

Other Ovidian elements abound in *Dream*: sometimes as event, sometimes as image or nuance.[1] More often than not, Shakespeare is not following a specific passage but drawing on

---

1   See Staton; Taylor, 'Ovid'; Barkan, *Gods*, 252–74, 'Diana', 353–9; Bate, 130–45. Most of the Ovidian parallels cited here are identified in these sources. Cody (127–41), more abstrusely, traces reflections of the Renaissance Neoplatonic reading of Ovid.

merged memories of several. Brooks (lxxxvi) notes Ovidian precedents for Titania's account of disordered nature (see 2.1.88–97n., 109n.), though Holland ('Theseus', 141) dismisses many such parallels as untenable. Ovid's stories of Echo and Narcissus (*Met.* 3.356–510; Golding, 3.427–642) and Salmacis and Hermaphroditus (*Met.* 4.285–388; Golding, 4.352–481) are reflected in Titania's aggressive wooing of Bottom. The story of Ino, assailed with snakes by the Fury Tisiphone (*Met.* 4.481–99), underlies Hermia's nightmare of the snake at her breast, while the story of Midas with his ass's ears (*Met.* 11.146–93; Golding, 11.164–216) suggests the gross comedy of Bottom's 'translation'. Staton (167–8) compares Oberon, Titania and Robin to Jupiter, Juno and Mercury, and the Indian boy to Ganymede, beloved by Jupiter to Juno's envy. Needless to say, the transformation of the flower love-in-idleness is deeply Ovidian. It remains a flower, but its appearance is changed supernaturally. The closest precedent is the mulberry in Ovid's account of Pyramus and Thisbe (*Met.* 4.125–7, 158–61; Golding, 4.150–2, 191–5): its fruit also changes from white to purple, though Quince's play makes no mention of the change and scarcely of the mulberry. In *Met.* 10.731–9 (Golding, 10.851–60), Adonis is changed into a blood-red flower, the anemone; in *Venus and Adonis* 1168, into a 'purple flower . . . chequered with white'. ('Red' and 'purple' were virtually interchangeable in sixteenth-century English.)

Beyond such specific analogies, the forest setting of *Dream* is charged with a living, sentient quality that is quintessentially Ovidian. It is also Spenserian. The wood near Athens is like a setting from *The Faerie Queene*, with more detail than Spenser commonly affords: animals that not only threaten but sustain the fairy order – the squirrel with nuts, snakes and bats with their skins for garments – and flowers everywhere, closely viewed with lyrical delicacy. The love-juice blends into this Ovidian setting, though it does not make anyone change shape. (The flower yielding it changes colour.) Shakespeare's wood

lacks the high seriousness infusing Spenser's settings even at
their most fanciful, but it has a subtler vitality. All its denizens,
even the plants, share in a pervasive sensate being:

> The moon, methinks, looks with a watery eye;
> And when she weeps, weeps every little flower . . .
>
> (3.1.189–90)

The fairies embody the spirit of this setting: they virtually
constitute a metaphor for it. A unique feature of *Dream* is rarely
noted. Oberon commonly has a castle and a glittering court,
even if fancifully scaled down in Drayton or Herrick. In *Dream*,
however, Oberon and Titania seem to have no habitation but the
woods. Titania refers to Oberon's fairy realm (2.1.65, 144), but
it is not a locatable presence in the play: it is an ambience, not a
site. In this respect at least, the fairies recall the classical wood
gods – fauns, satyrs, sileni – who are often compared to or even
assimilated with native fairies, as by Scot ('A Discourse vpon
diuels and spirits', ch. 21: *Discovery*, Scot, 521, sig. 2P5^r), Nashe
(*Terrors of the Night*, Nashe, 347) and Burton (1.2.1.2; 1.186–7).
Gavin Douglas says 'nymphs and fauns' are what his countrymen
call 'fairfolks' or 'elves' (Douglas, 8.6.6–7). In a passage that
Shakespeare takes over in *Tempest* 5.1.33, Golding translates
Ovid's *dique . . . nemorum* (gods of the woods, *Met.* 7.198) as
'Elves' (7.265). Golding (11.171) also renders Ovid's *teneris . . .
nimphis* (slender nymphs, *Met.* 11.153) as 'fayrye elves'.

Shakespeare turns the syncretic fairy lore of his times into a
sustained poetic creation mingling classical, medieval and
contemporary, remote and proximate, popular and elite. The
conflation of native spirits with classical deities supports
Cooper's contention (*Medieval*, 187) that 'Titania and Oberon
are much less Ovidian than Chaucerian': they act somewhat as
Venus, Mars and other gods do in *The Knight's Tale*. Shakespeare
implies, though he does not articulate, other parallels between
native and classical. Robin is quintessentially a creature of the
native folk imagination; yet there are classical nuances playing

about him. His shape-changing recalls the sea god Proteus; he can equally be compared to Mercury and, most saliently, to Cupid.[1] Purkiss (167–8) compares the swift ubiquitous Cupid in Greek Anacreontic lyrics and Seneca's *Phaedra* (titled *Hippolytus* in John Studley's translation in *Ten Tragedies*, 1581). Of the *Anacreontia*, only no. 31, where Cupid drives the lover through the woods, offers any real parallel; but the first chorus in Seneca's play (274–357), about Cupid's ranging the world, might have suggested Robin's putting a girdle round it. Both Robin and Cupid (in Oberon's vision) are anticipated in this account by Phaedra's Nurse:

> glyding through the Azure skies with slender
> ioynted arme
> His perlous weapons weildes at will, and working
> grieuous harme.[2]

Brooks (lxiii) notes a more precise parallel from the chorus in *Phaedra*. Among the countless victims of Cupid (consistently an 'elf' in Studley's rendering) are the ocean nymphs or Nereids: pierced with his arrow, they cannot quench their fire in the sea (*flammamque nequit relevare mari*, 337). This is reversed in Oberon's vision of 'Cupid's fiery shaft / Quenched in the chaste beams of the watery moon' (2.1.161–2).

Dream reflects Seneca's tragedies at other points as well; Burrow (184) even talks of an 'Ovidian–Senecan hybrid'. The disorder of the seasons recalls Seneca's *Medea* (see 2.1.101–14n.), and Theseus and Hippolyta's exchange on hunting and hounds echoes the opening of *Phaedra*. There is general precedent for Helena's obsessive, humiliating pursuit of Demetrius in Phaedra's pursuit of Hippolytus (*Phaedra* 233–41, 699–712). Not every borrowing is of tragic bent; but collectively,

---

1 Habib Tanvir found a parallel in the Indian love god Kamdev or Madan (see p. 33).
2 *Ten Tragedies*, fol. 59r (sig. I3ʳ); *Phaedra*, 199–201.

they suggest a subliminal tragic presence in this play of love and fairyland. Needless to say, the nuance is clearest in the play of *Pyramus and Thisbe*. Yet its tragic story is presented in burlesque mode, and Bottom's 'The raging rocks . . .' burlesques Studley's translation of Seneca (see 1.2.27–34n.).

Dream also links up with the other classical work called *Metamorphoses*, Apuleius' tale of the Golden Ass, translated by William Adlington in 1566.[1] This tells the story of a young man-about-town Lucius, turned into an ass by a botched magical experiment. It is a tale curiously commingling irony and fantasy, with much worldly realism and satire in a vein quite absent in *Dream*; but its witty and imaginative exuberance, and something of its supernatural aura, may have contributed to the play. Lucius' entertainment by a rich lascivious *matrona* (10.19–22) suggests Titania's advances to Bottom, especially her overt sexuality in 4.1; but as Carver (438) notes, the strident bestiality of Apuleius' account is toned down in Shakespeare, perhaps not least because Bottom, an ass only 'from the neck up', lacks the oversized member attributed to that beast. Carver considers the philosophical and mystical dimension of Apuleius' work equally inappropriate to *Dream*. Barkan ('Diana', 358), on the other hand, links Bottom's metamorphosis to Actaeon's in Ovid and Lucius' in Apuleius, both in their most Platonic and mystical guise. We need not follow Barkan all the way, but his summing up after Bottom's 'rare vision' captures the complexity of the outcome: 'The ass, who began as a fool, descended to jackass, and affirmed his humanity in the face of god and beast, has had an experience simultaneously beastly, human, divine.'

It is not an anomaly that a wood peopled by English fairies should be nominally located near Athens. It is touched by the mythic lights of ancient Greece and Rome, filtered through the

---

1   There is no evidence that Shakespeare knew Machiavelli's unfinished Italian poem *L'asino d'oro* (*The Golden Ass*, 1517), and no apparent resemblance between the two works.

composite culture of a later millennium. *Pace* generations of sentimental commentators, Shakespeare does not present the timeless spirit of the English countryside, if there be any such thing. Rather, he plays his part – perhaps the most crucial single part – in defining its changing spirit, as steered by changing cultural and class affinities.[1] Perhaps, as Reginald Scot observed (8.1, 8.6; Scot, 157–8, 166, sigs M7^{r-v}, N3^v), superstitious beliefs had actually dwindled through the influence of priests and religion. (Chaucer had satirically made the same point two hundred years earlier, in *The Wife of Bath's Tale*, 864–81.) The close, often fearsome reality of the fairy world as a living presence is exchanged for a new imaginative validation that is intellectually complex, artistically refined, and designed for a new public less affected by the disquietudes of folk belief.

This is different from earlier elite treatment of fairy lore, as by Giraldus (390–1), Walter Map (154–65, 314–23, 344–71) and Gervase of Tilbury (664–77, 718–43) in the Middle Ages. They had reported from the outside, perhaps with literal belief but without engaging the imagination. Shakespeare makes of the fairy world what it traditionally was not: a total imaginative artefact. He blends many disparate elements in the novel light of what Pierre Bourdieu (3–4) calls the 'pure gaze', that is

> the aesthetic disposition, the capacity to consider in and for themselves, as form rather than function, . . . everything in the world, including cultural objects . . . The 'pure' gaze is a historical invention linked to the emergence of an autonomous field of artistic production . . . The pure gaze implies a break with the ordinary attitude towards the world, . . . a social separation.

Dream affects this 'social separation' of the material of fairy lore from its context of popular belief, to implant it anew in the sensibility of a new urban theatrical public. Lyly's drama had

---

1   For two perceptive analyses, see Lamb ('Fairies') and Wall.

conjured up such a world well enough to please the London elite of a slightly earlier date. Shakespeare works a more radical and lasting transformation. He consolidates this fairy world within a new hegemony: Oberon over Robin, Ovid over romance writers and balladeers, courtiers and the bourgeoisie over rustics and 'mechanicals'. He also proposes an imaginative suspension of disbelief in place of country superstition. His material is validated within a new aesthetic which the play itself proceeds to reaffirm.

The structure of *Dream* is oriented to the new cultural bearings of the fairy world. Of the three classes of characters – courtiers, artisans and fairies – the first two are sharply if amicably opposed. The fairies bridge these disparate worlds by their hybridity. They affect the lovers as well as Bottom – in fact, the former much more lastingly. Oberon, no less than Theseus, decides the lovers' fates, which might be an argument for the same actor playing both roles. Courtiers and artisans take their place within a dramatic order flagged by the fairies. Hence every class of spectator can relate to the fairies in their own terms. *Dream* played to different types of theatres and audiences, whose individual viewers might themselves be divided in their beliefs and responses. Interiorizing the plurality, Lamb (*Popular*, 94) follows Montrose in postulating 'a heterodox theater within the subjectivities of members of the audience themselves, actively living out the contradictions staged before them'.

The fairies bear out the pastoral function of *Dream*. In Barber's words (145), they are 'creatures of pastoral, varied by adapting folk superstitions so as to make a new sort of arcadia'. From the secure aesthetic vantage of that fairy arcadia, courtly and urban patrons can pleasurably assimilate the concerns of 'the rabble', as a Quarto stage direction (4.2.0.1), probably from Shakespeare's own draft, describes them. Yet the new configuration is more complex than this suggests: as I argue later in this Introduction, *Dream* vindicates the popular ethos in many ways even while overriding the traditional terms of popular belief. Pastoral can be the site of challenging cultural engagements, arising from the basic encounter of 'simple' and 'complex man' in Empson's classic formulation (*Pastoral*, 18). *Dream* reflects many such encounters. I will approach its pervasive pastoral engagement, in the court no less than the wood, through the play of *Pyramus and Thisbe* and the uncertainties surrounding Theseus and Hippolyta.

Pyramus and Thisbe

There are many ironies working around the play of *Pyramus and Thisbe*. It is the most substantial Ovidian link in *Dream*, derived from *Met.* 4.55–166 (Golding, 4.67–201), but presented in burlesque. At the same time, it is a love-story with a sad ending. Burlesque and tragedy provide opposite but equally piquant contexts for the multiple marriages rounding off this romantic comedy. There is an obvious parallel between Pyramus and Thisbe and the eloping lovers in *Dream*, against a shared patriarchal setting. The ancient tragedy is diffused in the present comedy, but perhaps not entirely defused: its ominous implications reflect back on the lovers' predicament in the woods, and cast a shadow on the latter's future relations. The insouciant couples in Act 5 'fail to notice that they are watching what might have been their own plot', as Berry (72) remarks. The parallel between *Pyramus* and *Romeo and Juliet* has been amply noted, as between *Romeo* and *Dream* – plays close in date, foils to each other across the generic divide.

Pyramus presents new ways of shaping and subverting ancient texts and legends, thereby showing up *Dream* itself in a new light. The Ovidian narrative of *Pyramus* is melded with so many other elements that the final synthesis is almost as complex as that of the fairy subplot. Shakespeare would have known Chaucer's 'legend' of Thisbe in *The Legend of Good Women*, and may have drawn some phrases from it (see 5.1.146n., 179n.). He may also have known the moralized account in John Gower's *Confessio Amantis* (3.1331–1494), and

60

a briefer one in John Lydgate's *Reason and Sensuality* (3954–4001). There are Pyramus and Thisbe poems in two verse miscellanies, *A Gorgeous Gallery of Gallant Inventions* (1578) and *A Handful of Pleasant Delights* (1584). Shakespeare may have adapted (and enriched with internal rhyme) the stanza form of the lovers' dying laments in 'I. Tomson's' poem in the latter. A longer mythologized *Pyramus and Thisbe* by Dunstan Gale, involving Venus and Cupid, is known from a 1617 imprint, but its dedicatory letter is dated 1596. The story crops up in the most unexpected contexts. Muir (*Sources*, 32–3) cites a woodcut illustration on the title-page of several books published by Tottel, including the 1553 edition of Thomas More's *A Dialogue of Comfort against Tribulation*. Muir's claim (*Sources*, 39–45) for Thomas Moffett's *Of the Silkworms, and Their Flies*, read in manuscript, as a target of Shakespeare's parody has been scotched by Duncan-Jones ('Pyramus'). There is also an indifferent manuscript play of *Pyramus and Thisbe* in BL Add. MS 15227. The manuscript dates from the 1620s, but the play is adjudged 'possibly' sixteenth-century by Bullough (1.375). Much earlier in date (*c.*1528) is the still less distinguished *La Conusaunce damours*, 'The knowledge (or instruction) of love', with some (probably fortuitous) echoes in *Dream* (see 1.1.136n., 5.1.222n.).

Did Shakespeare have any specific target for his burlesque? Some of the works cited above might invite parody; but why should Shakespeare make the effort, unless as an unfathomable in-house joke? Even if there was such a target, Shakespeare is essentially satirizing not a particular work but the whole body of earlier drama that his own generation set out to supplant. The phrase 'very tragical mirth' (5.1.57) probably glances at Thomas Preston's *King Cambises*, described on the title-page as 'A lamentable tragedy mixed ful of pleasant mirth'. Quince's style and versification are distressingly close to the actual dramatic output of the 1560s and 1570s. Such plays were not always badly written by their own lights, but a once standard mode outdated and outclassed by Shakespeare's day.

As noted above, *Pyramus and Thisbe* touches on the 'serious' action of *Dream* and even *Romeo and Juliet*. Yet given the glaring conflict of register between them, can the one possibly uphold the purpose of the other? The style and staging of Quince's play seem to exclude any serious treatment of love, let alone other historical, philosophical or mystical concerns. Even critics who find such themes usually settle for their comic or burlesque treatment. Admittedly, from medieval religious drama to Elizabethan theatre, there is ample precedent for comic elements of deeply serious import. *Pyramus* too may be said to comment on the main action through reductive allusion and a species of parody. But the limits of such an interpretation emerge by contrast with Bottom's speech on his 'rare dream', buttressed by a very direct echo of the Bible (see p. 90 and 4.1.209–11n.). However different its idiom and its social and aesthetic register, that speech can be discussed on a par with the 'serious' action: its implications are not trivialized or devalued in rendering. The same cannot be said of the script and performance of *Pyramus and Thisbe*, though its metatheatrical function may be serious enough (see pp. 5, 97–101). *Pyramus* proclaims its own ineptitude. It is presented as a bad play by the dramatist of the serious play framing it. He might exploit the contrast to view all play-acting (including his own) in an ironic light. But to point the irony, he must retain the contrast: he cannot invest this travesty of serious theatre with serious *intrinsic* merit. Scholars might smuggle esoteric meanings into the text, but its idiom and dramatic context offer no ready basis for the exercise.

An outcome of this intrinsic unseriousness – or rather, the trivialization of intrinsically serious material – is that, as Dobson recounts ('Joke', 121–4; *Amateur*, 120–1, 199–202), this comic presentation of amateur theatricals has itself become a staple of amateur theatricals. This is not entirely ironic: it is as though amateurs recognize that the piece allows, indeed calls for an undemanding, appropriately flawed rendering. The burlesque thereby ceases to be sheer burlesque; it is vindicated in terms of a valued social activity, namely am-dram. This may mesh with professional theatre not only conceptually but in production: the 2016 touring RSC version had local amateur groups playing the artisans alongside professionals in all other roles. The burlesqued content is valued as a performative mode, a humane and social institution balancing its equivocal standing as art. 'The best in this kind are but shadows; and the worst are no worse, if imagination amend them' (5.1.210–11).

Theseus and Hippolyta:
Plutarch, Chaucer and Shakespeare

Shakespeare read Plutarch's life of Theseus in Thomas North's Englishing of Amyot's French version. More direct inspiration for his presentation of Theseus came from Chaucer's *The Knight's Tale.* Chaucer draws on Theseus' war with the Amazons and marriage to their queen, whom he calls Hippolyta. He also provides another major strand of *Dream*, two lovers vying (and literally fighting) for the hand of the same woman. Shakespeare converts this into a symmetrical design of two men and two women. As Robin Goodfellow says, 'Two of both kinds makes up four' (3.2.438), a promisingly even number. Its permutations allow more love-tangles but also general happiness at the end, dispelling the sombre, incipiently tragic ending of *The Knight's Tale.* Lysander and Demetrius fight but, unlike Chaucer's Palamon and Arcite, they need not: there are matches for both. Their scuffles in the wood are pointless and comical.

Dream has other features readily traceable to Chaucer.[1] The rite of maying is closely woven into the *The Knight's Tale.* In Part 2, Theseus, Hippolyta and Emily go hunting in the grove where Arcite, come to celebrate the rite, is fighting Palamon. In

---

1   Thompson (88–94) summarizes most of them, while Cooper (*Medieval*, 212–19) adds a set of subtler parallels.

Dream too, Theseus and Hippolyta, hunting in the wood, encounter the lovers apparently out a-maying (4.1.131–3). *Dream* has characters called Egeus and Philostrate, besides details like the image of the lark (*KnT* 1491, *Dream* 1.1.184). Egeus, Theseus' father, is mentioned in Plutarch and other accounts, usually spelt 'Aegeus' (as in North) but invariably 'Egeus' in editions of Chaucer down to 1600. 'Philostrate' was the disguised Arcite's assumed name in *The Knight's Tale* (1428).

How does Chaucer's Theseus differ from Plutarch's? As a story-teller rather than a chronicler, Chaucer presents a much more selective, compact picture of Theseus than Plutarch, seeing him primarily as a judicious and humane ruler. His martial ardour and prowess are never in doubt; he postpones his return home with his new-won queen to fight the cause of the Theban widows. But he projects a courtly ethos of private values and relationships rather than warfare and policy; by exercising his authority in this respect, he decides the characters' destinies. Shakespeare's Theseus is a low-key figure by contrast, no longer the determining force behind the events. He plays little more than the customary background role of ruler-figures in comedy, first to allow and then to resolve the complications of the lovers' fate. His only other role is the private one of lover and prospective bridegroom, and patron of outdoor and indoor recreations; above all to oversee his own wedding celebrations, giving a public dimension to a private event. In fact, he seems committed to a formal public stance over everything, including the rather stilted addresses to his bride-to-be. Even his most humane gestures carry an air of disengagement, as in the unusual patience and sympathy he shows towards Hermia in the first scene, or his plea for charity and even 'noble respect' for the artisans' play. He had even thought of a fatherly word with the fickle Demetrius (1.1.111–14); but his 'self-affairs' stood in the way, and his first verdict on Hermia is uncompromisingly harsh – needlessly so, seeing how easily he reverses it at the end. His actions as ruler relate solely to these private issues; his martial role is a matter of occasional report. It was highlighted in Reynolds and Kemble's 1816 production and some subsequent ones, feeding the growing imperialist discourse of the age couched in a faux classicism. There is nothing in *Dream* to support such concerns.

According to Plutarch, Theseus was a 'protectour of the oppressed, and dyd curteously receiue their requests and petitions that prayed to haue ayde of him' (36.2; North, 19, sig. B4[r]).[1] As the founder of Athenian democracy, he fostered 'a common weale or populer estate' whose three classes (nobles, tillers and artisans) were 'equall in voyce' (ch. 24–5; North, 13, sig. B1[r]), with mutual respect and interaction. This may be reflected in *Dream* in Theseus' relaxed encounter with the actor-artisans, very different from the lofty image of the new Renaissance monarch – including England's own, if one probes behind the rhetoric about Good Queen Bess. But Theseus' charity does not survive the test: he joins with the others in jeering at the players in their full hearing. Mitigating remarks like 'The best in this kind are but shadows' (5.1.210) and 'in courtesy, in all reason, we must stay the time' (5.1.248–9) seem little more than form. They are spawned by a somewhat pontificating self regard and a complacent trust in his subjects' allegiance, the underbelly of an easy courtesy born of privilege.

In other words, Theseus' princely refinement and graciousness prove somewhat thin on close view, though they never give way. There is the same noncommittal moderation in the way *Dream* presents his relations with women. The Theseus of legend has a dismal record of raping and philandering. Oberon names some of the victims (2.1.78–80): Perigouna, Aegle, Ariadne, Antiope. The last is Plutarch's name for the Amazon queen whom Theseus married. Hippolyta, in Plutarch, is a different woman who negotiates a peace between Theseus and the Amazons (27.4; North, 15, sig. B2[r]); elsewhere, she is

---

1   North's Plutarch, 1579 edition, with chapter numbers from the Loeb edition.

Antiope's sister. But Statius, hence Boccaccio and Chaucer, name the queen as Hippolyta. In *Dream*, the presence of both names adds to the irony, making Hippolyta herself a notional victim of seduction and violence. As Levine (210) notes, Theseus describes the way he 'won [her] love' as a species of rape: 'with my sword, / . . . doing thee injuries' (1.1.16–17). Shakespeare also ignores Plutarch's account (28.1–2; North, 15, sig. B2^r) that Theseus abandoned Antiope/Hippolyta for Phaedra, thereby provoking fresh wars with the Amazons. In fact, he does not mention Phaedra at all, or her disastrous courting of her stepson Hippolytus. But for those in the know – like Shakespeare and at least some among his audience – there is irony in Oberon's blessing that Theseus' issue 'Ever shall be fortunate' (5.1.396).

In Peter Holland's paradox ('Theseus', 145), 'Hippolytus cannot be ignored, but does that mean he should be noticed?' The same may be said of Theseus' abduction of Helen (Plutarch's comparison of Theseus and Romulus, 6.1; North, 43, sig. D4^r), to which Maguire (79–83) draws attention. These are uneasy nuances, never spelt out let alone stressed. Montrose speaks for many critics in detecting in *Dream* a narrative of 'sexual and familial violence, fear, and betrayal' ('Fantasies', 121). To others, however, Theseus is a model of order and reason threatened, if at all, by Bottom and his crew.[1] Both critical camps can relate Theseus to Elizabeth, the resemblance complicated by the latter's female sex. Many disquieting suggestions play around Theseus the patriarch, but Shakespeare never drives them home. In particular, there is much to question but little to seize on in Theseus' relations with Hippolyta; at most, we may sense an unstated play of differences. Earlier sources offer two opposite accounts of the war between Theseus and the Amazons (see Tyrrell, 4–5, 15–17, 90–3). In one, Theseus initiates the expedition – as explained by Boccaccio, to quell the Amazons'

---

1   See Olson, Brooks (cii–cv), Ormerod.

'unnatural' revolt against their menfolk. In the other version, the Amazons invade Athens and lay siege to the Acropolis; they are repulsed, but the conflict ends in a truce. Given either history, much might be read into the circumstances of the marriage or the very fact that it takes place, but the play neither compels nor excludes a hostile reading. Hippolyta's implicit dissent can be plausibly read only into the first scene. In 4.1.111–17, she talks with Theseus as an equal (possibly in a competitive spirit) on the traditionally masculine topic of hounds and hunting. (This carries another ominous nuance: in Seneca's *Phaedra* 110–11, Theseus' next wife, the tragic Phaedra, is seen as passionately fond of hunting.) In 5.1, Hippolyta holds a relaxed debate with her husband on reason and imagination, and joins the party in barracking Quince and his men. The change might be owing to adaptation on Theseus' side, or on Hippolyta's, or on both. It remains matter for speculation, beyond the evidence offered by the play.

On balance, Theseus remains an unproblematized figure. This might itself be a factor in the bigger problem raised by the play: that things are not questioned enough, that complexities are glossed over by the play of fancy. I will return to these matters (see pp. 95, 106–7). Within the narrative, Theseus is a self-regarding, well-disposed patriarchal ruler, his good intentions untested by circumstance. Many doubts and ambiguities play about him, but Shakespeare does not press them. In *Dream* Shakespeare is doing mildly, almost casually, what he later does devastatingly in *Troilus and Cressida*: take a classical story from Chaucer and subvert it for his own purpose. But he returns to *The Knight's Tale* near the end of his career, in *The Two Noble Kinsmen*. *Kinsmen* was co-authored by John Fletcher; we should be cautious how much Shakespeare we read into it. The broad resemblances between *Kinsmen* and *Dream* have been noted by Potter (17–18): 'their lovers and hunters escaping into the forest, their rivalry of two men for one woman, their depiction of spectacularly incompetent performances and the comic figures . . . who attempt to stage them'. Such parallels are found not only in *Dream* but also in *Two Gentlemen of Verona* and *Love's Labour's Lost*. More ingeniously, Barr unveils a set of nuances shared 'intratemporally' by *The Knight's Tale*, *Dream* and *Kinsmen*, populating *Dream* with the absent Emily and Arcite.

Insofar as *Kinsmen* is admissible evidence, it points away from *Dream*. It has fewer ambiguities, more clear-cut themes. *Kinsmen* opens where *Dream* ends, with Theseus' wedding. The wedding song opening the play is full of flowers, and warns off all 'sland'rous' and 'boding' birds (1.1.19–21), like the snakes and hedgehogs in Titania's lullaby; but as with the lullaby, hindrances break out, here from the very start of the play. In *Dream*, the wedding rites proceed without incident; in *Kinsmen*, they are interrupted by the Theban widows' supplication to Theseus to avenge their wrong. Egeus' entry at the start of *Dream* is a much milder interruption. Theseus' martial role is asserted from the start in *Kinsmen*, and dramatically affirmed by his leaving for Thebes, delaying the consummation of his marriage. This is a crucial departure from Chaucer, his source in Boccaccio, and the latter's source in Statius, in all of which the marriage took place earlier; the widowed queens intercept Theseus' triumphal return from his Scythian expedition, with Hippolyta as his wedded wife. *The Knight's Tale* and *Dream* had omitted Boccaccio's long opening narrative of Theseus' war against the Amazons, as well as Statius' and Boccaccio's account of the Theban campaign. *Kinsmen* revives these issues, drawing retrospective attention to the earlier avoidance. But despite this reinstatement of Theseus as warrior, the order he represents is more seriously questioned than in *Dream*. Above all, *Kinsmen* takes a more searching view of the institution of marriage, and is more assertive of female independence and otherness.[1] However we view Theseus and Hippolyta's

---

1   See Maguire, 83; Roberts, 127–39.

relationship in *Dream*, his dominance is never in doubt: her past exploits are merely a foil to set it off. But in *Kinsmen*, Hippolyta's martial past is recalled at length by the Second Queen, who credits her with more power over Theseus than he over her (1.1.87–8). Also, *Kinsmen* presents Emilia's openly homoerotic affection for her childhood friend Flavina (1.3.49–82). By contrast, the childhood bond between Hermia and Helena (3.2.198–214) is an ineffectual memory, recalled in 1.1.214–16 to soothe the lovesick Helena but powerless to reconcile them when they fight for the same man in 3.2.

All the above scenes in *Kinsmen* are generally credited to Shakespeare. Parallels in scenes ascribed to Fletcher carry an underlying difference. Theseus and Hippolyta go hunting (3.5.94), but the maying rites and country sports are much more a rustic and communal event. The scene introducing them (3.1) might be Shakespeare's work, but the more elaborate treatment in 3.5 is probably Fletcher's. The entertainment for the rulers is simply a morris dance. The audience praise the performance, and there is little or no satire or banter.

It is hard to return an unqualified 'Yes' to Nuttall's question (51), 'Does the Theseus of myth figure in the *theatrical* experience of *A Midsummer Night's Dream*?' (Nuttall's italics) – or, we may add, in the thematic design. There is still greater uncertainty about the play's minor sources; their use can be neither proved nor disproved. Like Oberon, the wise woman Felicia in Montemayor's *Diana* and Gil Polo's *Diana Enamorada* has two potions, one to induce and the other to eradicate love (*Diana*, 186–9, 375); but they work only on those who take them knowingly. Besides, Yong's English translation of *Diana* had not appeared by 1598 (when Meres refers to *Dream* as an extant work: see p. 283), though it may have been composed earlier and read by Shakespeare in manuscript. As Brooks (lxxxi) points out, a closer match is the 'hearbe . . . *Anacamsoritis*' in Lyly's *Euphues and His England*:

69

'whosoeuer toucheth it, falleth in loue, with the person shee [*sic*] next seeth' (Lyly, 2.115.11–13).

There is a telling set of parallels, first noted by Coghill (41–58), with Anthony Munday's *John a Kent and John a Cumber* from the late 1580s. This play has two pairs of true lovers (who never change their loyalties) and two unwanted but parentally favoured suitors. The lovers escape into the country to meet up by moonlight. There are two magicians of whom the superior, John a Kent, favours the lovers. His boy assistant prefigures Robin, but the magician himself does so even more with his love of mischief and love-tangles, in which he finds sport:

> help, hinder, giue, take back, turne, ouerturne,
> deceiue, bestowe, breed pleasure, discontent.
> yet comickly conclude, like Iohn a Kent.
>
> (135–7)

One of his magic feats is to lead two young men (not the lovers) astray in the woods and send them to sleep. There is also a group of comic rustics given to theatricals, preparing a show for the double wedding and manipulated by the magicians. Set out in this way, the parallels to *Dream* seem closer than they are. *John a Kent* presents a different kind of magic more akin to sorcery, centred on two rival magicians as in Greene's *Friar Bacon and Friar Bungay*. On a balanced view, we can only say that *John a Kent* offers a set of motifs broadly matching those in *Dream*. Shakespeare might have recalled them, especially if the play (rather dated by the time of *Dream*) had links with Shakespeare's previous company, Lord Strange's Men, as its editor Pennell suggests (Munday, 46–7). But it has also been argued that *John a Kent* is of later date, and borrows from *Dream* rather than the other way about (see Arrell, 81–2).

In looking for precedents, we may find one in Shakespeare's own earlier *The Two Gentlemen of Verona*. Here also, two young men fall in and out of love with two young women, both men pursuing one of the women while the other remains constant and is finally rewarded. The crucial action takes place in a wood, though one that foreshadows *As You Like It* rather than *Dream*. There is a Duke (of Milan) who disposes matters happily at the end, but nothing corresponding to the fairies, the artisans or the Theseus–Hippolyta plot. Among the chief sources of *Two Gentlemen* is Montemayor's *Diana*, strongly suggesting that Shakespeare knew Yong's unpublished translation and might have recalled it in *Dream*.

The fact that *Dream* does not have a single defined source does not mean that Shakespeare's invention was working in a vacuum. Rather, the field was open for many elements to enter, combining differently at different points. And beyond the evident sources, there is a penumbra of possible ones: perhaps a precedent for a single line, perhaps a rough model for a motif or episode. There is seldom reason to think that these minor sources had a greater hidden impact; even the major ones are worked into strikingly new compounds by the complex chemistry of the play.

THEMES AND DESIGNS

Pastoral: the forest

This Introduction has twice referred to pastoral: with respect to the setting and action of the fairy scenes, and to the encounter of classes at the performance of *Pyramus and Thisbe*. *Dream* is a pastoral play at many levels. First of all, it is pastoral in the obvious sense of leading us out of the court into the wood. Pastoral is not folk literature. Its cradle is a courtly or urban milieu: the pastoral poet creates a pleasurable rural fiction as a foil to the stress and disorder of urban life. The pastoral fiction is controlled by the elite imagination; it is the product of a sophisticated ethos. Since Theocritus and Virgil, pastoral poetry has presented one world, the rustic, directly, but implicitly set it against another, the urban or courtly. In pastoral drama and romance, both worlds are directly incorporated in a cyclic narrative: the characters pass from court to country and back to a new and happier court, their original problems having been resolved during the pastoral sojourn (perhaps after more complication in the first instance). Pastoral classically presents shepherd life, but more broadly this contrast of court and country: two opposed communities, differently defining (or ignoring) man's place in nature. *Dream* revises the literal terms of the convention. It features no shepherds, indeed no rustics: Bottom and his comrades are townsfolk who 'work for bread upon Athenian stalls' (3.2.10). The natural woodland setting, representing the rural side of the pastoral equation, harbours only supernatural beings and animals, while the human mix of classes and communities, divided between town/court and country in conventional pastoral, belongs entirely to the courtly and urban world. There are no human dwellers in the wood.

This is a complex and inventive variant of the basic pastoral design. All pastoral leads us into what Northrop Frye (*Perspective*, 142–3) calls a 'green world': a 'symbol of natural society . . . associated with things which in the context of the ordinary world seem unnatural, but which are in fact attributes of nature as a miraculous and irresistible reviving power'. In *Dream*, the natural and the supernatural are most clearly linked in a context of destruction rather than revival, in the turmoil in nature following Titania's quarrel with Oberon:

> The spring, the summer,
> The childing autumn, angry winter change
> Their wonted liveries; and the mazed world,
> By their increase, now knows not which is which.
>
> (2.1.111–14)

Nature is also tinged with the supra-natural in Oberon's description of Titania's bower, as in the fairies' lullaby for their queen, in which lowly creatures are endowed with a new mystery of being. The pervasive presence of water and dew, night and the moon, is reflected both in literal description and in imagery passing into pathetic fallacy:

> The moon, methinks, looks with a watery eye;
> And when she weeps, weeps every little flower . . .
>
> (3.1.189–90)

Dew (here the moon's tear-drops) is an imaginative presence in the play no less than the moon (see also 2.1.9–15, 4.1.52–5, 5.1.405). The moonlight fluctuates in metaphoric nuance between full and feeble, the magically engaging and the merely illusory. So too is the dew associated (perhaps at the same time) with both pearls and tears, the resplendence of nature and the melancholy tinging all illusion.

Nuttall (57) sees night itself as a transforming factor: *Dream* is 'a Nocturnal Pastoral, itself, generically, a strange thing'. The dominance of the moon is generally recognized. From Theseus' opening lines, it should be shining residually or not at all during the time-span of the play. But besides Quince's assertion that it 'doth shine' on the supposedly new-moon night of the wedding (3.1.49), it is in evidence throughout the action, presiding over it visually, metaphorically and mythically. The 'cold fruitless moon' of virginity (1.1.73) acquires a rarer mystique as the 'watery moon' dissipating Cupid's shaft shot at the 'fair vestal' (2.1.161–4). In 2.1.103–5, the moon's very pallor signals her angry destructive power. The moon was thought to govern not only the tides but also menstruation. Evoking another event of the female body, Cupid's dart turns the white flower 'purple with love's wound', suggesting hymeneal bleeding after loss of virginity. Oberon's 'dream' thus touches on the suppressed anxieties that erupt in Hermia's dream (2.2.149–54). Titania and Oberon meet by moonlight (2.1.60), as do Titania and Bottom and indeed Hermia and Lysander (1.1.209–10). But as Smidt points out (131–2), to the lovers the forest is a place of darkness rather than moonlight; and Oberon commands Robin to 'overcast the night' still further (3.2.355) before Demetrius and Lysander start brawling.

The moon is and is not all things to everyone under its sublunary spell. This is paradoxically possible because the play was acted by daylight on the Elizabethan open stage. All kinds of moons can be conjured up verbally because there is no question of visually recreating any of them. Complex calculations, involving both celestial and human calendars, have been made to rationalize these lunar anomalies, perhaps thereby to date the play or link it to a particular wedding. Such exercises can acquire a certain circularity. It seems best to take the moon as a sentient presence matching the mood of each character or situation. We are back at the idea of a dynamic, animated nature. The pastoralism of *Dream* is not Virgilian but Ovidian: that is to say, pastoral only in the extended sense of evoking a living, unspoilt, even unsettling order of existence beyond the restrictive human dispensation, an order closely linked to external nature and, even there, embodying beings and forces beyond the physical. Ecocritics today have found in *Dream* an insight into the dynamic and interactive processes of nature. Watson (55) talks of the 'hidden symbiotic universe' of the play. Turner (*Helix*, 34) cites Titania's speech about nature in disarray to ask: 'Is 'nature' a place, like a wood, or river, or sea, or glen? Or is it a system of relationships: a series of causes, effects, and transformations that are difficult to see or locate in any tangible way?'

A place can be owned or governed; but as we are all too aware today, human control is marginal to the 'system of relationships' constituting nature. Who owns the wood, Theseus or Oberon? Officially, of course, it is Theseus' hunting preserve, while for Oberon and Titania it is only a stopping-point on their worldwide coursing. Yet Theseus merely sets the seal on the play's final order as determined by Oberon's 'night-rule' in the 'haunted grove' (3.2.5).[1] This is one aspect of the broader polarity of reason and imagination, reality and art, prose and poetry, order and subversion, courtly and popular perception, and many other binaries operating in the play. Young (154, 114) compiles an 'impressive list' of such 'oppositions', balanced in two columns and brought to 'reconciliation and commitment' at the close. In fact, the elements cross sides, merge and change partners; the binaries can even merge. As Snodgrass (218) more acutely observes, none of the play's four worlds – rulers, lovers, fairies, artisans – can be seen as central: 'they exist only in their balanced relationship to one another', as the play's four couples do among themselves. It might be added that the balance is a shifting and precarious one, resting on the ironic manipulation of the nuances of those relationships.

These shifts and uncertainties link up with the anomalies in the play's time-scheme. Theseus awaits 'Four happy days' to his wedding (1.1.2), but the action accounts for only three. In the opening scene (Day 1), Hermia and Lysander decide to elope 'tomorrow night' (1.1.164). Presumably also on Day 1, the artisans agree to meet 'tomorrow night' (1.2.93) in the wood. Act 2, then, starts on the night of Day 2, and the events in the wood continue through the night. Theseus and Hippolyta encounter the lovers in the wood on the morning of Day 3 (4.1). Their marriage celebrations continue into the same night. As Holland observes (note on 1.1.2), the anomaly is 'effectively invisible in performance' – or, one may add, in normal reading; it is best seen as one of Shakespeare's many inconsistencies of time-scheme. But it admirably suits the fairy milieu of the forest, located outside time. It belongs with the openly supernatural nature of the setting, which alone could fitly account for the strange events that take place there. Characters

---

1 Marienstras (20–36) shows how in that age, legal ownership was underlain by an older concept of the forest as a wild natural space. Shakespeare transfers this legal history to an imaginative plane.

fall in and out of love, fight and make up, by the power of love-juices and invisibility spells. Such magical pastoral reduces the psychological subtlety of the plot but imbues it with a different mystique, deepening and extending the expected contours of a love-comedy set in a green world.

Equally, it reshapes, disrupts and blurs those contours. The same actors are often cast as Theseus and Oberon, or Hippolyta and Titania. There are illuminating parallels between the fairy and human pairs, but they show up only against the differences. Bill Alexander (Stratford, 1986) tellingly doubled Hippolyta with Titania but not Theseus with Oberon, thus making the play 'Hippolyta's dream': Oberon and Bottom afford her a fantasy life that Theseus cannot. Danny Scheie (Santa Cruz, 1991) doubled Hippolyta with Oberon and Theseus with Titania. Already in 1846, Ulrici (154) had observed how in *Dream*, 'the principal spheres of life are made mutually to parody one another in mirthful irony'. The outwardly insecure, effectively dominant Oberon contrasts with the opposite condition of Theseus. The belligerent Titania suffers an open ignominy spared the discreet Hippolyta. The characters most insensitive to the woodland setting, namely the lovers, have their lives most radically changed by it. The fairy world reflects and redefines the human order while seeming to contrast with it – in fact, extends that order by virtue of the contrast, bringing out something new, different and elusive of definition. 'It seems to me / That yet we sleep, we dream' (4.1.192–3).

Dreamers and lovers

As early as 1794, Walter Whiter (158) coined the memorable phrase 'distemper'd *Dream*' to describe the play. The status of *Dream* as dream is an obvious critical concern. The dream world can be linked to the fairy world and even to the processes of nature as extended and magnified in the wood. For Mangan (160) the play's narrative and imagery take on 'the logic of a dream' in the way they manipulate 'fairies, spirits, magic, animal transformations, inexplicably changed affections'. The last is a crucial item: there can be metamorphoses of the mind as well as the body. Titania is transformed no less than Bottom.

A dream is illusory and ephemeral. Yet it engages deeply with reality, in forms that seem alien and unreal because they stem from the hidden reaches of the mind. It is thus possible to eat the cake of dreams and have it too. In Shakespeare's age no less than our own, a dream could be viewed as a sign, the surrogate for a reality outside itself, a hidden unconscious world briefly brought to surface. But as Greenfield ('Madness', 333) observes, these surrogates can be independent entities as well, 'valid verbal, visual, and emotional constructs'. By moving into a 'green world' that is also a magical world, *Dream* turns the constructs of the mind to visible, accessible yet ephemeral forms that leave us doubting their demonstrated reality. Theseus recognizes this but misses the point in his celebrated speech on the lunatic, the lover and the poet. In truth, the heightened representation of reality can only be ephemeral, attained in spells, thus apparently *lacking* in sustained reality. Lysander says as much of love: 'Swift as a shadow, short as any dream', even while 'unfold[ing] both heaven and earth' (1.1.144–6). This is the first of several occurrences of the variously charged word 'shadow' – fairy, actor, illusion – set against 'dream'. Even their final settled love seems to the lovers like a dream (4.1.191–3). Dunn (20–2) sees the entire fairy plot as the Indian boy's dream or fantasy. In Mark Lamos's production (Washington, 2003), the boy dreaming the play was Hippolyta's son from her earlier life. And what are we to make of the very English boy viewing (or dreaming) the action in Adrian Noble's film?

An unusual number of people spend an unusual amount of time sleeping through the action, in or outside the audience's view. But the only actual dream is Hermia's, of the snake at her breast (2.2.149–54). In Freudian terms, this opens up the insecurity at the heart of her love,[1] shared by all the lovers through their changing relationships. Many other happenings seem dream-like to those experiencing them. For the restored Titania, her encounter with Bottom is a series of 'visions' (4.1.75).[2] Even after the love-tangles have been sorted out, Demetrius sees his state as a continuing dream (4.1.191–3): his uncertainty, shared by the rest, extends to their seemingly final partnerships, although their earlier misadventures are dismissed (whether confidently or evasively) as 'dreams' (4.1.198). Above all there is Bottom's dream, or what he considers one. He recalls it as an unreal but uniquely precious experience, beyond the normal reach of apprehension: 'The eye of man hath not heard, the ear of man hath not seen, man's hand is not able to taste, his tongue to conceive, nor his heart to report what my dream was' (4.1.209–12). It is 'More than cool reason ever comprehends', to borrow Theseus' words (5.1.6). For Theseus, this elusive experience is the province of the poet. Bottom too thinks his vision would be fitly embodied in a poem, a ballad by Quince called 'Bottom's Dream', to be incorporated in a play. The general transformation of experience in art is further adapted to stage representation. I will return to these matters.

Despite its dream-like or phantasmagoric quality, the action is defined on clear lines. This is largely achieved by presenting love as a matter of encounters and interactions rather than affect or sensibility. The reality of love in *Dream* is depressingly unedifying. For a classic 'romantic comedy' featuring four couples, there is little amorous sentiment, let alone insight into the psychology of love. There is also an unusually strong presence of what Evans (37) calls 'discrepant awarenesses': ignorance among the couples of the reality of their states, which is known to the audience. This blindness to their own condition

1 See the Freudian analysis in Holland, 'Dream', 76–82. See also Hutson, 183–7.
2 It is tempting to distinguish between 'dream' and 'vision', but they seem to be used almost synonymously, as by Oberon (3.2.371), Bottom (4.1.203–5) and Robin (5.1.415–18).

is doubtfully dispelled even at the close. Not only the four young lovers but Theseus and Hippolyta, and Titania and Oberon (with Bottom making up the triangle) act out their relationships within a frame of dramatic irony. Yet this irony releases a sustained theatrical energy in the way the couples impact on each other. The mere presence of four varied couples generates patterns of convergence and contrast. It becomes a structural principle, within the broader principle of three (if not four) sets of characters: the courtiers (young and mature), the artisans and the fairies.

The problem with drawing patterns is that it emphasizes design over analysis. The couples serve too much as counters in a plot. Their chief energy seems invested in a war of the sexes, commencing at court (indeed in the play's pre-history, in Theseus' battle with the Amazons) and vastly extended in the forest. Orgel (88–94) finds a more aggressive eroticism at work. This is manipulated by magic in the service of patriarchal control: that 'men can be *made* to betray their loves and women can be *made* to love asses' (Orgel's italics) is perversely pertinent to the play's aim of ensuring 'suitable and mutually satisfactory marriages' (90). The later *As You Like It* also features four pairs of lovers in an equally structured plot, but endowed with more active personalities. They influence the outcomes of their own loves to a much greater extent. In *Dream*, on the contrary, Demetrius and Lysander are notoriously alike. Hermia and Helena differ somewhat in nature as well as appearance. Hermia is more confident, demanding and belligerent ('though she be but little, she is fierce': 3.2.325), if only because of her mortification at being doubly loved, then doubly scorned. Helena's more acquiescent, self-doubting nature, even to the point of abjection ('Use me but as your spaniel': 2.1.205), may have been aggravated by Demetrius' initial rejection. But neither temperament is explored in depth, and apart from Helena's self-abasement, we learn nothing of the nature of their affection. The men fall in and out of love passively, under the effect of the love-juice; the women remain constant, but accept their changing status helplessly though under strident protest. No doubt all four are victims of magic, but this seems to expose an innate fickleness in the men and a beleaguered possessiveness in the women. They go through a kind of non-coital orgy, turn and turn about. It leaves them, as Berry (46) acutely notes, in a paradoxical state of isolation from each other: they share a 'private despair that only the audience can perceive is communal'.

In his unusually full study of the lovers alone, Girard extends the idea, seeing them as 'mimetic lovers' (*Envy*, 36) engaged in a 'game of imitation and rivalry' ('Myth', 192). Their peer group implodes and collapses: in the doomed task of asserting their identities by emulating and competing with another in the group, they end up alienated from themselves. Hence their final adjustment seems as chance-directed, or at least externally induced, as their conflicts and estrangements. It cannot expunge the shadow of darker alternatives, diverted but not exorcized. 'There is nothing to suggest comedy' in the lovers' quarrels, Peter Brook told his actors. It is 'black farce', 'a nightmare' (Selbourne, 13). Other productions have grossly physicalized the emotional violence in the lovers' cross-encounters: in Hall's and Lepage's stage versions (or Lang's in Germany), and with readier cinematic resources in Hoffman's and Noble's films.

The play as it stands does not bear out violence in Theseus and Hippolyta's relationship, except in sporadic reminders of their battles in the field. Given the dramatic context, we may infer reservation or even resentment on her side, but hardly the vehement rebelliousness or alienation found in some modern productions: first, perhaps, in Langham's (Old Vic, London, 1960), followed *inter alia* by Ciulei's Hippolyta, disarmed but still assertive; Hancock's, initially caged; and Beier's, initially naked, shooting arrows at the moon – all three played by black actresses. In Adrian Noble's film, Hippolyta slaps Theseus as she flounces out, incensed by his judgement in Hermia's case. Nothing in the text bears out such interpretations. On Theseus'

16 Hippolyta (Lindsay Duncan) slaps Theseus (Alex Jennings) in Adrian Noble's film, 1996

side, there is a casual possessive self-assurance almost amounting to emotional blindness. Even that may be matter for conjecture, read into the dialogue by the assumptions of later centuries. We hardly learn anything of the nature of their relationship.

Oberon's authority is flouted by Titania. He reasserts his power by making her fall in love with an ass. It abases her, but abases him no less. Titania's abjection is compensated by a vindication of female sexuality. Paster (139–43) views Titania and Bottom as a Freudian mother–child dyad, their love as scatological infantilism. But even here, Hinely's nuanced Freudian reading (134) finds a 'grotesquely tender and erotic madonna and child', 'transfigured . . . into something touching, even charming'. Their outrageous amour takes on a romantic and lyrical quality, almost a kind of innocence. There are touches of tenderness and even poetry in the relationship, beyond the merely grotesque or sordid:

> Sleep thou, and I will wind thee in my arms . . .
> So doth the woodbine the sweet honeysuckle

> Gently entwist; the female ivy so
> Enrings the barky fingers of the elm.
>
> (4.1.39–43)

The play's few snatches of romantic lyricism emanate not from a human lover but from a fairy addressing an ass. This does not make the encounter less preposterous in cold light, as summed up in one of Shakespeare's most chilling lines:

> Methought I was enamoured of an ass.
>
> (4.1.76)

To be 'enamoured of' meant not only to love but, more usually, to be loved by someone. Why this unfounded claim to Bottom's love? It may reflect Titania's sexual egotism, or a wish to deny her initiative in the relationship, now that she sees it in its true light. It may also be an oblique hit at her 'lord', suggesting even after their reconciliation that Bottom afforded her a satisfaction that Oberon cannot, as implied in Alexander's production (see p. 76). However we interpret the phrase, it carries a strong sense of violation. It is a disturbing admission of the mortifying depth of Titania's sexuality, which cannot but reflect on her newly revived love of Oberon. He on his part shows no jealousy, repugnance or humiliation, nothing but a detached delight in the 'sweet sight' (4.1.45) of her lying embowered with an ass. His sense of control and mastery seems to leave no room for jealousy: he is secure in his possession. Read deeply, the complexities of Titania's love, as brought out in her line above, compromise every lover in the play.

Patriarchy

The ethos of patriarchy explains why *Dream* can tie up all its love-plots as early as the fourth act. More than most subsequent Shakespearean comedies, the play operates from start to finish within a framework of patriarchy, paradoxically yet inevitably imposed on its varied repertoire of sexuality. All love-tangles and disputes can thus readily be resolved, especially if helped along by a little magic. The overarching patriarchal order is too evident to miss. At court, the power of patriarchy is more apparent than the power of love. How far it is mitigated by the end of the play depends in part on whether Egeus is absent from the wedding revels as in the quartos, or conducting them as in the Folio text. (On this subject, perhaps overstressed in some recent readings, see 5.1.0.1n., 44–58n.) This is because Egeus sees the daughter as the father's property in the crudest terms. Since theatrical practice made it acceptable, he has physically belaboured Hermia in some productions, perhaps beginning with Alexander's (1986). In fact, his stand goes beyond Elizabethan norms, where family consent, though customary, was not legally required, and love between the prospective couple was accepted as a crucial factor. Even the Puritan Robert Cleaver, who held that children were their fathers' goods, placed some limits on the latter's right to marry them off (Greaves, 160–1). Hermia's plight in *Dream* is more a trope of the woman's position under patriarchy than a historically valid situation. Theseus agrees that physical procreation endows the male parent with power of life and death over his progeny: 'By him imprinted, and within his power / To leave the figure, or disfigure it' (1.1.50–1). The mother is conspicuously absent from this dispensation. 'Hermia and Helena have no mothers', remarks Montrose ('Fantasies', 117). Hawkes (13–15) points to a line of absent women, spectres from a suppressed matriarchal discourse: Lysander's dowager aunt; Hermia's, Helena's or indeed Pyramus' and Thisbe's mothers; Hippolyta's earlier identity as Amazon queen.

Even the rebellious Hermia is ready to submit to a husband, provided it is a man of her choice (1.1.79–82nn.). Both she and Helena are voluble enough in the forest; but having achieved the married state, they do not utter a word in the last act. There is no hint that this is owing to repression, protest or alienation. By this point, Hippolyta too seems to have overcome any earlier resistance to her marriage. She now speaks with relaxed confidence, sometimes in good-natured contest with her husband, whether about hunting-dogs or the poetic imagination. Oberon consummately proves his power over Titania. Going far beyond Petruchio in *The Taming of the Shrew*, he subdues his wife by reducing her to bestiality. It is patriarchy at its most salacious and sadistic. She on her part addresses him as 'my lord' (4.1.98), the very term she had earlier contested (2.1.63–4). Feminist critics have seen the subjugation and degradation of women written into the terms of the play. For Levine (211–12), in *Dream* sexual violence is 'virtually a function of existence itself', coercing female appetites and violating the bonds between women. This compromises the closure of the comic action in terms of a patriarchal order.

The play advances a series of challenges to patriarchy that are defeated yet never quite dispelled. Hermia does not merely resent her father's orders; she protests against them in open court and argues her case. Decorously at court but unabashedly in the forest, she asserts her own sexuality, as Helena does openly from the start. The latter, indeed, harms the cause of her sex by abasing herself in love: 'I am your spaniel, and Demetrius, / The more you beat me, I will fawn on you' (2.1.203–4). Titania's abasement too is disturbingly total while it lasts; yet it is powered by an assertive sexuality (even if artificially roused), and she controls Bottom by virtue of her royal station and magic powers. Again, however we read the bride Hippolyta, she retains an aura of the Amazons and their ethos. Amazonian woman-power was a threat to the patriarchal state as well as to personal manhood. Theseus' victory over the Amazons marks the triumph of patriarchy over a matriarchal order. Thenceforth, the Amazon could be seen as a type of the unruly woman, and as Roberts argues, of all things 'wild', subversive and marginal.[1] But as Roberts also notes,

1 See Roberts, 101–5, 127–9; Wright, 'Amazons', 445–54; Loomba, 191–3.

Elizabethan literature equally admits the virtuous warrior-woman, a fit subject of love like Spenser's Britomart. Both aspects are present in Hippolyta. There is warrant in that age for seeing Hippolyta as a valiant warrior, even excelling Theseus: '*Hippolita* dissipated the troupes of great *Theseus*, dismounting himselfe [i.e. unseating him from his horse] in the fight, yet afterward (on meere grace) made him her husband.'[1]

The matriarchal subtext admits of many extensions. One is lesbian. The play presents two such potential bonds: between Titania and her votaress, and between Hermia and Helena in their schooldays. How far is the two girls' battle in 4.2 a cover for their anguish at the rupture of their old bond, and how erotically is that bond to be viewed? I have cited above the contrastingly decisive treatment of Emilia and Flavina in *The Two Noble Kinsmen* (see p. 69). Here is one more path glimpsed but not pursued in the subtextual play of themes. There is no clearly erotic dimension to Titania's relationship with her 'votaress' (2.1.123–37); but there is the sense of a fulfilled, self-sufficient female bonding, even a sisterhood like the original Titania or Diana's train. The members of this sisterhood can be mothers rather than virgins, reversing the barrenness of the monastic sorority with which Theseus threatens Hermia (1.1.70–8). Titania shares emotionally in her companion's pregnancy, and the boy becomes a surrogate for the child she cannot have (Calderwood, 417–18). Bottom, then, can be seen as *his* surrogate. Oberon's designs on the child are an attack on this matriarchal world, setting off a parental tussle between Titania and Oberon: Dunn (22–4) and Raman (240–54) weave the whole plot into an oedipal design. Though he never appears in the play, some critics see the boy as

---

1   Anthony Munday(?), *A Woman's Worth* (1599), fol. 5ʳ (sig. B5ʳ), trans. of Alexandre de Pontaymeri's *Paradoxe apologique . . . que la femme est beaucoup plus parfaite que l'homme* (1594).

important or even central to the plot. He has regularly featured in stage and screen versions, in many avatars from a dusky turbaned child (*inter alia* in Reinhardt's film) to a sybaritic youth in Danny Scheie's production (Santa Cruz, 1991).

The boy's Indian provenance is also matter for question. For Europeans in that age, 'India' was a remote half-mythic, half-romantic land concocted by merging reports and myths about both East and West 'Indies' (see Chaudhuri, 'India'). 'The farthest steep of India' (2.1.69) suits an eastern continental location, while the seaside scene with Titania and her votaress suggests the Caribbean, as Buchanan argues on both geographical and historical grounds. There are sharper colonial associations as well, for which the West Indies would provide the more obvious context at that date. Any extended reference to England's eastern trade would be anachronistic: the East India Company received its charter only in 1600. What postcolonial critics like Loomba (184–91) and Raman (243–5, 269–75) postulate is an alleged trait already in the national psyche that allows the exotic boy to be both spoil and commodity. Either way, he is the site of conflict and power-play. This would apply equally to the Native American prince that Ralegh brought back from Guiana (see p. 289). Colonial mercantilism is conflated with race; with gender too, for this 'India' is Titania's matriarchal realm, now colonized by a patriarchal order. Loomba most clearly demonstrates the age's notion of the female body as a colonizable site.

Raman makes two other acute points. He sees in the non-appearance of the Indian boy the 'invisibility of colonial history' in early modern Europe (275). He also argues (255–62) that a nascent capitalist ethos, advocating freedom in the civic and economic sphere, was merely redefining traditional patriarchy. Tennenhouse (111–14) finds a similar move from the old patriarchy to the new monarchy, and Erlich (65–6, 72–3) from the old to the new aristocracy in early modern England. In other words, the lovers' romantic fulfilment is framed within a subtler but no less confining social regimen. We may accept this premise the more readily because their happy unions are brought about by magic rather than free choice. The magical changes conceal the hard political realities of the age.

Carnival, class, court

The confusions in the forest, of judgement no less than relationships, are the very stuff of carnival. Robin, their connoisseur and often proximate cause, sums up the carnivalesque in the word I have already applied to Titania and Bottom's encounter, 'preposterously' (3.2.121) – literally, placing last what should be first: as it were, advancing the rear, in the spirit of a rude gesture to which he reduces even 'The wisest aunt telling the saddest tale' (2.1.51; see 54n.).[1] Robin has affinities outside the fairy world. He recalls the clever scheming slave of classical comedy and the Vice of medieval religious drama. Though Bottom is the formal 'clown' in the play, Robin can be seen as a variant of the clownish servant, a combination of Speed and Lance in *The Two Gentlemen of Verona*. In this multiple capacity, Robin serves as chorus and spectator even while intervening crucially in the action.[2] This double role is made possible by his emotional distance from the events he engages in. as Grady (294) puts it, he is an 'anthropologist from Mars'. (For all we know, he travels to that planet.) He has no stake in the outcome of his antics, and unlike Oberon, no interest in his victims' fate. His actions seem impelled by a motiveless delight in the 'preposterous', like a

---

1 Patterson entitles her chapter on *Dream* 'Bottom's Up'. Amazingly, this sense of *bottom* (*OED n.* 8) is effectively unrecorded till 1796, but sixteenth-century pronunciation allowed a pun on *ass* and *arse*.

2 Weimann (194) notes the association of the comic actor Richard Tarleton with Robin in *Tarlton's News out of Purgatory . . . Published by an Old Companion of His, Robin Goodfellow* (1590): stage clown, supernatural spirit and choric satirist are brought together.

benevolent Iago's. He has gifted a word to the language: the nineteenth-century coinage 'puckishness', meaning a disengaged volatility of being, as much energy and ingenuity as mischief.

Thus Robin epitomizes the reworking of accustomed experience in the green world: radical, redefining, yet illusory. In a context of May and Midsummer, it almost compels a connection with the ritualized, festive subversion of order we call carnival. Barber's seminal account of Shakespeare's 'festive comedy' has been extended since Bakhtin's *Rabelais and His World* appeared in English translation in 1968. Carnival, in Bakhtin's classic account, 'grants the right of a certain freedom and familiarity, the right to break the usual norms of social relations' (200–1). It is formalized disorder, a conventional breaking of convention. The established order allows itself to be briefly defied so as to absorb the forces that might have destabilized it. Hence its purport is not negative: 'it tends to embrace both poles of becoming in their contradiction and unity' (203). It mocks the 'old authority and truth' with a greater 'universality and sober optimism' (212).

Carnival is the essence of many popular festivals. In Shakespeare's day, such festivals were generally prevalent in the countryside, though condemned by the Puritans. At least three underlie the action of *Dream*: May Day, Midsummer and St Valentine's Day. The last, occurring in February, is mentioned in passing (4.1.138) but can be seen as underlying the dance of lovers. The other two are central, though maying is mentioned only twice in the text (1.1.167, 4.1.132) and Midsummer still more obliquely in 2.1.82. (Its presence in the title may be authorial or accidental.) But summer seems to be the notional season in Titania's account of the disorder in nature (2.1.82, 110), besides the fluid context of her splendid declaration, 'The summer still doth tend upon my state' (3.1.149). Maying, too, was not confined to the first of May. Shakespeare is evoking the conjunct spirit of both festivals, besides related ones like Whitsuntide, St Peter's Day and St John's Day (the last conflated with the pagan Midsummer). Most of these festivals originate in fertility rites and have strong magical and supernatural associations. No less important is their rite of disorder, a temporary overthrow of the social hierarchy. Not only the dominant mores but the dominant classes are challenged by the humbler orders and their practices. It is a severely controlled exercise, but the ideas it plants in the social consciousness may acquire greater potency. As playwright of a censored stage under an authoritarian monarchy, Shakespeare was clearly alive to the subversive potential of his 'preposterous' material. *Dream* exposes, even if it glosses over, many fault-lines in the fabric of society, especially as relating to class and gender – fault-lines, ultimately, in human nature itself. Potts (26) observes that the Bottom–Titania antithesis is at the heart of *all* comedy: 'It is a profound revelation of human nature: of the paradox by which extreme fastidious refinement exists in us side by side with the vulgarest fleshly processes and propensities.'

Dream is Shakespeare's first play (with few to follow) having ordinary working people as major characters. This element in the play's compound can create a telling dramatic effect. Barry Jackson recalls scenes from *Dream* performed by working-class schoolchildren in worn clothes, with 'midday meals in pudding basins wrapped up in bandana handkerchiefs, precisely as one saw their fathers in those days in the Black Country'. Jackson professes to those children an 'unpayable debt for an idea' ('Producing', 79). Christine Edzard's film version *The Children's Midsummer Night's Dream* (2001) was acted entirely by schoolchildren from London's deprived East End. Such productions serve as a kind of material metaphor for the proletarian element implanted in the play by the presence of the artisans. More subtly and pervasively, there is much other material drawn from subaltern culture: the fairy lore to start with, though radically changed in orientation as argued above (pp. 58–9).

To consider these elements in the play's design, I shall return to the basic premises of pastoral outlined earlier and apply them to the play's proletarian anchorman, Nick Bottom. Pastoral sets common people and popular culture against the ethos of the dominant elite. In his classic study of pastoral, Empson defines it as the 'complex' man's response to the 'simple': 'I am in one way better, in another not so good' (*Pastoral*, 19). Empson illustrates this equivocal mode from *Dream*:

> The simple man becomes a clumsy fool who yet has better 'sense' than his betters and can say things more fundamentally true; he is 'in contact with nature', which the complex man needs to be, so that Bottom is not afraid of the fairies . . .
>
> (18)

In fact, Bottom is the only human to encounter the fairies. He is so untuned to the supernatural that he can engage with it not only without fear but without losing a jot of his native identity, except in the external detail of a headpiece or so. Waking from his dream, he confusedly echoes St Paul's words in 1 Corinthians 2.9 (see 4.1.209–11n.). Other verses from the same Epistle draw a contrast between the simple and the complex man:

> But God hath chosen the foolish things of the worlde, to confounde the wise: and God hath chosen the weake things of the worlde, to confound the things which are mightie.
>
> (1 Cor. 1.27)

Shakespeare's closest reversion to the vein of Bottom's 'dream' speech is in Caliban's dream of the 'sounds and sweet airs' of Prospero's island:

> The clouds, methought, would open and show riches
> Ready to drop upon me, that when I waked
> I cried to dream again.
>
> (*Tem* 3.2.141–3)

90

This articulates the pathos of the excluded. The same pathos lingers about Bottom in Arthur Rimbaud's poem ('Bottom', *Illuminations*) who, as ass, goes 'brandishing my grievance' (*brandissant mon grief*), like his earlier incarnations of a bird dragging its wing and a bear with its fur hoary from grief.[1] Shakespeare's Bottom, in contrast, assimilates the supernatural to the mundane with aplomb, and wants to enshrine the combination in a ballad of 'Bottom's Dream'. The experience does not awe him; he cites it to outscore his companions: 'Masters, I am to discourse wonders; but ask me not what' (4.2.28–9). He also blithely flaunts the insight which troubles Helena (1.1.234) and eludes the besotted Titania altogether: 'to say the truth, reason and love keep little company together nowadays' (3.1.139–40). He is utterly insensitive to the power of stage illusion in presenting the lion and moonshine; but his literalism is a reflection on stage illusion itself. It is the same stolid literalism to which Corin in *As You Like It* later lends dignity: 'that the property of rain is to wet and fire to burn; that good pasture makes fat sheep; and that a great cause of the night is lack of the sun' (3.2.24–7). Hence Bottom is unfazed by the sniping of his social betters during their performance, even while Quince and Starveling are awed into garbling their lines. Despite the sniping, the encounter of unequals is on remarkably equal footing. This may owe something to Theseus' magnanimity, but no less to the unassailable security that the artisans, especially Bottom, derive from their class position.

In three important studies, Montrose (*Purpose*, chs 8–11), Parker (*Margins*) and Patterson all engage with the politics implicit in the play: Montrose with gender and power politics, Parker with class and gender, and Patterson with the politics of popular festival. These strands cannot be separated. We may group them under the general head of 'inversion politics'. There is a complex balance of opposites here. Among Bottom's

1   Rimbaud, 148–9; see also Riffaterre, 101–5.

appellations in stage directions and speech headings is 'Clown'. There can be little doubt that the company's clown Will Kemp played Bottom. But 'clown', at that day, meant not only a jester but more basically a rustic, hence a boor or socially inferior person. As a social inferior, he could be a figure of fun or contempt. As a jester, the amusement he inspired would be more equivocal: contemptible like the antics of 'naturals' or mentally disadvantaged persons, but also delectable like a witty jester's jibes at his social betters. It is the classic pastoral balance between persons of opposed station.

Bottom has traditionally been seen as a complete fool, lovable or otherwise. Cox (77) calls him Shakespeare's 'greatest purely metaphoric characterization': the man simply *is* an ass. And yet he is not: when he externally becomes one, he 'combines humanity and asshood', as Allen (108) remarks, 'and thus comments obliquely upon the peculiar qualities of each species in comparison with the other'. The symbolism of the ass extended many ways, though commonly signifying dullness, sloth and obstinacy. Valeriano (fol. 87[r]) depicts the ignorant and dull (*ignarus*) man with the head of an ass. Della Porta thrice repeats a drawing of a human fool's head alongside an ass's, showing their common features: a round high forehead, large ears and thick lips.[1] Della Porta also ascribes to the ass other signs of stupidity like a large head and face, fleshy cheeks and a deep loud voice. Bottom displays many of these physical features though not all. The iconographer Cesare Ripa (333) says an ass-head (carried by a woman representing obstinacy) stands for ignorance. Bottom's ass-head has been represented onstage in a variety of ways: from full-scale realistic ones – some with moving eyes, ears and mouths, thereby robbing the actor of scope for facial play – to minimal coverings for the head, nose or ears, as in Hall, Brook and Alexander's productions.[2]

---

1   della Porta, 61, 70, 93; see also 49, 87, 91, 92, 105 and Baumbach, 82–3.
2   For a full account, see Griffiths, 145–6.

Liber duodecimus. 87

PIERIVS VALERIANVS AD PETRVM CVR-
SIVM, ROM. CIVEM, DE IIS QVÆ PER ASINVM,
MVLVM ET CAMELVM SIGNIFICANTVR
EX SACRIS ÆGYPTIORVM
LITERIS.

 E forte commentitia ea putes, Petre Curfi lepidifsime, quæ multa adèo nudiuster tius Cytorio in iugo tuo, vbi bona pars Academiæ cænabamus, à veteribus tam Ægyptijs, quàm Græcis, atq; etiã Latinis, super Asini significationibus tradita comemoraueram, curæ precium fore duxi, quantu solicitudine præstare potui, primo quoq; tempore pleniori obsequio tibi satisfacere. Videbaris enim illa, quod facile animad uerti, attentioribus admodum auribus haurire, & auidiuscule, vt ita dicam, deglutire : sed vix adduci poteras scriptores illos veteres in Asino perscrutando fuisse adèo curiosos: & quoniã vm bra etiam eius in vanisimi negotij prouerbium cesserat, reliquum etiam corpus paruipenden dum existimabas. Collegi igitur tam ea, quæ tum memoriter disserueram, quàm quæ alias spar sim à me fuerant ea re super adnotata, eorum citatis testimonijs, qui talia memoriæ prodidere, vbi tantum res deposcere videbatur: nam minus omnia tunc ex tempore dicere ag gresso succur rebant. Quare tunc non pauca prætermissa sunt, quæ recitata longe maiori tibi admirationi sis tura fuerant: quæ quidem nunc, qualitercunq; à me conscripta sint, benigne accipias velim. Et si minus tibi lucubratio ipsa satisfecerit, vt quæ nimium properata non ita omnia complecti po tuerit, voluntatem tamen animumq; meum existimes, quantum in me fuit, tibi amico tam ve teri, tam probo, satis plurimùm facere studuisse : non enim recens mea erga doctrinam & inge nium tuum beneuolentia, firmaq; atq; constans amicitia, quæ ab ipso primùm die, quo Romam diu patria cariturus applicui, cœpta, mirificum in dies accepit incrementum : accessit & tam vnanime concorsq; contubernium, couictiusq; per annos aliquot iucundisimus. Ita ego pluribus atq; ijs non leuibus de causis tibi semper coiunctisimus, scripta cogitationesq; meas comunicare tecum maxime conueniens existimani: quòd optimi integerrimiq; amici, qualis es tu, vt melio res euadamus in causa sunt, si quid admoneant: vel, vt alacriores ad lucubrandum accedamus efficiunt, si probent. Sedenim quid oneris gerat Asinus inspiciamus.

IGNARVS HOMINVMQVE LOCO-
RVMQVE.

 VM PRIMIS autem rerum omnium ignarũ per aselli cipitem hominem ab Ægy ptijs sacerdotibus significa ri, & Horus & plerique alij prodidere : eamcɟ imperitiã in eo præcipuè notari uolebant, quæ pluri mum ex solitaria accidit educatione, quippe cùm quis tanquam Aglaus alter, intra pri uatos parietes semper altus & educatus, pe dem è domo, uel è patria nunquam tulisset fo ras, oportere scilicet hunc parũ experientem  esse, & officiorũ hospitalium inscium. Israël itacɟ diu apud Ægyptios educatus, & hieroglyphicân optimè peritus, cùm Isacharem filium suum asinum appellas̄ *Gen.49.*

O 3

17 Man with ass's head, *Hieroglyphica*, Pierio Valeriano, 1556

It is now more usual to focus on Bottom's native wit and sheer capacity for unshaken survival, a Rabelaisian heroism of the humble. Already in 1905, G.K. Chesterton (363) had offered a sparkling account of Bottom in this light. A little later, J.B. Priestley (3–6) anticipated Hoffman's film by endowing Bottom with a 'shrewish wife', and viewing him as 'the romantic, the poetical, the imaginative man' as well as 'a piece of humorous, bewildered flesh'. Much has been made of his garbled echo of St Paul.[1] Such confusion might be natural in anyone faced with the numinous. Bottom's speech has been taken as a secularizing parody of the religious. But that is to give it too much of a single thrust, ignoring the balance of contextual opposites – combining St Paul and Apuleius, as Kott phrases it (*Translation*, 32) – reflected in a confusion of the senses: 'The eye of man hath not heard, the ear of man hath not seen, man's hand is not able to taste, his tongue to conceive' (4.1.209–11). This confusion has been related to 1 Corinthians 12.17. The burlesque acquires a deeper dimension through the biblical echoes, while those in turn are validated in a new context of meaningful folly. The force of other, mysterious worlds touches even the untaught and incorrigible. Bottom's speech evokes the hallowed figure of the blessed fool whose ignorance is more godly, and perhaps more perceptive, than conventional wisdom. In the unironic praise of virtuous spiritual folly concluding his *Praise of Folly* (translated by Thomas Chaloner in 1549), Erasmus quotes several passages from 1 and 2 Corinthians, including that underlying Bottom's speech, though the ass finds only brief mention as Christ's chosen mount (sig. S1ʳ). But Cornelius Agrippa's *Of the Vanity and Uncertainty of Arts and Sciences* (translated by James Sandford, 1569) has a whole chapter (ch. 102, fols 183ᵛ–185ᵛ, sigs 3A3ᵛ–3B1ᵛ) praising the ass in Christian terms. Despite his general volubility, Bottom finds his dream inexpressible. As Miller observes (267),

---

1 On Bottom's speech, see Miller, 264–8.

it is notable not for its higher meanings, if any, but for 'the multivalency of the perspective': credulity and scepticism, acceptance and rejection, folly and wisdom. This free-ranging 'multivalency' may be the key mode of the play as a whole.

Patterson (59–62) links the inversion politics of the play to the inversion rituals of folk festivals. She takes from the anthropologist Victor Turner the idea of 'liminality', whereby 'the lower social strata become privileged, and bodily parts and biological referents, conceived as the source of regenerative energy, are revalued' (61). Bottom's physical grossness is obvious enough, though there is something frank and endearing about it. Patterson follows Bakhtin in linking 'the lower bodily stratum' with May Day rituals, morris dances and such popular festive practices derived from fertility rites. Within this associative framework, the 'festive plots' of *Dream* grow increasingly transgressive. Early modern England saw a steady line of protests and riots by the working classes, sometimes at Midsummer. Yet Penry Williams ('Tensions', 62) is right in seeing an absence of 'serious social upheaval' in Elizabeth's reign, which he ascribes to political rhetoric and social cohesion rather than to coercive governance. This reassuring picture is confirmed from an unexpected quarter, in Karl Marx's sarcastic dismissal of Britain's endemic political compromises. No less than four times, Marx illustrates his point from *Dream*: 'the lion of opposition' becomes 'Snug the mediator'.[1] Conservative European politics recalls for Marx the farcical deflation of the serious seen in *Pyramus and Thisbe*. Earlier, Heinrich Heine had compared the rulers of France after the 1848 revolution to the amateur players, especially Snug, anxious to establish he was not a real lion (Prawer, 31).

Dream carries no message of political revolution. The classes seem to coexist in essential harmony, give or take a little banter.

---

1   *Contribution to the Critique of Hegel's Philosophy of Law*: Marx, 3.87–8. For the other passages see 13.26, 16.463, 17.35.

The reflection of Elizabethan court culture is even harder to gauge, though *Dream* has been fertile ground for allusion-hunters. They have invariably destroyed their case by overkill and tenuous argument: the only point generally granted is that Oberon's 'fair vestal' is Queen Elizabeth. Hackett's exhaustive search has not unearthed any other solid link between Elizabeth and *Dream*; she leaves the issue as 'tantalizingly mysterious' (*Elizabeth*, 132). The Queen's subtextual presence is another matter: her quasi-mythic mystique is embedded in the play, as also the iconography of her court pageantry (see pp. 286–8). The royal allusion modulates the treatment of virginity, excluding the fair vestal from the love-charged universe in a rare compliment to her maiden state. For the rest, virginity is consistently linked to frustrated love, to images of water, dew and the moon: pallid, insubstantial, tearful, 'fruitless' (1.1.73). The virgin moon goddess Diana or Cynthia was a standard figure for the Queen, hence 'the watery moon' is an equivocal phrase implanted even in the 'fair vestal' passage (see 2.1.162n.). Later, the moon looks with a 'watery eye' (3.1.189) on Titania and Bottom. It is weeping, but is it also purblind or rheumy-eyed?

Yet as Orgel (85–6) points out, it is the vestal's virginity that endows the flower with the gift of inducing love. Titania is another name for Diana, hence applicable to the Queen (see pp. 52–3). It would be political blasphemy to show her coupling with an ass-headed yokel: that was the unspeakable (though subconsciously potent) commoner's fantasy embodied in a dream recounted by the astrologer and herbalist Simon Forman (Montrose, 'Fantasies', 109–12). Clearly, there can be no close identification of Titania with England's Queen. Further, Titania is roundly victimized by Oberon. Elizabeth's position as female (moreover virgin) head of a monarchy created a piquant conflict between her identities as monarch, hence inviolable, and as woman, hence assailable; as also between the rightful monarch (legitimized in patriarchal terms) and the Amazonian unruly woman. Shakespeare skilfully negotiates these oppositions by isolating the inviolable virgin queen in the 'fair vestal'. The description of the vestal recalls the iconic 'sieve' portrait of Elizabeth (Yates, 115–18). Most germane, perhaps, is a line from Petrarch's *Triumph of Love* (3.145) inscribed in the portrait, indicating the Virgin Queen's passage from the Triumph of Love to the Triumph of Chastity. But across the play, Shakespeare works a nuanced, ambiguous critique of the royal icon – virginal goddess, female patriarch, queen of the realm and womanly victim of her position – in terms of myth and image as he could not have done directly. Of course it is not a consistent political critique. Shakespeare weaves certain political motifs of his time into the complex design of the play, in a tangential, fictive reworking with no explicit commitment to any position. The motifs are freshly validated at the level of myth, and by application to contexts other than their own.

Theatre, art and illusion

Dream is Shakespeare's first play to take theatrical presentation as one of its themes. For all its fairy fancy, the play bears on serious issues within the politics of theatre as well as the wider politics of society. At one level, the workmen's performance of *Pyramus and Thisbe* exposes the philosophical and aesthetic deficiencies of the dramatic form. At another, it mirrors the class politics and cultural misalliances of Elizabethan theatre.

The artisans are characters of comedy in Aristotle's sense, people adjudged worse than the average and calling for reductive treatment (*Poetics* ch. 5). But their inclusion in the play raises rather more complicated issues. 'Rude mechanicals' formed a sizeable part of the clientele of the Elizabethan playhouse. Will Shakespeare, like Will Kemp and Richard Burbage, might have been admired by his working-class patrons, but the workers' social standing was more secure and assured by law. In fact, actors ran the risk of being taken for vagabonds if they did not legitimize their position by joining a trade guild. The genial but unflagging satire directed at the artisans, Bottom in particular, thus carries a charge of comradely laughter towards social coequals, even if gratifyingly below one's own intellectual level. Within the play, Quince and Bottom regard their companions in much the same light. The courtiers (no doubt like their real counterparts in the audience) take a more radically dismissive view of the artisan-actors. Their good humour masks a crushingly patronizing dismissal, untroubled by the subversive potential of their inferiors. Hence the social harmony remains intact, but the demoralizing effect on the artisans appears in Quince's stage fright and Starveling's resentful confusion, though Bottom does not lose his aplomb. He speaks with the one-upmanship of the insider in the know:

> THESEUS The wall, methinks, being sensible, should
>   curse again.
> BOTTOM No, in truth, sir, he should not. 'Deceiving
>   me' is Thisbe's cue.

> (5.1.181–4)

But the real riposte, if any, must lie in the *Dream* audience's reaction to the reactions of the audience of *Pyramus and Thisbe*. How far did they – how far do we – share in, and how far demur from, the barracking to which the palace audience subject their entertainers?

As explained above (pp. 4–5), *Pyramus and Thisbe* resembles the household performances of local amateur players in the 'big house', though during rehearsal, Quince refers to features of the London public stage (3.1.3–4). Our response to the play-within-the-play is thus rendered complex. We cannot take it at face value as a critique of the politics of Shakespeare's theatre. At the most proximate level, Shakespeare is targeting amateur players in household entertainments. At the next level, he is satirizing the cruder drama of an earlier (though still extant) phase of the public theatre. At both levels, he can share the amusement of Quince's courtly audience. Only at a third level does he bring his own theatre into focus. When the Chamberlain's Men played in big houses, their reception was no doubt outwardly different from that accorded to Quince's company, just as their performance must have been. But at this third level, Shakespeare is also presenting, however transmogrified, the ambiguous cultural and class relations between his own cohort and its elite audience and patrons. He had encountered the real-life equivalent of Philostrate, Master of the Revels, no less than that of Quince the producer or even Bottom, Snout and Starveling. He would have seen, even if he was not, 'an unperfect actor on the stage / Who with his fear is put besides his part' (*Son* 23.1–2), like the wretched Starveling playing Moonshine. 'The best in this kind are but shadows', says Theseus (5.1.210). This agrees with Shakespeare's own view of the actor-dramatist's function in Sonnet 110.5–6: 'Most true it is that I have looked on truth / Askance and strangely.' The Sonnets were written over an indeterminable span of the 1590s, probably overlapping with the date of *Dream*. Lines like the above link Shakespeare's poetic life with his experience of the theatre. They seem relevant to the concerns of *Dream*.

Beyond class politics, *Pyramus* is richly significant for the aesthetics and epistemology of theatre, most readily by the insights it offers into *Dream* itself. It highlights the internally mimetic and self-referential function of all drama. On different planes, both Quince's men and their audience serve metadramatic roles. The players in *Pyramus* are actors at two removes – Kemp (if it was he) playing Bottom playing Pyramus;[1] their audience within the play at only one – actors playing Theseus, Hippolyta and the rest. But the latter have a second role too, transporting them outside the play: they represent the actual audience watching *Dream*. It is especially important that this 'real' audience should be involved with the

---

1   Montrose (*Purpose*, 191) adds that a professional is playing an amateur.

action, for they enjoy a total advantage of knowledge over the characters. I have earlier noted the 'discrepant awarenesses' pervading the love-relations (see p. 78): the lovers do not know the reality of their own states. Even the fairies are prone to error: Oberon cannot control, and Robin does not even realize, the confusions they work. Titania is victim to the most egregious delusion in the play. The only ones who know the 'truth' are the spectators, who know it to be a fiction. This may be true of all drama, but *Dream* makes it unusually apparent.

Quince's troupe finds stage representation an insoluble challenge. They think stage illusion can work so well that the audience will take Snug for a lion. To obviate the risk, they make Lion declare he is a man. They also think their audience (unlike Shakespeare's own) must actually see moonlight to assume its presence. Here their final recourse is symbolic, employing not merely a lantern (which would be metonymic) but a man announcing he is Moonshine. The two strategies are actually contrary. Lion dispels the illusion of his role, Moonshine tries feebly to advance it by means of the lantern. These are the two chief and opposed arguments of Plato, the Puritans and other opponents of the stage: they charge it with presenting palpable lies, but also with disguising those lies as truths. If we can accept a man for a lion, then why not a bush for a bear (5.1.22)? The answer must be that we knowingly accept the first as a convention of representation, while the bush seems a bear by a 'literal' error of sight. In both cases, illusion is validated by the action of the mind; rightly or wrongly, we see what we want to see or think we see – comprehending what we apprehend, in Theseus' words (5.1.5–6, 19–20). Whether it really exists is beside the point: it does and does not. In Wallace Stevens's poem 'Peter Quince at the Clavier', the player speaks of a music of the mind, of feeling not sound. '*We come not to offend, / But with good will,*' says Shakespeare's Quince (5.1.109–10). He and his companions want to please the audience with a play, whether or not they have the ability; he is pleading their intention, not their performance. As ruler and patron, Theseus can commend his dutiful subjects by that criterion: 'Out of this silence, yet I picked a welcome' (5.1.100).

As philosopher, however, Theseus seems to deny the same defence to the lunatic, the lover and the poet, who also press the claims of the non-existent. Theseus is not romantically extolling these personages in his celebrated speech.[1] He is satirizing their unreal imaginings, hence implicitly deriding the quasi-Platonic views of Shakespeare's time about love, poetic inspiration and the divine furor of poets and visionary philosophers. A source readily available to Shakespeare was Sidney's *A Defence of Poetry* (published 1595):

> Only the poet, . . . lifted up with the vigour of his own invention, doth grow in effect another nature, in making things either better than nature bringeth forth, or, quite anew, forms such as never were in nature . . .
>
> *(Prose*, 78.22–6)[2]

Theseus' observations on the poet carry a strain of this serious idea, which Romantic critics stressed out of context when interpreting this passage. It would be simplistic to see Theseus as taking a merely rationalist stand against the action of the imagination (a term which, in any case, did not mean in Shakespeare's time what it does today: see 5.1.8n.). For Theseus 'imagination bodies forth / The forms of things unknown', and 'the poet's pen / Turns them to shapes' (5.1.14–16). In other words, the poet validates the imaginary forms *as forms*: they are authentic mental constructs even if they correspond to nothing material. Such a position is not really contrary to Hippolyta's. Far from advancing the exclusive claims of the

---

1   On Theseus' speech, see Nemerov, 'Marriage'; Girard, *Envy*, 66–9; on the illusionism of the play-within-the-play, Clare, 121–4.

2   The passages are associated in Oxf[2] 6.

imagination in either the older or the modern sense, she argues for the reality of the 'fairy toys'. However, her test of reality is not hard fact but the consent of many people in what may be a shared illusion – again, a mental construct:

> And all their minds transfigured so together,
> More witnesseth than fancy's images
> And grows to something of great constancy . . .
>
> (5.1.24–6)

As Gurr observes (*Company*, 146), these words could describe the collective experience of a theatre audience. Is that experience real or unreal? From an external perspective, the audience's acceptance validates the dramatist's fiction, as an artefact incorporating the 'fairy toys' to its own artistic purpose. It is this acceptance of the play as artefact that Robin begs of the audience in the epilogue, even while stressing the unreality of the action. Theseus' illusions can thus be Hippolyta's realities, for such entities straddle the line between the real and the unreal. They include the creations of poetry and drama, needless to say, but the supposedly external world no less, validated in the last analysis only by our shared perception of it.

All such qualified realities resemble creations of the dream state. At much the same time as Theseus' pronouncements in *Dream*, Mercutio in *Romeo and Juliet* declared dreams to be 'children of an idle brain, / Begot of nothing but vain fantasy' (1.4.97–8). His context is another fairy tale, that of Queen Mab. The substance of drama resembles a dream: both consist of forms that are real and not real, a visible representation enshrining a fiction. Theseus' words are again pertinent: 'The best in this kind are but shadows' (5.1.210). Robin talks of 'we shadows' (5.1.413) in his final speech, spoken (like all or most epilogues) half as Robin and half as the actor playing him. The fairy world becomes a metaphor for the world of the theatre, as also a metonym when actors play fairies. In Robin's speech, 'shadows' are interfused with dramatic illusion, as accustomed reality plays hide-and-seek with dreams. Ultimately, reality itself is called in question, like the Red King's dream in *Through the Looking-Glass*. We agree to accept something as real without being certain that it is so, or perhaps (as with theatre) even when we know it is not. To suspend disbelief in this way is not to believe; it is to say 'Let's pretend.' If we can say it of the fairies, why not of the humans whose lives are transformed by the fairies? If stage appearance can serve to represent reality, how real is reality itself?

The reality of *Dream* appears to be a series of presumptive fictions, contained one within another like a nest of Chinese boxes (an image first applied to *Dream* by Auden (57) in a somewhat different context). The play's structure has often been viewed in this light. In a 2008 play in the South Indian language Malayalam, whose title translates as *A Midsummer Night of Love*, the dramatist P. Balachandran presents four actors *qua* actors playing Bottom, Quince, Snout and Starveling. One of them asks, 'Isn't there a play within Shakespeare's play?' Another responds: 'That is to say, isn't Shakespeare's play within the play we're acting now? And isn't the other one within that play?' (Harris, 'Character', 179). This is one jump behind Peter Brook's notion (*Acting*, 24) of 'the play-within-the play within the play within the play'. Norman Holland ('Dream', 75) views the play as a 'dream of a dream of a dream'. In fact, Robin invites the audience to look back on the play as a dream:

> Think but this, and all is mended:
> That you have but slumbered here
> While these visions did appear.
> And this weak and idle theme,
> No more yielding but a dream . . .
>
> (5.1.414–18)

This decisively links the dream to the notion of stage representation. Pollard (2–3) sees the audience as waking up at this point from *their* theatrical dream, for which the love-juice provides a metaphor and Bottom's words find a new application: 'let the audience look to their eyes' (1.2.22).

The action in the woods, hence the entire love-plot – driven by illusion, creating illusion in turn – is like a play stage-managed by Robin and Oberon. 'What, a play toward?' says Robin, coming upon the artisans' rehearsal.

> I'll be an auditor;
> An actor too, perhaps, if I see cause.
>
> (3.1.74–5)

By this point, he is not talking about Quince's play of Pyramus but a 'play' of Bottom the weaver that he will set in motion by his magic. At the same time, viewed externally, he is himself a figure in a third play, that devised by Shakespeare. So is Oberon; but within the action, Oberon guides (or trouble-shoots) Robin's devices, the producer behind the stage-manager. Besides activating events by the love-juice, he devises settings ('I know a bank': 2.1.249, alluding to the 'discovery space' on the actual stage), presents stage tableaux ('Seest thou this sweet sight?': 4.1.45, again indicating the 'discovery space'), and determines the plot ('Ere he do leave this grove, / Thou shalt fly him, and he shall seek thy love': 2.1.245–6). On a post-Elizabethan stage, he also controls the lighting: 'Hie therefore, Robin, overcast the night' (3.2.355). Theseus would play the same controlling role in his sphere, though it proves to be rather restricted. He starts the play with a call for staged festivities ('pomp': 1.1.15) and ends by announcing a fortnight's revels (5.1.359–60). All these pointers impart a strong metatheatrical function to the action as a whole. The events are evidently managed or contrived by characters within the play; equally, they constitute an unreal and illusory sequence. This ambivalence in the action affects the play's status as a play. It sees itself as a construct of 'shadows', a term applicable to dreams, fairies and plays.

The comedy of compromise

In 1964 there appeared a book that, with much else, bestowed on *Dream* a new compelling, sensational quality: pervasive sexuality ('the most erotic of Shakespeare's plays', 73), animal eroticism 'in a quite literal, even visual sense' (79), 'the fearful visions of Bosch and . . . the grotesque of the surrealists' (82). It addressed both outward and inward concerns: it was both political and psychoanalytic. The book did not emanate from the anglophone West; it was Jan Kott's *Shakespeare Our Contemporary.* To Kott in communist Warsaw, Shakespeare's relevance in the modern world assumed this Freudian and surrealist guise, and Western response was swayed by the very exoticism of Kott's shock-treatment. The production history of *Dream*, recounted earlier, bears this out (see pp. 27–9). Peter Brook wrote a preface for the English translation of Kott's book. It may no longer be widely read, but it had a lasting impact on Shakespearean theatre and on many critical groupings: feminists, cultural materialists, postcolonialists, psychoanalytic critics, all players in the 'inversion politics' of global culture.

Does Kott's reading unveil some deeper reality of the play? Does *Dream* really evince this heightened, garish quality of imagination? Are its illusions quite so decisively imbued with the grotesque? Or did Marx, notionally holding sway over Kott's Poland, more correctly discern in it a classic British compromise, aesthetic as well as political? (See p. 95.) I would argue for a subtler blend of the two approaches. In *Dream*, Shakespeare assumes a deliberate inconclusiveness that deflects all questions and ambiguities in the comic-romantic close: the questions raised in the course of the play are not sustained, or even defined so consistently as to disturb. This is evident in the very lines of the plot. The threat posed by patriarchy to the lovers' union dissolves in marriage, but patriarchy is thereby reaffirmed. The lovers' own inner demons are subdued but not decisively expelled in the pairing-off at the close. Titania's inglorious amour ends in reconciliation with Oberon, while Theseus and Hippolyta's love is outwardly untroubled all through. Bottom is unfazed from beginning to end. The enactment of *Pyramus and Thisbe* turns on class disparities, but reconciles them in a mutually acceptable exercise for aristocrats and plebs. Class, gender and locale provide major sites of a curious formal feature of the play: a deconstructive subtext, in continuous operation but shifting from issue to issue without focusing on any. In this as in every other way, the value-structure supporting the narrative is undermined but never quite toppled. The knotty issues latent in the action are not resolved, or even brought to the point of seriously demanding a resolution. The harmony of the close leaves many discords out of account, but attention is not drawn to them.

I would therefore call *Dream* a comedy of compromise. Shakespeare's earlier comedies do not invite the name because they do not raise such issues in the first place – or if they do, they resolve them more directly, even ruthlessly, as in *The Taming of the Shrew*. In *Dream*, Shakespeare's achievement lies in holding the balance between several major plots, each with a set of challenging implications. These implications are variously followed up but not brought to closure. Bottom's solecism seems appropriate in this context: 'I will roar you as gently as any sucking dove' (1.2.77–8). This might apply to the dramatist's strategy in raising yet circumventing momentous issues. For Kavanagh (155) it is the theatrefolk's strategy to keep their peace with the empowered class; they can only challenge the hegemony by a 'surreptitious voice'. Their predicament is exemplified in the play-within-the-play. Quince's men can only play tragedy as comedy; they cannot afford to be taken too seriously.

This fuzziness of dramatic texture – or, if we prefer, a strategic reticence of speech – paradoxically ensures the neatness of the play's broad structure, the way it aestheticizes folk belief, and the harmony it presents between the classes.

Contrary nuances are never strong enough to confuse that structure. A potentially centrifugal cluster of three major plots (four, if we separate Theseus and Hippolyta from the young lovers) is skilfully integrated. Shakespeare was working towards this formal goal in *Two Gentlemen* and *Love's Labour's Lost*; in *Dream*, he achieves it. The neatly interlaced plot aligns the themes to certain set conclusions, leaving no more than a play of alternatives beneath the surface. One can turn the play's fabric inside out to see these loose ends tucked away underneath. But though much is suggested, little is worked out or even strongly articulated. The thematic design is shot through with aberrant hints and tantalizing sallies, but they do not materially break up the design. Freedman evokes Freud's analogy of the magic writing-pad on which one can make marks and erase them, yet leaving a trace. The Freudian analogy obviously applies to the substance of dreams. The play's intellectual structure is dream-like, 'mapping both knowledge and that which escapes it', 'stag[ing] visions only to discredit them' (Freedman, 172).

This 'unstable fusion of practicality and dream' (Nemerov, 'Bottom', 556) can also be seen as a function of poetic language, conveying meaning with suggestive approximation but not conclusive seriousness, setting contraries against each other. In its most compelling subtext, *Dream* can be seen as a play about poetry. I have argued elsewhere in this Introduction (see pp. 101–4, 115) that the aesthetics of poetic perception are not only implicit in *Dream* (that would be true of all poetic drama) but are a manifest presence shaping the setting and action, emerging as an explicit theme in the exchange between Theseus and Hippolyta in 5.1. This appears particularly in the way Shakespeare works the material of fairy lore into a new imaginative synthesis with elements drawn from Ovid and Chaucer. Even more intricate is the commingling of the world of nature, the dream state and the condition of love with magic and illusion. This imaginative compound overlies and moderates the play of such material subtexts as the social, the political or the ethical, and such issues as class and gender.

Hence the ending of *Dream* can reaffirm the familial and patriarchal order in terms of the formal aesthetics of comedy. The seemingly facile conclusion might inspire unease, but we should ask how far Shakespeare takes stock of our concern. The botched tragedy of *Pyramus and Thisbe* enhances the genial close of the framing comedy, precisely because it is botched. The lion and the wolf, the spirits wandering from their graves, the exhausted ploughman and the wretch staring death in the face: all these figures are evoked by Robin but excluded from the 'hallowed house'. *A Midsummer Night's Dream* fulfils itself as a comedy of harmony – or reverting to my earlier term, a comedy of compromise. Perhaps the one implies the other.

LANGUAGE AND VERSE

Scholars broadly agree that *Dream* belongs to the mid-1590s, when Shakespeare was entering his first mature phase (see p. 290). By 1594, he was a 'sharer' in the Chamberlain's Men. This may have prompted a new proprietary confidence over the very medium of his art. He continues to exploit his skill in rhyme while exploring more seriously than before the superior dramatic possibilities of blank verse. This verse repertoire is now matched with a new range of prose dialogue, from the earthily popular to the wittily urbane. He also truly starts to integrate the verse with the action, eschewing description and euphony for their own sake, 'play[ing] the solo instruments of the lyric against the groundswell of the narrative', in Peter Thomson's phrase (108). Thomson traces to this combination the birth of the Shakespearean 'character'. Another crucial circumstance must not be overlooked, the banding together of an exceptional team of actors: there may not have been a Bottom without a Will Kemp. All these factors combine in the first distinctively Shakespearean synthesis of verse drama: a balance of action, character and poetry where each element interacts with the others and provides formal support for them.

The plays chiefly in question are *Love's Labour's Lost*, *Dream*, *Romeo and Juliet* and *Richard II*. Whatever their precise order, these plays seem to form a 'natural group', in Anne Barton's phrase: 'lyrical and ornate, various and highly patterned in their verse forms' (*Riv* 174). One of their outstanding features is a new versatile prosody, with subtly expressive variations in verse-flow, more run-on lines and intricately varied pauses in mid-verse.[1] But each play has its own blend of prosodic features in accord with the subject-matter: in *Dream*, for instance, a distinctive use of short verse-lines and musical patterns. *Dream* also has a high proportion of rhymed verse: 36% of the text, marginally more than blank verse (798 and 746 lines respectively).[2] The play interweaves the two in its own way, and makes limited but deft use of stanzaic forms.[3] Onstage, the rhymed dialogue lends pace and vitality to the lovers' scenes that might appear flat on reading. At the same time, the rhyme

1   Overflows or run-on lines comprise only 13% of all verse lines in *Dream*, no more than in some earlier plays, as against 18% in *Love's Labour's Lost*, 20% in *Richard II*, and increasingly more in most later plays (Chambers, *Shakespeare*, 2.401). These figures may not be precisely borne out by the text of this edition. Analysis of pause patterns is always unreliable, as it is often hard to place the pause. Oras's detailed study, extended by Jackson ('Pause'), follows the punctuation of the earliest text of each play. The heavy pointing of Q1 might have affected the curious findings about *Dream*: a high match in pause count with *Romeo and Juliet* and *Love's Labour's Lost*, but also with *King John*, *1 Henry VI* and *The Comedy of Errors*. Conversely, *Romeo* and *Love's Labour's Lost* do not have *Dream* among their top matches, while *John* and *1 Henry VI* do. Interestingly, these results partly anticipate Hope and Witmore's computational analysis using the program Docuscope, whereby *Dream*, *Comedy* and most surprisingly *The Tempest* share their rhetorical register with the history plays rather than the other comedies. Computer analysis of generic and thematic features is an uncertain enterprise; but if the computer throws up unexpected results, we may ask whether there is any undetected factor to account for them.

2   This is exceeded only in *Love's Labour's Lost* (over 41%), with virtually twice as many rhymed as blank lines (Chambers, *Shakespeare*, 2.398, substantially confirmed by Spevack).

3   On the nuances of the verse-forms, see Doran, *Language*, 14–16.

(especially when arranged in stanzaic patterns) reflects their immature ardour by imparting an overdone, stilted or contrived touch, perhaps to comic or ironic effect:

LYSANDER
    Fair love, you faint with wandering in the wood,
      And to speak troth, I have forgot our way.
    We'll rest us, Hermia, if you think it good,
      And tarry for the comfort of the day.
HERMIA
    Be it so, Lysander. Find you out a bed,
    For I upon this bank will rest my head.

                         (2.2.39–44)

When Titania courts Bottom, her rhymed speeches (including ten lines with a single rhyme in two variants, 3.1.159–68) provide the sharpest possible contrast to Bottom's prose. Oberon too speaks eight lines with a single rhyme (4.1.84–91) after his reconciliation with Titania. All through the play, the use of rhyme, whether in couplets or stanzas, is carefully modulated to the dramatic tempo and context, even in its most extensive application in the lovers' scenes (see 1.1.171–251n., 2.2.39–55n., 3.2.122–33n.). It does not seem plausible to argue that these passages are relics of an earlier rhymed version of the play: they are too well co-ordinated for that. It is also hard to imagine how the rest of the play would have read in rhyme, and why Shakespeare should have radically rewritten those sections alone.

In the fairy scenes, Shakespeare employs a short rhymed line, in couplets or sometimes stanzas. One such instance, the lullaby for Titania (2.2.9–28), is the only formal song in the play (apart from Bottom's comic effort, 3.1.121–4, 126–9). Other sequences (like the fairy's lines at the start of 2.1) may also have been sung or at least chanted, as very likely were the verses uttered by Oberon and Robin while administering the love-juice (2.2.31–8, 84–7; 3.2.102–9). The final run of such short lines (5.1.381–412) accompanies a dance, and the last one before that (4.1.92–101), where Oberon, Titania and Robin all join, follows a dance and signifies their renewed concord. But there are several other passages (2.2.70–83; 3.2.110–21, 396–9, 437–41; 5.1.361–80, 413–28), almost entirely spoken by Robin, in a style compounded of frolic, magic and whimsy:

> Captain of our fairy band,
> Helena is here at hand,
> And the youth mistook by me
> Pleading for a lover's fee.
> Shall we their fond pageant see?
> Lord, what fools these mortals be!
>
> (3.2.110–15)

We may also place 3.2.448–63 here rather than with the love-juice spells. Such verse places the fairies on a removed, fanciful, aesthetically ordered plane, like a verbal equivalent of the dances that are their customary occupation. It is used discreetly to underpin the fairy scenes: by and large, the fairies speak blank verse like the other characters, and can thus operate at the same level of seriousness. The occasional spell of short lines merely reminds us that they belong to another world and are magically intervening in the action.

The fairy verse is a special instance of a general feature of *Dream*, the alignment of the dramatic verse with the action. The different verse registers, and especially the use of rhyme, can be attuned to subtle nuances of stage business or speakers' emotions as described above. They can also be modulated to reflect energetic action and sharp turns and twists, as best brought out in the scene where Robin leads Demetrius and Lysander through the dark forest (3.2.401–30). The lovers' earlier wrangle at 3.2.335–44 is another good example:

> LYSANDER   Now she holds me not.
> Now follow, if thou dar'st, to try whose right,
> Of thine or mine, is most in Helena.

DEMETRIUS
  Follow? Nay, I'll go with thee, cheek by jowl.
                    [*Exeunt*] *Lysander and Demetrius.*
HERMIA
  You, mistress, all this coil is long of you.
  Nay, go not back.
HELENA   I will not trust you, I,
  Nor longer stay in your curst company.
  Your hands than mine are quicker for a fray;
  My legs are longer, though, to run away.   [*Exit.*]
HERMIA
  I am amazed, and know not what to say.   [*Exit.*]

All the characters command a wide repertoire of pauses, line-
lengths and sentence-structures. Robin can be as sharply
epigrammatic ('Lord, what fools these mortals be!': 3.2.115) as
Theseus: 'Saint Valentine is past. / Begin these wood-birds but
to couple now?' (4.1.138–9). Equally, the verse can be swept up
in a descriptive flow, as even in this vituperative speech by
Titania:

  And never, since the middle summer's spring,
  Met we on hill, in dale, forest or mead,
  By paved fountain or by rushy brook,
  Or in the beached margin of the sea
  To dance our ringlets to the whistling wind,
  But with thy brawls thou hast disturbed our sport.
                                                (2.1.82–7)

Here setting, action and relationships combine in inseparable
compound with the verse-movement.

Less than 22% of *Dream* (470 out of 2,174 lines: Chambers,
Shakespeare, 2.398) is in prose, but Shakespeare employs it in
an innovative way, in a new equation with the verse. Among
earlier plays, *Love's Labour's Lost* has an exceptional amount of
prose (1,051 out of 2,785 lines, nearly 38%), and is unusual in

the diversity of characters that speak it, including royalty and aristocrats. But virtually all this prose is contrived in some way, matching the artificiality of the play's ambience, unlike the relaxed banter of the courtiers watching the play in *Dream*. Prose of an everyday or popular mode is found earlier in *The Taming of the Shrew*, more memorably in *The Comedy of Errors* and *The Two Gentlemen of Verona*, and even earlier in Jack Cade's revolt in *2 Henry VI*. The Nurse's snatches of prose in *Romeo and Juliet* may or may not be earlier in date. Homely prose acquires a new vigour and importance in *Dream*: for the first time, it is central to the design, privileged to create the most individualized character in the play. The prose bringing Bottom's yokel-like ebullience to life is anticipated, if at all, by Christopher Sly in the Induction to *Shrew*; but Sly is absent from the play itself.

Bottom's prose displays not only rude vigour but an earthy fancifulness – an oxymoron he makes real:

> Good Master Mustardseed, I know your patience well.
> That same cowardly giantlike Ox-beef hath devoured
> many a gentleman of your house. I promise you, your
> kindred hath made my eyes water ere now. I desire you
> more acquaintance, good Master Mustardseed.
>
> (3.1.182–7)

Such energy of utterance is entirely compatible with the overall imaginative and lyrical mode of *Dream* which, aided no doubt by the fairy setting, has inspired a remarkable amount of music down the ages (see pp. 39–41). The imagery also contributes to this vein. At this stage of Shakespeare's art, he can still expand the occasional image for its own sake in a flight of almost digressive lyricism:

> Your eyes are lodestars, and your tongue's sweet air
> More tunable than lark to shepherd's ear
> When wheat is green, when hawthorn buds appear.
>
> (1.1.183–5)

There are other striking images in the lovers' dialogue: an impressive series in Demetrius' lament at the brevity of love (1.1.143–8), a more succinct one in Helena's account of her plight:

> Apollo flies, and Daphne holds the chase;
> The dove pursues the griffon; the mild hind
> Makes speed to catch the tiger . . .
>
> (2.1.231–3)

We may also think of Hermia's fancy of the moon piercing through the earth (3.2.52–5), or the details whereby Demetrius brings new life to the cliché of a snow-white complexion: 'That pure congealed white, high Taurus' snow, / Fanned with the eastern wind . . .' (3.2.141–2). But such 'detachable' images of a purely figurative kind are surprisingly few, and largely confined to the lovers' speeches. Those in the fairies' dialogue, like the simile of geese and choughs in Robin's account of the fleeing artisans (3.2.20–3), are a small adjunct to the spate of literal references to nature. Theseus employs imagery in an illustrative rather than imaginative vein, like the rose on the 'virgin thorn' (1.1.76–8) or the father's image imprinted on the child as in wax (1.1.49–51). Hippolyta hardly uses images; nor do the artisans.

The intensive pictorial effects of *Dream* draw largely on the actual objects of the woodland setting, with special focal points like the moon and dew (see pp. 72–4). Titania and Oberon look very closely at flowers: 'hoary-headed frosts / Fall in the fresh lap of the crimson rose' (2.1.107–8), or

> And that same dew, which sometime on the buds
> Was wont to swell like round and orient pearls,
> Stood now within the pretty flowerets' eyes
> Like tears that did their own disgrace bewail.
>
> (4.1.52–5)

The evocative quality of the literal setting of nature, drawn out through pathetic fallacy, turns it into a trope: the setting becomes a metaphor for its own spirit, which is to say that metaphor joins function with metonymy. I noted earlier that in this period Shakespeare works his first syntheses of a play's dramatic substance with its language and imagery. *Dream* achieves this end to an unusual degree by the accident of its subject-matter, if it is an accident. We may wonder whether Shakespeare devised the subject (for *Dream* has no defined source) as a custom-made vehicle for the vein of imagination he wished to explore: the very terms of the fable allowed him to mesh his verse and visual effects with the action in the closest possible way, most evidently through the woodland setting and the fairies' dialogue.

The verse and language of *Dream* show a degree of organic cohesion that we commonly ascribe to much later plays (*Macbeth*, for example, with its pattern of darkness, night and disorder). *Dream* cannot match the profound melding of action, character, themes, verse and imagery achieved by the later Shakespeare; but quite early on even among the comedies, it brings together all the formal elements of poetic drama in a remarkably well-knit structure, employing a fable whose literal terms generate their own appropriate imagery and versification. Shakespeare has found the key to a dramatic mode that works equally on the page and the stage: action whose direct theatrical appeal is mediated through a web of words that only yields its secrets on repeated visits. He has created the conditions for being at once a theatrical and a literary dramatist.

A MIDSUMMER NIGHT'S DREAM

THE COURTIERS

THESEUS	*Duke of Athens*
HIPPOLYTA	*Queen of the Amazons, now Theseus'* *bride*
EGEUS	*a courtier, Hermia's father*
HERMIA	*Egeus' daughter, in love with Lysander*
HELENA	*in love with Demetrius* 5
LYSANDER	*in love at different times with Hermia and Helena*
DEMETRIUS	*in love at different times with Helena and Hermia*
PHILOSTRATE	*a courtier, in charge of court entertainments*

Other lords and courtiers

THE ARTISANS

Nick BOTTOM	*a weaver; Pyramus in the play-within-the-play* 10
Peter QUINCE	*a carpenter; producer and Prologue of the play-within-the-play*
Francis FLUTE	*a bellows-mender; Thisbe in the play-within-the-play*
Tom SNOUT	*a tinker; Wall in the play-within-the-play*
SNUG	*a joiner; the Lion in the play-within-the-play*
Robin STARVELING	*a tailor; Moonshine in the play-within-the-play* 15

THE FAIRIES

OBERON	*King of the Fairies*
TITANIA	*Queen of the Fairies*
ROBIN GOODFELLOW	*a puck*
PEASEBLOSSOM, COBWEB, MOTE, MUSTARDSEED	*fairies in Titania's train* 20
Another FAIRY	

Other fairies in Oberon's and Titania's trains

THE COURTIERS For sources and implications of their classical names, see Herbert, *Oberon*, 17–22.

1 **THESEUS** the half-legendary founder and first ruler of Athens. Shakespeare needed to look no further than Chaucer's *KnT* for the anachronistic title 'Duke', often applied to ancient rulers in medieval times. He may or may not have known of an actual Duchy of Athens set up by Christian rulers after the Crusades. In QF SDs and SPs, Theseus is referred to varyingly as 'Theseus' and 'Duke'.

2 **HIPPOLYTA** The Amazons were a race of female warriors most commonly said to dwell in Pontus, the region south of the Black Sea. Their queen Hippolyta (alternatively Antiope) is a figure compounded from many sources, hence there are many versions of her history and career; see pp. 65–7 for her war with Theseus, and for the name Hippolyta vis-à-vis Antiope. The name is uniformly spelt 'Hippolita' in Q2 and F, varied with 'Hyppolita' in Q1. In QF SDs and SPs, she is referred to varyingly as 'Hippolita' and 'Duchess'.

3 **EGEUS** Shakespeare may have derived the name from that of Theseus' father, spelt 'Aegeus' in North's Plutarch but invariably 'Egeus' in early editions of Chaucer. F extends his role by giving him charge of the wedding entertainment in 5.1 in place of Philostrate.

4 **HERMIA** The name recalls Hermione, Helen of Troy's daughter, contrasted with Helen in a line from Ovid (see 2.2.117n.), hence arguably, by extension, with Helena in *MND*.

5 **HELENA** Critics (most extensively Maguire) have tried to link her name through her name with Helen of Troy, though clear parallels are hard to trace. (However, see 2.2.117n., 3.2.137n.) Snyder (70) compares the later Helen of *AW*, another rare instance of a woman who actively woos instead of being wooed. In both cases, the choice of name is Shakespeare's own, not derived from any source.

6 **LYSANDER** There are two Lysanders in Plutarch, one the famous Spartan admiral, neither bearing any resemblance to Lysander in *MND*.

7 **DEMETRIUS** There are fourteen Demetriuses in Plutarch, which might unconsciously have suggested the name. None of them bears any resemblance to the character in *MND*.

8 **PHILOSTRATE** The name assumed by Arcite in disguise in *KnT*. In F, his role is reduced to a brief silent appearance in 1.1, with Egeus taking over his speaking part in 5.1.

THE ARTISANS usually called the 'mechanicals'. But as the word in this obsolete and class-biased sense is used only once in the play, and that derisively (by Robin, 3.2.9), it is best replaced by the neutral 'artisans'.

10 **BOTTOM** In QF SDs and SPs, referred to varyingly as 'Bottom' and 'Clown', or 'Pyramus' when playing that role in the play-within-the-play (see Wiles, *Clown*, 74 on the fluctuation of SPs). His name derives from 'bottom', the core or clew round which the weaver's yarn is wound (*OED n.* 24a). On the evidence of *OED*, the obvious physical sense seems to have been virtually untapped till 1796. But it was so evident in France shortly after that date that the name was considered untranslatable on grounds of propriety, and the English 'Bottom' generally retained (Riffaterre, 102). The word was applied to the female pudenda in Shakespeare's time, as in *VA* 236.

11 **QUINCE** The name derives from 'quines' or 'quoins', wooden wedges used by carpenters. For other suggested associations, chiefly involving the fruit quince, see Parker, 'Quince'.

12 **FLUTE** The name alludes to his high-pitched feminine voice. Wilson (102) suggests he mended the bellows of 'fluted church-organs'; but ordinary bellows, commonly used at the time, would provide the obvious livelihood appropriate to his station.

13 **SNOUT** The name alludes to the spout of a kettle, a utensil a tinker would commonly mend. It probably also indicates the length of his nose.

14 **SNUG** The name alludes to the snug fit of his joinery. *OED* does not record the adjective 'snug' in this sense (*adj.* 1d) before 1838; but other uses (as verb and

adjective) from the late 16th century onward denote compactness, nestling or lying closely – especially with reference to a ship's fittings, a traditional part of the joiner's output. Snug is the only artisan whose first name remains unknown.

15 **STARVELING** The name alludes to the proverbial thinness of tailors; cf. Francis Feeble in *2H4* 3.2.159–61, 268–70. The part may have been created for John Sincklo (Sincler or Sinclair), who is recorded as playing the 'thin-man' parts of a Beadle (and perhaps Shadow) in *2H4* (Q text, 5.4.0.1) and 'Master Doomsday's son' in Marston's *The Malcontent*; perhaps also Pinch in *CE*, Robert Faulconbridge in *KJ*, the Apothecary in *RJ* and Slender in *MW*. His name appears in the F texts of *3H6* (3.1.0.1) and *TS* (Induction 1.87). See Gaw, 302–3; Greg, *Problem*, 116, *Folio*, 115–16.

16 **OBERON** In QF SDs and SPs, referred to varyingly as 'Oberon' and 'King'. The name and basic identity derive from Auberon, King of the Fairies in the medieval romance *Huon of Bordeaux* and other works including *FQ* (2.1.6.8–9, 2.10.75.8–9); also in the entertainment for the Queen at Elvetham in 1591. See pp. 50–1, 287.

17 **TITANIA** In QF SDs and SPs, referred to varyingly as 'Titania' and 'Queen'. Not a traditional name for the Fairy Queen, it was derived by Shakespeare from Ovid,

Met. (see p. 52). As Golding does not use the name, Shakespeare must have drawn on the original Latin. This makes it the more likely that he would follow the probable anglicized Latin pronunciation of his place and time, somewhat like 'Tie-táy-niay'; but something closer to the usual modern 'Tit-áh-nia' is also possible (Kökeritz, *Pronunciation*, 352; Cercignani, 302). Benjamin Britten, in his opera of the play, spells 'Tytania' to indicate a long diphthongized first syllable (Godsalve, 61), presumably without reference to the occasional spelling 'Tytania' in Q1.

18 **ROBIN** In QF SDs and SPs, referred to varyingly as 'Robin Goodfellow', 'Robin' and 'Puck'. (On the textual implications if any, see pp. 297, 304, 307.) 'Robin' seems to be his name, and 'puck' the type of spirit with which he is basically identified. 'Goodfellow' probably began as a sobriquet meant to please him (2.1.40n.). On his complex origins, see pp. 44–5.

19–22 **PEASEBLOSSOM, COBWEB, MOTE, MUSTARDSEED** The names reflect their tiny insubstantial forms. On 'Mote' (spelt 'Moth' in QF), see 3.1.156n. Taking 'Moth' to mean the insect, Reynolds and Sawyer (518–20) observe that all four fairies are named after items of traditional medicine, though in Peaseblossom's case for disappointed love rather than physical illness.

A MIDSUMMER
NIGHT'S DREAM

[1.1] *Enter* THESEUS, HIPPOLYTA, [PHILOSTRATE,] *with others.*

THESEUS

Now, fair Hippolyta, our nuptial hour
Draws on apace. Four happy days bring in
Another moon; but O, methinks, how slow
This old moon wanes! She lingers my desires,
Like to a stepdame or a dowager   5
Long withering out a young man's revenue.

HIPPOLYTA

Four days will quickly steep themselves in night,
Four nights will quickly dream away the time;
And then the moon, like to a silver bow

[1.1] This is sometimes visualized as a formal court scene (cf. 5.1.0.1n.). Foakes thinks Theseus and Hippolyta enter in procession and occupy chairs of state to hear Egeus' formal complaint. Benson, Daly and Granville-Barker staged the scene in this manner. But it seems more likely to be a quiet conversation interrupted by Egeus, as staged by Alexander and Noble.

2 **Four happy days** On the play's time-scheme, see p. 75.

4 **lingers** prolongs, delays (*OED v.* 7)

5–6 **stepdame ... revenue** a widow paid a jointure or dower out of her late husband's wealth, thus blocking or reducing the income of his young heir; perhaps recalling Horace, *Epistles* 1.1.21–2, about a young ward under his mother's control. Those favouring the Earl of Derby's wedding as the play's occasion see a reference to the previous Earl's widow, who delayed the new Earl's succession by claiming to be pregnant with a possible heir (see pp. 284–5).

6 **withering out** (1) rendering futile through delay; (2) 'causing to dwindle' (Wells), diminishing: applicable to the widow as well as the revenue (Holland). The plant metaphor is more pronounced in 76–8.

7 **steep** imbue, submerge (in rest or sleep: *OED* steep *v.¹* 3a); 'be absorbed' (Wells). Cf. 'steeped our sense / In ... Lethe', *AC* 2.7.107–8; *TN* 4.1.61.

9 **bow** The bow usually associated with love and marriage is Cupid's, as in 2.1.155–64. Associating it with the moon, hence with the virgin moon-goddess Cynthia or Diana, impairs the idea of fulfilled love.

[1.1] *Rowe (*ACT I. SCENE I.*); Actus primus. F; not in Q* 0.1 PHILOSTRATE] *Theobald; not in QF* 7 night] nights *Q2, F* 8 nights] *Q1, F;* daies *Q2*

Now bent in heaven, shall behold the night   10
Of our solemnities.
THESEUS   Go, Philostrate,
Stir up the Athenian youth to merriments;
Awake the pert and nimble spirit of mirth,
Turn melancholy forth to funerals.   14
The pale companion is not for our pomp.   [*Exit Philostrate.*]
Hippolyta, I wooed thee with my sword,
And won thy love doing thee injuries;
But I will wed thee in another key,
With pomp, with triumph, and with revelling.

Enter EGEUS, HERMIA, LYSANDER *and* DEMETRIUS.

EGEUS
Happy be Theseus, our renowned duke.   20
THESEUS
Thanks, good Egeus. What's the news with thee?
EGEUS
Full of vexation come I, with complaint
Against my child, my daughter Hermia.

10 **Now** used proleptically, treating the future as the present, to convey a sense of vivid anticipation. Emending to 'New' is unnecessary.
in heaven where marriages are proverbially made (Dent, M688)
11 **solemnities** ceremonies, celebrations; perhaps the formal ceremony of marriage, in contrast to *merriments* (12)
13 **pert** 'lively, sprightly' (*OED adj.* 4)
14 **Turn . . . forth** turn out of doors, banish (to seek out funerals rather than weddings)
15 **pale companion** a feeble-spirited participant in our revels; *pale*, bloodless, spiritless. *Companion* is used contemptuously (*OED n.¹* 5).
15 SD *An exit (missing in QF) is required here for Philostrate to carry out Theseus' order. With his departure, Theseus turns to

Hippolyta and addresses her more intimately.
16–17 These lines carry a suggestion of violence, even rape, emphasized by the phallic connotations of *sword*. See p. 66.
19 **With . . . triumph** denoting both the spirit of celebration and the actual festivities (*OED* pomp *n.¹* 1a, 2a; triumph *n.* 3, 4); cf. *triumphantly*, 4.1.88. A *triumph* originally celebrated victory in battle: Theseus' defeat of Hippolyta in war lurks behind their new relationship.
19.1 *The Q entry for Helena is wrong: she enters at 179.1. This may be a single 'massed entry' for characters appearing at different points of the scene.
20 **renowned** renownèd
22 **vexation** used in a stronger sense than now

10 Now] New *Rowe*   15 SD] *Theobald; not in QF*   19.1] *Rowe; Enter* Egeus and his daughter Hermia*, [and Q]* Lysander *[and Q1]* [Helena *Q], and* Demetrius. *QF.*

122

Stand forth, Demetrius. My noble lord,
This man hath my consent to marry her.   25
Stand forth, Lysander. And my gracious duke,
This man hath bewitched the bosom of my child.
Thou, thou, Lysander, thou hast given her rhymes
And interchanged love-tokens with my child;
Thou hast, by moonlight, at her window sung,   30
With faining voice, verses of feigning love,
And stolen the impression of her fantasy;
With bracelets of thy hair, rings, gauds, conceits,
Knacks, trifles, nosegays, sweetmeats (messengers
Of strong prevailment in unhardened youth),   35
With cunning hast thou filched my daughter's heart,
Turned her obedience, which is due to me,
To stubborn harshness. And, my gracious duke,
Be it so she will not here before your grace

24, 26 *Stand forth, Demetrius ... Stand forth, Lysander** QF print these words in italics and centred like SDs, but they are clearly part of the dialogue, serving to fill out two lines of blank verse.

28 **Thou ... thou** Egeus tends to repeat words when excited; cf. 4.1.153–8.
rhymes verses of love and courtship. Harrison interprets as 'love spells' to suit *bewitched.*

29 **interchanged** exchanged

31 **faining** 'feigning', pretending, deceitful; but also longing, desiring (*OED* fain *v.¹*) and 'sing[ing] softly' (*OED* feign *v.* 12a). QF spell 'faining' at both points, but the varying spellings adopted here bring out the wordplay.

32 **stolen ... fantasy** 'fraudulently impressed your image upon her imagination' (Clemen); implicit images of (1) stamping false coinage: Lysander has created a false love in Hermia; (2) taking a wax impression of a key (with which to *filch* Hermia's

heart, Warburton). The soft wax is Hermia's *unhardened* (35) heart.
stolen compressed to one syllable or nearly so (QF 'stolne'); cf. 2.1.22, 65, 191; 3.2.51, 284; 4.1.155.
fantasy fancy, love, especially light or passing love (cf. *fantasies*, 2.1.258); also the faculty whereby impressions of external objects are imprinted on the mind (*OED* 1a, b)

33–5 On courtship gifts as tokens of intent to marry, see Cressy, 263–6.

33 **bracelets ... rings** common love-tokens
gauds trinkets, finery (*OED n.²* 2), with a root sense of trickery or deceit (1a); cf. 4.1.166.
conceits 'fancy article[s]' (*OED n.* 9a), with a suggestion of trickery (10a); hence 'clever gifts' (Norton³)

34 **Knacks** trifles, knick-knacks, again with a root sense of trickery or deceit (*OED n.²* 1)

35 **unhardened** tender, inexperienced; earliest *OED* citation

39 **Be it so** if it be that

24 Stand forth, Demetrius] *centred and italicized,* QF   26 Stand forth, Lysander] *centred and italicized,* QF   27 man] *om. F2*   28 rhymes] *(*rimes *QF)*   31 faining ... feigning] *Ard²;* faining ... faining *QF;* feigning ... feigning *Rowe*   32 stolen] *(*stolne *QF)* fantasy] *(*phantasie *Q1)*

Consent to marry with Demetrius,   40
I beg the ancient privilege of Athens:
As she is mine, I may dispose of her,
Which shall be either to this gentleman,
Or to her death, according to our law
Immediately provided in that case.   45

THESEUS
What say you, Hermia? Be advised, fair maid.
To you your father should be as a god,
One that composed your beauties; yea, and one
To whom you are but as a form in wax,
By him imprinted, and within his power   50
To leave the figure, or disfigure it.
Demetrius is a worthy gentleman.

HERMIA
So is Lysander.

THESEUS   In himself he is;
But in this kind, wanting your father's voice,

---

41 **privilege** a right or power granted by law. Shakespeare may or may not have known of an Athenian law of Solon's time, long after Theseus, granting a father power over his children's lives (Warburton), or of such regional laws in France in his own day (Sokol, 37). He certainly knew Arthur Brooke's *Romeus and Juliet*, 1954–5: 'if children did rebell, / The parentes had the power, of lyfe and sodayn death' (Bullough, 1.336). But in England at the time, no-one could lawfully be forced to marry, or prevented from marrying whom they wished (Cressy, 256).

42 **dispose of** (1) 'do what one will with' (*OED* dispose *v.* 8a); (2) 'get done with, settle' (*OED* 8b, first cited from *Tem* 1.2.225 but found earlier in *TGV* 5.4.157), hence marry off a daughter (*MW* 3.4.68). The modern sense of getting rid of material goods is later in date, though

Egeus clearly considers his daughter to be his property.

45 **Immediately** (1) at once; (2) not allowing mediation or intervention
    provided laid down, stipulated: a legal term (*OED v.* 1)

48 **composed** generated, begot

49 **form in wax** the imprint of a seal in wax (unlike the illicit image in 32)

51 **leave** leave intact. Warburton relates to Fr. *relever*, *enlever*, to chase or adorn in relief.
    disfigure 'deform, deface' (*OED v.* 1a), or even totally destroy the 'figure' or form: an 'appalling metaphor' (Hawkes, 13), ironically anticipating Quince's malapropism in 3.1.55. On the motif of 'disfiguring', see Hawkes, 20–3.

54 **kind** 'respect, regard' (Crystal)
    voice 'Support or approval' (*OED n.* 3c, earliest citation)

53] *one line, Q*

The other must be held the worthier.   55

HERMIA

I would my father looked but with my eyes.

THESEUS

Rather your eyes must with his judgement look.

HERMIA

I do entreat your grace to pardon me.
I know not by what power I am made bold,
Nor how it may concern my modesty   60
In such a presence here to plead my thoughts,
But I beseech your grace that I may know
The worst that may befall me in this case
If I refuse to wed Demetrius.

THESEUS

Either to die the death, or to abjure   65
For ever the society of men.
Therefore, fair Hermia, question your desires,
Know of your youth, examine well your blood
Whether, if you yield not to your father's choice,
You can endure the livery of a nun,   70

56–7 the first of many references to the disjunction between eye and mind, or passion and reason; cf. 232–7 (and 235n.), 2.2.119–24, 3.1.139–40, 3.2.134–5, 5.1.4–22 (and 4n.).

59 **power** Hermia contrasts the power impelling her, presumably from within, to her father's *power* over her (50) or even Theseus' *presence* (61).

60 **concern** affect, be important to (*OED v.* 3a)

61 **In ... presence** i.e. before the Duke, but perhaps more generally 'in public', even suggesting the theatre audience

63 **The worst** Holland cites the proverb 'To know the worst is good' (Dent, W915).

65 **die the death** be put to death (*OED* die *v.¹* 2c), in Shakespeare always by sentence of law (Wright); cf. *AC* 4.14.26, *Cym* 4.2.96.

65–6 **abjure ... men** Egeus had not mentioned this alternative. He may not have known of it, or have deliberately concealed it; or Theseus may be modifying the allegedly inviolable

law as he speaks, from a latent sympathy for Hermia evident in his mild tone.

67 **question your desires** ask yourself, decide what you want

68 **Know of** think of, consider; or perhaps 'find out from, consult'
blood disposition, inclination (*OED n.* 11); cf. 74n., 135n.

70–8 a curious mixture of pagan (see 72–8n., 89n.) and Christian elements in a notional setting of ancient Greece. North's Plutarch (3.3: North, 2, sig. A1ᵛ) speaks of a 'Nunne' in the temple of Apollo in Theseus' time. In Marlowe's *Hero and Leander* (1.45), Hero is '*Venus* Nun'. In Shakespeare's England, there were no nuns after Henry VIII's dissolution of monasteries and convents.

70 **livery** generally explained as a nun's habit, but could mean any food or clothing provided to workers (*OED n.* 4), hence convent rule generally; used dismissively, as livery was usually supplied to servants

For aye to be in shady cloister mewed
To live a barren sister all your life,
Chanting faint hymns to the cold fruitless moon.
Thrice blessed they that master so their blood
To undergo such maiden pilgrimage;   75
But earthlier happy is the rose distilled
Than that which, withering on the virgin thorn,
Grows, lives and dies in single blessedness.

HERMIA

So will I grow, so live, so die, my lord,
Ere I will yield my virgin patent up   80
Unto his lordship whose unwished yoke
My soul consents not to give sovereignty.

71 **For aye** for ever
    shady dark, hidden
    mewed shut up or confined, usually in a
    cage or prison
72–8 These lines would offend the virgin
    Queen before whom the play was
    supposedly performed. They project the
    most barren and negative associations of
    the moon, variously present through the
    play, and by implication of Diana, moon-
    goddess and goddess of virginity,
    commonly identified with Elizabeth. In this
    notionally pagan setting, Hermia is
    envisaged as Diana's votaress; cf. 73, 89,
    3.1.191n., and the restrictive image of
    convent life in *MM* 1.4.1–14.
73 **fruitless** barren, unproductive; perhaps
    because moonlight, unlike sunlight, does
    not make crops grow. Cf. 2.1.158n., 162n.;
    3.1.191n.
74 **blessed** blessèd (cf. 2.2.95, 3.2.392, 4.1.73;
    5.1.394); consistently distinguished by
    spelling in QF from one-syllable *blest*,
    2.1.102, 5.1.409
    blood fleshly appetites or passions (*OED*
    n. 13); cf. 68n., 135n.
75 **pilgrimage** journey through life: a
    commonplace, from Genesis 47.9
76 **earthlier** by contrast in one's earthly life
    distilled with the perfume extracted: a
    trope of sexuality. It is better to be

'plucked' or 'deflowered' than to die on the
stalk. This also suggests the transmission
of one's beauty and vitality to one's
children. Cf. *Son* 5.9–14, 6.2, and
Parolles's jocular arguments against
virginity in *AW* 1.1.133–9.
77 **withering** extends the sense of prolonged
    frustration; cf. *withering out* (6).
    thorn rose bush; metaphorically, a cause of
    pain or distress (*OED n.* 2).
78 **single** celibate, but also implying 'Slight,
    poor' (*OED adj.* 12b); cf. 'your wit single'
    (*2H4* 1.2.184).
80 **patent** privilege or distinctive right, as for
    trade or the issue of licences: 'my
    entitlement to my virginity' (Folg). Patents
    could be bestowed or transferred, usually
    to a 'lordship', a courtier or aristocrat.
81 **his lordship** the authority or control of that
    man (who marries her against her will). A
    general declaration: *his* does not indicate
    Demetrius but any such man.
    unwished yoke (unwishèd) unsolicited or
    undesired subjection. For *yoke* denoting the
    marriage bond, implying both union and
    subjection, see *OED n.*[1] 8b. 'Hermia does
    not refuse to subordinate herself. Rather, she
    asserts the far more limited privilege of
    choosing the man to whom she is to be
    subject' (Raman, 261). The patriarchal order
    is left intact with the woman's consent.

76 earthlier happy] earthly happier *Capell*

THESEUS

Take time to pause, and by the next new moon,
The sealing day betwixt my love and me
For everlasting bond of fellowship,   85
Upon that day either prepare to die
For disobedience to your father's will,
Or else to wed Demetrius as he would,
Or on Diana's altar to protest,
For aye, austerity and single life.   90

DEMETRIUS

Relent, sweet Hermia; and Lysander, yield
Thy crazed title to my certain right.

LYSANDER

You have her father's love, Demetrius.
Let me have Hermia's. Do you marry him.

EGEUS

Scornful Lysander, true, he hath my love,   95
And what is mine, my love shall render him;
And she is mine, and all my right of her
I do estate unto Demetrius.

LYSANDER

I am, my lord, as well derived as he,
As well possessed; my love is more than his,   100
My fortunes every way as fairly ranked
(If not with vantage) as Demetrius';

---

84 **sealing day** the day of sealing or
concluding the contract of marriage
85 **fellowship** companionship
88 **he** her father, not Demetrius
would wishes
89 **Diana's** Diana was the goddess of
virginity. Pagan elements are again merged
with the Christian.
protest vow, declare
92 **crazed title** (crazèd) unsound or invalid
claim to possession (*OED* crazed 3, earliest
citation), as against Demetrius' *certain*

right; but *crazed* also = mad
98 **estate unto** bestow or settle upon, as
though Hermia is his property (*OED* estate
v. 3, earliest citation)
99 **derived** descended: earliest *OED*
citation
100 **possessed** endowed with possessions;
propertied, rich. This sense is not recorded
in *OED*, but cf. *Son* 29.6.
101 **fairly ranked** favourably placed or
regarded
102 **with vantage** more favourably

94 Hermia's] Hermia *(Tyrwhitt, 50)*   102 Demetrius'] *Hanmer;* Demetrius *QF*

And (which is more than all these boasts can be)
I am belov'd of beauteous Hermia.
Why should not I then prosecute my right? 105
Demetrius, I'll avouch it to his head,
Made love to Nedar's daughter Helena
And won her soul; and she, sweet lady, dotes,
Devoutly dotes, dotes in idolatry
Upon this spotted and inconstant man. 110

THESEUS

I must confess that I have heard so much,
And with Demetrius thought to have spoke thereof;
But being over-full of self-affairs,
My mind did lose it. But Demetrius, come,
And come, Egeus; you shall go with me. 115
I have some private schooling for you both.
For you, fair Hermia, look you arm yourself
To fit your fancies to your father's will;
Or else, the law of Athens yields you up
(Which by no means we may extenuate) 120
To death, or to a vow of single life.
Come, my Hippolyta. What cheer, my love?

---

105 **prosecute** exercise (*OED* 1c)

106 **to his head** to his face (*OED* head *n.¹* P1.l)

107 **Nedar** The name recurs only once (4.1.129), and has not been convincingly traced to any source.

109 **idolatry** in Shakespeare, always the infatuation of love; cf. *TGV* 4.4.198, *LLL* 4.3.72.

110 **spotted** stained, tarnished; cf. 2.2.9n.

113 **self-affairs** my own affairs – especially, no doubt, his wedding. Earliest *OED* citation of the prefix *self-* with this function (*OED* self- 5a). Cf. 'self-breath' (one's own words), *TC* 2.3.169; 'self-danger' (to one's own self), *Cym* 3.4.146.

114 **lose** forget (*OED* v.¹ 5d)

116 **schooling** instructions, advice – perhaps on their treatment of Hermia and Helena; even 'reprimand' (Deighton, citing *1H4* 3.1.187,

'Well I am schooled.')

117 **arm** prepare (*OED* v.¹ 1c, earliest citation clearly in this sense)

118 **fancies** desires, especially light affections; cf. 32n. (*fantasy*), 155n., *MV* 3.2.63–8.

120 **extenuate** mitigate, moderate (*OED* v. 4b). Yet Theseus readily rescinds the punishment at 4.1.178–80.

121 **vow** This religious context contrasts with the word's later application to vows of love (175; 3.2.124–33, 153, 199). Cf. the contrasting 'votaresses' in 2.1.123, 163.

122 **What cheer** '[W]hat is your state or mood?' (*OED* cheer *n.¹* 3b), suggesting that Hippolyta may be displeased at Theseus' decision. In productions since Tree's in 1900, she has often mimed her displeasure, made sympathetic gestures to Hermia, or left the stage ahead of Theseus.

Demetrius and Egeus, go along.
I must employ you in some business
Against our nuptial, and confer with you   125
Of something nearly that concerns yourselves.

EGEUS

With duty and desire we follow you.
                    Exeunt [all but] Lysander and Hermia.

LYSANDER

How now, my love? Why is your cheek so pale?
How chance the roses there do fade so fast?

HERMIA

Belike for want of rain, which I could well   130
Beteem them from the tempest of my eyes.

LYSANDER

Ay me! for aught that I could ever read,
Could ever hear by tale or history,
The course of true love never did run smooth;
But either it was different in blood –   135

---

123 **go along** come with me (Schmidt)
124 **business** three syllables
125 **Against** 'in preparation for' (*OED prep.* 10)
126 **nearly** closely, intimately; again, presumably about Hermia and Helena
127 *SD Some commentators argue that Hermia would not be allowed to stay behind with her forbidden suitor. Fleay proposed starting a new scene here, though *Manet* (for *Manent*, 'they remain') in the F SD suggests a continuation of the same scene. In Peter Hall's film, a sympathetic Theseus draws the company away to allow the lovers a chance to talk.
128–49 The sound-structure of these lines is closely analysed by Sitwell (187–9). In Brook's production, they were accompanied by a guitar.

128 **your** Lysander breaks the silence with a formal *your* before the lovers switch to the intimate *thou*. Their exchanges in later scenes fluctuate between the two forms according to context; see 2.2.39–55n.
129 **How chance** How does it happen, why is it – a superfluous question in the circumstances
130 **Belike** probably
131 **Beteem** *OED* (*v.¹* 2a, earliest citation) explains as 'accord, grant'; but 'make teem, fill to overflowing' (not in *OED*) seems more appropriate.
132 **Ay me** Alas. Q 'Eigh' could be a variant of 'ay' (interjection) but not 'ah' in the sixteenth century.
135 **blood** birth, family rank. Cf. 68n., 74n.: three different senses of the word within 68 lines.

---

126 yourselves] (your selues *QF*)   127 SD] *Cam; Exeunt. Q; Exeunt. (right margin) / Manet Lysander and Hermia. (centred, next line) F*   131 my] mine *F*   132 Ay me] (Eigh me); *not in F; Hermia F2;* Ah me *Johnson*   I could ever] euer I could *F*

HERMIA

O cross, too high to be enthralled to low!

LYSANDER

Or else misgrafted in respect of years –

HERMIA

O spite, too old to be engaged to young!

LYSANDER

Or else it stood upon the choice of friends –

HERMIA

O hell, to choose love by another's eyes!   140

LYSANDER

Or, if there were a sympathy in choice,
War, death or sickness did lay siege to it,
Making it momentany as a sound,
Swift as a shadow, short as any dream,
Brief as the lightning in the collied night   145

136–40 an interesting adaptation of stichomythia, line-by-line ripostes between two speakers originating in classical tragedy. Unusually, the speakers are here in agreement. For a more typical instance, see 194–201. These lines are also an instance of isocolon, where the parts of a sentence are exactly balanced in length and structure.

136 **cross** pain, affliction
   high in rank
   ***low** Theobald's emendation matches the antithesis of *old . . . young* (138). Halliwell (*Introduction*, 69) compares *VA* 1139: [Love is] 'Ne'er settled equally, but high or low'. *La Conusaunce damours* (see p. 61) has an eloquent plea to allow young people to marry for love, 'both persones of hye and lowe degre' (sig. B4ᵛ).

137 **misgrafted** (QF 'misgraffed') wrongly grafted, like a plant; ill-matched. Only citation for 'misgraffed' in *OED*; *misgrafted* is first recorded from 1738.

139 **friends** The Q and F readings probably draw on different sources. *Friends* (kinsfolk, relations, *OED n.* 3; cf 219n.) makes better sense; cf. *TGV* 3.1.106. Taylor (Review, 333) suggests the F reviewer wrote 'merit' in the margin of his annotated Q2 copy to replace *else it*, but the compositor mistakenly substituted it for *friends*.

141 **sympathy** affinity (*OED n.* 1); here, mutual love

143–8 The four similes make the same point but are arranged in a climax, three brief ones building up to an elaborate, clinching image.

143 **momentany** a word then current, of slightly earlier origin than 'momentary'. 'Momentary' was growing commoner by the early sixteenth century, hence the deliberate or inadvertent change in F.

144 **Swift . . . shadow** A shadow is not necessarily swift: perhaps implying its transience relative to the body that casts it. Chambers evokes 'the shadow of a cloud passing over the fields'.

145 **collied** coal-black

136 low] *Theobald;* loue *QF*   137 misgrafted] *(*misgraffed *QF)*   139 else it] merit *Oxf (Taylor, Review, 333)*   friends] merit *F;* men *Collier MS, 99*   140 eyes] eie *F*   143 momentany] momentarie *F*

That, in a spleen, unfolds both heaven and earth,
And ere a man hath power to say 'Behold',
The jaws of darkness do devour it up:
So quick bright things come to confusion.

HERMIA

If then true lovers have been ever crossed,   150
It stands as an edict in destiny.
Then let us teach our trial patience
Because it is a customary cross,
As due to love as thoughts and dreams and sighs,
Wishes and tears, poor fancy's followers.   155

LYSANDER

A good persuasion; therefore hear me, Hermia.
I have a widow aunt, a dowager,
Of great revenue, and she hath no child.
From Athens is her house remote seven leagues,
And she respects me as her only son.   160

---

146 **spleen** outburst, fit of passion (*OED n.* 7a)
    unfolds lays open, reveals
147–8 Cf. *RJ* 2.2.119–20: 'Too like the
    lightning which doth cease to be / Ere one
    can say "it lightens"'.
149 **confusion** destruction. Baxter (24) points
    out the tragic undertone of this line, suiting
    RJ rather than *MND*. Cf. 'Brightnesse falls
    from the ayre': Nashe, *Summer's Last Will
    and Testament* (1592), line 1590 (Nashe,
    3.283).
150 **ever** always
    crossed thwarted
151 **edict in destiny** judgement of fate
152 **teach . . . patience** learn to suffer patiently
    trial trouble, misfortune
153 **customary** This antedates the earliest
    OED citation in a non-legal sense (*adj.* 1a),
    from *Cor.*
154 **due to** (1) caused by; (2) owed to, as an
    offering or tribute
155 **fancy's followers** accompaniments or
    consequences of love; cf. 118n.

156 **persuasion** argument, used jocularly.
    Hermia had advocated patience, while
    Lysander now proposes action.
157–8 The QF commas build up a climax: each
    item increases the aunt's attraction as a
    source of support.
157 **dowager** See 5–6n. This supportive
    dowager counters the earlier unfavourable
    image (Holland).
158 **revenue** Often read as 'rèvenue', but the
    usual 'rèvénue' (as at 6) scans just as well,
    as in *R2* 1.4.46, *R3* 3.7.157.
159–60 Transposing the lines makes for a more
    logical sequence, but not a more probable
    or natural one. *TxC* compares *Lear*
    2.2.398–9 (the last two lines on a quarto
    page, as here), which editors have also
    suggested transposing.
159 **leagues** A league (commonly used in
    poetical contexts) is usually taken as three
    miles.
160 **respects** (1) regards, considers (*OED v.*
    4b); (2) values

159–60] *transposed Keightley (Johnson)*   159 remote] remou'd *F*

131

There, gentle Hermia, may I marry thee,
And to that place the sharp Athenian law
Cannot pursue us. If thou lov'st me, then
Steal forth thy father's house tomorrow night;
And in the wood a league without the town,   165
Where I did meet thee once with Helena
To do observance to a morn of May,
There will I stay for thee.

HERMIA   My good Lysander,
I swear to thee by Cupid's strongest bow,
By his best arrow with the golden head,   170
By the simplicity of Venus' doves,
By that which knitteth souls and prospers loves,

162 **sharp** harsh, severe
164–5 Echoes the Pyramus and Thisbe story in
  Golding, 4.106–8: 'To steale out of their
  fathers house ... / to meete without the
  towne'. The parallel between Lysander and
  Hermia's plan and Pyramus and Thisbe's in
  the play-within-the-play has often been
  noted.
164 **forth** out of (Blake, 5.4.2)
165 **league** See 159n. The place is only a
  mile away according to Quince (1.2.94
  and n.).
  without outside
167 **do observance to** observe the rites of. The
  phrase occurs four times in *KnT*, twice
  (1045, 1500) with reference to Maying. Cf.
  observation, 4.1.103.
  May On the presence of May and
  Midsummer in this play, see p. 88.
169–75 The stylized figure of anaphora, six
  constructions all beginning *By*, seems

natural in Hermia's impassioned flow.
170 **the golden head** induces love, and the
  leaden arrow flight from love (*Met.* 1.468–
  71; Golding, 1.567–8)
171–251 The verse switches to rhyme as the
  dramatic tempo quickens: Hermia and
  Lysander settle their course of action, and
  Helena's entry adds more complication.
171–2 Singer transposes the lines, making
  'that ... loves' refer to Cupid's golden
  arrow.
171 **simplicity** innocence. Doves were
  proverbially 'simple' as having no gall
  (Dent, D573, D574).
  Venus' doves Doves draw Venus' chariot
  in *Met.* 14.597 (Golding, 14.680) and,
  alongside swans, in many other sources.
  They are said to be sacred to Venus in
  Aelian, *De animalium natura* 10.33. See
  VA 153, 1190; *Luc* 58; Chaudhuri, 'Venus'.
172 **loves** The rhyme demands Q1 *loves*.

163 lov'st] *F;* louest *Q*   167 to] for *F*   171–2] *transposed Singer*[3]   172 loves] loue *Q2, F*

And by that fire which burned the Carthage queen
When the false Trojan under sail was seen,
By all the vows that ever men have broke   175
(In number more than ever women spoke),
In that same place thou hast appointed me,
Tomorrow truly will I meet with thee.

LYSANDER
Keep promise, love. Look, here comes Helena.

Enter HELENA.

HERMIA
  God speed, fair Helena. Whither away?   180
HELENA
Call you me fair? That fair again unsay.
Demetrius loves your fair: O happy fair!

173–6 These reminders of male falsehood may be meant to exhort Lysander to behave differently; they are ironically appropriate given his future conduct. Shakespeare may have recalled Chaucer's apprehensions as Thisbe goes to meet Pyramus (*Legend of Thisbe, LGW*, 798–801).

173–4 Aeneas, the Trojan leader, voyaged in search of new lands after the fall of Troy. Reaching Carthage, he professed love to its queen Dido, but abandoned her to pursue his mission; Dido thereupon burnt herself on a pyre (*Aen.* Bks.1, 4). This is an anachronistic allusion, as Aeneas is of later date than Theseus. Mentioning Dido and Aeneas makes Hermia think of male betrayal, perhaps fearing the same of Lysander. Critics have noted an undercurrent of allusion through *MND* to Marlowe's *Dido, Queen of Carthage*, chiefly relating to Titania's love of Bottom: see Connolly.

173 **fire** both literal and a metaphor for passionate love
   Carthage used as an adjective (Blake, 3.3.3.1(c))

174 **under sail** i.e. sailing away from Carthage,

abandoning Dido. In *Aen.* 4.586–8 but not Chaucer's *Legend of Dido (LGW)* or Marlowe's *Dido*, it is the sight of Aeneas' departing sails that leads Dido to immolate herself (Brooks).

177 **appointed me** arranged or agreed with me

180 **God speed** God grant you success; may you prosper. Perhaps also a play on *speed*: Helena attempts to withdraw swiftly on seeing Hermia with Lysander (hence *Whither away?*).

182–93 There have been a dozen musical settings of this passage. In Garrick's *Fairies*, 182–5 (slightly modified) with 192–3 constitute an 'air'.

182 ¹**fair** beauty; ²**fair** a beautiful form or person. Cf. *Son* 18.7, 'And every fair from fair sometime declines'. Q 'your' makes readier sense than F 'you': 'your beauty, not mine', perhaps specifically 'your kind of beauty', shorter and darker (see 2.2.118, 3.2.257, 325–6), hence conventionally judged less beautiful (cf. *Son* 127). Helena, blonde by implication in the text and by stage convention, is ironically envying the 'fairness' of the dark Hermia.

174 Trojan] *(Troian;* Troyan *Q2, F)*   182 your] you *F*

Your eyes are lodestars, and your tongue's sweet air
More tunable than lark to shepherd's ear
When wheat is green, when hawthorn buds appear.   185
Sickness is catching; O, were favour so!
Your words I catch, fair Hermia; ere I go,
My ear should catch your voice, my eye your eye,
My tongue should catch your tongue's sweet melody.
Were the world mine, Demetrius being bated,   190
The rest I'll give to be to you translated.
O teach me how you look, and with what art
You sway the motion of Demetrius' heart.

HERMIA

I frown upon him, yet he loves me still.

HELENA

O that your frowns would teach my smiles such skill!   195

---

183 **lodestars** The lodestar is the pole star or a guiding star. The suggestion of two pole stars is a sarcastic extravagance.
air song, music
184 **tunable** tuneful, melodious
186 **favour** (1) beauty; (2) a gracious act, i.e. requiting love
187–9 *The Q wording (compatible with the punctuation adopted here) implies 'I hear your words, but cannot replicate the charms you hold for Demetrius.' *OED* glosses *catch* here as 'acquire by sympathy or imitation' (*v.* 34, earliest citation), but there is play on two other meanings: (1) apprehend, hear (*v.* 35a); (2) take infection (*v.* 33). *Ear* and *voice* relate differently from *eye* and *eye*, *tongue* and *tongue*, but the overall sense covers all three pairs. All alternative readings and punctuation imply 'If attractiveness were infectious like sickness, I would wish to be infected with the charms you hold for Demetrius.' But this sense derives from the F2 reading 'Ide' ('I'd') at 187, attempting to interpret the ambiguous punctuation of QF. Punctuated

as here, the earlier reading makes sense.
188–9 This is the first of many rhymes between words now taking different terminal vowel sounds. Cercignani argues (see 303–7 for these specific sounds) that such apparent 'eye-rhymes' or imperfect rhymes (especially if conventional) might have been exact rhymes in earlier pronunciation.
190 **bated** subtracted, excepted
191 **translated** (1) transferred (*OED v.* 1), referring to *The rest*; (2) transformed (*OED v.* 4) into *you*, i.e. Hermia; cf. 3.1.115. On the theme of 'translation' in the play, and especially this passage, see Saenger 70–2.
192 **with what art** an implicit accusation. Helena is as attractive as Hermia (227); the latter must be practising some trick or ploy for Demetrius to prefer her.
193 **sway the motion** control the movement, as the angelic 'intelligences' control the planetary spheres in the Ptolemaic system (see 2.1.7n.).
sway control, rule; but also suggesting 'divert', lead off course (*OED v.* 6a)
194–201 See 136–40n.

---

186 so!] *Theobald;* so, *QF*   187 Your words] Your's would *Hanmer*   I catch] Ide catch *F2*   Hermia;]
Collier; Hermia, Q1; Hermia Q2, F   go,] go; *Pope*   191 I'll] I'd *Hanmer*

HERMIA

    I give him curses, yet he gives me love.

HELENA

    O that my prayers could such affection move!

HERMIA

    The more I hate, the more he follows me.

HELENA

    The more I love, the more he hateth me.

HERMIA

    His folly, Helena, is no fault of mine.   200

HELENA

    None but your beauty. Would that fault were mine!

HERMIA

    Take comfort: he no more shall see my face.

    Lysander and myself will fly this place.

    Before the time I did Lysander see,

    Seemed Athens as a paradise to me.   205

    O then, what graces in my love do dwell,

    That he hath turned a heaven unto a hell!

LYSANDER

    Helen, to you our minds we will unfold.

    Tomorrow night, when Phoebe doth behold

    Her silver visage in the watery glass,   210

    Decking with liquid pearl the bladed grass

---

197 **affection** in an intensive sense: powerful emotion, passion (*OED n.*¹ 1b)

201 Helena implies sarcastically that only Demetrius' folly makes him find Hermia beautiful.

204–7 sung as an 'air' in Garrick's *Fairies*

206–7 The apparent paradox is explained in a MS revision in the late seventeenth-century Smock Alley Theatre prompt-book: 'for since I cannot with Lysander be, / at Athens, tis a perfect hell to me' (*Promptbooks*, 7.1.7, 17). Johnson suggests Hermia is trying to console Helena by saying she too has her problems. Helena ironically repeats the idea to express her frustrated love in 2.1.243.

206 **graces** fortunate or blessed traits, said ironically

209 **Phoebe** Diana the moon-goddess, hence the moon, here reflected in water (210). Since Diana has already been named as the goddess of virginity (89), it is ironical that Lysander should associate her with their elopement.

210 **glass** mirror

211 **bladed** This gives a vivid pictorial sense of each blade of grass gleaming with a dewdrop; cf. 2.1.15.

200 no fault] none *Q2, F*   205 as] like *Q2, F*   207 unto a] into *Q2, F*

(A time that lovers' flights doth still conceal),
Through Athens' gates have we devised to steal.

HERMIA

And in the wood, where often you and I
Upon faint primrose beds were wont to lie　　　　　215
Emptying our bosoms of their counsel sweet,
There my Lysander and myself shall meet,
And thence from Athens turn away our eyes,
To seek new friends and strange companies.
Farewell, sweet playfellow. Pray thou for us,　　　　　220
And good luck grant thee thy Demetrius.
Keep word, Lysander. We must starve our sight
From lovers' food till morrow deep midnight.　　　　　*Exit.*

LYSANDER

I will, my Hermia. Helena, adieu.
As you on him, Demetrius dote on you.　　　　　*Exit.*

HELENA

How happy some o'er other some can be!　　　　　226
Through Athens I am thought as fair as she,
But what of that? Demetrius thinks not so;

---

212 **still** always; i.e. it is the customary time for elopement
213 **devised** arranged, contrived
215 **faint** probably referring to the flowers' colour rather than their scent; cf. 'pale' primroses in *WT* 4.4.122, *Cym* 4.2.220.
　　wont accustomed
216 telling each other all our secrets
　　*****sweet** QF 'sweld' (swelled) makes sense and suits *Emptying*, but rhyme demands *sweet*; cf. 219n.
219 **new friends** unlike the hostile ones in 139. *Friends* changes meaning from the earlier 'relatives' to the usual modern sense: an implicit culture-shift in defining relationships, from the family thrust upon one to the circle one acquires oneself.

*****companies** As with 'sweet' (216), rhyme demands *companies* (easily misread as *companions*, taking a smudge above the *e* as a contraction for *n*). Theobald concomitantly emends QF *strange* to 'stranger' to preserve the metre (comparing *R2* 1.3.143, 'stranger paths of banishment'); but slightly irregular metre is a feature of the text, esp. in Q1. (See pp. 308–9.)
220 **thou** Till now, Hermia and Lysander have addressed Helena by the strained and formal *you*. At the moment of parting, Hermia opens up with the more intimate *thou*.
225 **dote** i.e. may he dote
226 **other some** some others (Blake 3.3.2.7(j)). QF 'othersome' was a standard compound at the time.

---

216 sweet] *Theobald;* sweld *QF*　219 strange companies] *this edn;* strange companions *QF;* stranger Companies *Theobald*　223 SD] *(Exit* Hermia. *QF)*　225 dote] dotes *F*　SD] *(Exit* Lysander. *QF subst.)*　226 other some] *(*othersome *QF)*

He will not know what all but he do know.
And as he errs, doting on Hermia's eyes,   230
So I, admiring of his qualities.
Things base and vile, holding no quantity,
Love can transpose to form and dignity.
Love looks not with the eyes but with the mind,
And therefore is winged Cupid painted blind.   235
Nor hath love's mind of any judgement taste:
Wings and no eyes figure unheedy haste.
And therefore is love said to be a child,
Because in choice he is so oft beguiled.
As waggish boys in game themselves forswear,   240
So the boy Love is perjured everywhere.
For ere Demetrius looked on Hermia's eyne,
He hailed down oaths that he was only mine;
And when this hail some heat from Hermia felt,
So he dissolved, and showers of oaths did melt.   245

231 **admiring of** marvelling at, struck by
232–41 Helena's words prefigure the action in
    the woods, as regards the human lovers but
    still more Titania and Bottom, with Robin
    playing Cupid (see p. 56).
232 **quantity** (1) weight, substance; (2)
    proportion (to the love inspired). Cf. *Ham*
    3.2.161, 'women's fear and love hold
    quantity'.
233 **transpose** transform
    form 'proper figure', 'good order' (*OED n.*
    8, first cited from *KJ* 3.3.101); 'good
    semblance' (Schmidt)
234–9 another 'air' in Garrick's *Fairies*,
    concluding the scene
234 **with the mind** This might suggest true or
    sincere love, but is made to imply the
    opposite.
235 **Cupid painted blind** Cupid was notorious
    for causing unsuitable love-matches
    against reason and judgement. Panofsky
    (122–4) cites 234–9 as 'paraphrasing the
    good old [medieval] "moralizations"'. The
    irrationality of love is a recurrent theme of

MND: see 56–7n. Neoplatonists, however,
    saw the blind Cupid as figuring a higher,
    non-material love (Wind, ch. 4). Kott
    (*Translation*, 33–9) cites a mystical reading
    of the Cupid and Psyche story in
    Apuleius.
236 **taste** (1) the smallest jot or sample (*OED
    n.*[1] 3c); (2) perception, discernment (*OED
    n.*[1] 6)
237 **figure** stand for, symbolize
    unheedy reckless, undiscerning
239 **beguiled** deluded, mistaken (*OED* 2)
240 **waggish** mischievous (*OED* 1, earliest
    citation)
241 **perjured** in an active sense: committing
    perjury, deceitful
242 **eyne** eyes. The old plural was archaic by
    this time, but is used by Shakespeare for
    rhyme or a deliberately archaic effect
    (Hope, 1.3.1).
243 **hailed down** poured down like hail. Folg
    (xxii) suggests a pun on 'hale', draw or pull
    down.
245 **So** thereupon (*OED* 11)

229 do] doth *F*   239 is so oft] is oft *Q2;* is often *F;* often is *F2*   244 this] *Q1, F;* his *Q2*

I will go tell him of fair Hermia's flight.
Then to the wood will he tomorrow night
Pursue her; and for this intelligence
If I have thanks, it is a dear expense.
But herein mean I to enrich my pain,   250
To have his sight thither and back again.   *Exit.*

[1.2]   *Enter* QUINCE, SNUG, BOTTOM, FLUTE,
         SNOUT *and* STARVELING.

QUINCE   Is all our company here?
BOTTOM   You were best to call them generally, man by
     man, according to the scrip.
QUINCE   Here is the scroll of every man's name, which is
     thought fit through all Athens to play in our interlude   5
     before the duke and the duchess on his wedding day
     at night.

---

248 **intelligence** information
249 **dear expense** (something obtained at) heavy
     cost: Demetrius' thanks will add to Helena's
     woe by proving his love for Hermia.
250 **enrich** obtain some gain from; adorn or
     make attractive
[1.2] This scene presumably takes place at the
     house of one of the artisans, perhaps
     Quince (as specified in Capell's SD). A
     public place seems unlikely, as they wish
     to keep their plan secret (97).
1   **company** Quince may mean not only their
     band but, somewhat grandly, a company of
     actors.
2   **generally** meaning the opposite,
     individually or by name: the first of
     Bottom's many misadventures with words.
     Treadwell suggests the word Bottom is
     groping for is 'severally' (= separately,
     OED 1a). The malapropism suits the

speaker, though *generally* might be a
misreading for *severally* in the copy. It is
comical to take a roll-call of such a small
group, but it serves to introduce the artisans
to the audience.
3   **scrip** a small piece of paper with writing.
     The reference is not to the play-text but to
     a list of actors; cf. *scroll* (4), a list of names
     (*OED n.* 2b). It is different from the *parts*
     given to the actors (62, 92), and the
     'prompt copy' that Quince uses during
     rehearsal in 3.1.
5   **interlude** a play, especially a short sketch
     or skit, usually comic; by this time, without
     the original sense of a brief item
     punctuating a longer entertainment or a
     meal. Cf. 5.1.154n.
     day at night not quite contradictory, but
     clumsy phrasing of a sort habitual to the
     artisans

---

248 this] his *F*   **1.2** [1.2] *Capell (SCENE* II.*); not in QF*   0.1–2] *Rowe; Enter* Quince, *the*
Carpenter; [and Q1] Snugge, *the Ioyner; [and Q1]* Bottom, *the Weauer; [and Q1]* Flute, *the Bellowes*
mender; [and Q1] Snout, *the Tinker; and* Starueling *the Tayler. QF*   3 to] *Q1, F; not in Q2*

BOTTOM First, good Peter Quince, say what the play treats on; then read the names of the actors; and so grow to a point. 10

QUINCE Marry, our play is 'The most lamentable comedy and most cruel death of Pyramus and Thisbe'.

BOTTOM A very good piece of work, I assure you, and a merry. Now good Peter Quince, call forth your actors by the scroll. Masters, spread yourselves. 15

QUINCE Answer as I call you. Nick Bottom, the weaver?

BOTTOM Ready. Name what part I am for, and proceed.

QUINCE You, Nick Bottom, are set down for Pyramus.

BOTTOM What is Pyramus? A lover, or a tyrant?

QUINCE A lover that kills himself most gallant for love. 20

BOTTOM That will ask some tears in the true performing of it. If I do it, let the audience look to their eyes. I will move storms; I will condole, in some measure.

---

10 **grow to a point** 'come to the purpose' (Schmidt)

11 **lamentable comedy** Shakespeare is parodying earlier titles like *A New Tragical Comedy of Apius and Virginia* and Thomas Preston's *A Lamentable Tragedy Mixed Full of Pleasant Mirth [about] Cambyses, King of Persia*; cf. 5.1.56–7. He may also be recalling the satire of 'mongrel tragi-comedy' in Sidney's *Defence of Poetry* (published 1595: *Prose*, 114.36). Wilson detects Shakespeare's deeper scepticism about 'the conventional classification of drama', famously reflected in Polonius' catalogue (*Ham* 2.2.333–6). The oxymoron also reflects the links between the main comic action and the tragic play-within-the-play, and the unintentionally comic enactment of the latter.

13–14 **good ... merry** perhaps more parody. The title-page of Skelton's *Magnificence* (1533) describes it as 'A goodly interlude and a mery' (Steevens, Var 1793).

15 **spread yourselves** spread out, arrange yourselves – perhaps in a circle around Quince, or in a row as Schmidt suggests. The officious Bottom may be telling the others to disperse so that he can himself get closer to Quince.

19 **lover ... tyrant** the two chief identities for the lead role of a play
tyrant any king or ruler, not necessarily oppressive (*OED* 2)

20 **gallant** For adverbs without a final *-ly* see Hope, 1.2.5; Blake, 5.1.2.1, 5.1.2.2(i), 5.1.3.1(iii); Crystal, 269. Cf. 46; 3.1.2; 4.1.24.

22 **look to** take care of (i.e. not strain them by too much weeping)

23 **storms** of either grief or applause (Ard¹)
condole 'grieve, lament' (*OED* 1); cf. *condoling* (37).
in some measure earliest *OED* citation (measure *n.* 4d) of the modern meaning 'to some degree, somewhat'; but the context suggests 'in quite some measure', 'to a great degree'.

10 grow] grow on *F* 20 gallant] gallantly *F*

To the rest yet, my chief humour is for a tyrant.
I could play Ercles rarely, or a part to tear a cat in, to   25
make all split.
    The raging rocks
    And shivering shocks
    Shall break the locks
        Of prison gates,   30
    And Phibbus' car
    Shall shine from far,
    And make and mar
        The foolish Fates.

24 **To ... yet** but in a general way. The Oxf
punctuation suggests that Bottom tells
Quince to address the other actors, but
immediately reverts to talking about
himself.
    humour 'inclination, fancy' (Wells);
mood. A fashionable word at the time: see
its use by Nym in *H5* (e.g. 3.2.26–7) and
MW (e.g. 1.1.154–5). Bottom is affecting
sophistication.
25 **Ercles** distortion of '(H)eracles' or
Hercules, perhaps with Seneca's *Hercules
Oetaeus* especially in mind (see 27–34n.).
Hercules seems to have been played onstage in a ranting, blustering vein. Wright
compares Sidney, 'with a voice like him
that plays Hercules in a play' (*Old Arcadia*,
31.30–1), and Greene, *A Groatsworth of
Wit*, '*Hercules* . . . terribly thundred on the
stage' (Greene, 12.131). A two-part
Hercules was acted by the Admiral's Men
in May 1595 (Henslowe, 29). Shakespeare
may be satirizing the rival company,
especially (as Harrison suggests) their
chief tragedian Edward Alleyn; cf.
3.1.125n., 4.2.34n., 5.1.286n.
    rarely splendidly, excellently
    tear a cat 'rant and bluster' (*OED* tear *v.*[1]
1d, earliest citation). Steevens (Var 1778)
cites several instances from early
seventeenth-century plays, including the

character called 'Tear-cat' (for his vaunted
'valour') in Middleton and Dekker's *The
Roaring Girl*. The phrase suggests violent
gesticulation (Kittredge).
26 **split** rend asunder by grief or pain (*OED v.*
3a, first cited from *R3* 1.3.299). But Farmer
(Var 1778) cites Beaumont and Fletcher,
The Scornful Lady 2.3.113, 'Two roring
boyes of *Rome* that made all split', alluding
to Nero and Caligula as fashionable bullies
or ruffians. Cf. also 'split the ears of the
groundlings' (*Ham* 3.2.10). 'Split with
laughter' would be an apt ironic nuance
(cf. 5.1.68–70), but the phrase is not
recorded in *OED* before 1688.
27–34 These lines are no doubt meant as a
quotation, whether from an actual play or
concocted by Shakespeare: Bottom could
hardly be shown as extemporizing eight lines
of rhyming verse. Shakespeare is satirizing
his duller contemporaries. Rolfe observes
that the lines recall John Studley's translation
of *Hercules Oetaeus*, with its alliterative
doggerel as well as specific details like
'Phoebus carre' (*Ten Tragedies*, fol. 188ʳ; sig.
2B6ʳ), 'roring rocks' and bursting hell's gates
(fol. 195ᵛ; sig. 2C5ᵛ). The alliteration
produces a stilted, archaic effect, harking
back to medieval alliterative verse.
31 **Phibbus' car** Phoebus or the sun-god's
chariot. 'Phibbus' is Bottom's distortion.

24 To ... yet] To the rest. – Yet *Oxf*   26–7 split. The] *Theobald (*split – "the*); split the *QF*   27–34] *so
lined and indented, Johnson; prose QF; within quotation marks, Theobald*

This was lofty. Now name the rest of the players. This   35
is Ercles' vein, a tyrant's vein. A lover is more
condoling.

QUINCE   Francis Flute, the bellows-mender?

FLUTE   Here, Peter Quince.

QUINCE   Flute, you must take Thisbe on you.   40

FLUTE   What is Thisbe? A wandering knight?

QUINCE   It is the lady that Pyramus must love.

FLUTE   Nay, faith, let not me play a woman. I have a
beard coming.

QUINCE   That's all one. You shall play it in a mask, and   45
you may speak as small as you will.

BOTTOM   And I may hide my face, let me play Thisbe
too. I'll speak in a monstrous little voice: 'Thisne,

37 **condoling** 'moving, affecting' (Crystal); earliest *OED* citation as adjective, but the definition 'expressing sympathy in sorrow' seems inappropriate here. Cf. *condole* (23).

40 **take . . . you** take charge of or play the part of Thisbe

41 **wandering knight** knight errant, a knight travelling in search of tasks or adventures. As Bottom is playing a lover, Flute hopes for this other heroic role, however unsuited to his appearance and voice.

44 **beard coming** may indicate wishful thinking on young Flute's part; often delivered after a hesitant pause. Flute's protest would be especially comic to the original audience if uttered by a boy actor known for playing female roles (Foakes). On this entire passage, see Fisher, 182–4.

45 **That's all one** It's all the same, it doesn't matter.
    mask part of an upper-class woman's normal outdoor costume. Chaucer's Thisbe is 'ywympled [veiled and bonneted] subtyly' (*Legend of Thisbe*, *LGW*, 797) when she goes to meet Pyramus at night.

46 **small** 'Thin, shrill, piping' (Onions); cf. *MW* 1.1.44, 'speaks small like a woman'.

47 On Bottom's desire to play all roles, see p. 4; cf. Holofernes offering to play three of

the Nine Worthies (*LLL* 5.1.134). Wiles (*Clown*, 35) suggests that early comic actors like Tarlton and Kemp would extend or revise their parts, and deviate from the script to address the audience directly, creating 'a conflict of interests between clown and poet'. Cf. 3.1.33–42, 5.1.183–6, 217–24. Shakespeare may be having a dig at his comic lead.
    And 'an', if; cf. 70, 78.
    hide my face i.e. behind a mask, so that he is not mistaken for Pyramus

48 **monstrous** unnaturally: a loose intensifier like modern 'terribly', but anticipating Bottom's later transformation. Though anything unnatural could be *monstrous*, the common implication of giant size clashes comically with *little*; cf. *smallest monstrous mouse*, 5.1.218. For adverbs without a final *-ly*, see 20n.
    little thin, high-pitched (Schmidt); cf. 3.1.124n. and *small*, 46.
    ***Thisne** Thisbe (whose role Bottom assumes here) would not call herself by her own name. Malone first arranged the speech as though Bottom were playing both roles, *Thisne* representing Pyramus' amorous baby-talk and *Ah . . . lady dear* Thisbe's response.

40 Flute] *not in Q2, F*   48–50] *Norton³ after Malone; Thisne, Thisne, ah Pyramus, my louer deare, thy Thysby* deare, and Lady deare. *QF*

Thisne!' – 'Ah, Pyramus, my lover dear! Thy Thisbe
dear, and lady dear.'   50

QUINCE   No, no. You must play Pyramus; and Flute, you
Thisbe.

BOTTOM   Well, proceed.

QUINCE   Robin Starveling, the tailor?

STARVELING   Here, Peter Quince.   55

QUINCE   Robin Starveling, you must play Thisbe's
mother. Tom Snout, the tinker?

SNOUT   Here, Peter Quince.

QUINCE   You, Pyramus' father; myself, Thisbe's father;
Snug the joiner, you the Lion's part; and I hope here   60
is a play fitted.

SNUG   Have you the Lion's part written? Pray you, if it
be, give it me, for I am slow of study.

QUINCE   You may do it extempore, for it is nothing but
roaring.   65

BOTTOM   Let me play the Lion too. I will roar that I will
do any man's heart good to hear me. I will roar that I
will make the duke say, 'Let him roar again, let him
roar again.'

QUINCE   And you should do it too terribly, you would   70

56–9 Pyramus and Thisbe's parents do not
appear in the performance in Act 5 (but see
5.1.343–4). Either Quince or Shakespeare
could have changed his mind or simply been
inconsistent, as Shakespeare often was.
Kittredge suggests revision by Quince, as
also in omitting the dialogue spoken during
the rehearsal (3.1.77–82, 88–92, 98–9) and
adding the characters of Moonshine and
Wall (3.1.54–66). The changes make for
variety: repeating the same dialogue in
Act 5 would be 'wearisome' (Furness, Var
115). The lovers' parents play an active
role in the *Gallery* poem and the medieval
French versions of the story underlying

it (van Emden); so do the fathers in the
play in BL Add. MS 15227 (see p. 61).
On the absence of the mothers, see
p. 83.

61 **fitted** properly set up; perhaps suggested
by Quince's profession of carpenter

63 **study** memorizing, as an actor learns a part
(*OED n.* 5c, earliest citation as noun in this
sense). Cf. *Ham* 2.2.477, 'study a speech of
some dozen lines'.

66–9 Daly and Brook introduced a roaring
contest here between Bottom and Snug.

66 **that** so that

70 **And** See 47n.

terribly fearsomely, causing terror

53–4] *one line, Q*   60 here] there *F*   62–3 if it be] if be *F*   70 And] If *Q2, F*

fright the duchess and the ladies, that they would
shriek, and that were enough to hang us all.

ALL   That would hang us, every mother's son.

BOTTOM   I grant you, friends, if you should fright
the ladies out of their wits, they would have no more   75
discretion but to hang us. But I will aggravate my
voice so, that I will roar you as gently as any sucking
dove; I will roar you and 'twere any nightingale.

QUINCE   You can play no part but Pyramus; for Pyramus is
a sweet-faced man, a proper man as one shall see in   80
a summer's day, a most lovely gentlemanlike man:
therefore you must needs play Pyramus.

BOTTOM   Well, I will undertake it. What beard were I
best to play it in?

QUINCE   Why, what you will.   85

BOTTOM   I will discharge it in either your straw-colour
beard, your orange-tawny beard, your purple-in-grain

---

73   no doubt spoken in a confused clamour, not
in chorus

76   **discretion** power to moderate a law; option
aggravate meaning the opposite,
'moderate'. Mistress Quickly makes the
same mistake in *2H4* 2.4 163.

77   **roar you** roar to show you or oblige you:
the old 'ethical dative' (see Hope, 1.3.?1)

77–8   **sucking dove** confusing two harmless
creatures, a sitting dove and a sucking
(suckling) lamb. Smith ('Dove') cites an
actor's confusion in speaking 'As is the
sucking lamb or harmless dove' (*2H6*
3.1.71) as reported in Robert
Chamberlain's(?) *A New Booke of Mistakes*
(1637), 51 (sig. D2ʳ), wrongly ascribing the
line to Marlowe's *Edward II*.

78   **and** 'an', as if; cf. 47, 70.

79   **You ... Pyramus** In many productions
(e.g. Brook's, and Noble's film) Bottom
walks off in a huff at this point and is
cajoled back.

80   **proper** fine, excellent; handsome

80–1   **In ... day** in the best circumstances,
given the best possible choice (proverbial:
Dent, S967). Wright compares *H5* 3.6.63,
4.8.23.

83   **undertake** like *discharge* (86), a weighty
word suggesting a much graver challenge
than amateur theatricals

86–9   On the variety of false beards used by
Renaissance actors, see Fisher, 163–5.
Brook's production turned these lines into a
song. The use of *your* expresses an 'easy
familiarity' (Hope, 1.3.2b); cf. 'Your worm'
(*Ham* 4.3.21), 'Your serpent of Egypt' (*AC*
2.7.26).

86   **discharge** execute, perform; cf. *undertake*,
83n.

87   **orange-tawny** 'dull yellowish-brown'
(*OED adj.* a); cf. 3.1.122. Donaldson (13)
compares Sir Thopas's saffron-coloured
beard in Chaucer (*Sir Thopas*, *CT*, 1920).
purple-in-grain a shade of red, originally
a fast (*in grain*) dye from certain insects;
see Linthicum, 7.

74   if] if that *F*   78   roar you and] roare and *F*

beard, or your French-crown-colour beard, your perfit yellow.

QUINCE   Some of your French crowns have no hair at all,   90
and then you will play bare-faced. But masters, here are your parts; and I am to intreat you, request you and desire you to con them by tomorrow night, and meet me in the palace wood a mile without the town by moonlight. There will we rehearse; for if we meet   95
in the city, we shall be dogged with company, and our devices known. In the meantime, I will draw a bill of properties such as our play wants. I pray you, fail me not.

BOTTOM   We will meet, and there we may rehearse most   100
obscenely and courageously. Take pains, be perfit. Adieu.

---

88 **French-crown-colour** golden like the French coin, the *écu* or crown
perfit Q *perfit* was the older and commoner (not necessarily uneducated or vulgar) version, used by the artisans; Demetrius uses the later Latinate *perfect* (3.2.137). Cf. the contrast of *lantern* and *lanthorn* (see 3.1.55n.). Cf. also the artisans' use of popular forms like *byrlakin* and *parlous* (3.1.12).

90 **French crowns** bald pates caused by syphilis, the 'French disease'. It also destroyed facial hair; hence *bare-faced* (*OED* 1, earliest citation), whose metaphorical sense 'open' (hence bold, audacious) is first cited from *Mac* 3.1.121.

92 **parts** scrolls with a single actor's speeches and the preceding cues, from which he would learn his part
am to have to, must (*OED* be *v.*[1] 18a)

93 **con** learn by heart

94 **palace wood** a wood owned by the Duke, not one adjoining his palace: it is variously a mile or a league from the city (see next note).
mile Lysander's appointed place was a league away (1.1.165); but as he loses the way (2.2.40), they may have ended up in a different place – if we seek consistency at all.

without outside

96 **dogged with** pursued or pestered by. It is comical that Quince should expect their amateur effort to attract a crowd of fans.

97 **devices** plans
draw a bill make a list

98 **properties** props, stage furnishings
wants requires

98–9 **fail me not** don't miss your appointment with me

101 **obscenely** *Obscene* was a very new word in the 1590s, meaning 'offensive, loathsome'. It could be wrongly derived from *scene* (Lat. *scaena*, stage), hence 'off-scene' or 'out of sight', suiting the context; but is here probably another of Bottom's solecisms, shared with Costard in *LLL* (4.1.142). It might also be a malapropism (or misprint) for 'obscurely', in secret or hiding.
courageously vigorously, spiritedly (*OED* courageous 3, last recorded 1577)
perfit word-perfect, with all the lines memorized. For the form, see 88n.

102 **Adieu** The French word is a comic affectation in Bottom, contrasting with the homely *perfit*. Cf. his use of *Monsieur* and *Cavalery* (4.1.8–23).

---

88 French-crown-colour] French-crowne colour'd *F*   perfit] perfect *F*   95 will we] we will *Q2, F*
100 most] more *Q2, F*   101 perfit] perfect *F*

QUINCE   At the duke's oak we meet.

BOTTOM   Enough. Hold, or cut bowstrings.   *Exeunt.*

[2.1]   *Enter a* FAIRY *at one door, and* ROBIN GOODFELLOW
                      at another.

ROBIN
    How now, spirit, whither wander you?

FAIRY
          Over hill, over dale,
              Thorough bush, thorough brier,
          Over park, over pale,
              Thorough flood, thorough fire,   5

---

103 **duke's oak** presumably a forest landmark,
a large tree especially associated with
Theseus; cf. 'Herne's oak' named after a
legendary hunter in *MW* 4.4.38.

104 **Hold ... bowstrings** whether the
bowstring holds or breaks (Warburton) –
i.e. whatever befall; but 'cut bowstrings'
may be slang for 'castrate'. Malone
compares the proverb 'Hold, or cut
codpiece point' (Dent, C502, first recorded
1678). Godshalk offers a military
explanation: archers beating a retreat
would discard their heavy crossbows after
cutting the strings to prevent their pursuers
from using them.

[2.1] The F act division marks a decisive
change of venue to a wood, inaugurating
the pastoral sequence (see pp. 71–6,
320–1). The familiar SD 'A Wood near
Athens' stems from Capell, expanding
Pope's 'The [Theobald's 'a'] Wood'.

0.1 The two doors were probably at the back of
the stage, leading out from the tiring-house
(see p. 6). Oberon and Titania, with their
trains, enter the same way at 59.1. This
may be a stage convention to indicate
chance encounters, but it divides the
quarrelling Oberon and Titania, with their

respective retinues, into two visually
opposed camps.

1–17 Brooks compares the dialogue between
Cupid and Diana's nymph in Lyly's
Gallathea 1.2.

1   **spirit** The term is repeatedly used to cover
the varied population of the fairy world: cf.
16; 2.2.7; 3.1.148, 155; 3.2.4, 388. The
fairy is addressing a supernatural creature
of another sort.
     whither wander you? recalls the proverb
'Wit, whither wilt thou?' (Dent, W570); cf.
AYL 4.1.156.

2–15 *The short rhyming lines suggest a song,
though the last two lines grade into the
following pentameters; cf. 249–56n.
Sitwell (190) would print 2–5 as two long
lines (as in QF) to bring out the pace of the
fairy's flight and a sense of 'stretching of
wings'. Gooch and Thatcher list 44 musical
settings, often as a free-standing song
sometimes wrongly attributed to 'Puck'.

2–3 Halliwell-Phillipps (*Memoranda*, 6)
compares *FQ* 6.8.32.1 (published 1596),
'Through hils and dales, through bushes
and through breres'.

3   **Thorough** archaic variant of 'through'

4   **pale** fence, boundary

2.1 [2.1] *Rowe (*ACT II. SCENE I.*); Actus Secundus. F; not in Q*   0.1 ROBIN GOODFELLOW] Puck *or*
Robin-goodfellow *Rowe; Robin Goodfellow, a puck Oxf*   1+ SP] Puck *(throughout the play) Rowe;* ROBIN
(throughout the play) Oxf   2–9] *so lined, Pope; QF line* brier, / fire: / sphere: / greene. / *Indented,
Capell*   3, 5 Thorough ... thorough] through ... through *Q2, F*

I do wander everywhere
Swifter than the moon's sphere,
And I serve the Fairy Queen
To dew her orbs upon the green.
The cowslips tall her pensioners be.   10
In their gold coats, spots you see:
Those be rubies, fairy favours;
In those freckles live their savours.
I must go seek some dew drops here,
And hang a pearl in every cowslip's ear.   15
Farewell, thou lob of spirits; I'll be gone.
Our queen and all her elves come here anon.

6   **everywhere** stressed by an exhausted fairy
in Hoffman's film; cf. 15n.

7   **moon's sphere** the innermost (carrying the
moon) of the crystalline spheres thought to
revolve round the earth in the Ptolemaic
system; but here, perhaps simply the moon.
The fairy must travel faster than the moon
to complete her tasks before it sets. Cf. 176
and 4.1.96–7 for the speed, and 3.2.378–95
for the time allotted to fairy activities.
moon's May be pronounced in two
syllables, as emended by Steevens, for a
more regular rhythm; but such regularity is
uncalled-for, especially in a song or chant
(see pp. 308–9).

9   **dew her orbs** usually taken as 'water the
fairy rings with dew' (see *OED* orb *n.¹* 6a,
first citation after 1460). Fairy rings are
round patches of mushrooms growing in a
field, thought to be caused by fairies
dancing in a ring. Steevens (Var 1778)
notes how in Olaus Magnus' *Historia de
Gentibus Septentrionalibus* (*History of the
Northern Peoples*, 1555) fairies are said to
parch the circles on which they dance; this
fairy may be appointed to water them. But
'dew her orbs' might also mean to sprinkle
(*OED* dew *v.* 3) the dewdrops (*orbs* or
globes of moisture), as 15 indicates.

10   **tall** brings out the fairy's tiny size by
contrast: see p. 49.

pensioners sumptuously dressed royal
bodyguards, like those attending Elizabeth

12   **Those** the spots
rubies 'the crimson drops / I'th' bottom of
a cowslip' (*Cym* 2.2.38–9)
favours signs of (royal) favour, decorations

13   **freckles** specks; cf. 'freckled cowslip', *H5*
5.2.49.
savours fragrance (*OED n.* 2)

15   Pearl earrings were a male fashion of the
time, as borne out by a supposed portrait of
Walter Ralegh, and another of Prince
Henry by Isaac Oliver. Such ornaments
would suit the richly dressed *pensioners*.
pearl i.e. dewdrop. The idea that pearls
originate from dew stems from a
misreading of Pliny's *Natural History*,
9.54 (trans. Holland, 1601, 1.254: sig. Z1ᵛ).
Dodypoll (see p. 48) has fairies 'Hanging
on euery leafe an orient pearle' (Act 3: sig.
E4ʳ). Cf.1.1.211n.
every stressed by the fairy in Hall's
1959 production as an exhausting chore;
cf. 6n.

16   **lob** bumpkin, lout; also a type of fairy,
sometimes identified with the hobgoblin to
which Robin is allied (see p. 44).
spirits See 1n.

17   **elves** as Foakes notes, used broadly of all
fairies of both sexes
anon soon, in no time

7   moon's] *(Moons QF); moones Var 1778 (Steevens)*

ROBIN

The king doth keep his revels here tonight.
Take heed the queen come not within his sight;
For Oberon is passing fell and wrath   20
Because that she, as her attendant, hath
A lovely boy stolen, from an Indian king:
She never had so sweet a changeling.
And jealous Oberon would have the child
Knight of his train, to trace the forests wild.   25
But she perforce withholds the loved boy,
Crowns him with flowers, and makes him all her joy.
And now, they never meet in grove or green,
By fountain clear or spangled starlight sheen,
But they do square, that all their elves, for fear,   30
Creep into acorn cups and hide them there.

FAIRY

Either I mistake your shape and making quite,

18 **keep** hold, observe
20 **passing ... wrath** surpassingly fierce and
angry
   wrath only adjectival use in Shakespeare,
though current in the period
22 **lovely boy** The Friend is so addressed in
Son 126.1 (Sinfield, 74).
   stolen one syllable (F 'stolne'); see 1.1.32n.
Q1 comma after *stolen* makes *hath stolen* a
compound verb, implying Titania has
herself stolen the child and not simply
obtained one stolen by others. As Brooks
notes, this is compatible with 123–37.
   Indian On this 'India', with its
'implications about race and early modern
England's mercantilist and/or colonialist-
imperialist ideology' (Hendriks, 41), see
127n. and p. 86. The Indian boy might
have been suggested by a South American
tribal prince brought to England by Walter
Ralegh.
23 **changeling** three syllables. Usually a fairy
child left among humans, but here a human
child taken by fairies (the only instance
under *OED* 3). Such thefts were a matter of
common belief. Spenser's Redcrosse

Knight (*FQ* 1.10.65) and Sir Arthegall (*FQ*
3.3.26) were so stolen, and 'Chaungclings'
(*FQ* 1.10.65.9) may apply to Redcrosse as
well as the fairy child left in exchange
(Brooks). Latham (158) cites the fairies'
'stolen children' in Fletcher, *The Faithful
Shepherdess* 1.2.104, and the 'Faies' and
'Elves' dancing 'With each a little
Changeling, in their armes' in Jonson, *The
Sad Shepherd* 2.8.52–4.
24–7 On the Freudian implications read into the
relations between Titania, Oberon and the
child, see pp. 85–6.
24 **jealous** envious (of Titania's possession of
the child); but as 61, 63, 81 indicate,
Oberon is also sexually jealous about
Titania.
25 **trace** range, traverse
26 **perforce** forcibly
   loved lovèd
27 **Crowns ... flowers** as she later crowns
Bottom (4.1.3); see p. 85).
29 **fountain** spring; cf. 84.
   sheen bright, shining
30 **square** quarrel (*OED v.* 8a)
32 **making** appearance (*OED n.*[1] 5a)

22 stolen,] stollen, *Q1;* stollen *Q2;* stolne *F*

147

Or else you are that shrewd and knavish sprite
Called Robin Goodfellow. Are not you he
That frights the maidens of the villagery,   35
Skim milk, and sometimes labour in the quern,
And bootless make the breathless housewife churn,
And sometime make the drink to bear no barm,
Mislead night-wanderers, laughing at their harm?
Those that Hobgoblin call you, and sweet Puck,   40
You do their work, and they shall have good luck.
Are not you he?

ROBIN   Thou speak'st aright:

---

33 **shrewd and knavish** mischievous and roguish. Any more sinister sense seems inappropriate.

34–41 For Robin's activities in relation to fairy lore, see p. 44.

34 **Robin Goodfellow** On the names Robin Goodfellow and Puck, see List of Roles 18n. On their occurrence in the text, see pp. 297, 304, 307.

35 **villagery** countryside, rural community (earliest *OED* citation); three syllables (villag'ry), as indicated by the spelling in all editions from Q2

35–9 F3 'fright' and Malone's proposed 'Skims, labours' etc. mark unnecessary attempts to rationalize the syntax. Grammatical inconsistency in verb endings was common in the period and is natural at any time in long sentences. The QF forms *Skim, labour* etc. reflect the shift from a 'who' to a 'you' construction (Abbott, 415).

36 **Skim milk** steal the cream from the top of the milk
quern handmill for grinding corn, but here perhaps a variant of 'churn' (for butter: not in *OED*). The *labour* appears to be mischievous; but Scot (4.10; 85, sig. H3ʳ) cites 'grinding of malt or mustard' among Robin Goodfellow's services to the householder.

37 **bootless** fruitlessly: Robin's spell prevents the butter from forming.

38 **sometime** sometimes; cf. 47.
barm yeast to ferment ale, hence the resulting 'head' or froth. Kittredge (*Witchcraft*, 167–70) cites stealing milk (often directly from the cow) and interference with brewing and butter-making as common tricks of goblins and other spirits.

39 **Mislead night-wanderers** one of the commonest pranks of the puck, merging into the will-o'-the-wisp or *ignis fatuus*. Cf. 3.1.102–7; see Briggs, *Vanishing*, 120; Young, 21.
harm distress

40 **Hobgoblin** 'Rob(in) the Goblin' (cf. 3.2.399): a beneficent spirit of the class of brownies, doing housework for a small reward of food (Briggs, *Vanishing*, 8); but according to Scot (7.2; 131, sig. L2ʳ), both he and Robin Goodfellow were once held 'terrible' by the people. Here the names seem to be personal appellations for Robin rather than generic.
Puck a spirit originally identified with the devil; but Robin clearly finds the name pleasing, perhaps by the addition of *sweet*. It was common folk practice to neutralize a feared or hated name by a conciliatory epithet.

---

33 sprite] spirit *Q2, F* 34 not you] you not *Q2, F* 35 frights] fright *F3* villagery] *(*Villageree *Q1;* Villagree *Q2, F)* 36–9 Skim . . . labour . . . make . . . make . . . Mislead] Skims . . . labours . . . makes . . . makes . . . Misleads *Collier (Malone)* 42–3 Thou . . . night] *so lined, F; one line, Q* 42 speak'st] *Q2, F;* speakest *Q1*

I am that merry wanderer of the night.
I jest to Oberon, and make him smile
When I a fat and bean-fed horse beguile,   45
Neighing in likeness of a filly foal.
And sometime lurk I in a gossip's bowl
In very likeness of a roasted crab,
And when she drinks, against her lips I bob,
And on her withered dewlap pour the ale.   50
The wisest aunt telling the saddest tale
Sometime for three-foot stool mistaketh me;
Then slip I from her bum, down topples she,
And 'Tailor' cries, and falls into a cough;
And then the whole choir hold their hips and laugh,   55

45 **bean-fed** i.e. fat from indulgent feeding

46 **filly foal** female foal, attracting the male horse. Spirits could disturb horses in their stalls (Kittredge, *Witchcraft*, 219).

47 **gossip's bowl** perhaps not the vessel but the drink, a spiced ale or gossip-cup; *she* (49) indicates the drinker is also in mind. *Gossip*, one of a friendly group of women (originally attending a birth: *OED n.* 2b, earliest citation, but this association seems inappropriate here); cf. *gossiped* (125).

48 **very** exact
   crab crab-apple, roasted to spice a drink

50 **dewlap** loose skin at the throat (*OED* 1b, earliest application to humans); but perhaps 'hanging breast' (Schmidt), or even a woman's private parts (Rubinstein, 75, as part of a bawdy double meaning running through this account).

51 **aunt** 'An old woman; a gossip' (*OED* 2, only citation)
   saddest most solemn

52 **three-foot** three-legged. 'Measuring three feet' (*OED*, earliest citation) seems untenable.

54 **'Tailor'** Editors were long content with Johnson's tentative reference to a tailor's squatting posture, like the 'aunt's' after her

fall. The word might mean a thief (from Middle English *taillard*, 'one with a tail', a term of abuse: Clemen). Nares (869) cites *Cornu-copiæ. Pasquil's Night-Cap* (1612), 1 (sig. B1ᵛ): 'Theeuing is now an occupation made, / Though men the name of Tailor doe it giue.' It may also be an error for 'tak[e]s on' (shouts, makes a fuss; cf. 3.2.258n.); but is most likely a play on *tail*, buttocks ('Oh, my bum!': Brooks, citing Hulme, 99–101), or indeed vagina (Partridge, *Bawdy*, 196; Williams, 3.1355–8) The exclamation from the 'wisest aunt telling the saddest tale' proves to have indelicate nuances. Cf. 'tailer' in Dekker, *The Honest Whore 1*, 5.2.260.

55–6 Brooks takes QF 'loffe' (laugh), *waxen* (increase, grow louder), *neeze* (sneeze) as archaisms suiting the old 'aunt's' tale. For the archaic plural verb-ending *-en* in *waxen*, see Hope, 2.1.8a. 'Loffe', with 'coffe' to underscore the rhyme, is the most persistent survivor of all non-modern spellings in the sample Shakespearean texts tracked by Howard-Hill ('Printers', 18) through the seventeenth century. 'Loffe' could also mean 'fart' (Rubinstein, 144).

55 **choir** 'chorus', band, company (*OED n.* 6)

46 filly] silly *Q2, F*   50 dewlap] *(dewlop QF)*   54 'Tailor'] *(tailour QF); rails or Hanmer; tail-sore (Rann)*   cough] *(coffe QF)*   55 choir] *(Quire QF)*   laugh] *(loffe QF)*

And waxen in their mirth, and neeze, and swear
A merrier hour was never wasted there.
But room, fairy. Here comes Oberon.

FAIRY

And here my mistress. Would that he were gone.

Enter [OBERON] *at one door with his train, and* [TITANIA]
at another with hers.

OBERON

Ill met by moonlight, proud Titania.   60

TITANIA

What, jealous Oberon? Fairies, skip hence.
I have forsworn his bed and company.

OBERON

Tarry, rash wanton. Am not I thy lord?

TITANIA

Then I must be thy lady; but I know
When thou hast stolen away from fairy land   65
And in the shape of Corin, sat all day

---

56 **waxen** Farmer (Var 1793) suggests *yexen*
from *yex*, hiccup (*OED v.* 2) – or perhaps
sob (*v* 1), i.e. shed tears of merriment.
57 **wasted** spent
58 **room** make room, stand back
59 F4 *we* is attractive, but *he* (Oberon) suits
the speaker, who serves Titania.
59.1 See 0.1n.
61 ***Fairies** Theobald's plural seems justified:
Titania makes a motion of leaving with her
train. In QF, the *-s* ending might easily
have been passed over for the *s* in *skip*. But
Titania may be telling the first fairy, her
servant, to move away from Oberon's
servant Robin (Wells).
63 **wanton** 'wilful creature' (Crystal; cf. *OED
n.* 1); also a lascivious or promiscuous
person, especially female (*OED n.* 2), no

doubt alluding to Titania's alleged
relationship with Theseus (76). Cf. 99n.,
and see Maguire, 87 on the nuances of the
word in this scene.
thy Oberon and Titania generally address
each other as *thou*. Occasional shifts to *you*
may be arbitrary, or may imply moments of
especially distant or sarcastic formality.
63–4 **lord … lady** implying the husband's
authority but also the wife's 'claim to his
devotion' (Brooks). If Titania is to
acknowledge Oberon as her husband, he
must accept her as his wife and not run
after other women (Kittredge).
65 **stolen** one syllable (F 'stolne'); see 1.1.32n.
66–8 **Corin, Phillida** typical names from
pastoral poetry. Oberon, in the guise of a
mortal man, courts mortal women.

---

56 waxen] yexen *Var 1793 (Farmer)*   59] *F lines* Mistris: / gone. /   he] we *F2*   59.1 OBERON] *Malone;
the King of Fairies QF;* Oberon *King of* Fairies *Rowe*   TITANIA] *Malone; the Queene QF*   60] *F lines*
Moone-light, / *Tytania.* /   61+ SP TITANIA] *Capell; Queen. (subst.) QF*   61 Fairies] *Theobald;* Fairy
QF   65 hast] wast *F*   stolen] *(stollen Q; stolne F)*

Playing on pipes of corn, and versing love
To amorous Phillida. Why art thou here
Come from the farthest steep of India,
But that, forsooth, the bouncing Amazon,   70
Your buskined mistress and your warrior love,
To Theseus must be wedded; and you come
To give their bed joy and prosperity.

OBERON

How canst thou thus for shame, Titania,
Glance at my credit with Hippolyta,   75
Knowing I know thy love to Theseus?
Didst not thou lead him through the glimmering night
From Perigenia, whom he ravished?

---

67 **corn** oat straws
versing love composing or singing love-poems

69 ***steep** slope, mountain. As Himaeus or Emodus, the Himalayas were known to Europeans since classical times. Q1 *steppe* may be 'step', reach or extent, 'utmost limit in travel' (Onions; not in *OED*). The modern 'steppe' is first recorded from *c.*1670.

70–80 Krieger (56) notes how these cross-relations support Theseus-Oberon, Hippolyta–Titania parallels – as, one may add, stressed by doubling casting in many modern productions.

70 **But that** only because
forsooth in truth, to speak frankly
bouncing strapping, spirited

71 **buskined** wearing buskins, a boot worn by hunters and also tragic actors. The word suggests the sensational appearance of the warrior queen, who is fond of hunting (see 4.1.111–17). Spenser cites buskins as part of an Amazon's costume (*FQ* 5.5.3.1). Treadwell (101) takes them as a sign of masculinity in women.

72 **must be** will be, is going to be: virtually the simple future tense (Blake, 4.3.7.10; Hope, 2.1.2c), but with a hint of something

deeply desired or expected

75 **Glance at** 'cast aspersion on' (*Riv*)
credit good name
with using, citing the case of

77–80 Bevington ('Dark Side', 90) suggests Titania did not simply draw Theseus away from these women, but induced him to 'ravish and then reject' them as a way of expressing her own 'mysterious affection'. See also 5.1.3n.

77 **glimmering night** 'the night faintly illuminated by stars' (Steevens, Var 1778). *Glimmer* meaning to shine intermittently or flicker (*OED* 2a) is virtually a Shakespearean innovation; cf. 5.1.381, *Mac* 3.3.5 and (as a noun) *CE* 5.1.315. Cf. also 3.2.61n. But the phrase might imply that Titania led Theseus astray like a will-o'-the-wisp; hence Warburton's emendation 'glimmering, through the night'.

78 **Perigenia** Gk *Perigoune* (*Perigouna* in North), abducted but honourably treated by Theseus after he killed her father, the brigand Sinnis (Plutarch, 8.2–3; North, 5, sig. A3ᵛ). The Latinate form *Perigenia* in QF seems deliberate and worth retaining; cf. *Antiopa* (80).
ravished ravishèd

---

69 steep] *Q2, F;* steppe *Q1;* step *Capell*   77 not thou] thou not *F*   through the glimmering] glimmering, through the *Warburton*

And make him with fair Aegles break his faith,
With Ariadne, and Antiopa?   80
TITANIA
These are the forgeries of jealousy;
And never, since the middle summer's spring,
Met we on hill, in dale, forest or mead,
By paved fountain or by rushy brook,
Or in the beached margin of the sea   85
To dance our ringlets to the whistling wind,
But with thy brawls thou hast disturbed our sport.

79 ***Aegles** Aegle, a nymph for whom Theseus forsook Ariadne (Plutarch, 20.1, 29.2; North, 10, 16: sigs A5ᵛ, B2ᵛ). North's version of the name, *Aegles*, is used here as closer to QF 'Eagles'. Cf. Thomas Cooper, *Thesaurus* (1584), sig. 7A3ʳ: 'Aegle, gles, A Nymph.'

80 **Ariadne** daughter of King Minos of Crete. She eloped with Theseus after helping him slay the monster Minotaur, but was abandoned by him and finally married Dionysus.
Antiopa Latinate form (cf. *Perigenia*, 78) of 'Antiope', Hippolyta's sister (sometimes identified with her). Theseus had a son by her, but abandoned her for Phaedra (Plutarch, 27.4–5; North, 15, sig. B2ʳ). On the Antiope/Hippolyta binary, see pp. 65–6.

81 **forgeries** fabrications, lies

82 **middle summer's spring** start of midsummer (*spring*, start or origin); but the juxtaposition of *summer* and *spring* suggests the confusion of seasons described in 106–14.

83 **we** As 86–7 indicates, Titania does not mean herself and Oberon, but herself and her train.
mead meadow

84 **paved** (pavèd) 'with a pebbly bottom' (Doran)
fountain spring
rushy 'Full of or covered with rushes' (*OED adj.¹* 3)

85 **beached** (beachèd) covered with 'beach' or shingle (earliest *OED* citation, the only other before 1889 being *Tim* 5.2.101)
margin QF 'margent' was the usual form at the time, and always in Shakespeare.

86 **ringlets** circular dances (supposedly creating fairy rings): *OED* 2, earliest citation
whistling piping, as though in accompaniment

87 **brawls** clamours, disputes; but here, perhaps a kind of dance (*OED* brawl *n.³* 2a), more energetic and raucous than *ringlets* – a subtler invasion of Titania's space than open dispute. Whiter (102–5) suggests a play on both senses.
sport (1) diversion, recreation; (2) merriment, mirth

79 Aegles] *Chambers;* Eagles *QF; Ægle / Rowe*   85 margin] (margent *QF)*

Therefore the winds, piping to us in vain,
As in revenge have sucked up from the sea
Contagious fogs, which, falling in the land,   90
Hath every pelting river made so proud
That they have overborne their continents.
The ox hath therefore stretched his yoke in vain,
The ploughman lost his sweat, and the green corn
Hath rotted ere his youth attained a beard.   95
The fold stands empty in the drowned field,
And crows are fatted with the murrain flock.

88–114 For climatic aberrations in the 1590s and their bearing on the play's date, see p. 288. For Turner (*Helix*, 34) this passage foreshadows the modern concept of nature's complex ecology, where 'many local factors quickly combine to produce effects that are impossible to anticipate and very difficult to model'.

88–97 Echoes Ovid's account of Deucalion's flood (*Met.* 1.262–73; Golding, 1.311–24), with details from Ceres' anguish at the rape of Proserpina (*Met.* 5.477–86; Golding, 5.595–604), the plague of Aegina (*Met.* 7.538–51; Golding, 7.671–706), and possibly Seneca's account of the plague of Thebes (*Oedipus*, 41–51, 133–48).

88, 93, 103 The repeated *therefores* build up to a climax; but Barber (146) takes the repetition as a petulant attempt to force a connection that does not exist.

88 **piping** whistling, howling (*OED v.¹* 7b, earliest citation), but also in a musical sense (see next note). 'Piping wind' occurs several times in Gavin Douglas's *Aeneid* (Douglas, 3.2.3, 177; 6.3.101; 7.1.17).
in vain because Titania and her train could not dance to the *piping* of the winds. Furness compares Matthew 11.17: 'We have piped vnto you, and ye have not daunced' (cf. Luke 7.32).

90 **Contagious** 'Pestilential, breeding disease' (Cam²)

91 **Hath** apparently singular verb with plural subject, especially common with a relative marker (*which*); cf. 3.1.77n., 3.2.97n. See Hope, 1.4.2i.
pelting paltry, insignificant (*OED adj.¹*); perhaps also driving, onrushing (owing to the unseasonal rain: *OED adj.²* 2). For the easy change to *petty* in F, cf. 'every pelting petty officer' (*MM* 2.2.113).

92 **overborne** overflowed, but also 'oppressed, overpowered', agreeing with *proud* (91): a vivid pathetic fallacy
continents confines, banks

93–5 The farmer's futile labours recall, in a grimmer key, Robin's tricks on the housewife (36–8). Summer rain 'beats down the wheat, making it rot' (Ladurie, 289). On the bad harvests of 1594–7, see p. 288.

93 **stretched** strained to pull (the plough)

95 **his** the usual earlier possessive case of 'it', but here perhaps a deliberate personification
beard the bristles on ripe ears of grain; cf. *Son* 12.7–8, 'summer's green ... with white and bristly beard'.

96 **fold** sheepfold
drowned drownèd

97 **murrain** dead of the murrain or sheep-plague; spelt 'murrion' in QF, indicating a different scansion

91 Hath] Have *Rowe²*   pelting] petty *F*   97 murrain] (murrion *QF*)

The nine men's morris is filled up with mud,
And the quaint mazes in the wanton green,
For lack of tread, are undistinguishable.   100
The human mortals want their winter here;
No night is now with hymn or carol blest.
Therefore the moon, the governess of floods,
Pale in her anger, washes all the air
That rheumatic diseases do abound.   105

98–102 Montrose (*Purpose*, 184) sees here 'the disruption of traditional cultural practices'.

98 nine men's morris (pattern outlined in the soil for) a game, an 'elaborate noughts and crosses' (Brooks) played with pegs or pebbles
filled up The phrasal verb 'fill up' seems virtually a Shakespearean coinage, providing *OED* with six of the eight earliest citations (though not this passage) covering five senses. 'To stop up ... (a hole) by filling' (*OED* 8), illustrated from *1H4* 3.2.116, seems most suitable here. However, the QF spelling 'fild' also suggests 'filed', i.e. 'defiled' or befouled (*OED* file *v.²* 1a): cf. 'filed my mind', *Mac* 3.1.64.

99 quaint intricate (*OED adj.* 3a)
mazes tracks made by dancers, human or fairy, or maze-like trails followed in a race
wanton green luxuriant grass, hiding the *mazes*. Unlike Oberon (see 63n.), Titania uses *wanton* with a positive suggestion of growth and abundance.

100 tread footsteps
undistinguishable faint, indiscernible (earliest *OED* citation); cf. 4.1.186.

101–14 Cf. the disorder wrought by Seneca's Medea: 'I have changed the pattern of the seasons: the summer earth has frozen under my spells, and Ceres was compelled to see a winter harvest' (*Medea*, 759–61). Nosworthy (105) cites the great untimely frost in Athens in Demetrius' time (Plutarch, *Life of Demetrius*, 12.3–4; North, 946–7, sigs 4K5ᵛ–6ʳ). Another source might lie in an event of Demetrius' time whereby (using North's English names for the months) March was renamed November and then August (ch. 26; North 953, sig. 4L3ʳ).

101 human mortals apparent tautology suiting a fairy speaker; cf. 135, 3.2.115. Whether fairies were regarded as mortal is unclear. Some certainly suffered death, including Oberon in *Huon of Bordeaux*.
here Theobald's conjectural suggestion of 'cheer' (chear) – winter or Christmas festivities – is widely adopted in the light of 102, taking *want* as 'lack'. But it seems too early for humans to miss the winter: the fairies' dispute began in early summer (82), and the same disordered summer appears to be continuing (109–11). Perhaps *here* = here and now, right away (*OED adv.* 5a): 'The summer is so bad, that men wish it were winter' (Chambers). They have missed out on the festivities of summer but are not getting those of winter either. Whatever the precise meaning, the situation reverses Titania's vaunt as queen of eternal summer (3.1.149).

102 hymn or carol A carol could be either a religious or a secular song; here perhaps Christmas carols, popular from at least the fifteenth century.
blest so spelt in QF (also in 5.1.409), indicating pronunciation in one syllable; see 1.1.74n.

103 governess ruler, controller. The moon was held to govern tides.

104 Pale ... anger another aspect of the 'watery moon'
washes makes wet or damp (*OED v.* 7a)

105 That so that
rheumatic (rhéumatic: Cercignani, 39) producing rheum or watery discharge through eyes and nose (catarrhs); or perhaps simply caused by damp

98 filled] *(*fild *QF)*   101 here] cheer *Hanmer (Theobald)*

And thorough this distemperature, we see
The seasons alter: hoary-headed frosts
Fall in the fresh lap of the crimson rose,
And on old Hiems' thin and icy crown
An odorous chaplet of sweet summer buds   110
Is, as in mockery, set. The spring, the summer,
The childing autumn, angry winter change
Their wonted liveries; and the mazed world,
By their increase, now knows not which is which.
And this same progeny of evils comes   115
From our debate, from our dissension:
We are their parents and original.

106 **thorough** through, because of
  distemperature imbalance, disorder (of
  both climate and body as well as the root
  cause, Titania and Oberon's quarrel).
  Scansion demands four syllables,
  'distémp'rature', balancing Q1 two-syllable
  thorough to produce a regular pentameter.
107–11   suggests an unequal mating: an
  advance hint of Titania's liaison with
  Bottom, especially her crowning him with
  flowers (4.1.3)
107 **hoary-headed** This antedates the first
  OED citation (hoary *adj.* S2), from
  Jonson's *Every Man in His Humour*
  (1598).
109–11 The cold summer is so like winter that
  its white buds seem to garland the latter's
  head like snow and frost.
109 **Hiems'** winter's, personified as an old man
  as in *Met.* 2.30 (Golding, 2.36–9), 15.212–
  13 (Golding, 15.233–5)
  *****thin** QF 'chin' is possible: Golding (2.39)
  describes winter's 'gray and hoarie bearde'
  as well as 'snowie frozen crowne', details
  absent in Ovid (*Met.* 2.30). In *Aen.* 4.250–
  1, Mount Atlas' chin and beard are stiff
  with snow. But a chaplet round the chin is
  hard to visualize, and *t* and *c* are easily
  confused in the secretary hand, making
  Tyrwhitt's emendation plausible. *Thin*
  probably = thin-haired (Steevens compares

R2 3.2.112, 'thin and hairless scalps': Var
68); but in *Met.* 11.159 (Golding, 11.178),
often thought to have influenced this line,
Mount Tmolus has hollow temples (*cava
tempora*).
  crown the top of the head, not royal
  headgear
110 **odorous** fragrant
112 **childing** fecund, fruitful; cf. *Son* 97.6,
  'teeming [i.e. pregnant] autumn, big with
  rich increase'.
  change probably meaning 'exchange'
  (*OED v.* 3a, first recorded in modern
  English from *RJ* and *LLL*)
113 **wonted liveries** accustomed garb or
  appearance
  mazed (mazèd) bewildered
114 **their increase** the produce or crops (*OED*
  increase *n.* 7a) of the seasons; cf. 112n. and
  Son 97.6.
115 **progeny** offspring (hence *parents*, 117),
  sinisterly born of *dissension* rather than
  union
116 **debate** quarrel
  dissension usual 4-syllable pronunciation
  of the time
117 **parents and original** This links Oberon
  and Titania with Adam and Eve: their
  quarrel re-enacts the Fall (Garber,
  Shakespeare, 221).
  original source, cause

106 thorough] through *Q2, F* 107 hoary-headed] hoared headed *Q2, F* 109 thin] *Halliwell (Var 1778,
Tyrwhitt)*; chinne *QF*; chill *(Theobald, Letter, 232)* 112 childing] chiding *F4* 115–16] *so lined, F2;
QF line* euils, / dissention: /

OBERON

Do you amend it then; it lies in you.
Why should Titania cross her Oberon?
I do but beg a little changeling boy   120
To be my henchman.

TITANIA   Set your heart at rest.
The fairy land buys not the child of me.
His mother was a votaress of my order;
And in the spiced Indian air by night,
Full often hath she gossiped by my side,   125
And sat with me on Neptune's yellow sands
Marking th'embarked traders on the flood,
When we have laughed to see the sails conceive
And grow big-bellied with the wanton wind,
Which she with pretty and with swimming gait   130

---

119 **cross** thwart, oppose
121 **henchman** squire, page (*OED* 1b); in
   particular, a royal page or 'child of
   honour', an office abolished by Elizabeth
   in 1565. The Queen's decision may be
   implicit in Titania's refusing Oberon the
   boy's services.
   Set . . . rest be assured (*OED* rest *n.*[1] P6.a)
   without the modern nuance 'Don't worry',
   unless it be meant sarcastically
122 **The fairy land** Oberon's entire kingdom;
   cf. 144.
123–37 a moment of female bonding in a
   patriarchally dominated play, a 'glimpse of
   women . . . rejoicing in their own special part
   of life's power' (Barber, 156), explaining
   Titania's dismay at the destruction of
   nature's cycle of *increase* (114). See also
   Levine, 213; Hackett, *MND*, 29.
123 **votaress** vowed follower of a deity or
   religious order; here and in 163, two
   syllables, 'vot'ress' (Q1 'Votresse'). Titania
   being Diana's name, the word recalls the
   goddess's virgin train, but Titania's 'order'
   is non-celibate and non-reclusive. On the
   opposition of religious and other vows, see
   1.1.121n.
124 **spiced** (spicèd) fragrant, presumably with
   the scent of spice plants of the East Indies

Indian air If this is where Titania spent
   time with her votaress, it seems likely the
   Indian king was the boy's father, from
   whom Titania stole the child after the
   mother's death.
125 **gossiped** sat chatting like a gossip or boon
   companion; cf. 47n.
126 **Neptune's yellow sands** the sea-beach, the
   ocean-god's territory. 'Yellow sands'
   suggests a tropical, or more specifically
   Caribbean, setting, of which Shakespeare
   would have learnt from the accounts of
   voyagers. Cf. *Tem* 1.2.376; also *Aen.* 6.643.
127 This has been linked to a colonial traffic
   with the Indian boy as a human commodity
   (Hendriks, 52–3; Loomba, 183–91;
   Raman, 244–5, 272–4): see p. 86. But as
   Buchanan (59) argues, the 'rich
   merchandise' would, in that age, carry
   much stronger associations of the West
   Indies, as would the idyllic, Golden-Age-
   like scene described here.
   embarked traders (embarkèd) merchants
   on board ship. *Trader* meaning 'trading
   vessel' is not recorded before 1616.
   flood sea
129 **wanton** lascivious (hence making the sails
   pregnant). Malone compares *Oth* 4.2.79,
   'The bawdy wind that kisses all it meets'.

Following (her womb then rich with my young
   squire)
Would imitate, and sail upon the land
To fetch me trifles and return again
As from a voyage, rich with merchandise.
But she, being mortal, of that boy did die,   135
And for her sake do I rear up her boy;
And for her sake, I will not part with him.

OBERON

How long within this wood intend you stay?

TITANIA

Perchance till after Theseus' wedding day.
If you will patiently dance in our round   140
And see our moonlight revels, go with us;
If not, shun me, and I will spare your haunts.

OBERON

Give me that boy, and I will go with thee.

TITANIA

Not for thy fairy kingdom. Fairies, away.
We shall chide downright if I longer stay.   145
   Exeunt [Titania and her train, and Oberon's train].

---

131 **Following** imitating, resembling
   squire used humorously: 'young gallant'
135 Roughly one per cent of women died in childbed in the late sixteenth century (Schofield, 248–50). The pain and risks associated with pregnancy made it a standard trope for mortality (Cressy, 28–31). **mortal** (1) human; (2) subject to death. Cf. 101n.
138–9 The isolated rhyming lines produce the effect of a sharp exchange.
138 **stay** probably a noun, object of *intend*
140 **patiently** calmly, without losing your temper
142 **shun** avoid, keep away from

spare avoid (*OED v.*[1] 7b)
145 **chide downright** quarrel openly
145 *SD QF allow no exit for Oberon's followers. But they are probably not present during the ensuing dialogue between Oberon and Robin, and certainly not when Oberon eavesdrops on Demetrius and Helena after that. They could hardly have left at Titania's command in 61, for her own fairies remain till 145. We must assume that Oberon's train leaves at the same time, either by taking Titania's command as applying to them, or at a gesture from Oberon when he calls Robin (148).

136 do I] I doe *F*   145 SD *Titania and her train*] Malone *after* Theobald (Queen *and her Train*) *and Oberon's train*] this edn.

OBERON

Well, go thy way. Thou shalt not from this grove
Till I torment thee for this injury.
My gentle puck, come hither. Thou rememberest
Since once I sat upon a promontory,
And heard a mermaid on a dolphin's back   150
Uttering such dulcet and harmonious breath
That the rude sea grew civil at her song,
And certain stars shot madly from their spheres
To hear the sea-maid's music.

ROBIN   I remember.

---

146 **from** depart from, leave
147 **injury** often explained as 'insult', but the general meaning 'harm, loss' seems appropriate; cf. 3.2.148n.
148–68 It seems futile to speculate on possible historical allusion in these lines, and unnecessary to postulate allusion at all, beyond a general reference to Queen Elizabeth. See the accounts in Var and Hackett, *Elizabeth*, 114–20.
149 **Since** 'With verbs of recollection: When; the time when' (*OED conj.* 3b, earliest citation). See Abbott, 132.
150–4 On possible borrowings from Elizabethan pageants, see pp. 287–8. Oberon's account is best taken to reflect the general aesthetics of court pageantry rather than a specific event.
150 **on . . . back** 'Mermaid' (QF 'Mearemaide', from *mere*, sea) could mean a siren – of human form, without a fish-tail, hence needing to ride a dolphin. Sometimes farfetchedly taken to recall Arion, the ancient poet and musician thrown into the sea by sailors but rescued by a dolphin charmed by his song. Frances Yates suggests the

figure might stand for Elizabeth, like the vestal at 158: 'the one complimenting her virginity, the other her charms' (Brooks lxvii).
151 **breath** song; extending *OED* 9a, 'utterance, articulate sound'. Cf. 'a contagious breath' (catchy tune), *TN* 2.3.53.
152 **rude** barbarous, churlish
civil civilized, urbane. The rough sea is calmed by the music. There may be an allusion to English naval power: like Elizabeth, the sea-maid brings peace to the seas (Edgecombe). But the mermaid's song is 'both civilizing and disordering' (Levine, 214), as it dislodges stars from their spheres.
153 **certain stars** probably 'fixed stars' as opposed to planets. But in the Ptolemaic system, all such stars were placed in a single sphere; the plural *spheres* suggests conflation with planetary orbits in the Copernican system. See 7n., 3.2.61n.; cf. *Luc* 1525, 'And little stars shot from their fixed places'.
madly also used of the effect of the magic love-juice (171)

---

150 mermaid] (Mearemaide *subst. QF*)   154+ SP] *Oxf ; Puck (subst.) QF*

OBERON

That very time I saw (but thou couldst not)   155
Flying between the cold moon and the earth
Cupid, all armed. A certain aim he took
At a fair vestal, throned by west,
And loosed his love-shaft smartly from his bow
As it should pierce a hundred thousand hearts.   160
But I might see young Cupid's fiery shaft
Quenched in the chaste beams of the watery moon,
And the imperial votaress passed on
In maiden meditation, fancy free.

155 **but ... not** rarely explained. For Barber (148), the myth of Elizabeth is thus raised to a 'more sublime and occult' level, visible only to the fairy king.

157 **all armed** fully armed, i.e. supplied with his arrows. Brooks compares the armed Cupid, flying among the stars above the sea, in Seneca, *Phaedra* (*Hippolytus*), 198–203, 332–7.
     certain Cupid's *certain aim* is deflected just as the *certain stars* (153) abandon their orbits.

158 **vestal** virgin: originally virgin priestesses of Vesta, goddess of the hearth, but Venus' priestesses were virgins too. A clear allusion to Queen Elizabeth, though some have noted a lukewarm, equivocal quality in the praise. The fine balance between two compliments, to the Queen's virginity and her beauty or (implicitly sexual) attractiveness, is here tilted towards the former; cf. 150n. But Titania's 'order' values motherhood (123), contrasting with the sterile chastity symbolized in the *cold* (156) and *watery* (162) *moon*. The royal compliment 'is at odds with the values of the rest of ... *Dream*' (Hackett, *MND*, 29).
     throned thronèd
     by west a common phrase (*OED* by *prep.* 9c); F *the*, perhaps added to regularize the metre, is uncalled-for (see pp. 308–9). England is west of Athens; cf. *western*, 166.

159 **loosed** shot (*OED* loose *v.* 4a)
     love-shaft earliest *OED* citation, perhaps the model for its later use
     smartly briskly, vigorously

160 **As** as though

161 **might see** was able to see (*OED* may *v.*¹ 4), as though by some special power; cf. 155n.

162 **watery moon** the moon reflected in the water, hence suggesting the paleness of the *cold moon* (156) itself, hence the weak unsatisfying nature of chastity; cf. 1.1.73n., 3.1.191n. As Diana is the moon-goddess, this implication tells against the chaste Diana-like figure of the vestal.
     watery two syllables, 'wat'ry' (Q1 'watry')

163 From the QF spelling, the syllabification seems to be 'And th'imperial vot'ress passèd on'.
     imperial royal, but also 'majestic; august' (*OED adj.* 5a)
     votaress This votaress is presumably Diana's (with whom Elizabeth was often identified); but compare the virgins vowed paradoxically to Vesta and Venus, and contrast Titania's votaress (see 123n., 158n.).

164 **fancy free** free of thoughts of love. 'Fancy free' suggests an absolute construction, 'her fancy remaining free'; F2's *fancy-free* is a compound adjective, 'free of fancy'.

155 saw] say *Q2, F*   157 all armed] alarm'd *Theobald (Warburton)*   158 by west] by the West *F*
163 Votaress] *(*Votresse *QF)*   164 fancy free] fancy-free *F2*

159

Yet marked I where the bolt of Cupid fell: 165
It fell upon a little western flower,
Before milk-white, now purple with love's wound,
And maidens call it love-in-idleness.
Fetch me that flower: the herb I showed thee once.
The juice of it, on sleeping eyelids laid,   170
Will make or man or woman madly dote
Upon the next live creature that it sees.
Fetch me this herb, and be thou here again
Ere the Leviathan can swim a league.

ROBIN
I'll put a girdle round about the earth   175
In forty minutes.   [*Exit.*]
OBERON   Having once this juice,

---

165 **bolt** arrow
166 **western** See 158n.
167 **Before ... purple** like the transformed
  mulberry fruit in Ovid's account of
  Pyramus and Thisbe (*Met.* 4.125–7, 158–
  61; Golding, 4.150–2, 191–5). Cf. also the
  'purple flower ... chequered with white' to
  which the dead Adonis is metamorphosed
  in *VA* 1168. Shakespeare reworks these
  tales of death into the setting of a romantic
  comedy.
  purple first used of the colour of blood
  in *FQ* 2.6.29.9, then in *3H6* 5.6.64 (*OED
  adj.* 2c)
  love's wound suggests loss of virginity.
  The arrow misses the virgin but deflowers
  the flower (Carroll, 163).
168 **love-in-idleness** easy or precipitous love,
  suiting 'love's wound'; but perhaps futile
  (idle) or frustrated love, again suggesting a
  dissatisfying chastity; cf. 3.1.191n. Also,
  'idleness' = folly, delirium (*OED* 3), like
  Titania's infatuation with Bottom. The wild
  pansy or heart's-ease is traditionally called
  'love-in-idleness' in Warwickshire and
  Gloucestershire (Tatlow, 113). For parallels
  in Montemayor and Lyly, see pp. 69–70.

169 **herb** plant bearing the flower
171 ¹**or** either
  madly Cf. 153n.
174 **Leviathan** a biblical sea-monster (Job
  41.1–34) usually identified with the whale,
  as explicitly in the Bishops' Bible. Job
  41.32 implies it has a turn of speed, making
  the sea foam and seethe. The satanic
  implications of Psalms 74.15 and Isaiah
  27.1 seem irrelevant.
  league See 1.1.159n.
175 **put ... earth** go all round the earth: a
  common expression after *MND*, but
  probably not in earlier use. Chapman's
  Bussy d'Ambois 1.1.23 predates the
  examples in *OED* girdle *n.¹* 3b and
  Allusion-Book, 1.117, 303, but not *MND*.
176 **forty minutes** Compare the fairy's speed
  (7) and Oberon's (4.1.96–7), apparently
  also encircling the earth.
176–87 This speech is formally a soliloquy but
  functionally a piece of exposition. It is a
  relic of an older dramatic practice whereby
  characters declare their intentions, even
  ignoble ones, for the audience's benefit.
  Clemen (*Tragedy*, 51) calls this particular
  variant a 'Planning-speech'.

175–6 I'll ... minutes] *so lined, Pope; one line, QF*   175 round about] about *Q2, F*   176 SD] *F2; not
in QF

I'll watch Titania when she is asleep
And drop the liquor of it in her eyes.
The next thing then she, waking, looks upon,
Be it on lion, bear, or wolf, or bull,   180
On meddling monkey or on busy ape,
She shall pursue it with the soul of love.
And ere I take this charm from off her sight
(As I can take it with another herb),
I'll make her render up her page to me.   185
But who comes here? I am invisible,
And I will overhear their conference.

Enter DEMETRIUS, HELENA *following him.*
[*Oberon stands apart.*]

DEMETRIUS

I love thee not, therefore pursue me not.
Where is Lysander and fair Hermia?
The one I'll stay; the other stayeth me.   190

---

177 **when ... asleep** to see when she falls
asleep
180–1 As Foakes notes, these animals belong to
a wild forest rather than a pastoral wood,
lending an ominous touch both to the
setting and to Oberon's intentions; cf.
228n., 2.2.35n., 5.1.361–4n.
181 **meddling ... busy** implying mischievous
curiosity (cf. 'busybody')
182 **soul** 'chief part and quintessence'
(Schmidt): deepest or purest love
186 **I am** a customary construction implying 'I
am doing or becoming this at once'; cf.,
e.g., *TN* 4.2.121, *Ham* 3.2.302, *Mac* 1.7.80.
invisible The Henslowe papers list 'a robe
for to goo invisibell' (Henslowe, 325); but
no such device is mentioned here, or for
Prospero and Ariel in *Tem*. 'These
"invisible" appearances seemingly require
nothing more elaborate ... than for the
actor to say that he or she is invisible.'

(Bevington, 'Hearing', 101)
187 **conference** talk
188–244 Except briefly at 199–201, 214–19
(see 199–201n., 202n.), Demetrius
addresses Helena by the familiar,
contemptuous *thou*, and she him by the
adoring and respectful *you*. (Cf. Demetrius'
you and Hermia's *thou*, 3.2.43–81n.)
Griffiths (129–31) records how these lines
(like 2.2.45–69) were commonly cut in
earlier times, often on grounds of propriety,
but are nowadays played up for their
comic, grotesque or sadistic/masochistic
potential.
190 **stay** cause to stop or pause. Demetrius
would stop Lysander from pursuing
Hermia, but would himself stop to view
and woo her (or: she prevents Demetrius
from stopping Lysander, as she loves the
latter). The emendation *slay ... slayeth* is
attractive but uncalled-for.

---

177 when] *Q1, F;* whence *Q2*   179 then] when *Q2, F*   183 from off] off from *Q2, F*   187.2 *Oberon
stands apart*] *this edn; not in QF*   190 stay ... stayeth] slay ... slayeth *Theobald (Thirlby)*

Thou toldst me they were stolen unto this wood;
And here am I, and wood within this wood,
Because I cannot meet my Hermia.
Hence, get thee gone, and follow me no more.

HELENA

You draw me, you hard-hearted adamant;   195
But yet you draw not iron, for my heart
Is true as steel. Leave you your power to draw,
And I shall have no power to follow you.

DEMETRIUS

Do I entice you? Do I speak you fair?
Or rather do I not in plainest truth   200
Tell you I do not, nor I cannot love you?

HELENA

And even for that do I love you the more.
I am your spaniel, and Demetrius,

---

191 **stolen** one syllable (QF 'stolne'); cf. 1.1.32n.

192 ¹**wood** mad; cf. 4.1.139n.

195–244 Brooks notes many echoes in Helena's speeches (most clearly in 243–4) of Phaedra's pleas to Hippolytus in Seneca's *Phaedra* (*Hippolytus*), 233–41, 700–3, 710–12.

195–7 Demetrius attracts Helena like adamant, and his heart is as hard; yet he is not like adamant in that he does not draw Helena to him and embrace her, though her heart is true as steel (modified from Ard¹). Doran best expresses a further nuance: Helena's heart is 'not base iron but refined steel, which will hold its temper'.

195 **adamant** combines the senses of a supremely hard substance (often identified with the diamond) and an attracting agent, the lodestone. Both qualities are proverbial (Dent, A31.1, A31.2).

197–8 'If you leave (discard, put off) your power to attract, I will no longer be led to follow you.'

199–201 Demetrius adopts the more formal *you* here and at 214–19; perhaps because at these points, Helena's abject advances make him feel the need to be more aloof and formal. Cf. 188–244n.

199 **speak you fair** (1) speak to you in a kind or civil manner; (2) say you are beautiful

201 *****nor** Q reads 'not', no doubt by mistaken repetition of the two preceding *not*s.

202 Except for the intimately pleading appeal in 2.2.88–90, the Q2, F reading here marks the only point where Helena addresses Demetrius (or indeed Lysander or Hermia) by the familiar *thee*, though he generally addresses her so, first in contempt and from 3.2.138 in the presumed intimacy of love (see 188–244n.). For his addressing Helena as *you*, see 199–201n. For the rest, the lovers seem to use *thou* and *you* towards each other indiscriminately; possible local reasons have been suggested at various points of this commentary. See also Stansbury, 61. On nuances of *thou* and *you* generally, see Hope, 1.3.2b; Crystal, 450–1.

---

191 stolen] *(stolne QF)*   unto] into *F*   201 not, nor] *F;* not, not *Q*   202 you] thee *Q2, F*

The more you beat me, I will fawn on you.
Use me but as your spaniel: spurn me, strike me,   205
Neglect me, loose me; only give me leave,
Unworthy as I am, to follow you.
What worser place can I beg in your love
(And yet a place of high respect with me)
Than to be used as you use your dog?   210

DEMETRIUS

Tempt not too much the hatred of my spirit;
For I am sick when I do look on thee.

HELENA

And I am sick when I look not on you.

DEMETRIUS

You do impeach your modesty too much,
To leave the city and commit yourself   215
Into the hands of one that loves you not,
To trust the opportunity of night
And the ill counsel of a desert place
With the rich worth of your virginity.

204 a proverbial trait of the spaniel (Dent, S705), as of a woman (and a walnut tree: the three are associated in Tilley, W644). Dent compares Lyly, *Euphues* (1.249.7–8); 'the kinde Spaniell, which the more he is beaten the fonder he is'. Cf. also *TGV* 4.2.14–15, where a man (Proteus) says *his* love increases 'spaniel-like' the more his mistress scorns him. This is the lowest point of Helena's self-abjection in love, often shown on stage by her grovelling at Demetrius' feet or crawling after him; cf. 3.2.225n.

205 Use . . . as treat me no better than

206 loose *Loose* and *lose* were variants of both words now distinguished by these spellings. Both meanings are relevant: (1) turn me loose, send me away; (2) forget me (cf. 1.1.114); hence (combining both

senses) banish me from your thoughts (Kittredge). Q1 always spells 'lose' as *loose*, sometimes suggesting both modern words. The sense *loose* seems especially relevant here.

208 worser The double comparative was common in Early Modern English (Hope, 1.2.3); cf. 'worser part', *Ham* 3.4.155.

210 used (usèd) treated. 'To use like a dog' (Dent, D514) is proverbial for ill-treatment.

212 sick The sight of Helena makes Demetrius feel ill. The implication of nausea (*OED adj.* 2a) is first noted from Jonson's *Bartholomew Fair* (1614).

214 impeach 'call in question', 'discredit' (*OED v.* 3, earliest citation)

217 opportunity to a possible attacker

218 ill . . . place the temptation posed by the deserted place

206 loose] lose *Q2, F*   210 use] doe *F*

HELENA

　　Your virtue is my privilege, for that　　　　　　220
　　It is not night when I do see your face.
　　Therefore I think I am not in the night,
　　Nor doth this wood lack worlds of company,
　　For you in my respect are all the world.
　　Then how can it be said I am alone,　　　　　　225
　　When all the world is here to look on me?

DEMETRIUS

　　I'll run from thee and hide me in the brakes,
　　And leave thee to the mercy of wild beasts.

HELENA

　　The wildest hath not such a heart as you.
　　Run when you will, the story shall be changed:　　230
　　Apollo flies, and Daphne holds the chase;
　　The dove pursues the griffon; the mild hind
　　Makes speed to catch the tiger: bootless speed,
　　When cowardice pursues, and valour flies.

220 **privilege** immunity, exemption (*OED n.* 2a)
　　for that because
221–4 Johnson compares a poem once
　　attributed to Tibullus (4.13 or 3.1): '*Tu
　　nocte vel atra / Lumen, et in solis tu mihi
　　turba locis*' ('You are a light to me in
　　the dark night, and company in solitary
　　places'). Steevens compares Psalms
　　139.11, 'Yea, the darkenes is no darkenes
　　with thee, but the night is as cleare as the
　　day', and Malone *2H6* 3.2.362, 'For where
　　thou art, there is the world itself.'
223 **worlds** large numbers: *OED n.* 19a(b)
224 **respect** regard, judgement
227 **brakes** bushes
228 **wild beasts** The forest is again presented as
　　a savage and dangerous place; cf.180–1n.
229 Malone (citing 'S.W.') compares Ovid,

Heroides, 10.1 (Ariadne to Theseus, a
context relevant to *Dream*): '*Mitius inveni
quam te genus omne ferarum*' ('Gentler
than you I have found every race of wild
beast').
231–3 an impassioned series of parallels, like
　　Demetrius' in 1.1.143–8; see p. 114.
231 Apollo pursued the nymph Daphne, who
　　was saved by being turned into a laurel tree
　　(*Met.* 1.452–566; Golding, 1.545–700).
　　holds the chase pursues
232 **griffon** a mythical creature, half eagle and
　　half lion; also the vulture
233 **bootless speed** futile or unavailing speed,
　　that cannot reach its target
234 **cowardice** fear, timorousness (like
　　Helena's); cf. 3.2.302.
　　valour flies said sarcastically of Demetrius

220 privilege: for that] privilege for that. *Var 1778 (Tyrwhitt)*

DEMETRIUS

    I will not stay thy questions. Let me go;   235
    Or if thou follow me, do not believe
    But I shall do thee mischief in the wood.   *[Exit.]*

HELENA

    Ay, in the temple, in the town, the field
    You do me mischief. Fie, Demetrius!
    Your wrongs do set a scandal on my sex.   240
    We cannot fight for love as men may do;
    We should be wooed, and were not made to woo.
    I'll follow thee, and make a heaven of hell,
    To die upon the hand I love so well.   *Exit.*

OBERON

    Fare thee well, nymph. Ere he do leave this grove,   245
    Thou shalt fly him, and he shall seek thy love.

---

235 **stay** wait for, abide
   questions speeches (usually singular in this sense)
236–7 **believe / But** expect anything other than that
237 **mischief** serious harm or injury: a much stronger sense than usual today; cf. 'hellish mischief', *1H6* 3.2.38.
   *SD An exit for Demetrius is clearly called for. Capell, followed by most editors, inserts it after 242. Rowe changes Q2, F *Exit* (for Helena) after 244 to plural *Exeunt*. It is dramatically more effective to have Demetrius rush away at 237 and Helena direct her reply, half to herself, after his disappearing figure.
238 **temple ... town ... field** respectively the most sacred, most frequented and most open of places (Deighton)
240 **set ... sex** make me behave shamefully for a woman
241 **We ... love** ironically disproved in her encounter with Hermia, 3.2.192–344

241–6 Shakespeare often rounds off a stretch of blank verse with one or a few couplets. These lines also lead on to the different use of couplets in Oberon's song-like speech, 249–56.
243 **make ... hell** Helena, in her frustrated love, ironically repeats Hermia's words about the anguish of fulfilled love (1.1.206–7n.).
244 **die** As the nature of the threatened *mischief* is unclear, the sexual meanings of *hell* (vagina: Williams, 2.660) and *die* (experience orgasm: *OED v.*[1] 7d) are relevant. Helena seems to suggest she would find ecstasy even in being raped by Demetrius. See Hutson, 189–91.
   upon by means of (*OED prep.* 2c)
245–6 The rhyme *grove / love*, repeated at 259–60, 3.2.5–6, and many similar rhymes elsewhere in Shakespeare (e.g. 265–6), provide one of Cercignani's most persuasive cases (9, 184) for genuine rhyme based on earlier pronunciation.

237 SD] *Norton*[3]; DEMETRIUS *breaks from her, and Exit.* / Capell, *after 242; not in QF*   238 [3]the] and Q2, F   243 I'll] I *F*   244 SD] *Q2, F; not in Q1; Exeunt.* / Rowe.

Enter [ROBIN GOODFELLOW]. [*Oberon advances.*]

Hast thou the flower there? Welcome, wanderer.

ROBIN

Ay, there it is.

OBERON   I pray thee give it me.

I know a bank where the wild thyme blows,

Where oxlips and the nodding violet grows,   250

Quite over-canopied with luscious woodbine,

With sweet musk-roses and with eglantine.

There sleeps Titania sometime of the night,

Lulled in these flowers with dances and delight;

And there the snake throws her enamelled skin,   255

Weed wide enough to wrap a fairy in.

And with the juice of this I'll streak her eyes,

246.1 *Capell reasonably moved the QF SD to this position. Robin must appear before Oberon can address him.

249–56 As Wilson observes, the irregular yet deeply pleasing metre suggests a song, blending into pentameter by 253 if not earlier; cf. 2–15n. Attempts to regularize the metre are misguided. Gooch and Thatcher list 38 musical settings, often separately as a song.

All these flowers do not bloom (or the fruits in 3.1.160–1 ripen) at the same time in nature, but were supposed to do in Eden. For Garber (*Dream*, 72) this is an 'Eden-like' world, to be disturbed by Robin's (actually Oberon's) intrusion. The bower is also 'a synecdoche for the woman's body, which must be penetrated and invaded for the plot to advance' (Levine, 214). It can thus provide a womb-like retreat for Bottom, viewed as Titania's surrogate child rather than her lover; see p. 81.

249 **a bank** The Henslowe papers list two moss

banks (Henslowe, 320) among the properties of the Admiral's Men. The Chamberlain's Men may have had a similar provision. See 2.2.44n. on the function of the 'bank' in this play.

blows blooms

251 **over-canopied** covered, roofed, but suggesting luxuriance or excess

luscious sweet-smelling (*OED* 1a)

woodbine perhaps the convolvulus or bindweed rather than the more usual honeysuckle; cf. 4.1.41n.

252 **eglantine** a wild rose, also called the sweet-briar

253 **sometime of** (1) some part of; (2) sometimes at

255 **throws** casts, sheds (*OED* throw *v.*[1] 22, earliest citation)

enamelled shiny and colourful: combining *OED* 2, 3, first cited from *TGV* 2.7.28 and here, but found earlier in Sidney, *New Arcadia*, 11.1.

256 **Weed** garment

257 **streak** smear, anoint (*OED v.*[1] 5)

246.1 *Enter* ROBIN GOODFELLOW] *Oxf*[1]; Enter Pucke. *QF, after* 247; *placed here* Capell (Re-enter PUCK.) *Oberon advances*] *this edn; not in QF*   250 oxlips] Oxslips *Q2, F*   251 over-canopied] (ouercanopi'd *Q1;* ouercanoped *Q2;* ouer-cannoped *F*)

And make her full of hateful fantasies.
Take thou some of it, and seek through this grove:
A sweet Athenian lady is in love   260
With a disdainful youth. Anoint his eyes,
But do it when the next thing he espies
May be the lady. Thou shalt know the man
By the Athenian garments he hath on.
Effect it with some care, that he may prove   265
More fond on her, than she upon her love;
And look thou meet me ere the first cock crow.

ROBIN

Fear not, my lord; your servant shall do so.
          Exit [Robin. Oberon remains onstage at the back].

258 **hateful** (1) reprehensible (i.e. lustful); (2) monstrous, detestable (like the transformed Bottom). Cf. 4.1.48, 62.
    fantasies love-thoughts (Schmidt, citing 1.1.32); also imaginary shapes, like those seen by lovers (and lunatics and poets) in Theseus' speech, 5.1.5
264 **Athenian garments** Editors are silent as to what these may look like. Meagher (243–4) reasonably observes that anyone in a wood near Athens might be so dressed. The contrast, if any, can only be with fairy costume. Cf. *Athenian eunuch*, 5.1.45.
266 **fond** (1) loving; (2) foolish, infatuated. Cf. 2.2.92, 3.2.114, 317.
267 **first cock crow** when they must stop roaming: see 3.2.388–95n.
268 *SD Though F repeatedly has singular '*Exit*' where plural '*Exeunt*' (as here in Q)

is required (3.1.101; 3.2.338, 412; 4.1.185, 198; 5.1.150, 204), here F '*Exit*' may correctly mark the departure of Robin alone. As Holland suggests (note to 2.2.32), Oberon remains onstage to keep watch on Titania (as planned, 177) from the start of 2.2 till she falls asleep and the fairies disperse (2.2.30), leaving him free to approach her. Given the locational fluidity of the Elizabethan stage, this is consistent with the apparent change of venue: the bank that Oberon only talks about in 2.1 appears in 2.2. For F's retention of Q '*Enter Oberon*' after 2.2.30, cf. F '*Enter Oberon and Pucke*' at 3.2.344.1, and a second entrance for Oberon after 4.1.44.1, when in both cases they are already onstage (as indicated by earlier F SDs) and merely stepping forward.

258 fantasies] *(phantasies Q1)*   268 SD] *this edn; Exeunt. Q; Exit. F*

[2.2]　　　　*Enter* TITANIA *with her train,* [OBERON *hiding on one side.*]

TITANIA

Come, now a roundel and a fairy song;
Then for the third part of a minute, hence:
Some to kill cankers in the musk-rose buds;
Some war with rearmice for their leathern wings
To make my small elves coats; and some keep back　　5
The clamorous owl, that nightly hoots and wonders
At our quaint spirits. Sing me now asleep;
Then to your offices, and let me rest.

[2.2] 0.1 This scene commences in Titania's bower, probably a recessed 'discovery space' (see pp. 6–8) where Titania remains sleeping after 38. If Oberon has been watching from the close of the previous scene (see 2.1.268 SDn.), he is lurking at one side of the stage (cf. the start of 4.1). This would explain why the fairy on guard does not see him (apart from his possible invisibility, which may or may not have worked with fairy observers).
For the 'bank' as possible stage furniture, see 2.1.249n. and p. 8.

1 **roundel** 'A type of round dance' (*OED* 12, earliest citation). The word was long current for a song (*OED* 11), but Titania mentions the song separately.

2 **for** Theobald's emendation to *'fore* (before) is attractive. In *MND*, though not in fairy lore generally, the fairy world seems to operate in human time, and the third part of a minute is hardly enough for the tasks enjoined. But the scaling-down conveys the miniature proportions of the fairy world.

3 **cankers** caterpillars that destroy plants, canker-worms (*OED n.* 3); cf. 3.2.282.

4 **rearmice** bats

6 **nightly** (1) at night; (2) every night

7 **quaint** strange, curious (*OED adj.* 8). The owl is amazed by the antics of Titania's band.
spirits (1) fairies (see 2.1.1n.); (2) temperament, mood, hence vivacity, energy

8 **offices** tasks, duties

[2.2] *Capell (SCENE* II.*); not in QF* 0.1 TITANIA] Tytania *Queene of Fairies Q1; Queene of Fairies Q2, F* 0.1–2 OBERON . . . *side*] *this edn; not in QF* 1 SP TITANIA] *Queen. (subst.) QF* 2 for] *'fore Theobald* 4 leathern] *(lethren Q1)*

Fairies sing.

1 FAIRY

You spotted snakes with double tongue,
    Thorny hedgehogs, be not seen.   10
Newts and blindworms, do no wrong,
    Come not near our Fairy Queen.

CHORUS

Philomel, with melody,
    Sing in our sweet lullaby,
Lulla, lulla, lullaby; lulla, lulla, lullaby.   15
    Never harm, nor spell, nor charm,
    Come our lovely lady nigh.
    So good night, with lullaby.

2 FAIRY

Weaving spiders, come not here –
    Hence, you long-legged spinners, hence.   20
Beetles black, approach not near,
    Worm nor snail do no offence.

9–28 *As 9–12 and 19–22 have the same structure, Capell's allocation of singers is convincing and widely followed, as here. A SP for the first singer at 9 might have been left out of the Q1 copy in error, and later SPs mistakenly rationalized (in F, along the lines proposed in TxC, 281). As Seng (32) observes, the song is not simply a lullaby but a charm to ward off evil. It is the passage from *MND* most often set to music: Gooch and Thatcher list 116 settings in whole or part.

9–11 All these creatures are harmless (see *spotted*, 9n.) but were regarded as noxious and sinister, or just 'creepy-crawly' and repellent, as they are even today except the hedgehog. Snake, newt and blindworm (slowworm, a legless lizard) go into the witches' cauldron in *Mac*, and the hedgehog appears to be their familiar (*Mac* 4.1.2, 14–16).

9 **spotted** Of British species, the grass snake and smooth snake (both harmless) have indistinct spots, but the metaphoric sense 'stained, evil' seems paramount; cf. *spotted*, 1.1.110.
   double forked; for the crucial metaphoric implication, cf. 3.2.72–3.

13 **Philomel** the nightingale Philomela was turned into a nightingale after being raped by her brother-in-law Tereus (*Met.* 6.667–70; Golding, 6.841–8).

14 **sing in** join in.
    our F 'your' also makes sense: 'work your contribution into our song'.

19 **spiders** thought to be poisonous; they 'suck up [the earth's] venom' (*R2* 3.2.14).

20 **spinners** either spiders or, as perhaps in *RJ* 1.4.62, the crane fly or daddy-long-legs. Q2 'Spinders' is probably by erroneous overlap with *spiders* (19).

22 **Worm nor snail** again, harmless creatures commonly found repellent and (especially the generalized *worm*, also used of snakes) credited with malign and destructive powers

9–23] *so indented, Capell; uniformly indented, QF; italicized, Q2, F*   9 SP] *Capell; not in QF*   13 SP] *Capell; not in QF*   14 our] *your F*   19 SP] *F, Capell; 1. Fai. Q*   20 spinners] *Q1, F; Spinders Q2*

CHORUS

> Philomel, with melody,
> Sing in our sweet lullaby,
> Lulla, lulla, lullaby; lulla, lulla, lullaby.   25
> Never harm, nor spell, nor charm,
> Come our lovely lady nigh.
> So good night, with lullaby.   [*Titania*] *sleeps.*

1 FAIRY

> Hence, away; now all is well.   29
> One aloof stand sentinel.   [*Exeunt Fairies.*]

[OBERON *advances.*]

OBERON [*Squeezes the flower on Titania's eyelids.*]
> What thou seest when thou dost wake,
> Do it for thy true love take;
> Love and languish for his sake.
> Be it ounce or cat or bear,
> Pard, or boar with bristled hair   35
> In thy eye that shall appear
> When thou wak'st, it is thy dear.
> Wake when some vile thing is near.   [*Exit.*]

---

28 *SD It seems best to move the F SD to this point. Titania must be asleep before the Fairies leave her, perhaps drawing a curtain across the recess where she sleeps. She remains sleeping there till awakened by Bottom's song (3.1.125).

29–30 QF indent and F italicizes these lines as part of the song, which they clearly are not.

30 **aloof** in SDs, 'aside, afar off' (Dessen and Thomson, 5). The sentinel is unable to prevent Oberon's mischief. This may be an intended effect, or Shakespeare may simply have forgotten about him. In Benson's production and Moshinsky's and Noble's films, he is kidnapped by Oberon

or his followers. In Hoffman's film, Oberon distracts the female sentinel by holding a mirror to her face.

*SD An exeunt for the fairies is needed in view of Titania's command (8) and the First Fairy's injunction (29).

34 **ounce** lynx
   cat wildcat

35 **Pard** leopard. The wood again becomes a savage and sinister place; cf. 2.1.180–1n.
   with bristled hair Golding's phrase (14.323; *Met.* 14.279), describing the boar into which Macareus is transformed by Circe (also called Titania: see p. 53).

37 **it . . . dear** seem as though it is your beloved

---

23 SP] *Capell; not in QF*   melody] *Cam¹; melody, &c. QF*   24–8 *Cam¹; not in QF*   28 SD] *Capell, opp. 30; placed here, Kittredge; Shee sleepes. F, opp. 30; not in Q*   29–30] *so placed, Capell; indented QF*   29 SP] *F; 2. Fai. Q*   30 SD] *Rowe; not in QF*   30.1] *this edn; Enter Oberon. QF*   31 SD] *after Capell (to Tit. squeezing the Flower upon her Eye-lids.); not in QF*   31–8] *indented, Capell*

Enter LYSANDER *and* HERMIA.

LYSANDER

Fair love, you faint with wandering in the wood,
    And to speak troth, I have forgot our way.   40
We'll rest us, Hermia, if you think it good,
    And tarry for the comfort of the day.

HERMIA

Be it so, Lysander. Find you out a bed,
For I upon this bank will rest my head.

LYSANDER

One turf shall serve as pillow for us both,   45
One heart, one bed, two bosoms, and one troth.

HERMIA

Nay, good Lysander; for my sake, my dear,
Lie further off, yet. Do not lie so near.

39–55 Hermia and Lysander use the unexpectedly formal *you*, perhaps owing to her caution and his bashfulness, added to their tension at having lost the way. Only at the very end of their exchanges (65, 68), when they have agreed to lie down separately, do they venture on the more intimate *thy* and *thee*, (Cf. 1.1.128n.) The strain and formality are also reflected in the artificiality of the four-line stanza opening the dialogue, followed by couplets through the patterned action of the rest of the scene.

39–46 set as a song in Brook's production, accompanied by a guitar which resumed for 49–69.

40 **troth** truth. Here the form *troth* agrees with 46, 54 (where the rhyme requires it) and also suggests the special duty and frankness that Demetrius professes towards Hermia (see 46n.).

42 **tarry for** await

43 ***Be** Q1 *Bet* (better: *OED* bet *adj.* 2) makes sense; but as Q1 reads 'comfor' at 42, this seems a case of a misplaced *t* (Brooks).

44 **this bank** in whose inner recess Titania lies asleep (see 2.1.249n., 3.1.192n.). Hermia and Lysander settle down to sleep just outside the discovery space representing Titania's bower. This is also probably where Demetrius lies down to sleep at 3.2.87, and all the lovers at 3.2.428–47, leaving the forestage clear for other action. A defined area upstage thus becomes a magic space for the operation of the love-juice and its antidote.

45–69 Like 2.1.188–244, this dialogue was sometimes cut in earlier times for its supposed impropriety, but is now often played up for its comic potential.

46 **troth** a pledged or sworn relationship: cognate with *truth*. See 40n.

48 **off, yet** The *yet* need only mean 'still farther off', but perhaps also 'till we are married'. The comma in Q1 brings out this implication more pointedly. Even as regards physical distance, it suggests Hermia's first injunction was not effective enough; cf. *So far*, 64n.

38 SD] *Rowe (Exit* Oberon.*); not in QF*   39 wood] woods *Q2, F*   43 Be it] *Q2, F;* Bet it *Q1;* Be't *Pope*   48 off, yet] off yet *Q2, F*

LYSANDER

  O take the sense, sweet, of my innocence:

  Love takes the meaning in love's conference.   50

  I mean that my heart unto yours it knit,

  So that but one heart we can make of it:

  Two bosoms interchained with an oath,

  So then two bosoms, and a single troth.

  Then by your side no bed-room me deny;   55

  For lying so, Hermia, I do not lie.

HERMIA

  Lysander riddles very prettily.

  Now much beshrew my manners and my pride

  If Hermia meant to say Lysander lied.

  But gentle friend, for love and courtesy,   60

  Lie further off, in human modesty:

  Such separation as may well be said

  Becomes a virtuous bachelor and a maid,

  So far be distant, and good night, sweet friend.

  Thy love ne'er alter till thy sweet life end.   65

49 'Take my words in the innocent sense in which I mean them.'

50 'Love makes lovers interpret each other's words in a proper spirit' (*conference*, conversation, exchange) – i.e. Lysander's true love is a guarantee of his honest intentions. Theobald's transposition of *innocence* and *conference* makes the meaning clearer but is uncalled-for.

51 **it** i.e. love: 'Love knit our two hearts together.' Q2, F 'is' is an unnecessary emendation.

53 **interchained** (interchainèd) interlinked (*OED v.*, earliest citation). F replaces the unfamiliar coinage with the familiar *interchanged* – the clichéd conceit of an exchange of hearts.

56 **lying … lie** punning on *lie*, deceive

57 Hermia notes that Lysander's words need not mean he will not offer sex to Hermia, only that he will do so out of true and firm love.

58 **beshrew** be harmed or cursed, 'a mischief upon'

60 **gentle** noble, honourable

61 **human modesty** common decency

64 **So far** (1) at such a distance; (2) at this point of time: hinting at future intimacy, as in *yet* (48n.)

65–8 On the change to *thou*, see 39–55n.

65 **Thy love** perhaps referring to herself ('your beloved') rather than Lysander's love for her; but the latter possibility indicates a latent insecurity in her love; cf. 1.1.173–6n.

ne'er alter May (she or it) never change.

49–50 innocence … conference] conference … innocence *Theobald (Warburton)*   51 it] is *Q2, F*
52 we can] can you *F*   53 interchained] interchanged *F*

LYSANDER

  Amen, amen, to that fair prayer say I,
  And then end life, when I end loyalty.
  Here is my bed; sleep give thee all his rest.

HERMIA

  With half that wish the wisher's eyes be
     pressed.   *They sleep.*

Enter [ROBIN GOODFELLOW].

ROBIN

      Through the forest have I gone,   70
      But Athenian found I none
      On whose eyes I might approve
      This flower's force in stirring love.
      Night and silence! Who is here?
      Weeds of Athens he doth wear.   75
      This is he, my master said,
      Despised the Athenian maid;
      And here the maiden, sleeping sound
      On the dank and dirty ground.
      Pretty soul, she durst not lie   80

---

68 **all his rest** more riddling: (1) all the rest or
  refreshment afforded by sleep; (2) all the
  other gifts of sleep (except Lysander's
  company in bed)
69 **half that wish** Hermia does not want 'all
  [the] rest' Lysander wishes for her, but
  would share it equally with him.
  pressed pressed shut, closed
69 SD, *69.1 F has '*Enter Pucke*' centred
  and '*They sleepe*' in the right-hand margin
  on the same line, probably for lack of
  space. The second SD no doubt indicates

the earlier action. Cf. other SDs so placed:
in F at 4.1.198, and Q at 4.1.101.1–2. For
the normal arrangement, see F SDs at
1.1.127; 2.2.30, 87; 4.1.101, 101.1–2;
5.1.360, 360.1.

72 **approve** test, try out
74 **Night and silence** either a mild oath ('in
  the name of night and silence': cf. *KL*
  1.3.4, 'By day and night he wrongs me'),
  or an invocation to darkness and silence to
  conceal him.
77 **Despised** Despisèd

---

69 SD] *F, opp. 69.1 in right margin; not in Q*   69.1 ROBIN GOODFELLOW] *Oxf¹;* Pucke *QF*   70 SP] *Oxf;*
Puck QF   70–87] *indented, Capell*   71 found] finde *Q2, F*   72 On] One *F*

173

Near this lack-love, this kill-courtesy.
Churl, upon thy eyes I throw
All the power this charm doth owe.
[*Squeezes the flower on Lysander's eyelids.*]
When thou wak'st, let love forbid
Sleep his seat on thy eyelid.   85
So awake, when I am gone;
For I must now to Oberon.   *Exit.*

Enter DEMETRIUS *and* HELENA *running.*

HELENA
Stay, though thou kill me, sweet Demetrius.
DEMETRIUS
I charge thee, hence, and do not haunt me thus.
HELENA
O, wilt thou darkling leave me? Do not so.   90
DEMETRIUS
Stay, on thy peril. I alone will go.   *Exit.*
HELENA
O, I am out of breath in this fond chase.
The more my prayer, the lesser is my grace.
Happy is Hermia, wheresoe'er she lies,

---

81 The extra-long line emphasizes Robin's
disapproval. Alternatively, it can be
reduced in length by reading 'court'sy'.
Emendations omitting some words seem
uncalled-for.
   lack-love earliest *OED* citation (lack *v.*[1]
C1.c). Holland compares 'lack-brain' (*1H4*
2.3.14), 'Lack-beard' (*MA* 5.1.187).
   kill-courtesy For such verb-and-object
compounds, cf. 'carry-tale' (*LLL* 5.2.463),
'find-faults' (*H5* 5.2.270), 'Mar-text' (*AYL*
3.3.39).
83 **owe** own, possess
84–5 **let . . . eyelid** Let love rob you of sleep.
87.1 *running* i.e. Helena pursuing Demetrius,

who flies from her
88–91 Demetrius addresses Helena as *thou*, as
habitually (see 2.1.188–244n.); but Helena
addresses him so only here (except for Q2, F
thee at 2.1.202), perhaps in an impassioned
attempt to force the *thou* of intimacy.
89 **charge thee, hence** order you to go away
(*OED* charge *v.* 14a)
   haunt hang around, 'run after' (*OED v.* 4)
90 **darkling** in the dark
92 **fond** Cf. 2.1.266n.
93 'The more I plead (with Demetrius), the
less response I get.'
   grace reward or return in love: a fragment
of the language of courtly love

---

81 lack-love, this kill-courtesy] lack-love kill-curtesie *Johnson*   83 SD] *Dyce, after 82; not in QF*
91 SD] *F (Exit Demetrius.); not in Q*

For she hath blessed and attractive eyes.   95
How came her eyes so bright? Not with salt tears;
If so, my eyes are oftener washed than hers.
No, no: I am as ugly as a bear,
For beasts that meet me run away for fear;
Therefore no marvel though Demetrius   100
Do, as a monster, fly my presence thus.
What wicked and dissembling glass of mine
Made me compare with Hermia's sphery eyne?
But who is here? Lysander, on the ground?
Dead, or asleep? I see no blood, no wound.   105
Lysander, if you live, good sir, awake.

LYSANDER [*Wakes.*]

And run through fire I will for thy sweet sake.
Transparent Helena, nature shows art,
That through thy bosom makes me see thy heart.
Where is Demetrius? O, how fit a word   110
Is that vile name to perish on my sword!

95 **blessed** blessèd. See 1.1.74n.
    attractive having the power to draw and
    influence people (*OED adj.* 5, earliest
    citation)
96 **ugly as a bear** proverbial (Dent, B123.1)
101 **Do** the plural form, perhaps taking the
    beasts and Demetrius as a composite subject
    monster something unnatural, repelling
    even beasts; but perhaps also alluding to
    Demetrius, suggesting he is an unnatural
    being to spurn such ardent love
102 **glass** mirror, where Helena looked as
    beautiful as Hermia
103 **compare with** vie with (*OED v.¹* 4b)
    sphery celestial, like the heavenly bodies
    set in crystalline spheres in the Ptolemaic
    system (see 2.1.7n.).
    eyne eyes. See 1.1.242n.
107–38 Lysander first addresses Helena
    impulsively by the intimate *thy.* He then
    switches to the formal *you* of adoration,

and she answers with a *you* conveying
distance and caution.
108 The line is a syllable short, but balanced by
    Lysander drawing out the words to express
    his rapture. 'her shewes', probably to fill
    the line out metrically, may be interpreted
    as 'here shews' (so F?), or as an erroneous
    transposition of 'shows her' (Malone). This
    uncertainty makes the emendation seem
    even more unnecessary.
    Transparent metaphoric for frankness and
    virtue (see 109n.), but may also imply
    'delicately or radiantly fair'
    nature shows art The traditional
    opposition of nature and art is reconciled in
    this figure of ideal beauty and purity.
    Bodies are usually opaque, so Helena's
    'transparency' indicates a special creation
    on nature's part (Brooks).
109 **see thy heart** presumably in its purity or
    nobility, but also as an object of love

107 SD] *Rowe (Waking); not in QF* 108 shows] *(shewes Q); her shewes F; here shews F2; shews her*
Malone

HELENA

Do not say so, Lysander, say not so.

What though he love your Hermia? Lord, what though?

Yet Hermia still loves you; then be content.

LYSANDER

Content with Hermia? No, I do repent   115

The tedious minutes I with her have spent.

Not Hermia, but Helena I love.

Who will not change a raven for a dove?

The will of man is by his reason swayed,

And reason says you are the worthier maid.   120

Things growing are not ripe until their season;

So I, being young, till now ripe not to reason.

And touching now the point of human skill,

Reason becomes the marshal to my will

And leads me to your eyes, where I o'erlook   125

Love's stories, written in love's richest book.

---

113 an interesting double use of *what though*, first to start a concessive clause and then as a complete utterance by itself. Cf. *AYL* 3.3.47; see Blake, 5.3.2.8.

117 The line fills out metrically if *Hermia* and *Helena* are given due emphasis, spacing out *Hermia* over three syllables, making 'now' added in Q2, F unnecessary. Holland (note to 1.1.19.1), links the names Hermia and Hermione (Helen of Troy's daughter) to recall Ovid's *Ars Amatoria*, 2.699: '*Scilicet Hermionen Helenae praeponere posses*' ('Could you prefer Hermione to Helen?').

118 **raven** alluding to Hermia's darker appearance (cf. 'Ethiop', 3.2.257n.); but the raven was also a bird of ill omen. Juliet appears to Romeo like 'a snowy dove trooping with crows' (*RJ* 1.5.47). On the actor playing Hermia, see p. 9.

119 **reason** ironical. Reason is the faculty traditionally displaced by passions like love (cf. 3.2.134–5), the more so as Lysander's change of heart is magically induced; cf. 1.1.56–7n.

122 **till ... reason** not mature enough to attain to reason till now. *Ripe* can be either an adjective or a verb (ripen, grow mature).

123 **point** usually taken to mean the summit or pinnacle (*OED n.¹* 12), but perhaps simply a point of time or stage of growth (*OED n.¹* 1b); here, the age at which one acquires *skill* (reason, discrimination: *OED n.¹* 1)

124 **marshal** regulator, controller; but *leads me to* (125) suggests a court official arranging guests at a banquet (*OED n.* 4), here ushering Lysander into the presence of Helena's eyes.

125–6 For the eyes as a book teaching love, cf. *RJ* 1.3.87–8, 'his eyes. / This precious book of love'; *LLL* 4.2.108, 4.3.324–8.

125 **o'erlook** 'peruse, read through' (*OED* overlook *v.* 3)

117 I] now I *Q2, F*

HELENA

Wherefore was I to this keen mockery born?
When at your hands did I deserve this scorn?
Is't not enough, is't not enough, young man,
That I did never, no nor never can   130
Deserve a sweet look from Demetrius' eye,
But you must flout my insufficiency?
Good troth, you do me wrong; good sooth, you do,
In such disdainful manner me to woo.
But fare you well. Perforce I must confess   135
I thought you lord of more true gentleness.
O that a lady of one man refused
Should of another therefore be abused!   *Exit.*

LYSANDER

She sees not Hermia. Hermia, sleep thou there,
And never mayst thou come Lysander near.   140
For as a surfeit of the sweetest things
The deepest loathing to the stomach brings,
Or as the heresies that men do leave
Are hated most of those they did deceive,
So thou, my surfeit and my heresy,   145
Of all be hated, but the most of me;
And all my powers, address your love and might
To honour Helen, and to be her knight.   *Exit.*

---

132 **you** stressed: 'not only Demetrius but you too'
  flout mock, jeer at
  insufficiency inadequacy, lack (of qualities to attract Demetrius)
133 **Good troth** (1) God be my pledge or surety; (2) in truth (cf. *good sooth*), perhaps further suggesting a lover's pledge or trust. Cf. 40n., 46n.
136 **gentleness** nobility of spirit; courtesy, decency

139–45 Lysander now calls Hermia *thou* out of contempt, as earlier from intimacy.
141–2 a proverb (Dent, H560) deriving from Proverbs 25.15. Cf. *1H4* 3.2.71–2, 'They surfeited with honey and began / To loathe the taste of sweetness'; *RJ* 2.6.11–12.
144 **of** by (*OED prep.* 14)
  they the heresies: of all false doctrines (hence *deceive*), men most hate those they once subscribed to but have now abandoned.
147 **address** direct to a purpose

144 they] that *F*

177

HERMIA [*starting*]
> Help me, Lysander, help me: do thy best
> To pluck this crawling serpent from my breast.   150
> Ay me, for pity! What a dream was here!
> Lysander, look how I do quake with fear.
> Methought a serpent ate my heart away,
> And you sat smiling at his cruel prey.
> Lysander – what, removed? Lysander, lord –   155
> What, out of hearing, gone? No sound, no word?
> Alack, where are you? Speak, and if you hear;
> Speak, of all loves! I swoon almost with fear.
> No, then I well perceive you are not nigh.
> Either death or you I'll find immediately.   160
>> *Exit.* [*Titania remains lying asleep.*]

[3.1]   *Enter* [QUINCE, SNUG, BOTTOM, FLUTE, SNOUT *and*
          STARVELING. *Titania lying asleep.*]

BOTTOM   Are we all met?

QUINCE   Pat, pat; and here's a marvellous convenient
place for our rehearsal. This green plot shall be our

---

149 **thy** Hermia turns to Lysander in her sleep with a spontaneously intimate *thy*, but switches to the more distant *you* on noting his absence, and recalling his behaviour in her dream.

150 **serpent** Taylor ('Ovid', 53–4) cites the story of Ino, afflicted with snakes by the Fury Tisiphone (*Met.* 4.481–99; Golding, 4.605–30). Hackett (*MND*, 72) recalls the serpent bringing about the biblical Fall of Man. For the Freudian implications, see pp. 77–8.

154 **prey** act of preying, depredation (*OED n.* 4b)

155 **removed** in the original sense 'left,

departed'; cf. *Son* 116.4, 'with the remover to remove'.

157 **and if** old 'an if', if

158 **of all loves** in the name of all loves: 'a strong appeal or entreaty' (*OED* love *n.*[1] P1.b); cf. *MW* 2.2.108.

[3.1]   The artisans are presumably meeting as agreed at the 'duke's oak' (1.2.103). From Robin's words (73), this is near Titania's bower. All act and scene divisions for the action in the wood are fairly arbitrary; see pp. 320–1.

2   **Pat** 'On the dot, punctually' (Cam²)
     marvellous Cf. 4.1.24n. On adverbs without a final -*ly*, see 1.2.20n.

---

149 SD] *Capell; not in QF*   153 ate] *(*eate *QF)*   154 you] *yet F*   158 swoon] *(*swoune*); swound Q2; sound F*   160 SD *Titania . . . asleep] Ard²; not in QF*   **3.1** [3.1] *Rowe (*ACT III. SCENE I.*); Actus Tertius. F; not in Q*   0.1–2 QUINCE . . . STARVELING] *Rowe; the Clownes. QF*   0.2 *Titania . . . asleep] Cam after Rowe (The Queen of Fairies lying asleep.); not in QF*   2 marvellous] *(*maruailes *Q1; maruailous Q2, F)*

stage, this hawthorn brake our tiring-house; and we
will do it in action, as we will do it before the duke.   5

BOTTOM   Peter Quince!

QUINCE   What sayst thou, bully Bottom?

BOTTOM   There are things in this comedy of Pyramus
and Thisbe that will never please. First, Pyramus must
draw a sword to kill himself, which the ladies cannot   10
abide. How answer you that?

SNOUT   Byrlakin, a parlous fear.

STARVELING   I believe we must leave the killing out,
when all is done.

BOTTOM   Not a whit. I have a device to make all well.   15
Write me a prologue, and let the prologue seem to say
we will do no harm with our swords, and that Pyramus
is not killed indeed; and for the more better assurance,
tell them that I, Pyramus, am not Pyramus, but Bottom
the weaver. This will put them out of fear.   20

QUINCE   Well, we will have such a prologue, and it shall
be written in eight and six.

---

4   **brake** See 2.1.227n.
     tiring-house 'attiring-house' or dressing-room behind the stage, effectively the site of all backstage activities: the earliest *OED* citation, though the term must have been familiar in Elizabethan stage parlance. It occurs in *The Second Report of Doctor John Faustus* (1594), sig. E2ᵛ. Quince's words indicate how the forest scenes in *MND* were staged in the public theatre, though his own production would be in makeshift conditions in the duke's hall (see p. 5).

5   **in action** acting out the script, not merely reading it

7   **bully** 'a brisk, dashing fellow' (Schmidt): a hearty term of camaraderie, repeatedly used by the Host in *MW*: 'God bless thee, bully Doctor!' (2.3.16) etc.

12   **Byrlakin** 'by our ladykin' (the Virgin Mary): a mild oath

parlous a variant of 'perilous', perhaps already with something of its later popular or vulgar flavour

14   **when . . . done** after all

16   **Write me** write for me, to meet my plan or suggestion: the ethical dative (see 1.2.77n.). The tone reflects the officiousness which earlier made Bottom wish to act every role in the play.
     seem to say say something like this

18–20 On the implications for the theme of stage illusion, see pp. 97–104.

18   **more better** Such double comparatives were accepted practice (Hope, 1.2.3); cf. 'more safer', *Oth* 1.3.226.

22   **eight and six** alternate lines of eight and six syllables, as in the ballad metre; not the metre of the prologue as performed (5.1.108–17), but Bottom talks of Quince writing a ballad (4.1.213).

6 Quince] *quince Q2, F*   7 SP] *(Quin.); Peter Q2, F*

BOTTOM　No, make it two more. Let it be written in eight
　　and eight.

SNOUT　Will not the ladies be afeared of the Lion?　　　25

STARVELING　I fear it, I promise you.

BOTTOM　Masters, you ought to consider with yourself: to
　　bring in (God shield us) a lion among ladies is a most
　　dreadful thing; for there is not a more fearful wild-
　　fowl than your lion living, and we ought to look to't.　　30

SNOUT　Therefore another prologue must tell he is not
　　a lion.

BOTTOM　Nay, you must name his name, and half his
　　face must be seen through the lion's neck, and he
　　himself must speak through, saying thus, or to the　　35
　　same defect: 'Ladies', or 'Fair ladies, I would wish
　　you', or 'I would request you', or 'I would entreat
　　you, not to fear, not to tremble: my life for yours. If
　　you think I come hither as a lion, it were pity of my
　　life. No, I am no such thing. I am a man as other men　　40
　　are.' And there, indeed, let him name his name, and
　　tell them plainly he is Snug the joiner.

23–4 **eight and eight** Bottom 'cannot have too much of a good thing' (Wilson).

25 **afeared ... lion** For a likely allusion to the baptism festivities of Prince Henry of Scotland, see p. 289.

26 **fear** comically echoing *afeared* (25): Starveling fears the ladies' fear.

27 **yourself** The singular may be another of Bottom's solecisms (F replaces with 'your selues'), but it is an easy slippage in natural speech.

28 **God shield us** God forbid us, God protect us

29 **dreadful** causing dread, fearsome
fearful in the original sense of 'fearsome'; but the later sense 'frightened, timorous' was already current, producing a comic ambiguity reinforced by calling the lion a *fowl*. Cf. the lion that 'mouses' in the actual performance (5.1.262).

33–42 Bottom's advice is taken up in 5.1.217–24.

33 **'his** the actor's

36 **defect** for 'effect'

38 **my ... yours** proverbial. Dent (L260.1) explains as 'I'm sure, Assuredly', but the phrasing implies a much stronger pledge or oath.

40–1 **I ... are** proverbial (Dent, M395.1). Malone compares an incident, assumed to be at the Kenilworth revels (1575) though identified in the source only as 'a spectacle presented to Q: Elizabeth vpon the water', where a man playing Arion declared he was not such 'but eene honest Har[ry] Goldingham'. The incident is reported only in a manuscript (BL Harley MS 6395, fol. 36ᵛ), not in Robert Laneham's (or William Patten's) published account; but oral reports may have circulated locally.

---

27 yourself] *(your selfe Q);* your selues *F*　30 to't] *(toote);* to it *Q2, F*　42 them] him *F*

QUINCE   Well, it shall be so. But there is two hard things:
that is, to bring the moonlight into a chamber; for you
know Pyramus and Thisbe meet by moonlight.   45
SNOUT   Doth the moon shine that night we play our play?
BOTTOM   A calendar, a calendar: look in the almanac.
Find out moonshine, find out moonshine.

Enter [ROBIN GOODFELLOW] [*behind*].

QUINCE   [*consulting an almanac*] Yes, it doth shine that
night.   50
BOTTOM   Why, then may you leave a casement of the
great chamber window, where we play, open; and the
moon may shine in at the casement.
QUINCE   Ay, or else one must come in with a bush of

---

43   **there is** The *two hard things* are considered
as a single entity, hence *is*. In fact, Quince
mentions only one problem at this point;
the second, presumably, is representing the
wall (57).

46   *SP Q1 abbreviated the SP to the
ambiguous '*Sn.*', probably to fit a single
line at the foot of the page (sig D1ᵛ); Q2
and F followed mechanically. F2 took it to
mean Snug, but Snout is the voluble one
here. Cf. the progressive deviations from Q
to F2 in the SP at 60. The SP at 110, after
Snout's entry, also reads '*Sn.*' in QF.

48   **moonshine** 'Moonshine in the water' had
meant an empty or fanciful notion since
1468. The example of *MND* might have led
to *moonshine* alone being so used (*OED n.*
2a: first citation, 1624). 'Moonshine in the
water' (i.e. a reflection, not the real moon)
adds an ironic nuance to the serious and
romantic use of the image in *MND*,
including the 'fair vestal' passage
(2.1.162).

48.1   *The F SD seems to mark the point where

Robin creeps in and begins eavesdropping
on the artisans. See 71n.

49   It seems improbable that Quince should be
carrying an almanac. Perhaps he knows the
answer anyway, or perhaps the question
should not be raised.
it doth shine This contradicts Hippolyta's
saying it will be the silver of a new moon
(1.1.9–10). The fluctuations of the moon
seem to exceed normal Shakespearean
inconsistency and form a deliberate
imaginative design; see pp. 73–4.

51   **casement** a hinged section of a window
(*OED* 2a)

52   **great chamber** probably the hall of
Theseus' palace. In noblemen's mansions,
plays were usually performed in the
hall.

54–5   **bush ... lantern** The man in the moon
was visualized as carrying these objects
(and accompanied by a dog: see 5.1.134,
253), by a fanciful interpretation of the
dark patches on the moon.

54   **bush** bunch, bundle (*OED n.¹* 6a)

---

46 SP] *Cam; Sn. QF; Snug F2*   48.1] *Oxf (Enter Robin Goodfellow the puck, invisible); Enter Pucke. F;
not in Q   behind*] *this edn. (Theobald, in SD after 71); not in QF*   49 SD] *Oxf¹; not in QF*   51 SP] *Q2,
F; Cet Q1*

thorns and a lantern, and say he comes to disfigure or   55
to present the person of Moonshine. Then there is
another thing: we must have a wall in the great
chamber; for Pyramus and Thisbe, says the story, did
talk through the chink of a wall.

SNOUT   You can never bring in a wall. What say you,   60
Bottom?

BOTTOM   Some man or other must present Wall; and let
him have some plaster, or some loam, or some
roughcast about him, to signify Wall; and let him hold
his fingers thus, and through that cranny shall Pyramus   65
and Thisbe whisper.

QUINCE   If that may be, then all is well. Come, sit down
every mother's son, and rehearse your parts. Pyramus,
you begin. When you have spoken your speech,
enter into that brake; and so every one according to   70
his cue.

---

55 **thorns** thorn branches or twigs
lantern Q1 seems to distinguish between
lantern(e) and *lanthorne*, a popular form
born of folk etymology (perhaps from the
thin sheets of horn forming the lantern's
windows). *Lantern* is used by the relatively
well-educated Quince, here and at 5.1.134;
lanthorne by Starveling (5.1.234, 238, 252)
and, parodying him, the aristocrats (5.1.241,
254). Q2, F standardize to *lanthorne*
everywhere. Cf. 'lanthorne', *MA* 3.3.24, Q
and F (spoken by Dogberry) and *2H4*
1.2.49, Q and F (by Falstaff: see 5.1.234n.).
disfigure a mistake for 'figure', recalling
Theseus' sinister use of the word in 1.1.51.
Bottom is not the only malapropist in the
company.

56 **present** represent (as throughout the play)
person (1) role, character (*OED n.* 1, first
citation in a theatrical context); (2) body
(*OED n.* 4a) – a comically inept attribute of
something as unsubstantial as moonshine

60 SP Q1 '*Sno.*' (Snout) is obviously
correct; cf. 46n.

63 **loam** a mixture of sand, clay etc. used as a
building material

64 **roughcast** a mortar of lime and gravel used
to plaster walls
*and let The logical conjunction here is
'and'. QF 'or' would be an easy error after
the three previous *or*s in the same speech.

68 **rehearse** go over, polish your memories
(*OED v.* 7c). The other actors con their
parts while Bottom begins to act his. In the
1854 Broadway production, the
promptnotes make the artisans enter
'studying their parts' (Sprague, 52).

71 QF have the SD '*Enter* Robin' at this
point, where he first speaks. But the F SD
'*Enter Pucke*' at 48.1 may be Robin's
actual point of entry; cf. 3.2.344.1n., 463n.,
4.1.44.1n. See Ichikawa (213–4) and
Werstine (*Manuscripts*, 173–5, 385) on
such duplicated entry SDs.

---

55 lantern] lanthorne *Q2, F*   60 SP] *(Sno.); Sn. Q2, F; Snu. F2*   64 and] *Dyce (Collier MS, 103); or*
QF   71] *Here QF have SD Enter* Robin

ROBIN [*aside*]
  What hempen homespuns have we swaggering here,
  So near the cradle of the Fairy Queen?
  What, a play toward? I'll be an auditor;
  An actor too, perhaps, if I see cause.   75
QUINCE   Speak, Pyramus. Thisbe, stand forth.
BOTTOM
  Thisbe, the flowers of odious savours sweet.
QUINCE   Odours, odours.
BOTTOM
  . . . odours savours sweet.
  So hath thy breath, my dearest Thisbe dear.   80
  But hark, a voice. Stay thou but here a while,
  And by and by I will to thee appear.   *Exit.*

---

72 **hempen   homespuns** lowly people,
wearing cheap coarse material spun from
hemp: probably referring metaphorically to
their class affinity rather than literally to
their clothes, for they are skilled workmen.
Brooks finds an echo of 'Hemton hamten',
Robin Goodfellow's angry cry in *Scot*,
4.10 (85, sig. H3ʳ).
  swaggering strutting   about,   giving
themselves airs
73 **cradle** could be used of an adult's bed or
place of repose: *OED n.* 4, first cited from
VA 1185.
74 **toward** in progress, in the making
  auditor listener
77–99 On the absence of this dialogue in the
final play, see 1.2.56–9n.
77 'The flowers savour sweetly of odours.'
The plural *flowers* could take the singular
verb *savours* by the 'not infrequent'
practice of the time (Blake, 4.2.2(d)); cf.
hath, 2.1.91. Blake and Hope (2.1.8a) take
it as a genuine plural form of the verb.
Wells suggests *of* may be a colloquialism
for 'have', and Cam¹ that Shakespeare
wrote 'a' (which could mean both 'have'
and 'of'), leading to the confusion; cf. F 'a'

for Q *have* in 3.2.69.
  odious Dogberry in *MA* 3.5.15 makes the
opposite mistake: 'Comparisons are
odorous.'
  sweet sweetly. On adverbs without a final
-ly, see 1.2.20n.
78 ***Odours, odours** This, the F reading,
corrects not only Bottom's error but very
likely the Q1 printer's, followed in Q2. In
all versions, Bottom repeats Quince's testy
correction. Quince himself is prone to
malapropisms: see 55 and 4.2.12.
80 **hath** Rowe's emendation 'doth' follows
logically from 77, but Bottom may be
garbling his lines again.
  thy breath Golding (4.90) goes beyond
Ovid in saying Pyramus and Thisbe drew
'pleasant breath' from each other as they
talked through the wall (Rudd, 116).
81 **while** Theobald proposes 'whit' (a little
while, 'a bit') to rhyme with *sweet*. We
need not assume a regular rhyme-scheme
in these clumsy verses, but the 'rhyme' in
sweet and *whit* is inept enough for serious
consideration.
82 **by and by** directly, right away (*OED adv.*
3), rather than 'presently, in due course'

---

72 SD] *Cam¹; not in QF*   77+] *lines of play-within-the-play italicized, Malone; marked in margin,
Capell*   77, 79, 99 SP BOTTOM] *Cam; Pyramus (subst.) QF;* BOTTOM *as Pyramus / Wells*   77 *of*] have
Collier (conj.); ha' *Cam¹*   78 Odours, odours] *F;* Odours, odorous *Q*   80 *hath*] doth *Rowe²*   81 *while*]
whit *Theobald*   82 SD] *Exit. Pir. F*

ROBIN [*aside*]
  . . . A stranger Pyramus than ere played here.   [*Exit.*]
FLUTE   Must I speak now?
QUINCE   Ay, marry, must you. For you must understand   85
he goes but to see a noise that he heard, and is to come
again.
FLUTE

Most radiant Pyramus, most lily-white of hue,
  Of colour like the red rose on triumphant brier,
Most brisky juvenal, and eke most lovely jew,   90

---

83 The obviously wrong SP in Q may be due to confusion between 'Pu.' and 'Qu.' in the manuscript copy; but as Wilson notes, all other SPs in this scene name 'Robin', not 'Puck'. This does not necessarily bear out Wilson's theories of extensive revision; the line is not essential to the action, and might have been inserted later in the margin. Robin caps Bottom's last words by extending them into a longer sentence ('You will appear as a stranger Pyramus than before'). This may be the point where Robin decides to play his trick on Bottom (Var).
ere the spelling in QF; usually emended to 'e'er' (= ever), but the thrust of Robin's remark as explained above favours *ere*, earlier or hitherto. This also makes better sense of *here* – i.e. in this place so far.

83 *SD2 Robin needs an exit if he is to work the magic on Bottom's head and re-enter in time to speak 102–7; this seems the best point. However, QF SDs are unreliable throughout this passage (e.g. none has a re-entry for Bottom after 98); and the absence of *two* SDs, an exit and a re-entrance, might mean Robin remains onstage all through, transforming Bottom (who is offstage) by remote control. As there is magic at work, this need not conflict with the fact that the ass's head is removed physically (4.1.83).

85 **marry** (the Virgin) Mary: a mild oath or interjection
86 **see a noise** Quince confuses the senses no less than Bottom, as evident from the play-within-the-play; see 4.1.209–11, 5.1.191–2, 297, 344–5.
88–9 **lily . . . rose** obviously contradictory, perhaps with the ideal complexion of *mingled* red and white in mind (as ascribed to Adonis in *VA* 10); cf. 5.1.323–4n. Donaldson (11–12) compares Chaucer's *Sir Thopas*, 1915–17.
89 **triumphant** splendid, magnificent: an absurd description of the wild rose (Foakes)
  brier wild rose bush
90 **brisky** lively: first *OED* record. The next, from 1894, may be modelled on Shakespeare.
  juvenal first cited from Shakespeare (*LLL* 1.2.8, 12–13; 3.1.63): an earlier form of *juvenile* (first cited from 1625, as an adjective), usually with comic or ironic nuance. Cf. *jew* below.
  eke also: already an archaic word, a clumsy line-filler
  jew either empty padding (Wells), or an abbreviation of 'juvenile' or 'jewel'. Johnson suggests *jew* was a term of endearment; cf. 'my incony jew', *LLL* 3.1.132.

---

83 SP] *Oxf; Quin. Q; Puck F*   SD1] *Pope; not in QF*   ere] e'er *Rowe*   SD2] *Capell; not in QF*   84 SP] *Cam; Thys. QF*   85+ SP] *Pet. Q2, F*   88+ SP] *Cam; Thys. QF;* FLUTE *as Thisbe / Wells*

> As true as truest horse that yet would never tire,
> I'll meet thee, Pyramus, at Ninny's tomb.

QUINCE   Ninus' tomb, man. Why, you must not speak
that yet. That you answer to Pyramus. You speak all
your part at once, cues and all. Pyramus, enter; your   95
cue is past. It is 'never tire'.

FLUTE   O!
> As true as truest horse, that yet would never tire.

Enter [BOTTOM] *with* [*an*] *ass's head,* [ROBIN GOODFELLOW
following].

BOTTOM
> If I were, fair Thisbe, I were only thine.

QUINCE   O monstrous! O strange! We are haunted. Pray,   100
masters; fly, masters. Help!   [*Exeunt all except Robin.*]

91 Cf. the proverb 'A good horse becomes
never a jade' (Tilley, H645).
92 **Ninny** for 'Ninus' (see 93n.). *Ninny*
meaning a fool was a very new word (*OED
n.¹*, first cited from 1593), making this a
comic application of fashionable slang.
93 **Ninus** supposed founder of Nineveh. Ovid
(*Met.* 4.88; Golding, 4.108) names his
tomb as Pyramus and Thisbe's meeting-
place.
95 **cues and all** i.e. without waiting for
Pyramus' response to the cue *never tire.*
Stern (*Making*, 123–4) notes how the first
never tire (91) is a cue for Pyramus in the
play-within-the-play, and only the second
(98) for the actor playing Bottom – he must
ignore the first cue.
98.1–2 *Robin obviously re-enters at or about
this time if he is to speak 102–7. Oxf has
him lead Bottom in wearing his ass's head.
See 107.1n.
99 *This punctuation (after Malone) makes
readier sense, coming as a response to 98:

'If I were as true as you say, it would
always be to you.' The QF punctuation
might mean 'Even if I were as fair as you
say (in 88–90), I would still be true to you.'
Cam¹ takes the mispunctuation as an
intended comic effect – like, we may add,
Quince's in the Prologue (5.1.108–17).
100 **monstrous** in the literal sense of an
unnatural creature
   haunted in this sense (afflicted by ghosts
or spirits), first recorded from *RJ* 3.2.158
and here (*OED* haunt *v.* 5b)
101 *SD Bottom can remain onstage or rush
out after his companions to re-enter after
107, having lost them. F's SDs at 101 (for
'The Clownes', not excluding Bottom) and
107.1 accord with the latter alternative,
suggesting stage practice. That still leaves
a confusion in F SDs: there is no SD for
Bottom's entry after 98 or (if the F SD at
107.1 is relocated to 98) for his re-entry
after 107. The repeated, confused entrances
and exits find a parallel at 3.2.404–30.

93–6] *prose Q2, F; Q1 lines* speake / speake / tire. /   97–8] *so lined, Wells; one line, QF*   98.1–2] *this
edn after Capell (Re-enter* PUCK, *and* BOTTOM *with an ass' Head.); Enter Piramus with the Asse head. F,
after 107, Theobald (subst.), after 98; not in Q   ass's head*] *Hanmer; Asse head F; not in Q*   99   *were, fair
Thisbe,*] *Collier (Malone); were faire, Thysby, QF*   101   SD] *this edn; The Clownes all Exit. F; not in Q;
Exeunt all but Bottom and Puck / Alexander*

ROBIN

I'll follow you; I'll lead you about a round,
    Through bog, through bush, through brake, through
        brier.
Sometime a horse I'll be, sometime a hound,
    A hog, a headless bear, sometime a fire,   105
And neigh, and bark, and grunt, and roar, and burn,
Like horse, hound, hog, bear, fire, at every turn.   *Exit.*

Enter [BOTTOM].

BOTTOM   Why do they run away? This is a knavery of
them to make me afeard.

Enter SNOUT.

SNOUT   O Bottom, thou art changed. What do I see   110
on thee?
BOTTOM   What do you see? You see an ass-head of your
own, do you?   [*Exit Snout.*]

Enter QUINCE.

QUINCE   Bless   thee   Bottom,   bless   thee!   Thou   art
translated.   *Exit.*

102 **a round** a roundabout course; also,
punningly, a ring-dance: 'I'll lead you a
fine dance.' Robin combines his role as
will-o'-the-wisp (*fire*, 105; cf. 2.1.39n.)
with more elaborate shape-changing.
103 Robin echoes the Fairy's words at 2.1.2–5
in a different key.
105 **headless bear** Rahter cites *A true and most
dreadful discourse of a woman possessed
with the Devil* (1584), sig. A6ʳ⁻ᵛ, where an
apparition like a bear without head or tail
appears to a possessed woman. Simpson
(89–94) notes later parallels.
107.1 *The F SD at this point should come
after 98. F might have confused this SD

with one for Bottom's re-entry after 107.
See 101 SDn.
112–13 **ass-head ... own** a variant of 'a
fool's head of your own', a proverbial
retort to someone deriding another's folly
or oddity, as in *MW* 1.4.117 (Dent, F519;
cf. A388).
114 **Bless thee** evoking God's protection for
Bottom against evil forces
115 **translated** transformed (*OED v.* 4); cf.
1.1.191n., 3.2.32. Quince also unwittingly
conveys the extended sense 'metaphorical'
(see examples under *OED* translate *adj.*,
translated): Bottom's ass-head is a
metaphor of his mental state (see p. 92).

102 SP] *Puk. F*   107.1] *this edn; Enter Piramus with the Asse head. F (cf. 98.1); not in Q*   113 SD]
Dyce; Exit. (Capell, opp. 111); not in QF   113.1] QUINCE] *Peter quince Q2, F*

BOTTOM   I see their knavery. This is to make an ass of   116
me, to fright me if they could; but I will not stir from
this place, do what they can. I will walk up and down
here, and I will sing, that they shall hear I am not
afraid.   120

     The ousel cock so black of hue
       With orange-tawny bill,
     The throstle with his note so true,
       The wren with little quill.

TITANIA [*Wakes.*]

What angel wakes me from my flowery bed?   125

BOTTOM

     The finch, the sparrow and the lark,
       The plainsong cuckoo gray,
     Whose note full many a man doth mark,
       And dares not answer nay.
For indeed, who would set his wit to so foolish a bird?   130

---

116 **make . . . of** proverbial (Dent, A379.1)
121 Steevens (Var 1793) compares a line from
a catalogue of birds in 'A poeme of a
Mayde forsaken', *Arbor*, 9 (sig. B1ᵛ): 'The
Thrustle-Cock that was so blacke of hewe'.
ousel cock male blackbird
123 **throstle** thrush
124 **little quill** probably 'thin voice or song'
(not in *OED*, but *quill* = pipe, *OED n.¹* 3c;
for *little* see 1.2.48n.); but perhaps the
feeble wing-feathers of this small bird
(Schmidt)
125 Malone compares a celebrated line from
Kyd's *Spanish Tragedy*: 'What outcries
pluck me from my naked bed' (2.5.1). This
may be a simple echo or a parody. The
Henslowe papers record 29 performances
of Kyd's play between 1592 and 1597,
spanning the likely period of composition

of *MND*. Cf. 1.2.25n., 4.2.34n., 5.1.286n.
Titania looks out from her bower in the
recessed 'discovery space' at the back of
the stage, parting the curtain behind which
she lay, and comes downstage to greet
Bottom.
127 **plainsong** (singing) a simple melody – i.e.
an unvarying call, unlike the songs of other
birds; also, telling the plain truth (about
cuckoldry: see 129n.) Cf. Skelton, *Philip
Sparrow*, 427.
129 **dares not answer** The cuckoo's call is
supposed to signal cuckoldry, and no man
can be sure he has not suffered that way (cf.
LLL 5.1.889–90). Bottom misses the point
of even this well-worn jest.
130 **set . . . to** to engage with, pit his wits against;
echoing the proverb 'Do not set your wit
against a fool's' (Dent, W547)

121–4, 126–9] *lines alternately indented, Pope; whole song further indented and italicized,*
Capell   121 ousel] *(Woosell QF)*   124 with] *and* F   125 SD] *after Rowe (Waking.); not in QF*

Who would give a bird the lie, though he cry cuckoo
never so?

TITANIA

I pray thee, gentle mortal, sing again:
Mine ear is much enamoured of thy note.
So is mine eye enthralled to thy shape,   135
And thy fair virtue's force perforce doth move me
On the first view to say, to swear, I love thee.

BOTTOM   Methinks, mistress, you should have little
reason for that. And yet to say the truth, reason and
love keep little company together nowadays; the   140
more the pity that some honest neighbours will not
make them friends. Nay, I can gleek upon occasion.

TITANIA

Thou art as wise as thou art beautiful.

BOTTOM   Not so neither; but if I had wit enough to get out
of this wood, I have enough to serve mine own turn.   145

TITANIA

Out of this wood do not desire to go.
Thou shalt remain here, whether thou wilt or no.
I am a spirit of no common rate:

---

131 **cry cuckoo** utter its call of 'cuckoo'; but
also cry crazily or till crazy, 'cry itself
stupid'. See *OED* cuckoo *n.* 3; cf. *1H4*
2.4.344, 'ye cuckoo' (simpleton).

132 **never so** as never before; cf. 3.2.442n., but
here an 'absolute' construction without
adjective or adverb to follow.

133 **gentle** noble

134 Titania's ear, no less than Bottom's, is
deficient like Midas'; her mental
transformation compares with Bottom's
physical change. See 4.1.28n. and Folkerth,
95–6.

135 **enthralled** enthrallèd

136 **fair virtue's force** As *virtue* etymologically
suggests manhood or manliness (Lat. *vir*,
man), it is especially ironic as applied to

the ass-headed Bottom, no less than by its
usual meaning of merit or moral excellence.
It may also imply virility: the pronouncedly
sexual nature of Titania's interest in
Bottom is borne out by all that follows.
   perforce strongly, compellingly: clumsy
and almost tautological immediately after
force

139–40 Bottom's version of a general theme of
the play; see 1.1.56–7n.

142 **gleek** 'make a jest or gibe' (*OED v.* 2)

146–7 This can be rendered as a threat, as by
Judi Dench in Hall's 1962 revival: she
magically blocked Bottom's path whichever
way he turned.

148 **spirit** See 2.1.1n.
   rate class, rank (*OED n.¹* 12a)

135–7] *137 before 135, Q2, F*

The summer still doth tend upon my state,
And I do love thee; therefore go with me.   150
I'll give thee fairies to attend on thee,
And they shall fetch thee jewels from the deep,
And sing while thou on pressed flowers dost sleep;
And I will purge thy mortal grossness so,
That thou shalt like an airy spirit go.   155
Peaseblossom, Cobweb, Mote, and Mustardseed!

Enter four Fairies: PEASEBLOSSOM, COBWEB, MOTE *and*
MUSTARDSEED.

PEASEBLOSSOM
  Ready.
COBWEB   And I.
MOTE   And I.
MUSTARDSEED   And I.
ALL   Where shall we go?

149 **still** always, continuously. Such perennial summer (a traditional attribute of Paradise) contrasts with the untimely winter induced by her quarrel with Oberon; see 2.1.101n.
  tend upon serve as an attendant
  state rank
152 **jewels** two syllables
153 **pressed** pressèd
154 **purge . . . grossness** dissolve the weight of your mortal body
156 This line, in italics in Q2 (also, except *and*, in Q1), has been misread in F as part of the SD.
  Peaseblossom the flower of the pea plant: only *OED* citation (pease *n.* C1.a) before 1807
  ***Mote** The QF spelling *Moth* was widely

current for *mote* in the sixteenth century. Kökeritz, *Pronunciation* (320), says the name should 'be pronounced *mote* and preferably be so written'; Cercignani (120) would pronounce *mot*. Schäfer (13–14) notes how *mote* would convey a greater sense of 'lightness, grace and minuteness'. Holland adds that all Shakespeare's references to moths are uncomplimentary. Note also *moth* for 'mote' at 5.1.311 and F *moth* for Q *mote* in *LLL* 4.3.158, with a biblical pun on *mote* and *beam* (Matthew 7.3, Luke 6.41). In all early Shakespeare imprints where the word *mote* appears, it is spelt *mo(a)th*, except in *Luc* 1251: see White's list, Var 127. However, Bevington (164) thinks both meanings may be present.

156 Mote] *White; Moth QF*   156.1–2] *Ard² (subst.); Enter foure Fairyes. Q; Enter Pease-blossome, Cobweb, Moth, Mustard-seede, and foure Fairies. F*   157] *White; Fairies. Readie: and I, and I, and I. Where shall we goe? QF*   SPs] 1. Fair., 2. Fair. *etc.* / *Rowe*   ³And . . . go?] And I, Where shall we go? *Rowe*   SP ALL] *Capell*

TITANIA

Be kind and courteous to this gentleman.
Hop in his walks, and gambol in his eyes.
Feed him with apricots and dewberries,   160
With purple grapes, green figs and mulberries.
The honey-bags steal from the humble-bees,
And for night-tapers, crop their waxen thighs
And light them at the fiery glow-worms' eyes,
To have my love to bed and to arise;   165
And pluck the wings from painted butterflies
To fan the moonbeams from his sleeping eyes.
Nod to him, elves, and do him courtesies.

---

158 **kind** courteous (*OED adj.* 5a)
159–68 On this ten-line stretch of approximately rhyming lines, see p. 110. Titania's next speech (188–92) includes a lyrical quatrain.
159–60 resembles a phrase from Moffett's *Silkworms* (Muir, 'Pyramus', 151; *Sources*, 45). This might imply a borrowing in either direction, or merely a chance likeness; see p. 61.
159 **walks** paths, frequented places (*OED n.¹* 11a, 15). Cf. 5.1.31.
160–1 See 2.1.249–56n.
160 **apricots** QF have the usual sixteenth-century form 'apricocks'.
     dewberries variously identified, most often with the blackberry. The word was used in Warwickshire for 'mutant blackberries with just four or five very large drupelets' (Paul Taylor through Peter Holland, personal communication). The name blends with the play's imagery, where dew is a constant presence (see p. 73). Outside botanical works, the only earlier occurrence is in Marlowe's *Dido*

4.5.6 in a not dissimilar context, the Nurse's comic courtship of Cupid in the guise of Ascanius (Connolly, 146–9).
162–8 sung in Brook's production
162–3 **honey-bags**, **night-tapers** earliest citations in *OED*, the next from 1774 and 1894 respectively
162 **humble-bees** 'humming' or bumble bees
163 **crop** perhaps not 'cut off' (though butterflies have their wings plucked, 166) but (*OED v.* 3) 'gather, harvest' (the wax from the bees' thighs, to make candles)
164 **eyes** Glow-worms' light is not *fiery*, nor (as Johnson notes) located in their eyes. Such literal objections seem beside the point; or *eyes* may be 'oes', spangles or spots of light (cf. 3.2.188).
165 **have … bed** bring my love to bed
167 **fan … eyes** so that neither the light nor the touch of the moonbeams disturbs Bottom's sleep
168 **Nod** by way of salutation (*OED v.* 1a)
     courtesies (1) curtseys; (2) courteous acts generally. Cf. 4.1.20n.

160 apricots] *(Apricocks QF)*

PEASEBLOSSOM
Hail, mortal.

COBWEB   Hail.

MOTE   Hail.

MUSTARDSEED   Hail.

BOTTOM   I cry your worships mercy, heartily. I beseech   170
your worship's name.

COBWEB   Cobweb.

BOTTOM   I shall desire you of more acquaintance, good
Master Cobweb. If I cut my finger, I shall make bold
with you. Your name, honest gentleman?   175

PEASEBLOSSOM   Peaseblossom.

BOTTOM   I pray you commend me to Mistress Squash,
your mother, and to Master Peascod, your father.
Good Master Peaseblossom, I shall desire you of more
acquaintance too. Your name, I beseech you, sir?   180

MUSTARDSEED   Mustardseed.

BOTTOM   Good Master Mustardseed, I know your patience
well. That same cowardly giantlike Ox-beef hath

---

169 *It seems reasonable (and dramatically
effective) to divide this line between the
four fairies on analogy with 157. Admittedly
Bottom does not address Mote in the
ensuing dialogue; but that need not imply
the same oversight on the dramatist's part.

170–87 There is a very similar exchange
between some boys and fairies, punning on
the latter's names, in *Maid's Met.* 2.2.73–
83, probably imitating *MND*.

170 cry . . . mercy usually 'ask pardon', but the
context suggests the French sense 'thank'
(*merci*). Bottom addresses Cobweb and
Mustardseed as 'Monsieur' in 4.1.8–23.

173 desire . . . acquaintance wish to know you
better. The constructions 'desire someone
of something' and 'desire something of
someone', as in the F reading of 179, were
both possible (see *OED* desire *v.* 5b, 6b).

174 If . . . finger Cobwebs were commonly
used to stanch bleeding from small wounds.
174–5 make . . . you venture to trouble you
(*OED* bold *adj.* 3)
177 Squash an unripe peapod
178 Peascod a ripe peapod; cf. *TN* 1.5.153, 'as
a squash is before 'tis a peascod'. The word
suggests 'codpiece' (Norton³); *Squash*
applied to the female heightens the
innuendo.
181 F repeats 176 after this line, presumably in
error.
182 your patience often interpreted as his
resignation at being 'devoured', but more
likely an ironic reference to the smarting or
irritant quality of mustard.
183 Ox-beef Beef, itself an item of food, is
comically said to 'devour' (presumably
absorb or soak in) mustard.

---

169 PEASEBLOSSOM . . . ²Hail] *Dyce;* 1. *Fai.* Haile mortall, haile. *QF;* 1. *F.* Hail, mortal! 2. hail! *Capell*
SP MOTE] *White;* 2. *Fai. QF;* 3. *Capell; Moth. / Dyce* SP MUSTARDSEED] *Dyce;* 3. *Fai. QF;*
4. *Capell* 179 you of] of you *F* 181] *F adds (on next line) / Peas.* Pease-blossome.

devoured many a gentleman of your house. I promise
you, your kindred hath made my eyes water ere   185
now. I desire you more acquaintance, good Master
Mustardseed.

TITANIA

Come, wait upon him; lead him to my bower.
The moon, methinks, looks with a watery eye;
And when she weeps, weeps every little flower,   190
Lamenting some enforced chastity.
Tie up my lover's tongue, bring him silently.   [*Exeunt.*]

186 **desire . . . acquaintance** The use of *desire*
with a double object is unusual and
apparently unnoted. An 'of' might have
dropped out after *you* (supplied by Dyce by
analogy with 173, 179).

189 **watery eye** The moist pallor of the moon's
reflection in water (2.1.162n.) is here
extended to the actual moon: its poetically
conceived tears contrast with Bottom's
mustard-induced ones. Dew was thought to
fall from the sky, hence called the moon's
tears. Stephen Bat(e)man, in the
encyclopedic *Batman upon Bartholomew*
(1582: fol. 161ᵛ, sig. 2E5ᵛ), cites Ambrose
as calling the moon the 'mother of dew'
(Kittredge). The line might indicate
impending daybreak, as at 3.2.378–80. In
that case, *enforced chastity* (191) suggests
the frustration of lovers at daybreak, as in
the conventional *aubade* or dawn poem, or
RJ 3.5.1–50: Titania wants to make the
most of the night while it lasts.

191 **enforced chastity** (enforcèd) a telling
ambiguity: (1) violated chastity; but in the
context, more likely (2) forcefully imposed

chastity or thwarted love, as suffered by
nuns and perhaps virgin queens (see
1.1.72–8n.). This view of chastity brings
out Titania's own amorous bent (Andrews).

192 **bring him silently** a surprising command,
seeing Titania is *enamoured of* [Bottom's]
note (134). Perhaps she is rethinking her
views after hearing him speak or even
make 'asinine noises' (Wells). This would
impart additional comic irony to the scene
and to their relationship. The rhyming line
is like an ironic afterthought tagged to the
poetic quatrain preceding it. In Hall's film,
the fairies muzzle a braying Bottom with a
string of leaves.

Titania and Bottom now retreat to her
bower in the 'discovery space', perhaps
behind a curtain, while the events of 3.2
take place on the main stage. The entire
action in the wood is thus split between
two sectors of the stage: the main stage
occupied by the lovers and Theseus' band,
as well as Oberon and Robin; and the
'discovery space' at the back, occupied by
Titania and Bottom. See 2.2.44n.

186 you] your *F3;* you of *Dyce*   190 ²weeps] weepe *Q2, F*   192 lover's] love's *Pope*   SD] *Rowe; Exit. QF*

[3.2]   *Enter* [OBERON].

OBERON

I wonder if Titania be awaked;
Then what it was that next came in her eye,
Which she must dote on in extremity.

Enter [ROBIN GOODFELLOW].

Here comes my messenger. How now, mad spirit?
What night-rule now about this haunted grove?   5

ROBIN

My mistress with a monster is in love.
Near to her close and consecrated bower,
While she was in her dull and sleeping hour,
A crew of patches, rude mechanicals
That work for bread upon Athenian stalls,   10
Were met together to rehearse a play

[3.2] 0.1 *SD Oberon seems to enter *solus* (alone) here, and Robin after 3, as in F. But Robin may enter earlier as in Q, though Oberon does not notice him till 3.

3 **in extremity** to the utmost; perhaps even reflecting Latin *in extremis*, to the point of death

5 **night-rule** Commentators interpret variously as 'revels of the night' and '(dis)order of the night'. Kökeritz ('Night-rule') offers etymological support for the former sense, but the latter provides the broader meaning required here.

6–34 Granville-Barker (1914, 37) describes this as 'both in idea and form, in its tension, climax, and rounding off, a true messenger's speech'. The rhyme conveys Robin's excited narration.

6 *Rowe's punctuation (full stop after *love*) gives 6 an epigrammatic impact clinched by the rhyme in *grove / love*, and opposes the exclusiveness of the *close and consecrated*

bower to *A crew of patches*. Line 7 also goes better with 'Were met' (11).

7 **close** enclosed, hence hidden, secluded (*OED adj.* 4)

consecrated carries strong implications of sanctity, making Titania a kind of goddess; but perhaps used loosely to mean 'secret'. Shakespeare characteristically couples this long Latinate word with the short (though still Latinate) *close*, underpinned by the alliteration.

9 **patches** (1) people in patched clothes (Johnson compares '*ragamuffin*, or *tatterdemalion*'); (2) fools (*OED n.²* 1), the two meanings bridged by (3) clowns, dressed in patches or motley. Cf. *patched fool*, 4.1.208.

rude crude, boorish

mechanicals (*OED n.*1, earliest citation) artisans, manual workers

10 **work for bread** earn their living

stalls small shops or workplaces

[3.2] *Capell (SCENE* II.*); not in QF* 0.1] F (*Enter King of Pharies, solus.); Enter King of* Fairies, *and* Robin goodfellow. *Q* 3.1] *Oxf; Enter Pucke. F; not in Q* 6 SP] *Oxf; Puck QF* love.] *Rowe;* loue, *QF* 7 bower,] *Q2, F;* bower. *Q1*

Intended for great Theseus' nuptial day.
The shallowest thickskin of that barren sort,
Who Pyramus presented in their sport,
Forsook his scene and entered in a brake,   15
When I did him at this advantage take:
An ass's nole I fixed on his head.
Anon his Thisbe must be answered,
And forth my minic comes. When they him spy,
As wild geese that the creeping fowler eye,   20
Or russet-pated choughs, many in sort
Rising and cawing at the gun's report,
Sever themselves and madly sweep the sky,
So at his sight away his fellows fly;
And at our stamp, here o'er and o'er one falls,   25

---

13 **shallowest** stupidest (*OED adj.¹* 6c).
Barring a single other early instance,
Shakespeare virtually initiates this
metaphoric use, first in *3H6* 4.1.62.
thickskin 'a person dull or slow of feeling'
(*OED*)
sort (1) band, company (*OED n.²* 17a); (2)
class, station (*OED* 11a)
14 **sport** theatrical performance (*OED n.¹* 2b);
cf. 119, 4.2.17.
16 **advantage** vulnerable position
17 **nole** head, 'noddle'
fixed fixèd
18 **Anon** presently, by and by (*OED adv.* 5)
answered answerèd
19 **minic** shortened form of 'minikin', a
person (usually female) of mincing or
affected behaviour (*OED* minikin *adj.¹* 1a);
'One who apes or fools about' (Onions).
The word suits the artificial playing style
of the mechanicals. Cf also *OED* minikin
n.² 2, (someone with) a high or shrill voice,
as in *KL* 3.6.43. See 1.2.48n.: Bottom
might have been playing even Pyramus'
condoling role in a *monstrous little voice*.
F *mimic* (*OED n.* 1, 'A mime, a burlesque
actor') gives excellent sense, but was a

very new word at the time, less used than
'minikin'.
20 **eye** watch closely, look out for (*OED v.* 1c)
21 **russet-pated** 'Russet' could mean any
shade of grey or brown, from the cloth of
that name (Linthicum, 86). The jackdaw
(see below) has a grey head.
choughs formerly, any small bird of the
crow family, especially the jackdaw
in sort in a band (*OED* sort *n.²* 17b)
23 **Sever** disband, scatter
25 **stamp** earliest *OED* citation for the sense
'blow with the foot' (*n.³* 1a), though the
corresponding verb is much older. Johnson
assumed that fairies could not stamp hard;
hence following Theobald, he conjectured
'stump [of a tree], upon which they
stumble'. (An 'a' could be misread as a
contracted *our*.) But the story of
Rumpelstiltskin tells otherwise, and Scot
(4.10; 85, sig. H3ʳ) reports a Robin
Goodfellow who used to, but will no
longer, 'stampen'; cf. also Oberon's *rock
the ground* (4.1.85). The *our* is a self-
glorifying plural. Var's 'at one stamp', i.e.
in a rush, feet pounding together, is possible
(*OED v.* 2e, 'to walk noisily', 'tramp').

---

19 minic] *(Minnick)*; Minnock *Q2*; Mimmick *F*   25 our stamp] a stump *Johnson*

He 'Murder' cries, and help from Athens calls.
Their sense, thus weak, lost with their fears thus
　　strong,
Made senseless things begin to do them wrong;
For briers and thorns at their apparel snatch –
Some sleeves, some hats; from yielders, all things
　　catch.　　　　　　　　　　　　　　　　　　30
I led them on in this distracted fear,
And left sweet Pyramus translated there;
When in that moment, so it came to pass,
Titania waked, and straightway loved an ass.

OBERON

This falls out better than I could devise.　　　35
But hast thou yet latched the Athenian's eyes
With the love-juice, as I did bid thee do?

ROBIN

I took him sleeping (that is finished too)
And the Athenian woman by his side,
That when he waked, of force she must be eyed.　　　40

26　**'Murder' cries** best taken as an interjection expressing alarm; cf. *Oth* 5.1.27. The phrase 'cry [etc.] murder' is not recorded till 1713.

27　'Their senses being weakened by their strong fears' (so that they do not see objects like briers and thorns, or perhaps take them as spirits)

28　**senseless** inanimate

30　**from ... catch** Instead of yielding to them as before, all things now catch at them. But *yielders* might refer to Bottom's companions: 'Everything snatches at or from those who have yielded to fear.'

32　**translated** transformed; cf. 3.1.115.

33–4 In Brook's production, Robin sings these lines at the climax of his account.

36　**latched** possible senses: (1) leached, moistened (*OED* leach *v.²* 1, citing this passage); (2) caught and held fast 'as by a charm or spell' (Onions); (3) caught, snared (*OED* latch *v.¹* 2b)

38　**that ... too** I have completed that task too.

40　**of ... eyed** she was sure to be seen (by him)

26　'Murder'] murther *QF*

Enter DEMETRIUS *and* HERMIA. [*Oberon and
Robin stand apart.*]

OBERON

Stand close. This is the same Athenian.

ROBIN

This is the woman, but not this the man.

DEMETRIUS

O, why rebuke you him that loves you so?
Lay breath so bitter on your bitter foe.

HERMIA

Now I but chide; but I should use thee worse,   45
For thou, I fear, hast given me cause to curse.
If thou hast slain Lysander in his sleep,
Being o'er shoes in blood, plunge in the deep
And kill me too.
The sun was not so true unto the day   50
As he to me. Would he have stolen away
From sleeping Hermia? I'll believe as soon

---

41 **close** hidden, unseen

43–81 Throughout this passage, Demetrius addresses Hermia deferentially by the formal *you*, and she him by the hostile and contemptuous *thou*; cf. 2.1.188–244n.

44 **breath** words, utterance; perhaps further, 'judgement or will expressed in words' (*OED* 9a)
    bitter ... bitter a play on (1) stinging, harsh (*OED adj.* 7); (2) virulent, hateful (*adj.* 6a)

45 ¹**but** only
    use thee worse i.e. attack or beat you, not merely scold you

48 **o'er shoes** up to the ankles, so that one might as well pass deeper in; cf. *TGV* 1.1.24, *Mac* 3.4.135–7. 'Over shoes over boots' is proverbial (Dent, S379, S380).

49 This may be the relic of an incomplete or deleted line – another sign that Q1 derives from the author's draft. Or it may indicate a choking pause in Hermia's speech, or her offering her breast for Demetrius to strike (Furness); cf. *CE* 1.1.61, *Mac* 1.2.41–2. See Abbott, 511.

50–5 Hermia had doubts about Lysander's love when it seemed most secure (1.1.173–6n., 2.2.65n.); now that it is genuinely in doubt, she stridently declares her trust in him. Cf. 247.

50 Cf. *TC* 3.2.172–3, 'As true ... / As sun to day'.
    true faithful, attached

51 **stolen** one syllable, though here QF all spell 'stollen'. See 1.1.32n.

40.1–2 *Oberon ... apart*] *Ard²* (*They stand apart.*), *after* 42; *not in QF* 48–9] *so lined, Rowe²; one line, QF* 51 stolen] *(stollen QF)*

This whole earth may be bored, and that the moon
May through the centre creep, and so displease
Her brother's noontide with th'antipodes. 55
It cannot be but thou hast murdered him.
So should a murderer look: so dead, so grim.

DEMETRIUS

So should the murdered look, and so should I,
Pierced through the heart with your stern cruelty.
Yet you, the murderer, look as bright, as clear 60
As yonder Venus in her glimmering sphere.

HERMIA

What's this to my Lysander? Where is he?
Ah, good Demetrius, wilt thou give him me?

DEMETRIUS

I had rather give his carcass to my hounds.

HERMIA

Out, dog, out, cur! Thou driv'st me past the bounds 65
Of maiden's patience. Hast thou slain him then?
Henceforth be never numbered among men.

53–5 The moon will pierce through the centre of the earth to the opposite side, where it is noon. The *antipodes* are conceived as the location opposite to the speaker's, rather than the southern hemisphere.

53 **whole** solid (Wilson, citing *Mac* 3.4.20, 'Whole as the marble')
   bored pierced through

54 **displease** disturb, vex

55 **Her brother's** i.e. the sun's. Diana the moon-goddess and Apollo the sun-god were siblings.

57 **dead** pale, deathly; cf. *2H4* 1.1.71, 'So dull, so dead in look'. Pope's emendation to 'dread' is plausible but unnecessary.

58 **murdered** F 'murderer' is no doubt by eye-skip with 'mutrherer' (*sic*) in the previous line.

61 **yonder Venus** presumably the morning star (cf. 107n.); still shining at 380, which hardly allows time for the intervening action. Such typically Shakespearean slippages argue against those who would impose a strict time-scheme or astronomical pattern on the play.
   glimmering shining brightly (*OED v.* 1); last *OED* citation from 1533, but used in this sense in *1H6* 2.4.24. Cf. 2.1.77n.
   sphere one of the crystalline spheres surrounding the earth in the Ptolemaic system; but here, perhaps Venus' orbit in the Copernican system. See 2.1.7n., 153n.

62 **What's this to** What has this to do with

65 **bounds** Q2 'bonds' also makes sense as 'constraints, obligations'

---

57 murderer] *(murtherer Q1, F)* dead] dread *Pope* 58 murdered] *(murthered Q1);* murderer *F* 60 murderer] *(murtherer Q1)* look] looks *F* 64 I had] Ide *Q2, F* 65 bounds] *Q1, F;* bonds *Q2*

O, once tell true: tell true, even for my sake,
Durst thou have looked upon him, being awake,
And hast thou killed him sleeping? O brave touch!　　　70
Could not a worm, an adder do so much?
An adder did it; for with doubler tongue
Than thine, thou serpent, never adder stung.

DEMETRIUS

You spend your passion on a misprised mood.
I am not guilty of Lysander's blood,　　　　　　　　75
Nor is he dead, for aught that I can tell.

HERMIA

I pray thee, tell me then that he is well.

DEMETRIUS

And if I could, what should I get therefor?

HERMIA

A privilege never to see me more.
And from thy hated presence part I so.　　　　　　　80
See me no more, whether he be dead or no.　　　　*Exit.*

DEMETRIUS

There is no following her in this fierce vein;
Here, therefore, for a while I will remain.
So sorrow's heaviness doth heavier grow

68　**once** just this once (implying he is a
　　habitual liar)
　　Q2, F omit one *tell true*, missing the
　　rhetorical point of the repetition. F2
　　emends conjecturally to correct the
　　resultant lame metre.
69–70　**being awake ... sleeping** referring to
　　Lysander
70　**brave touch** fine trick (*OED* touch *n.* 15)
71　**worm** snake: the original meaning
72　**doubler** more lying or treacherous, making
　　a metaphor of the adder's forked tongue;
　　cf. 2.2.9n.
73　**adder** Hermia might be identifying
　　Demetrius with the serpent that attacked
　　her in her dream (2.2.150).
74　**spend** expend, vent

misprised mistaken: only example in
　OED, but cf. *misprision*, 90n. Shakespeare
　often uses words from this root (literally
　'value wrongly') to imply misjudging,
　hence hating: cf. *AW* 3.2.30, *AYL* 1.1.160,
　MA 3.1.52.
mood anger (*OED n.¹* 2b); cf. *TGV* 4.1.50.
78　**And if** probably the old 'an if' (= if), rather
　　than 'and + if'; cf. 2.2.157n.
　　therefor for that (*OED* therefore *adv.* 1a,
　　b)
79　**privilege** a special right or exemption
80　***so** added by Pope for the necessary rhyme
84–5　Bankrupt of opportunity, sleep cannot
　　provide due relief to sorrow.
84　**heaviness ... heavier** punning on the
　　senses 'weight, quantity' and 'drowsiness'

68　¹true ... ²true] true *Q2, F;* tell true and *F2*　　69　have] a *F*　　78　therefor] *(*therefore *QF)*　　80–1] *so
lined, Pope; QF line* more; / no. /　　80　so] *Pope; not in QF*　　84　grow] *Pope;* growe. *Q;* grow: *F*

For debt that bankrupt sleep doth sorrow owe,   85
Which now in some slight measure it will pay,
If for his tender here I make some stay.
    Lie[s] down [and sleeps].

[*Oberon and Robin come forward.*]

OBERON

What hast thou done? Thou hast mistaken quite,
And laid the love-juice on some true love's sight.
Of thy misprision must perforce ensue   90
Some true love turned, and not a false turned true.

ROBIN

Then fate o'errules, that one man holding troth,
A million fail, confounding oath on oath.

OBERON

About the wood go swifter than the wind,
And Helena of Athens look thou find.   95
All fancy-sick she is and pale of cheer,
With sighs of love that costs the fresh blood dear.

---

85 **sleep** For the QF spelling 'slip(pe)', cf. the
    shift between *ship* and *sheep* in *TGV*
    1.1.72–3, *LLL* 2.1.218–20.
86 **it** sleep
87 **his** possessive of 'it'
    tender payment to discharge a debt (*OED*
    n.² 1b)
    make some stay stop for a while
    SD For the place where he lies down, see
    2.2.44n.
90 **misprision** mistake, misunderstanding; cf.
    misprised, 74n.
91 ¹**turned** reversed, undone
92 **that** in that, seeing that
92–3 **one . . . oath** 'For one man who is true in
    love, a million are false, breaking one oath
    by another.' Robin's defence is that by a

rare mischance, he has harmed the one true
lover among so many false ones.
93 **confounding** (1) mixing (*OED* 6), i.e.
    making contrary oaths; (2) destroying
    (*OED* 1), i.e. breaking or negating one oath
    by another. Cf. 128–33.
95 **Helena** an anomaly: Oberon has not heard
    Helena's name. It is not mentioned in the
    dialogue he overhears in 2.1.188–244.
    look take care to, be sure to
96 **fancy-sick** love-sick
    cheer face, countenance
97 **costs . . . dear** Each sigh was supposed to
    drain away a drop of blood; cf. *3H6* 4.4.22,
    'blood-sucking sighs'.
    costs For the apparently singular verb ending
    with a plural subject (*sighs*), see 3.1.77n.

85 sleep] *Rowe;* slippe *Q1;* slip *Q2, F*   87 SD Lies down] *Rowe;* Ly doune *QF*   and sleeps] *Dyce; not
in QF*   87.1] *Ard² (subst.); not in QF*

199

By some illusion see thou bring her here.
I'll charm his eyes, against she do appear.

ROBIN

I go, I go, look how I go,   100
Swifter than arrow from the Tartar's bow.   *Exit.*

OBERON [*Squeezes the flower on Demetrius' eyelids.*]
Flower of this purple dye,
Hit with Cupid's archery,
Sink in apple of his eye.
When his love he doth espy,   105
Let her shine as gloriously
As the Venus of the sky.
When thou wak'st, if she be by,
Beg of her for remedy.

Enter [ROBIN GOODFELLOW].

ROBIN

Captain of our fairy band,   110
Helena is here at hand,
And the youth mistook by me

98 **illusion** presumably a magical device. It remains a mystery how Robin produces Helena at 111, or whether she appears by coincidence.
99 **against . . . appear** in preparation for her coming
101 **Tartar's bow** Shakespeare was probably echoing Golding 10.687, 'as swift as arrow from a Turkye bowe', where Ovid (*Met.* 10.588) has '*Scythica . . . sagitta*', 'Scythian bow'. Ancient Scythia overlapped with later 'Tartary', and Turk and Tartar were popularly associated: see 263, and *OED* Tartar *n.*² 1. The Turks had a venerable tradition of archery, reaching its highest point during the Ottoman Empire, and known to Europeans from the time of the Crusades. 'As swift as an arrow' is proverbial by itself (Dent, A322).
102–21 An especially prominent example of short rhymed couplets in fairy speeches; cf. 4.1.92–101. See pp. 110–11.
102–9 These lines are sung as an 'air' in Garrick's *Fairies.*
102–3 as described in 2.1.165–8
104 **apple . . . eye** the pupil (thought to be spherical), or the whole eyeball (*OED* apple *n.* 6a)
106 **gloriously** 'brightly, lustrously' (*OED* 3)
107 **Venus . . . sky** i.e. the star rather than the goddess; cf. 61n.
109 **remedy** for his love-lorn state. It was a common Petrarchan conceit to describe the mistress's love as medicine for love-sickness.

99 do] doth *F*   101 SD] *Q2, F; not in Q1*   102 SD] *Dyce, after 103; not in QF*   102–21] *indented, Capell*   109.1] *Oxf¹; Enter Puck QF*   110+ (to 396) SP] *Oxf; Puck (subst.) QF*

Pleading for a lover's fee.
Shall we their fond pageant see?
Lord, what fools these mortals be!   115

OBERON

Stand aside. The noise they make
Will cause Demetrius to awake.

ROBIN

Then will two at once woo one:
That must needs be sport alone.
And those things do best please me   120
That befall preposterously.

Enter LYSANDER *and* HELENA. [*Oberon and
Robin stand apart.*]

LYSANDER

Why should you think that I should woo in scorn?
Scorn and derision never come in tears.

---

113 **fee** reward, perhaps in the form of a kiss; cf. Peele, *Arraignment of Paris*, 319, 'a lovers fee: they saie, unkist, unkinde'.

114 **fond** Cf. 2.1.266n.
   pageant performance in the theatrical sense, used as a satiric metaphor: 'foolish spectacle' (Onions). The word reflects on the actual performance of which this is a part. It also suggests that Oberon and Robin are staging a play with the lovers as unwitting actors (cf. 3.1.74–5).

115 **mortals** Robin seems to exclude the fairies from this category; cf. 2.1.101, 135.

119 **sport** (1) theatrical performance (cf. 14; *pageant*, 114); (2) fun, entertainment (cf. 5.1.90)
   alone (1) even by itself, without any added spice; (2) unique, in a class by itself

121 **preposterously**   (four   syllables, 'prepost'rously') literally 'back to front', hence 'confusedly, in a disordered way'.

Brooks's phrasing 'backside foremost' suggests a possible gesture by Robin. See pp. 87–8.

122–344 This sequence between the lovers, like others earlier, was often curtailed in Victorian productions on grounds of length as well as propriety. With changing social mores and gender relations, these scenes are now theatrically exploited for their incipient comedy and potential for stage action (see Griffiths, 41). This last may extend to horseplay, violence and physical degradation, perhaps most pronouncedly in Lepage's production.

122–33 a double measure of stanzaic verse; cf. 431–6n., 442–7. Like the long stretch of couplets that follows, it brings out the patterned, artificial quality of the lovers' convoluted relations. They are painfully in earnest, but conform to an externally controlled design.

121.1–2 *Oberon . . . apart*] *Ard²* (*They stand aside.*); not in *QF*   123 come] comes *F*

Look when I vow, I weep; and vows so born,
　　In their nativity all truth appears.　　　　　　　　125
How can these things in me seem scorn to you,
Bearing the badge of faith to prove them true?

HELENA

You do advance your cunning more and more.
　　When truth kills truth, O devilish holy fray!
These vows are Hermia's: will you give her o'er?　　130
　　Weigh oath with oath, and you will nothing weigh.
Your vows to her and me, put in two scales,
Will even weigh, and both as light as tales.

LYSANDER

I had no judgement when to her I swore.

HELENA

Nor none, in my mind, now you give her o'er.　　　135

LYSANDER

Demetrius loves her, and he loves not you.

---

124 **Look when** whenever (Eccles, 391)
　　I weep probably an impassioned hyperbole, not literal fact
　　vows so born absolute construction: 'vows being so born', 'when vows are so born'
125 **In their nativity** by the circumstances of their birth or origin. The tears testify to the sincerity of the vows.
127 **badge of faith** like retainers' badges with the crest of the master or family they serve; here, perhaps, the service is to fidelity itself (Brooks). Steevens (Var 1793) compares *Tem* 5.1.267–8, 'Mark but the badges of these men, my lords, / Then say if they be true.'
128 **advance** (1) display, flaunt (cf. *OED v.* 6a); (2) increase (*OED* 15)
129 A complete sentence with 'it is' understood.
　　devilish holy an oxymoron. Truth is holy,

but professed truths that undermine each other (like Lysander's successive vows to Hermia and Helena) are evil. The meaning of *truth* declines from the absolute sense in 125 to a mere vow, pledge or 'troth', which may be false.
131 because, as the next lines explain, both oaths are empty
133 **even** equal
　　tales lies
136 There is no rhyming line to follow, but Demetrius' waking words, immediately contradicting Lysander's, have a different and greater impact. Holland remarks how Demetrius wakes at this point as if 'he is conjured into the scene by his name', though neither Lysander nor Hermia was aware of his presence.

DEMETRIUS (*Wakes.*)

O Helen, goddess, nymph, perfect, divine,
To what, my love, shall I compare thine eyne?
Crystal is muddy. O, how ripe in show
Thy lips, those kissing cherries, tempting grow!   140
That pure congealed white, high Taurus' snow,
Fanned with the eastern wind, turns to a crow
When thou hold'st up thy hand. O let me kiss
This impress of pure white, this seal of bliss!

HELENA

O spite! O hell! I see you all are bent   145
To set against me for your merriment.
If you were civil and knew courtesy,

---

137 **Helen** Metre demands the absence of final -*a*, but thereby points a comparison with Helen of Troy – a comparison inherent in the name itself, argues Maguire (75). As the daughter of Zeus and Leda, Helen of Troy was both 'goddess' and 'nymph' as loosely applied to human women.
perfect perhaps an adverb, 'perfectly' (*OED adv.* 1); but the following comma in Q2, F suggests a climax, as does the structure of the line: 'not only humanly perfect but even divine'. Demetrius uses the more Latinate, educated form *perfect*, in contrast to the artisans' *perfit* (1.2.88, 101).

138 **eyne** See 1.1.242n.

139 **muddy** i.e. in comparison

140 **kissing** i.e. each other as they meet; but also implying 'fit to kiss, attracting kisses'

141 **congealed** (congealèd) thickly packed, hence intensely white
Taurus a range of mountains in Turkey, mentioned in Ovid (*Met.* 2.217; Golding, 2.275) and Seneca (*Phaedra*, 168)

142 **Fanned . . . wind** driven snow, snow sifted by the wind and made still more pure and white; cf. *WT* 4.4.369–70, 'the fanned snow that's bolted / By th' northern blasts

twice o'er'. By accident or design, *eastern* is geographically correct: the strong winds on the Taurus mountains blow from central Asia, to the east.
crow i.e. as black as a crow (in comparison with Helena's hand)

143 **hold'st ... hand** Foakes (following Talbert, 252–3) suggests Helena is making a gesture signifying 'No, no.' Demetrius might seize her hand and kiss it (see 144n.).

144 ***impress** QF 'Princesse' can apply to Helena, but not to her hand as the context demands. *Impress* agrees with *seal*: Demetrius kisses Helena's hand as he speaks, as though imprinting a seal on wax. Jumbled typesetting (perhaps owing to deletion or overwriting in manuscript copy), wrongly 'corrected' thereafter, could change *impress* into *princess*. Cf. *AC* 3.13.130–1: 'your hand, this kingly seal / And plighter of high hearts!' Staunton compares Beaumont and Fletcher's *Double Marriage* 4.3.48, describing Juliana's hand as 'white seale of vertue'.
seal mark of authentication (*OED n.*[2] 1b), besides the literal sense continuing from *impress*

146 **set against** attack (*OED* set *v.*[1] PV1.1)

---

137 SD] *F (Awa.), opp. 136; not in Q*   perfect, divine] *Q2, F;* perfect diuine *Q1*   144 impress] *Staunton (Collier);* Princesse *QF*   145 all are] are all *F*

You would not do me thus much injury.
Can you not hate me, as I know you do,
But you must join in souls to mock me too?   150
If you were men, as men you are in show,
You would not use a gentle lady so,
To vow and swear and superpraise my parts
When I am sure you hate me with your hearts.
You both are rivals and love Hermia,   155
And now both rivals to mock Helena.
A trim exploit, a manly enterprise,
To conjure tears up in a poor maid's eyes
With your derision! None of noble sort
Would so offend a virgin, and extort   160
A poor soul's patience, all to make you sport.

LYSANDER

You are unkind, Demetrius; be not so,
For you love Hermia: this you know I know.
And here with all good will, with all my heart,
In Hermia's love I yield you up my part;   165
And yours of Helena to me bequeath,
Whom I do love, and will do till my death.

---

148 **injury** (1) insult, taunt (*OED n.* 2), as in *injurious* (195), (2) harm generally; cf. 2.1.147n.
150 **join in souls** think alike, conspire
151 **show** external appearance
152 **gentle** (1) well-born, a 'gentlewoman'; (2) tender, soft-natured
153 **superpraise** earliest *OED* citation, super-3c(a)(i). Early Modern English introduced coinages in *super-* on a large scale; the novelty lends a satirical edge.
  parts (1) physical features; (2) qualities, faculties
155–7 Steevens (Var 1778) compares Juno's reproach to Venus (*Aen.* 4.93–5) about two gods, Venus and Cupid, joining to subdue

one woman, Dido.
157 **trim** neat, smart
159 **sort** kind, nature, 'with special reference to character, disposition, or rank' (*OED n.²* 2a, citing this passage)
160 **extort** torture, oppress (*OED v.* 3a)
162 **unkind** perhaps in the basic sense 'false to one's nature' (as Helena believes him to love Hermia, 163); cf. *unkindly*, 183.
164 **here** Q1 'heare' might be = 'hear'; but 'heare' for 'here' is a Shakespearean spelling (Wilson, 'Spellings', 138) that might occur in the authorial draft underlying Q1. (See p. 298.)
165 **part** share

151 were] are *F* 159 derision! None] *Theobald;* derision None, *Q1;* derision, none *Q2;* derision; none *F*
164 here] (heare*);* heere *Q2;* here *F* 167 till] to *Q2, F*

HELENA

Never did mockers waste more idle breath.

DEMETRIUS

Lysander, keep thy Hermia; I will none.
If e'er I loved her, all that love is gone.   170
My heart to her but as guestwise sojourned,
And now to Helen is it home returned,
There to remain.

LYSANDER   Helen, it is not so.

DEMETRIUS

Disparage not the faith thou dost not know,
Lest, to thy peril, thou abye it dear.   175
Look where thy love comes: yonder is thy dear.

Enter HERMIA.

HERMIA

Dark night, that from the eye his function takes,
The ear more quick of apprehension makes;
Wherein it doth impair the seeing sense,
It pays the hearing double recompense.   180

---

168 **mockers** (1) deceivers (*OED n.¹* 1); (2) scoffers

169 **I will none** I want no part (of Hermia).

170 **e'er** QF 'ere', possibly 'ere' = earlier; cf. 3.1.83n.

171 **guestwise** like a guest
sojourned travelled: *OED v.* 4, citing a single 1608 instance, but a possible sense here in view of *to*

172 **home returned** Demetrius originally loved Helena (1.1.106–10). Malone compares *Son* 109.5–6: 'if I have ranged, / Like him that travels I return again'.

173 Here or later (e.g. at 246), directors have made both men try to embrace Helena simultaneously. She ducks and escapes, and they fall into each other's arms (Griffiths, 160, 163).

174 **dost not know** referring not only to Demetrius' faith but Lysander's own: he has no notion of true love like Demetrius'.

175 **abye** pay for, suffer for; cf. 335.

176 **thy ... thy** No doubt stressed: 'There comes *your* love, Hermia; Helena is mine.'

177–8 Night makes one's hearing sharper even as it impairs the vision.

177 **his** the usual possessive of *it* at the time

178 **apprehension** perception (*OED* 5, earliest citation); cf. *apprehend*, 5.1.5.

170 e'er] *(ere QF)*   172 is it] it is *Q2, F*   173 Helen] *not in Q2, F*   175 abye] *(aby); abide Q2, F*

Thou art not by mine eye, Lysander, found;
Mine ear, I thank it, brought me to thy sound.
But why, unkindly, didst thou leave me so?

LYSANDER

Why should he stay, whom love doth press to go?

HERMIA

What love could press Lysander from my side? 185

LYSANDER

Lysander's love, that would not let him bide:
Fair Helena, who more engilds the night
Than all yon fiery oes and eyes of light.
Why seek'st thou me? Could not this make thee
  know,
The hate I bare thee made me leave thee so? 190

HERMIA

You speak not as you think. It cannot be.

HELENA

Lo, she is one of this confederacy.
Now I perceive, they have conjoined all three
To fashion this false sport in spite of me.
Injurious Hermia, most ungrateful maid, 195

183 **unkindly** See 162n.

185 **press** (1) impel, urge (cf. 184); (2) seize or force into service (*OED v.²* 1, 2)

186 **love** beloved, the person loved

188 **oes and eyes** small shining objects (*OED* O *n.³* 2b, eye *n.¹* 10c), here stars; punning on the letters *o* and *i* as in an old poetic refrain (see *OED* O *n.¹* 1b)
  oes 'o's, small round spangles; see Linthicum, 152–3.

189 **this** presumably embracing or kissing Helena

190 **bare** old past tense of *bear*

192–219 This impassioned outburst is formally underpinned by a pattern of repetitions and parallel constructions, in *all* (198–202), *both* (204–6) and *two* (211–13). Together

182 thy] that *F*

with the elaborate images in 203–14, this gives the childhood friendship an ideal, almost artificial quality, contrasting with their current animosity.

194 **false sport** misguided mirth, a bad joke (cf. 161, 5.1.90); but *false* also = deceitful
  in spite of in 'scorn or contempt' of (*OED* spite *n.* 5a), in order to spite

195 As Helena gets more and more indignant, her protest shifts from rhyme to the freer movement of blank verse: the opposite poetic strategy to that employed for the more patterned action of 2.2.88–160.
  Injurious offensive, insulting; cf. *Cor* 3.3.68, 'thou injurious tribune'.
  ungrateful as not recalling or valuing their past friendship

Have you conspired, have you with these contrived
To bait me with this foul derision?
Is all the counsel that we two have shared,
The sisters' vows, the hours that we have spent,
When we have chid the hasty-footed time   200
For parting us – O, is all forgot?
All schooldays' friendship, childhood innocence?
We, Hermia, like two artificial gods,
Have with our needles created both one flower,
Both on one sampler, sitting on one cushion,   205
Both warbling of one song, both in one key,
As if our hands, our sides, voices and minds
Had been incorporate. So we grew together
Like to a double cherry, seeming parted
But yet an union in partition,   210
Two lovely berries moulded on one stem;

196 **contrived** plotted, conspired
197 **bait** harass, torment
   derision four syllables, as then usual
198–210   rather surprisingly, the only lines
   in the play among Pope's chosen 'shining
   passages' in Shakespeare
198 **counsel** secrets (*OED n.* 5b)
201 **O, is** F2 makes the first of many attempts to
   regularize the metre. But it is regularized in
   any case by expressively pausing after *us*
   and prolonging *O*.
203 **artificial** usually explained as 'skilled in
   art'; but with due allowance for hyperbole,
   like . . . gods seems extravagant praise for
   two schoolgirls doing needlework. Perhaps
   artificial = made by art (*OED* 1a), like two
   classical gods presented as *incorporate*
   (208) in a painting or statue.
204 **needles** Some editors have suggested, with
   perhaps undue concern for metrical
   regularity, that this should be pronounced
   'needls', as often at the time.
208 **incorporate** conjoined in body; most
   familiarly in the hermaphrodite, combining
   Hermaphroditus (son of Hermes and

Aphrodite) and a nymph, taken as a symbol
of perfect sexual union (see *FQ* 3.12,
cancelled ending; 4.10.41). The sexual
association may not be irrelevant: Helena's
speech carries homoerotic nuances, as
more pronouncedly does Emilia's
friendship with her playfellow Flavina in
TNK 1.3.49–85. These lines briefly open up
an idyllic love between the two girls,
contrasting with their later tormented
relations with men and hence with each
other.
209 **seeming** perhaps an adverb, 'seemingly';
   or a participle, 'seeming to be'
210 **an union** At this time, 'a, an' retained
   something of the original sense of 'one'
   (Abbott, 79–80), which suits the context
   and justifies Q *an* before *u*. This nuance is
   lost in the modern 'a' in F. Cf. 'an union',
   Ham 5.2.249, F text.
   partition (four syllables) division. In view
   of 213–14, the heraldic sense 'division of a
   field into . . . parts' (*OED n.* 6) may be
   especially relevant.
211 **moulded** formed, shaped

201 O, is] O and is *F2*   210 an] a *F*

So with two seeming bodies but one heart,
Two of the first, like coats in heraldry,
Due but to one, and crowned with one crest.
And will you rent our ancient love asunder   215
To join with men in scorning your poor friend?
It is not friendly, 'tis not maidenly.
Our sex, as well as I, may chide you for it,
Though I alone do feel the injury.

HERMIA
I am amazed at your passionate words.   220
I scorn you not; it seems that you scorn me.

HELENA
Have you not set Lysander, as in scorn,
To follow me and praise my eyes and face?
And made your other love Demetrius,
Who even but now did spurn me with his foot,   225
To call me goddess, nymph, divine and rare,
Precious, celestial? Wherefore speaks he this

212 **two ... heart** the proverbial idea of 'one
soul in bodies twain' (Dent, B503.1)
213 ***first, like** Theobald's emendation, more
fully explained by Capell (*Notes*, 109),
refers to a coat of arms with two main
quarterings or shields (of two families
joined in marriage), topped by a single
crest (the husband's) to which both
quarterings relate or are 'due'. The
metaphor implies that contrary to this
patriarchal design, the two friends are
equal in regard, neither subservient to the
other.
214 **crowned** crownèd
215 **rent** rend, tear apart
220 **amazed**   (amazèd)   (1)   perplexed,

bewildered (*OED* 2); (2) astonished
***passionate** This F addition fills out the
metre. It may be the F editor's conjecture,
or derive from the new manuscript he
consulted, hence possibly authorial.
Marshall (560) thinks Helena is 'amazed'
not only at Hermia's vehemence but at her
expression of an incipient love for Helena.
225 **spurn ... foot** as, ironically, she had asked
him to do (2.1.205); cf. 313.
226 **goddess, nymph** See 137.
227 ***Precious, celestial** completing a climax;
cf. 'perfect, divine' (137), and the similar
pointing of Q2, F against Q1. But *celestial*
in Q1 may be a noun, meaning a god or
angel.

213 first, like] *Theobald (Martin Folks);* first life *QF*   220 passionate] *F; not in Q*   227 Precious,
celestial] *Q2, F;* Pretious celestiall *Q1*

To her he hates? And wherefore doth Lysander
Deny your love, so rich within his soul,
And tender me, forsooth, affection, 230
But by your setting on, by your consent?
What though I be not so in grace as you,
So hung upon with love, so fortunate,
But miserable most, to love unloved?
This you should pity rather than despise. 235

HERMIA

I understand not what you mean by this.

HELENA

I do. Persevere, counterfeit sad looks,
Make mouths upon me when I turn my back,
Wink each at other, hold the sweet jest up.
This sport, well carried, shall be chronicled. 240
If you have any pity, grace or manners,
You would not make me such an argument.
But fare ye well. 'Tis partly my own fault,
Which death or absence soon shall remedy.

232 **in grace** in favour (with the two men)
233 **hung upon** loaded, 'draped with': a graphic image of fawning suitors
237 **I do. Persevere** Q1 *I* was interpreted as *aye* in Q2, F (with 'do' meaning 'carry on as you are doing').
  Persevere persèver
  sad serious
238 **Make mouths** grimace mockingly (perhaps conflated with 'mow' = moue)
239 **Wink ... other** 'tip each other the wink' (Brooks), share the joke by winking; but *wink* could also mean 'shut one's eyes',

connive, as in *H5* 2.2.54–5, 'little faults . . . be winked at'.
  hold ... up continue, keep up
240 **carried** (1) carried out, executed; (2) continued, prolonged (*OED v.* 14b)
  chronicled recorded in history
242 **make me** make for me, foist on me: the ethical dative (see 1.2.77n.)
  argument contention, fracas
243 **fare ye well** For the compound 'faryewell' in Q2, cf. Q readings at *MV* 1.1.58, 103; 2.2.195.

237 I do. Persevere] I, do, perseuer *Q2, F*   243 fare ye well] *Q1, F;* faryewell *Q2*   my] mine *Q2, F*

LYSANDER

    Stay, gentle Helena; hear my excuse,   245

    My love, my life, my soul, fair Helena.

HELENA

    O excellent!

HERMIA [*to Lysander*]   Sweet, do not scorn her so.

DEMETRIUS [*to Lysander*]

    If she cannot entreat, I can compel.

LYSANDER

    Thou canst compel no more than she entreat.

    Thy threats have no more strength than her weak

        prayers.   250

    Helen, I love thee, by my life I do.

    I swear by that which I will lose for thee

    To prove him false that says I love thee not.

DEMETRIUS [*to Helena*]

    I say, I love thee more than he can do.

LYSANDER [*to Demetrius*]

    If thou say so, withdraw, and prove it too.   255

DEMETRIUS

    Quick, come.

HERMIA   Lysander, whereto tends all this?

---

247 **scorn her** Hermia still persists, perhaps desperately, in the notion that Lysander is jesting with Helena in offering her his love; cf. 50–5n.

248 'If you don't listen to Hermia's entreaty, I can force you to abandon your love for Helena.'

250 ***prayers** Theobald's emendation (moderating his preferred reading 'prays'

as a noun) contrasts *threats* with *prayers* to match *compel* and *entreat*, while QF 'praise' does not suit anything in the context.

252 **that ... thee** i.e. his life, perhaps suggesting he will sacrifice it in a duel

255 **withdraw** move elsewhere – i.e. away from the women, to fight a duel

256 **whereto** to what end or purpose

247 SD] *Capell, after* Sweet; *not in QF* 248 SD] *Oxf; not in QF* 250 prayers] *Theobald;* praise *QF* 254 SD] *Oxf; not in QF* 255 SD] *this edn; not in QF*

LYSANDER

Away, you Ethiop.

DEMETRIUS [*to Hermia*] No, no: he'll seem

To break loose, take on as you would follow,

But yet come not. [*to Lysander*] You are a tame

man, go.

LYSANDER

Hang off, thou cat, thou burr, vile thing let loose,   260

Or I will shake thee from me like a serpent.

257 **Ethiop** Ethiopian, hence African; alluding
to Hermia's dark hair and/or skin. See 263,
and 2.2.118.

257–9 **No ... go** Puzzling lines, perhaps more
so in F. If addressed wholly to Hermia or to
Lysander, it is hard to see what either of
them is visualized as doing. Taylor ('Crux',
49) and Oxf emend Q1 'heele' to 'yeeld',
which is palaeographically viable but does
not help the sense, and also retain F 'Sir' to
regularize the metre. Doran's 'you'll' for
he'll (257), anticipated by Thiselton,
makes for a consistent taunting of
Lysander. Sisson's 'he' for *you* at 258
(*Readings*, 1.129) carries the same taunt,
routed through Hermia rather than
addressed directly to Lysander.
The SDs in this edition (partly following
Folg) suggest a different solution without
emendation, in line with Treadwell's
interpretation: 'Demetrius is accusing
Lysander of only pretending to break free
from Hermia who is clinging on to him –
he is actually glad to be restrained because
he is too cowardly to go off to fight
Demetrius.' Most of the speech is
addressed to Hermia, only the last half-line
to Lysander. There are other instances in
this scene (251, 327) of speakers dividing a

speech between two addressees, without
any SD in QF to indicate the shift.

257–8 Brooks (158) observes plausibly that at
this date, Shakespeare would not admit a
weak enjambment like *heele / Seem*. It also
makes 257 short by a syllable, though such
irregular lines are common in the play,
especially in Q1. The Q2, F line division
creates an implausible series of irregular
lines.

258 **take on** make a fuss, grow agitated (*OED*
take *v.* PV1, take on 5). The equally
appropriate sense 'To pretend', act as
though (*OED* take on 7b) is first cited from
1645.

259 **come not** also in a sexual sense, taunting
Lysander with impotence; cf. *tame*
(impotent, castrated: Rubinstein, 269).

260 **Hang off** drop off me, let go
cat which clings by its claws
burr again, because Hermia is clinging to
him

261 **like a serpent** reversing the situation in
Hermia's dream, where the serpent might
be identified with Lysander; also,
somewhat far-fetchedly, taken to allude
to St Paul's shaking into the fire a viper
that had fastened on his hand (Acts
28.3–6).

257–8] *so lined, this edn; Q1 lines* Ethiop. / heele / follow; /; *Q2, F line* Ethiope. / loose; / follow, /
257 SD] *Folg; not in QF*   he'll] *(*heele *Q1;* hee'l *Q2);* Sir, *F;* sir! You *Kittredge;* you'll *Doran (Thiselton);*
sir, yield. *Oxf*   258 you] he *Sisson, Readings, 1.129*   259 SD] *this edn; Folg, after* loose, *258; not in QF*

HERMIA

Why are you grown so rude? What change is this,
Sweet love?

LYSANDER   Thy love? Out, tawny Tartar, out!
Out, loathed medicine; O hated potion, hence.

HERMIA

Do you not jest?

HELENA   Yes, sooth, and so do you.   265

LYSANDER

Demetrius, I will keep my word with thee.

DEMETRIUS

I would I had your bond; for I perceive
A weak bond holds you. I'll not trust your word.

LYSANDER

What, should I hurt her, strike her, kill her dead?
Although I hate her, I'll not harm her so.   270

HERMIA

What, can you do me greater harm than hate?
Hate me, wherefore? O me, what news, my love?
Am not I Hermia? Are not you Lysander?
I am as fair now as I was erewhile.
Since night you loved me, yet since night you left
    me.   275

---

262 **rude** in a strong sense: violent, harsh (*OED adj.* 2c)
263 **tawny** (root meaning, 'tanned') brown of any shade, hence dark or swarthy; cf. *Ethiop* (257).
    Tartar again wrongly thought to be dark-skinned
264 **loathed medicine** loathèd med'cine
    medicine implying something foul or bitter; perhaps also the Petrarchan notion of the woman's return of affection curing the lover's 'sickness' of love. Here, Hermia is the more hated as having once been loved; cf. 109n., 2.2.141–6 and nn.
    potion Q2, F 'poison' makes sense, but

seems to be a simplification by the editor or printer. *Potion* agrees better with *medicine*.
266 **my word** to fight with him (252–3)
267–8 **bond ... bond** a play on (1) written contract or assurance (rather than his mere word); (2) bond of love (for Helena); (3) restraining force (Hermia, who seems still to be clinging to Lysander; hence his retort in 269 that he cannot be violent with her)
272 **what news** 'What news is this?', i.e. 'What are you saying?'
275 **Since night** a night ago, it was only last night that. Schmidt finds it a 'peculiar' usage.

262–3] *Q2, F line* rude? / Loue? / out; / 264 potion] poison *Q2, F* 272 news] *(newes QF); means (meanes) Collier MS, 105*

Why then, you left me (O the gods forbid)
In earnest, shall I say?
LYSANDER   Ay, by my life,
And never did desire to see thee more.
Therefore be out of hope, of question, of doubt;
Be certain, nothing truer: 'tis no jest   280
That I do hate thee, and love Helena.

HERMIA [*to Helena*]

O me, you juggler, you canker-blossom,
You thief of love! What, have you come by night
And stolen my love's heart from him?
HELENA   Fine, i' faith.
Have you no modesty, no maiden shame,   285
No touch of bashfulness? What, will you tear
Impatient answers from my gentle tongue?
Fie, fie, you counterfeit, you puppet, you!

HERMIA

Puppet? Why so? Aye, that way goes the game.
Now I perceive that she hath made compare   290
Between our statures: she hath urged her height,

---

279 **of doubt** deleting *of* before *doubt* improves
  the metre, but such refinements seem
  uncalled-for. See pp. 308–9.
282 **juggler** deceiver, trickster (*OED* 3); but
  possibly a worker in magic (*OED* 2).
  Hermia is implying Helena might have
  used magic spells to attract Lysander; cf.
  1.1.27, 28n., 192n.
  canker-blossom a cankered blossom or the
  canker-worm itself (cf. 2.2.3), which has
  destroyed or stolen (hence *thief*) the heart
  of the flower; or possibly the 'canker-
  bloom' or wild rose that has colour but no
  scent, unlike the cultivated rose (cf. *Son*
  54.5–12).
283–4 Holland notes the irony of Hermia's
making the same charge against Helena as
Egeus against Lysander when the latter was
wooing her (1.1.27).
284 **stolen** one syllable (QF 'stolne'); cf.
  1.1.32n.
288 **puppet** doll, image ('typically small',
  OED n. 1b); a *counterfeit* woman. On
  the two women's respective heights, see
  p. 9.
289 **Why so?** often punctuated 'Why, so?' or
  'Why, so!' ('Oh, so that's how it is') or
  'Why, so:' ('Very well, if that's how it is');
  but the simple indignant protest 'Why
  should you call me so?' will serve.
  that ... game proverbial: 'to see which
  way the game goes' (Dent, W144.1)

---

279 of doubt] doubt *Pope*   282 SD] *Oxf; after* O me, *Ard²; not in QF*   284 stolen] *(*stolne
QF)   289 Why so?] why, so: *Theobald;* Why, so! *Kittredge;* Why, so? *Ard²*

And with her personage, her tall personage,
Her height, forsooth, she hath prevailed with him.
And are you grown so high in his esteem
Because I am so dwarfish and so low? 295
How low am I, thou painted maypole? Speak,
How low am I? I am not yet so low
But that my nails can reach unto thine eyes.

HELENA

I pray you, though you mock me, gentlemen,
Let her not hurt me. I was never curst; 300
I have no gift at all in shrewishness.
I am a right maid for my cowardice:
Let her not strike me. You perhaps may think
Because she is something lower than myself,
That I can match her.

HERMIA   Lower? Hark again. 305

HELENA

Good Hermia, do not be so bitter with me.
I evermore did love you, Hermia,
Did ever keep your counsels, never wronged you,
Save that in love unto Demetrius,
I told him of your stealth unto this wood. 310
He followed you; for love, I followed him.

---

292 **personage** appearance, stature (*OED* 2a):
satirical use of a long formal word,
repeated for good measure

296–8 In Massinger's *The Duke of Milan*
2.1.173–91, Marcelia and Mariana echo
this quarrel by taunting each other about
their stature.

296 **maypole** the pole round which May dances
were held, decorated with flowers and
often painted. A dig at Helena's height: 'as
tall as a maypole' is proverbial (Dent,
M778). *Painted* implies that Helena's fair
complexion is not her own, and that she is
sexually forward: Jonson refers to a
prostitute as a 'painted ladie' (*The Gypsies*

Metamorphosed, 1108).

300 **curst** shrewish, quarrelsome (*OED* 4); cf.
'Kate the Curst', *TS* 2.1.185.

301 **shrewishness** earliest *OED* citation

302 **right maid** truly a maiden – i.e.
inexperienced, as befits a virgin; a riposte
to Hermia's *painted* (see 296n.).
cowardice fear, timorousness; cf.
2.1.234.

307 **evermore** always, but unusually referring
solely to the past; cf. *MM* 4.2.145, *H8*
3.2.172.

308 **counsels** secrets; cf. *counsel*, 1.1.216.

310 **stealth** stealthy passage or departure (*OED*
3a, earliest citation); cf. 4.1.159.

299 gentlemen] *Q2, F;* gentleman *Q1*

But he hath chid me hence, and threatened me
To strike me, spurn me, nay to kill me too.
And now, so you will let me quiet go,
To Athens will I bear my folly back,   315
And follow you no further. Let me go.
You see how simple and how fond I am.

HERMIA

Why, get you gone. Who is't that hinders you?

HELENA

A foolish heart, that I leave here behind.

HERMIA

What, with Lysander?

HELENA   With Demetrius.   320

LYSANDER

Be not afraid. She shall not harm thee, Helena.

DEMETRIUS

No, sir, she shall not, though you take her part.

HELENA

O, when she is angry, she is keen and shrewd.
She was a vixen when she went to school;
And though she be but little, she is fierce.   325

HERMIA

Little again? Nothing but low and little?
Why will you suffer her to flout me thus?
Let me come to her.

---

312 **chid me hence** driven me away by railing
   at me
313 **spurn me** Cf. 225n.
314 **so** if, providing
   quiet referring to herself or her tormentors
   or both. For adverbs without a final *-ly*, see
   1.2.20n.
317 **fond** Cf. 2.1.266n.
320 The F SP '*Her.*' for the second speech is
   obviously wrong, as the first SP rightly
   reads '*Her[mia]*'.

323 **keen** fierce, cruel; insolent (*OED adj.*
   2c, d)
   shrewd shrewish
324 This contradicts 'the image of perfect
   childhood   friendship'   at   198–214
   (Holland).
327 **flout** mock, insult
328 **Let ... her** indicates that the men are
   physically holding her back from attacking
   Helena

320 SP HELENA] *Her. F*   323 ¹she is] shee's *Q2, F*

LYSANDER   Get you gone, you dwarf,
You minimus, of hindering knot-grass made,
You bead, you acorn.

DEMETRIUS   You are too officious   330
In her behalf that scorns your services.
Let her alone. Speak not of Helena,
Take not her part. For if thou dost intend
Never so little show of love to her,
Thou shalt abye it.

LYSANDER   Now she holds me not.   335
Now follow, if thou dar'st, to try whose right,
Of thine or mine, is most in Helena.

DEMETRIUS

Follow? Nay, I'll go with thee, cheek by jowl.
                    [*Exeunt*] *Lysander and Demetrius.*

HERMIA

You, mistress, all this coil is long of you.
Nay, go not back.

HELENA   I will not trust you, I,   340
Nor longer stay in your curst company.

---

329 minimus a very small person. A nonce-use: *OED*'s only citation before 1879, except in special contexts; probably italicized in QF to indicate its latinity, though as Theobald observes, this is the Latin masculine form.
hindering knot-grass An infusion of knot-grass, a common weed, was thought to stop bodily growth. Knot-grass also hindered the plough and was hard to uproot, hence is applicable to Hermia's clinging persistence.
330 bead . . . acorn very small objects
333–4 intend . . . her profess the least love towards her (*OED intend v.* 22: assert or claim, with an implication of deceit)
335 abye See 175n.

335 holds me not said of Hermia: (a) does not attract me; (b) does not hold me back, referring to her clinging to Lysander a while earlier
337 Of out of, as between; cf. *Tem* 2.1.30, 'Which, of he or Adrian'.
most greatest
338 *SD Q1 has no Exit for either Lysander or Demetrius. They may be covered by an '*Exeunt*' after 344 – like Lysander in Q2, which has an Exit for Demetrius after 338.
339 coil uproar, confusion
long of because of
340 go not back She wants Helena to remain so that she can abuse or attack her further.
341 curst hateful, detestable (*OED* 3a)

---

335 abye] abide *F*   337 Of] Or *Theobald*   338 SD] *F (Exit Lysander and Demetrius.); Exit. Q2; not in Q1*   341 Nor] *Q1, F; Not Q2*

Your hands than mine are quicker for a fray;
My legs are longer, though, to run away.   [*Exit.*]

HERMIA
I am amazed, and know not what to say.   [*Exit.*]

[*Oberon and Robin come forward.*]

OBERON
This is thy negligence. Still thou mistak'st,   345
Or else commit'st thy knaveries wilfully.

ROBIN
Believe me, king of shadows, I mistook.
Did not you tell me I should know the man
By the Athenian garments he had on?
And so far blameless proves my enterprise,   350
That I have 'nointed an Athenian's eyes;
And so far am I glad it so did sort,
As this their jangling I esteem a sport.

OBERON
Thou seest these lovers seek a place to fight.
Hie therefore, Robin, overcast the night;   355

343–4 *SDs Capell allows separate exits for Helena and Hermia after 343, 344 respectively, which is theatrically more effective. F has no exits at this point, and also lacks 344.

344 **amazed** in a maze: bewildered, confused (*OED* 2)

344.1 Oberon and Robin had remained at the back of the stage all along. Cf. 463n., 3.1.71n.

345 **still** always, continually

346 **knaveries** earliest *OED* citation for the weakened sense of roguishness or mischievous tricks (2a); but the angry Oberon probably intends the full force of the word.
wilfully deliberately (*OED* 4), with a tinge of 'perversely' (*OED* 5)

347 **shadows** (1) darkness; (2) spirits, illusions. The word may carry a theatrical implication, continuing the motif underlying 114 and made explicit in 5.1.210, 413 (see notes on all these lines).

351 **'nointed** anointed, smeared

350–3 **And so far ... That ... And so far ...
As** (1) to the extent that; (2) up till now because

352 **sort** befall, turn out

353 **jangling** quarrelling, bickering

355 **Hie** make haste
overcast the night recalls *Met.*14.369–71 (Golding, 14.416–20), where Circe conjures up darkness and fog while drawing Picus to his doom

343 SD] *Capell; not in QF*   344] *not in F*   SD] *Capell; Exeunt. Q; not in F*   344.1] *Wells (subst); Enter Oberon and Pucke. F; not in Q*   346 wilfully] *willingly F*   349 had] *hath Q2, F*

The starry welkin cover thou anon
With drooping fog as black as Acheron,
And lead these testy rivals so astray
As one come not within another's way.
Like to Lysander sometime frame thy tongue,   360
Then stir Demetrius up with bitter wrong,
And sometime rail thou like Demetrius,
And from each other look thou lead them thus
Till o'er their brows, death-counterfeiting, sleep
With leaden legs and batty wings doth creep.   365
Then crush this herb into Lysander's eye,
Whose liquor hath this virtuous property
To take from thence all error with his might,
And make his eyeballs roll with wonted sight.
When they next wake, all this derision   370
Shall seem a dream and fruitless vision,
And back to Athens shall the lovers wend
With league whose date till death shall never end.

356 **welkin** sky
   anon at once; cf. 2.1.17n.
357 **drooping** descending, settling on the ground
   Acheron a river of the underworld. 'As black as hell' is proverbial (Dent, H397).
358 **testy** 'Aggressive, contentious' (*OED* 1)
361 **wrong** insult, taunt (Schmidt; not in *OED*); cf. *1H6* 3.4.42, *KL* 4.2.13, 52.
363 **from** away from
364 **death-counterfeiting** A comma follows in all three early texts, suggesting it may not be a simple adjective but a descriptive phrase: 'sleep, by counterfeiting death', a proverbial idea (Dent, S527). Cf. 'this downy sleep, death's counterfeit' (*Mac* 2.3.76).
365 **batty** like a bat's: only *OED* citation before 1883
367 **virtuous** healing or beneficial, perhaps magically (especially used of plants: *OED adj.* 8b)

368 **his** the liquor's; see 177n.
369 **roll** turn in their sockets to allow sight (*OED v.²* 21a); cf. *Luc* 368, *MV* 3.2.116–18.
   wonted accustomed
370–1 Oberon predicts the lovers' actual reaction (4.1.191–3), and more tellingly (as Holland observes), Robin's account of the play's action (5.1.414–18).
370 **derision** perhaps meaning the jibes and abuse exchanged by the lovers; possibly a printing error for 'division', conflict
371 **fruitless** 'of no consequence in the world of reality' (Doran)
373 The line echoes the Anglican marriage service, where the couple pledge to stay together 'till deth vs depart' (= divide: *Book of Common Prayer*, Cambridge, 1549, sig. 2B3ʳ⁻ᵛ) – a piquant allusion from the lips of an 'immortal'.
   league (marriage) union
   date duration, term

Whiles I in this affair do thee employ,
I'll to my queen and beg her Indian boy;   375
And then I will her charmed eye release
From monster's view, and all things shall be peace.

ROBIN

My fairy lord, this must be done with haste,
For night's swift dragons cut the clouds full fast
And yonder shines Aurora's harbinger,   380
At whose approach ghosts, wandering here and
there,
Troop home to churchyards. Damned spirits all,
That in cross-ways and floods have burial,
Already to their wormy beds are gone.
For fear lest day should look their shames upon,   385
They wilfully themselves exile from light,
And must for ay consort with black-browed night.

---

374 **employ** For the chain of variants 'imploy ... apply ... imply' across QF, cf. the shift from 'heare' to 'here', 164. Q1 *imply* (= involve: *OED* 1) makes sense, but this usage is not recorded after 1475.

375 **I'll to** I'll go to

376 **charmed** (charmèd) enchanted, bound by a spell

377 **view** sight of, proximity to

378–82 In some productions (Guthrie, Barton, Caird) Robin shows real fear, adding another sinister touch to the woodland setting – the more so in occurring at the approach of daylight.

379 **night's swift dragons** In *Met.* 7.218–9 (Golding, 7.287–8), a chariot drawn by winged dragons descends in response to Medea's prayers to Night and Hecate. Cf. 'dragons of the night', *Cym* 2.2.48; and as drawing the moon's chariot, Marlowe, *Hero and Leander*, 1.108.

380 **Aurora's harbinger** the morning star. Aurora or Eos was goddess of the dawn. See 61n.

381–2 Cf. 5.1.369–72.

382 **Damned spirits** suicides buried in unconsecrated ground like cross-roads, or carried away on the stream (*floods*, 383) if they drowned themselves. Such spirits retreat even more hurriedly than those ceremonially buried in churchyards. This is another incursion of Christian beliefs in a notionally pagan setting: cf. 1.1.70–8n. **Damned** *Damnéd*

384 **wormy** infested with carrion-feeding worms

386–7 From Thirlby (224) onwards, it has been observed that these lines suit Oberon better. A misplaced SP is possible, but there is no ground for assuming it

386 **wilfully** (1) willingly, deliberately; (2) perversely, obstinately
exile F 'dxile' may incorrectly reflect a marginal revision to *exild* in the manuscript newly consulted (Brooks). 'Wilfully exiled' suggests the revolt of the fallen angels.

387 **ay** ever

---

374 employ] *(imploy);* apply *Q2;* imply *F*   379 night's swift] night swift *Q2;* night-swift *F*   384–5 gone: / ... upon,] gone, / ... upon; *Alexander*   385 lest] *(least QF)*   386 exile] dxile *F;* exil'd *Alexander (Thirlby, 224)*

OBERON

But we are spirits of another sort.
I with the morning's love have oft made sport,
And like a forester the groves may tread   390
Even till the eastern gate, all fiery red,
Opening on Neptune with fair blessed beams,
Turns into yellow gold his salt green streams.
But notwithstanding, haste, make no delay.   394
We may effect this business yet ere day.   [*Exit.*]

ROBIN

Up and down, up and down,
I will lead them up and down.
I am feared in field and town.
Goblin, lead them up and down.
Here comes one.   400

388–95 Oberon can be out till sunrise, whereas the unquiet spirits must return as soon as the morning star appears; cf. 2.1.267n.

388 **spirits** See 2.1.1n.

another sort Lander (46) compares Greenham, 74 (sig. F5ᵛ): 'hee thought they [fairies] were spirits: but he distinguished betweene them and other spirits, as commonly men distinguish betweene good witches and bad witches'.

389 **with ... sport** (1) jested at or with Tithonus, Aurora's eternally aged spouse; (2) hunted with Cephalus, whom Aurora loved and attempted to seduce (see 5.1.197n.); (3) dallied with Aurora herself

390 **forester** probably a forest-dweller (*OED* 3a) rather than a forest guard or gamekeeper like the one summoned by Theseus at 4.1.102

391 **eastern gate** Aurora's purple gates in *Met.*

2.113 (Golding, 2.152), opened to release the dawn light

392 **Neptune** i.e. the sea, whose god Neptune is **blessed** blessèd. See 1.1.74n.

395 *SD There is no SD marking Oberon's exit. This is the obvious place for one.

396–9 Q1 prints as two lines spanning the page, which might have misled Q2 and F into printing 396–400 as prose. No doubt sung by Robin, the lines provide an 'air' in Garrick's *Fairies*, and the nucleus of an item in the Duke Ellington album *Such Sweet Thunder.* This seems the point where Robin spreads darkness and fog as enjoined by Oberon.

396 **Up and down** obvious sexual overtones, perhaps accompanied with appropriate gestures by Robin; cf. 121n.

399 **Goblin** Presumably Robin likes the name, as he applies it to himself; cf. *Hobgoblin*, 2.1.40n.

395 SD] *Rowe (Exit Oberon.); not in QF*   396–400] *so lined, Pope; Q1 lines* ³down: / ⁴downe. / one. /; *prose Q2, F.*   396–9] *indented, Capell*

Enter LYSANDER.

LYSANDER
Where art thou, proud Demetrius? Speak thou now.

ROBIN
Here, villain, drawn and ready. Where art thou?

LYSANDER
I will be with thee straight.

ROBIN   Follow me then
To plainer ground.

> [*Exit Lysander, as though following Demetrius.*]

Enter DEMETRIUS.

DEMETRIUS   Lysander, speak again.
Thou runaway, thou coward, art thou fled?   405
Speak: in some bush? Where dost thou hide thy head?

ROBIN
Thou coward, art thou bragging to the stars,
Telling the bushes that thou look'st for wars,
And wilt not come? Come, recreant, come, thou child.
I'll whip thee with a rod: he is defiled   410
That draws a sword on thee.

DEMETRIUS   Yea, art thou there?

ROBIN
Follow my voice. We'll try no manhood here.   *Exeunt.*

401–30 Brook mounted Robin on stilts, with Demetrius and Lysander rushing about between his legs.

402 **drawn** with drawn sword

404 **plainer** clearer, more open (*OED adj.¹* 2a, c), hence suitable for a duel

404 *SD Demetrius' taunt (405–6) indicates that Lysander rushes off at this point to return at 412.1. Robin makes the two men play hide-and-seek with each other, as he confused the fleeing artisans in 3.1.102–7.

406 ***in some bush?** i.e. Are you hiding in a bush?

409 **recreant** one who admits defeat
child in obvious contempt; cf. Aufidius' addressing Coriolanus as 'boy of tears' (*Cor* 5.6.103).

412 **try no manhood** not test your courage or fighting skill

403–4] *so lined, Theobald; QF line* straight. / ground. / againe. / 404 SD] *Theobald (Lys. goes out, as following Dem.); not in QF* 406 Speak: . . . bush?] *Capell (subst.);* Speake . . . bush. *QF* 412 SD] *Exit. F*

[*Enter* LYSANDER.]

LYSANDER

He goes before me, and still dares me on;
When I come where he calls, then he is gone.
The villain is much lighter heeled than I: 415
I followed fast, but faster he did fly,   *shifting places*
That fallen am I in dark uneven way,
And here will rest me.   *(Lie[s] down.)*
                                    Come, thou gentle day,
For if but once thou show me thy gray light,
I'll find Demetrius, and revenge this spite.   [*Sleeps.*]   420

Enter ROBIN *and* DEMETRIUS.

ROBIN

Ho, ho, ho! Coward, why com'st thou not?
DEMETRIUS

Abide me, if thou dar'st. For well I wot,
Thou run'st before me, shifting every place,
And dar'st not stand nor look me in the face.
Where art thou now?
ROBIN   Come hither. I am here.   425
DEMETRIUS

Nay then, thou mockst me. Thou shalt buy this dear

412.1 *See 404n.
413 Oxf begins a new scene here. This seems unwarranted, given that the three characters are rushing in and out both before and after this point on a scenically indeterminate stage.
417 **That** so that
   fallen befallen, arrived at, rather than literally fallen down
418, 420, 429–30, 436, 446–7 *SDs See 2.2.44n. Dessen (73) finds a comic effect in the lovers lying down one by one without noticing the others, who are perfectly visible to the audience.

420 **spite** insult, outrage (*OED n.* 1)
421 **Ho, ho, ho** a cry attributed to Robin Goodfellow in several ballads (e.g. *Merry Pranks*) and the 1628 chapbook *Robin Good-Fellow*, where it is his standard utterance at the end of a prank
422 **Abide** (1) wait for – i.e. don't run away; (2) face, esp. in combat (*OED v.* 5)
   wot know
424 **stand** not just halt, but take up a fighting position (*OED v.* 10)
426 **buy this dear** pay dearly for this

412.1] *Yale after Theobald (*Lysander *comes back.); not in QF*   414 he is] hee's *Q2, F*   416 SD] *F; not in Q*   418 SD] *Rowe after F (lye down.); not in Q*   420 SD] *Capell; not in QF*   420.1 *Enter*] *F; not in Q*   425 now] *not in Q2, F*

If ever I thy face by daylight see;
Now go thy way. Faintness constraineth me
To measure out my length on this cold bed.   [*Lies down.*]
By day's approach look to be visited.   [*Sleeps.*]   430

Enter HELENA.

HELENA

O weary night, O long and tedious night,
Abate thy hours. Shine, comforts, from the east,
That I may back to Athens by daylight
From these that my poor company detest;
And sleep, that sometimes shuts up sorrow's eye,   435
Steal me a while from mine own company.
[*Lies down and*] *sleep*[*s*].

ROBIN

Yet but three? Come one more.
Two of both kinds makes up four.
Here she comes, curst and sad.
Cupid is a knavish lad,   440
Thus to make poor females mad.

---

430 'Expect me to come for you before daybreak.' There is obvious comedy in Demetrius' brave words even as he droops.

431–6, 442–5 Set to music and sung in Brook's production. As in 122–33, the stanzaic form brings out the artificial, manipulated nature of the lovers' movements, contrasting with Robin's staccato, whimsical verses.

432 **Abate** shorten, reduce

*Shine, comforts, Theobald's punctuation (partly anticipated in Q1) makes Helena evoke the 'comforts' of the coming day, perhaps specifically sunlight. This is better than asking the night to shine forth daylight, as the Q2, F punctuation implies.

434 **From** parting from, leaving behind

poor (1) meagre, unsatisfying – perhaps in ironic self-deprecation; (2) suffering, abject

detest probably in the original sense: revile, execrate (*OED v.* 1)

436 **steal me** release me, separate me: the ethical dative (see 1.2.77n.)

439 **curst** probably 'afflicted, as though under a curse'; perhaps 'cross, cantankerous', or even 'shrewish' (as at 300, 341), but this suits Hermia's earlier behaviour rather than her present state.

---

429 SD] *Capell (Rowe, opp. 430); not in QF*   430 SD] *Capell; not in QF*   432 Shine, comforts,] *Theobald;* shine comforts, *Q1;* shine comforts *Q2, F*   435 sometimes] sometime *F*   436 SD *Lies down and*] *Dyce; not in QF*   sleeps] *Rowe;* Sleepe. *QF*   437–41] *indented, Capell*

Enter HERMIA.

HERMIA

Never so weary, never so in woe,
  Bedabbled with the dew, and torn with briers,
I can no further crawl, no further go;
  My legs can keep no pace with my desires.   445
Here will I rest me till the break of day.   [*Lies down.*]
Heavens shield Lysander, if they mean a fray.   [*Sleeps.*]

ROBIN [*Squeezes the juice on Lysander's eyelids.*]

    On the ground
    Sleep sound.
    I'll apply   450
    To your eye,
  Gentle lover, remedy.
    When thou wak'st,
    Thou tak'st
    True delight   455
    In the sight
  Of thy former lady's eye;
And the country proverb known,
That every man should take his own,
In your waking shall be shown.   460
    Jack shall have Jill,
    Nought shall go ill,

---

442 **Never so weary** more weary than I ever was before. See Abbott, 52.
443 **Bedabbled** Cf. 'dew-bedabbled', *VA* 703.
445 'I cannot walk any further, as I would like to do.'
459–63 As Foakes points out, this is an amalgam of three proverbs: 'Let every man have his own' (Dent, M209), 'All shall be well and Jack shall have Jill' (Dent, A164), and 'All is well and the man has his mare again' (Dent, A153).
460 **In your waking** (the events) once you wake

441.1] *Q2, F (opp. 440); not in Q1*   446 SD] *Capell, after* me *(Rowe, opp. 447); not in QF*   447 SD] *Capell; not in QF*   448–57] *lines indented by rhyme-scheme, Warburton*   448–57] *so lined, Warburton; QF line* sound: / remedy. / tak'st / eye: /   448–62] *Further indented, Capell*   448 SD] *Rowe (Squeezing . . . Eye), after 452; not in QF*   451 To] *Rowe; not in QF*   461–2] *so lined, Johnson; one line, QF*

> The man shall have his mare again, and all shall
> be well.
>   [*Exit Robin. The lovers remain onstage, sleeping.*]

[4.1]   *Enter* [TITANIA, BOTTOM] *and* FAIRIES, *and* [OBERON]
         behind them.

TITANIA

Come sit thee down upon this flowery bed
While I thy amiable cheeks do coy,

463 *SD This edn follows all others in giving Robin an exit here. The F SD also indicates a break. But the absence of an exit in QF suggests the possibility that Robin might remain onstage in the background, advancing to meet Oberon at 4.1.44.1. The SD for his entry at 4.1.44.1 would then be another example of 'double entrance' SDs (see 3.1.71n.).

The lovers remain sleeping onstage all through the fairy sequence in 4.1.1–101 and the hunting scene that follows, waking at 4.1.137. *Act* in the F SD might mean the music played in the interval between acts (*OED n.* 9b), hence the interval itself (*TxC* 279, Holland: not in *OED*). Dessen and Thomson (2) adopt the former sense, Gurr (*Stage*, 217) and Bradley (30) the latter. *Act* also readily suggests the ensuing Act 4 (though they do not sleep right through it). *Pace* Holland, this last familiar meaning of *act* is cited in *OED* (*n.* 9a) from *c.*1520, but the meaning 'music during interval' (*n.* 9b) first from the present passage. Public-stage practice in the 1590s may not have incorporated act divisions, but such divisions with intervening music were a feature of indoor performances in private playhouses. The presence of this SD suggests the later popularity of *MND* at such venues, no doubt chiefly Blackfriars; act divisions had also spread to public theatres by the date of the F SD (see pp. 320–1). For another indication of the late date of the theatrical copy consulted for F SDs, see 5.1.125.3n. See also Hosley,

'Music-Room', 118–19.

[4.1] 0.1 The scene starts in Titania's bower in the 'discovery space', where she and Bottom had retreated at the end of 3.1 and presumably remained through 3.2 (though Titania emerged at least once: see 47). The curtain hiding the recess is now drawn aside to reveal them. (Hosley suggests ('Discovery', 37) that 'Enter' in Elizabethan SDs could mean 'is discovered'.) Oberon presumably enters and watches from the side; on a second SD for his entrance, see 44.1n. On Robin's possible presence, see 3.2.463 SDn. The lovers lie sleeping all this while, presumably to one side, leaving the forestage free first for the fairies and then for the hunting party (see 2.2.44n.).

1–4 Titania's romantic affection finds formal stanzaic expression: as with the lovers' stanzaic verses (3.2.122–33, 431–6, 442–7), ironically indicating the artificial, manipulated nature of her love.

1 echoed in Dekker's *The Shoemaker's Holiday* (1599–1600): 'Here sit thou downe vpon this flowry banke' (1.2.1)

2 **amiable** lovable, sexy
coy caress (*OED v.*[1] 2). Titania's behaviour in this scene recalls the lady's in love with Lucius-as-ass in Apuleius 10.19–22. (See p. 57.) Holloway compares the *flowery bed* and roses to those the slave-girl Photis lavishes on the human Lucius (Apuleius, 2.16). Clayton (*Hole*, 18) recalls the garlanded ass in Juvenal, *Satire* 11.97–8, around whom children romp rather like the fairies here.

463 SD *Exit Robin*] Rowe (*Ex.* Puck.*); not in QF   The lovers . . . sleeping*] Cam[2] (*subst.); They sleepe all the Act. F; not in Q   **4.1**   [4.1]* Rowe (*ACT IV. SCENE I.*); *Actus Quartus. F; not in Q   0.1–2*] *this edn after QF (Enter Queene of* Faieries, *and Clowne, and* Faieries: *and the king behinde them.*)

And stick musk-roses in thy sleek smooth head,
And kiss thy fair large ears, my gentle joy.

BOTTOM   Where's Peaseblossom?   5

PEASEBLOSSOM   Ready.

BOTTOM   Scratch my head, Peaseblossom. Where's
Monsieur Cobweb?

COBWEB   Ready.

BOTTOM   Monsieur Cobweb, good Monsieur, get you   10
your weapons in your hand, and kill me a red-hipped
humble-bee on the top of a thistle; and good Monsieur,
bring me the honey-bag. Do not fret yourself too
much in the action, Monsieur; and good Monsieur,
have a care the honey-bag break not. I would be loath   15
to have you overflown with a honey-bag, Signor.
Where's Monsieur Mustardseed?

MUSTARDSEED   Ready.

BOTTOM   Give me your neaf, Monsieur Mustardseed.
Pray you, leave your courtesy, good Monsieur.   20

---

3   **musk-roses** a sad decline for the flowers adorning Titania's bower (2.1.252, 2.2.3)

4   **gentle** inappropriate to Bottom in all possible senses: highborn, of noble spirit, courteous, or soft and tender

8   **Monsieur** Bottom is comically playing the already comic 'travelled Englishman' aping foreign ways and speech, here French and later (16, 22) Italian. See *AYL* 3.2.283–6, 4.1.30–4. Taylor ('Quince', 63) notes that 'Monsieur' and 'Cavaliero' were sobriquets associated with Kemp, who probably played the part of Bottom.

11   **kill me** kill for me, kill at my behest: the ethical dative (see 1.2.77n.). Cobweb is comically conceived as a knight; cf. 'Cavalery', 22.

12–13   **humble-bee, honey-bag** see 3.1.162–3nn.

16   **overflown** drowned, perhaps also suggesting drunkenness (*OED v.* 1d, first cited from Middleton, 1607)

19   The division as verse in Q2, F is clearly wrong. Bottom always speaks prose, except when playing Pyramus.
neaf clenched hand; cf. modern 'Give me your fist'.

20   **courtesy** As the variant spellings in Q1 and Q2, F indicate, the word combines the senses of modern *courtesy* and *curtsy* (cf. 3.1.168n.): Mustardseed is bobbing up and down in obeisance. It was usually (though not exclusively) women who curtsied: the feminine gesture suits the diminutive fairy.

5+ SP BOTTOM] *Rowe; Clowne (subst.) QF*   10 you] *not in Q2, F*   19–20] *Q2, F line Mustardseed. / Mounsieur. /*   20 courtesy] *(curtsie Q1; courtesie Q2, F)*

MUSTARDSEED   What's your will?

BOTTOM   Nothing, good Monsieur, but to help Cavalery
Cobweb to scratch. I must to the barber's, Monsieur,
for methinks I am marvellous hairy about the face;
and I am such a tender ass, if my hair do but tickle me,   25
I must scratch.

TITANIA

What, wilt thou hear some music, my sweet love?

BOTTOM   I have a reasonable good ear in music. Let's
have the tongs and the bones.

Music: tongs, rural music.

TITANIA

Or say, sweet love, what thou desirest to eat.   30

BOTTOM   Truly, a peck of provender. I could munch your
good dry oats. Methinks I have a great desire to a
bottle of hay. Good hay, sweet hay, hath no fellow.

22 **Cavalery** adapting Italian *cavaliere*,
knight, used of fashionable gallants (Nares,
145); cf. 'Cavaliero Slender', *MW* 2.3.67.

23 **Cobweb** It was Peaseblossom who had
earlier been asked to scratch Bottom's
head, but consistency is not Bottom's
strong point. The alliteration with *Cavalery*
also suits *Cobweb*.

24 **marvellous hairy** Foakes observes (note
to 1.2.86(–7) that Bottom must normally be
clean-shaven if he is irked by his hairiness.
This may also explain his interest in stage
beards (1.2.83–9, 4.2.34). On *marvellous*
as adverb, cf. 3.1.2n.; on adverbs without a
final *-ly*, see 1.2.20n.

28 **good ... music** Weavers were held to be
keen singers; cf. *TN* 2.3.57–8, 'a catch
[song] that will draw three souls out of one
weaver'. Halliwell (*Introduction*, 19–20)
first noted the parallel with Midas,
punished with ass's ears for preferring
Pan's rustic music to Apollo's.

29 **tongs ... bones** crude musical devices:
metal tongs struck with a key, and bone
clappers struck or rattled against each

other. Earliest *OED* citation for both words
in this sense, but the instruments no doubt
existed and were so named earlier. Inigo
Jones has figures holding them in his
designs for the 1637 masque *Britannia
Triumphans* (Var, Oxf¹). On music in this
scene, see 82 SDn.

30 **desirest** two syllables, 'desir'st'

31 **peck** a quarter bushel
provender dry fodder, like hay or oats.
Bottom's ass-like taste in food conflicts
with his human discomfort at his hairiness.
Apuleius' Lucius retains his appetite for
human food and drink even when turned
into an ass (10.13–16). But Scot,
recounting Bodin's story of a man turned
into an ass (5.3; 95, sig. H8ʳ), later alludes
to him as an ass-headed man who 'must
either eate haie, or nothing' (5.5; 99, sig.
I2ʳ).

33 **bottle** bundle
Good ... fellow Hunter (1.296) says this
imitates 'the snatch of an old song' praising
good ale.
fellow match, equal

23 Cobweb] Pease-blossom *Rann (Grey, 1.64)*   28 Let's] *Q1 (Lets); Let vs Q2, F*   29 SD] *F; not in Q*

TITANIA

I have a venturous fairy, that shall seek
The squirrel's hoard, and fetch thee new nuts.   35

BOTTOM   I had rather have a handful or two of dried
peas. But I pray you, let none of your people stir me.
I have an exposition of sleep come upon me.

TITANIA

Sleep thou, and I will wind thee in my arms.
Fairies, be gone, and be always away.   40

[Music stops. Exeunt Fairies.]

So doth the woodbine the sweet honeysuckle
Gently entwist; the female ivy so
Enrings the barky fingers of the elm.
O how I love thee! How I dote on thee!   *[They sleep.]*

---

34   **venturous** (vent'rous) bold, venturesome
37   **stir** disturb (*OED v.* 4)
38   **exposition** malapropism for 'disposition'
40   **always** perhaps 'all ways', in all directions
(Theobald)
40   *SD We may assume that the 'rural
music' stops when the attendant fairies
leave, on Bottom asking not to be
disturbed. An exeunt for the fairies is
obviously needed, and this is the
appropriate place. It also allows Titania
seclusion for greater intimacy.
41   **woodbine ... honeysuckle** It is often
contended that the two are the same plant,
as clearly in *MA* 3.1.8, 30 (see Var; Sisson,
Readings, 1.130). But both names are also
applied to other plants. The *woodbine* may
here be the bindweed or convolvulus
(Gifford, Var 1821). Cf. Jonson, *Vision of
Delight*, 162–3: 'How the blew Binde-
weed doth it selfe infold / With Honeysuckle'. In this 1617 masque, Jonson seems

to be echoing the *MND* line as he mentally
interpreted it. Wilson suggests 'bindweed'
in the copy was misread as *woodbine*. This
could result from partial deletion and
overwriting; cf. *impress/princess*, 3.2.144.
42–3   **the ... elm** By both biblical precedent
(Psalms 128.3) and classical (Catullus,
62.48–57), it is the vine that embraces the
elm (as in *CE* 2.2.174), proverbially
standing for the wife embracing her
husband (Dent, V61). But a parallel
convention uses the ivy to represent a more
aggressively sexual, often extra-marital
love (Demetz, 528–30).
42   **entwist** earliest *OED* citation
43   **Enrings** girds or embraces, but also 'puts a
(marriage) ring on' (*OED v.* 2, earliest
citation)
barky covered with bark: earliest *OED*
citation. The 'fingers' are branches. The
soft tendrils of the ivy are contrasted with
the rough bark of the tree.

34–5] *so lined, Hanmer; Q1 lines* hoord, / nuts. /; *Q2, F line* Fairy, / hoard, / Nuts. /   40   always] all ways
Theobald   SD *Music stops] this edn; not in QF*   Exeunt Fairies] *Capell; not in QF*   44   SD] *Capell; not
in QF*

[*Oberon advances.*] *Enter* ROBIN GOODFELLOW.

OBERON
Welcome, good Robin. Seest thou this sweet sight?   45
Her dotage now I do begin to pity.
For meeting her of late behind the wood,
Seeking sweet favours for this hateful fool,
I did upbraid her, and fall out with her;
For she his hairy temples then had rounded   50
With coronet of fresh and fragrant flowers,
And that same dew, which sometime on the buds
Was wont to swell like round and orient pearls,
Stood now within the pretty flowerets' eyes
Like tears that did their own disgrace bewail.   55

44.1 *Oberon had been present in the background from the start of the scene; he now advances to greet Robin. The latter, too, might have been present from the start: see 3.2.463 SDn. Their unexpected encounter, advancing from hiding-places at opposite corners, makes for comic stage business. F has a second entry for Oberon at this point. Cf. 3.1.71n.
Oberon's watching Titania and Bottom's love-play testifies to both cruelty and voyeurism. It is one of the most unsettling features in the presentation of love and sex in this 'dream-play'.

46 **dotage** folly (in earlier use, need not imply senility)

47 **behind** in the rear or interior of. Titania, then, has not been asleep all this time.

48 **favours** love-tokens. Q2 and F, probably confusing long *s* and *f*, read 'savours', justifiable as either 'aromas' (hence flowers) or '(food of) pleasing taste'.
hateful He had earlier desired such 'hateful' consequences (2.1.258n.); cf. 62.

49 **upbraid ... out** It seems Oberon belatedly feels jealous or humiliated by his consort's behaviour. That he did not do so all this time, and still delights in the *sweet sight* (45), is no doubt owing to his sense of power, akin to a sadistic personality disorder, in bringing Titania to this pass.

50–1 This description counters the image of winter's head crowned with meagre spring buds (2.1.109 11). However preposterous, Titania's love of Bottom restores an ampler spring.

50 **rounded** encircled

51–5 **coronet ... tears** Cf. 'crowne of fresh and fragrant floures', Golding, 2.33 (*Met.* 2.27), and *Shep. Cal.* 'December', 109–12, 'fragrant flowres ... dewed with teares'.

52 **sometime** once, formerly

53 **orient** brilliant, lustrous (like pearls from the orient or East). For dew as pearls, cf. 1.1.211, 2.1.14–15.

54 **flowerets** The word occurs in *Shep. Cal.* 'November', 83.

44.1] *Capell (subst.); Enter* Robin goodfellow. *Q; Enter* Robin goodfellow and Oberon. *F*   48 favours] *Q1;* sauors *Q2, F*   54 flowerets'] *(flouriets QF)*

229

When I had at my pleasure taunted her,
And she, in mild terms, begged my patience,
I then did ask of her her changeling child,
Which straight she gave me, and her fairy sent
To bear him to my bower in fairy land.   60
And now I have the boy, I will undo
This hateful imperfection of her eyes.
And gentle puck, take this transformed scalp
From off the head of this Athenian swain,
That he, awaking when the other do,   65
May all to Athens back again repair,
And think no more of this night's accidents
But as the fierce vexation of a dream.
But first I will release the Fairy Queen.
[*Squeezes the juice on her eyelids.*]
    Be as thou wast wont to be.   70
    See as thou wast wont to see.
    Dian's bud o'er Cupid's flower
    Hath such force and blessed power.
Now, my Titania, wake you, my sweet queen.
TITANIA [*Wakes.*]
    My Oberon, what visions have I seen!   75

56–7 more evidence of Oberon's sadistic sense of power
57 **patience** three syllables
58 **changeling** See 2.1.23n.
63 **transformed** transformèd
64 **swain** rustic (*OED* 4), but with an ironic tinge of 'country gallant or lover' (*OED* 5)
65 **other** commonly used in the plural (Abbott, 12)
66 **all** along with them, all together
67 **accidents** happenings, events (*OED n.* 5b), but tinged with the usual modern sense of 'mishaps'
68 **vexation** disturbance, confusion
72 **Dian's bud** No botanical support is needed for opposing Diana and Cupid, but

Shakespeare may have thought of the *Artemisia*, named after Artemis or Diana; and/or the vitex, *agnus castus* or 'chaste tree' in Pliny, *Natural History*, 24.38 and the pseudo-Chaucerian *The Flower and the Leaf*, 472–6 (included in Speght's 1598 edition of Chaucer). Thomas Bradshaw's *The Shepherd's Star* (1591) calls the amaranthus '*Dianas* herbe' (Otten).
*o'er *o'er* (o'r) gives the correct sense, and is easily misread as QF 'or'.
73 **blessed** blessèd. See 1.1.74n.
74–5 **my ... Oberon** The exchange of *my*s indicates renewed love and harmony between Oberon and Titania. Cf. Hippolyta's *my Theseus*, 5.1.1.

69 SD] *Ard²; touching her Eyes with an Herb. / Capell; not in QF*   70–3] *indented, Q1; italicized, Q2*   70 Be as] *Be thou as F*   72 o'er] *Theobald (Thirlby); or QF*   75 SD] *Wells; not in QF*

Methought I was enamoured of an ass.

OBERON

There lies your love.

TITANIA   How came these things to pass?

O, how mine eyes do loathe his visage now!

OBERON

Silence a while. Robin, take off this head.

Titania, music call, and strike more dead   80

Than common sleep of all these five the sense.

TITANIA

Music, ho, music, such as charmeth sleep.   *Music still.*

ROBIN [*Takes the ass-head off Bottom.*]

Now, when thou wak'st, with thine own fool's eyes
    peep.

---

76 **enamoured of** The recollection is even more disturbing than it seems. *Enamoured of* can mean 'in love with', and is so used by Titania in 3.1.134. In 78, Titania implicitly admits her earlier infatuation with the ass-headed Bottom. But *enamoured of* more commonly meant 'loved by': see *OED* of *prep.* 14, including the sectional note. For the implications, see p. 82.

79 **Silence** presumably meaning a halt to their speech; the 'rural music' must have stopped earlier (see 40 SDn.). Oberon does not wish to discuss Titania's experience further.

80–1 **strike ... sleep** make more deeply unconscious than in normal sleep

81 ***five** the four lovers and Bottom. QF 'fine' is explained by a minim error for 'fiue'.

82 **charmeth** magically induces

82 ***SD** *still* perhaps (1) continuing without a break (through the ensuing dance), as at 3.1.149 or 'Storm still' (*KL* 3.2.0), 'Alarum still' (*JC* 5.5.29); but more likely (2) soft, soothing (especially of music· *OED adj.* 3b) to 'charm' the sleepers, unlike the more lively music that Oberon demands for their dance (84). Both senses of *still* were used for music SDs (Dessen and Thomson, 216). This fairy music, marking the reconciliation of Oberon and Titania, contrasts with the crude music of tongs and bones while Titania was couching with Bottom. To accommodate such varied types of music in a short span is a challenge for the producer, and one or more are sometimes omitted.

78 do] doth *Q2, F*   his] this *Q2, F*   79 this] his *F*   81 sleep ... five] *Theobald (Thirlby);* sleepe: of all these, fine *QF*   82 SD] *F; not in Q*   83 SD] *Ard²* after *Cam¹ (he plucks the ass's head from him); not in QF*   Now] *not in Q2, F*

OBERON

    Sound music. Come, my queen, take hands with me,

    And rock the ground whereon these sleepers be.   85

    [*They dance.*]

    Now thou and I are new in amity,

    And will tomorrow midnight solemnly

    Dance in Duke Theseus' house triumphantly,

    And bless it to all fair prosperity.

    There shall the pairs of faithful lovers be   90

    Wedded, with Theseus, all in jollity.

ROBIN

        Fairy king, attend and mark:

        I do hear the morning lark.

OBERON

        Then, my queen, in silence sad,

        Trip we after night's shade.   95

        We the globe can compass soon,

        Swifter than the wandering moon.

84–91 The dance symbolizes the renewed concord of Oberon and Titania, hence of the natural order disturbed by their quarrel. Oberon also promises a dance at the human weddings to follow. Dance is a familiar symbol of both human and cosmic harmony; for an elaborate contemporary account, see Sir John Davies, *Orchestra* (written 1594, pub. 1596), stanzas 111–12. The eight consecutive lines with a single rhyme also convey agreement or concord.

85 rock the ground implies energetic dancing (as strikingly in Tim Supple's production), contrasting with the earlier sleep-inducing music; but Holland suggests a soothing dance to lull the sleepers, 'rocking' the ground like a cradle. Brook reduced the dance to a few sedate steps.

86 thou The intimate *thou* reflects their reconciliation.

87 tomorrow midnight Strictly, this should

mean not midnight of the day about to break but the one following it; but clearly, the former is meant.

solemnly ceremonially

88 triumphantly in a festive or ceremonial spirit; cf. *triumph*, 1.1.19n.

89 prosperity This agrees with 2.1.73; but Q2, F 'posterity' deserves consideration, especially in view of 5.1.395–404.

91 with Theseus at the same time as Theseus

92–101 Another notable example of the fairies' short rhymed couplets; cf. 3.2.110–21. See pp. 110–11.

92 attend listen (*OED v.* 1b)

94 sad regretful, as befits a last dance now that night is over. The usual explanation 'sober, serious' does not suit *Trip* (95), to dance or skip.

95 For the slightly irregular metre, see 2.1.7n. and pp. 308–9.

96–7 Cf. 2.1.7n., 175–6n.

85 SD] *Cam¹; not in QF*   89 prosperity] posterity *Q2, F*   92–101] *indented, Capell*   92 Fairy] Faire *F*   95 night's] the nights *Q2, F;* nightës *Oxf*

TITANIA

Come, my lord, and in our flight,
Tell me how it came this night
That I sleeping here was found   100
With these mortals on the ground.

Exeunt [Oberon, Titania and Robin. The lovers and
Bottom remain sleeping.]

Wind horns. Enter THESEUS, HIPPOLYTA, EGEUS *and*
[the Duke's] train.

THESEUS

Go one of you, find out the forester;
For now our observation is performed,
And since we have the vaward of the day,
My love shall hear the music of my hounds.   105

101 *SD Bottom continues to sleep in the 'discovery space' at the back; perhaps the fairies draw the curtain across it as they leave. Hence he remains undiscovered by Theseus and his band appear, as also by the lovers, and emerges only after their departure.

101.1 *The SD follows the logical order of events as in the F SD: horns are heard before Theseus and his band appear. Q has 'Winde horne(s)' in the right margin, and 'Enter *Theseus* and all his traine' centred on the same line. In such cases, the marginal SD represents the earlier action; cf. F SDs at 198n. and 2.2.69n. The Q2, F reading *hornes* is adopted rather than Q1 'horne' in accord with *horns* at 127 and 127 SD.

Productions that double Theseus with Oberon and Hippolyta with Titania face a challenge here, as one couple enters immediately on the other's exit. They

might openly change their outer garments, as in Brook's production, or else there must be some contrivance like rearranging the lines (e.g. bringing Bottom's speech forward from 189 to 92, giving the other actors time to change offstage). Cooper ('Anomalies', 7) suggests that winding the horn was an elaborate musical exercise, allowing enough time for a change of costume.

Wind blow

103 **observation** of the rites of May: a relic of *KnT*, like Theseus' love of hunting (*KnT* 1673–82); cf. *observance*, 1.1.167 and n.

104 **vaward** early part, start (*OED* 1c); cf. 'the vaward of our youth', *2H4* 1.2.177–8.

105 Continues the motif of music even in hunting, a version of the 'concord in discord' theme running through the play. See 111–17n., 117n., 122–3n., 142n., 5.1.60n.

101 SD *Oberon . . . Robin*] *Cam² (subst.); not in QF The . . . sleeping*] *this edn after Ard² (The four lovers and Bottom still lie asleep.); Sleepers Lye still. F, after 100; not in Q 101.1–2*] *this edn after Capell (Horns wind within. / Enter . . .* EGEUS, *and Train.); Enter Theseus and all his traine. (centred) Winde horne [hornes Q2]. (right margin) Q; Winde Hornes. (right margin) / Enter Theseus, Egeus, Hippolita and all his traine. (centred, next line) F*

Uncouple in the western valley, let them go.
Dispatch, I say, and find the forester.

                 [*Exit an Attendant.*]

We will, fair queen, up to the mountain's top,
And mark the musical confusion
Of hounds and echo in conjunction.   110

HIPPOLYTA

I was with Hercules and Cadmus once
When in a wood of Crete they bayed the bear
With hounds of Sparta. Never did I hear
Such gallant chiding; for besides the groves,
The skies, the fountains, every region near   115

---

106 **Uncouple** let loose (from being leashed or haltered in couples)

109 **confusion** (four syllables, like *conjunction*, 110) fusion, mingling (*OED* 7a, b), but with a hint of the usual sense of 'disorder' which, linked to *musical*, again suggests 'concord in discord'.

111–17 Hippolyta's hunting career recalls her past as the spirited Amazon queen. More radically, it aligns her with the huntress Diana, goddess of virginity, hence a figure opposed to marriage. Thus her presence alongside Theseus also presents a 'concord in discord'; cf. 5.1.60n.

111 **Hercules** Theseus' kinsman, admired by him as a model of valour (Plutarch, 6.6–7; North, 4, sig. A2ᵛ); see 5.1.44n. Hippolyta's recalling him as her associate underscores her (possibly competitive) spiritedness.
    Cadmus legendary founder of Thebes; in mythic chronology, earlier than Hercules, Theseus and Hippolyta. No classical source records a meeting of these characters.

112–13 **Crete . . . Sparta** both celebrated for their hounds. See Virgil, *Georgics*, 3.405 for Spartan dogs; *Met.* 3.206–25 (Golding, 3.245–72) and Seneca, *Phaedra*, 31–43 for Cretan and Spartan hounds, and descriptions of hunting-dogs generally that may underlie this passage. See also 109–10n.

112 **bayed** made (the bear) stand at bay, cornered it
    bear The proposed change to 'boar' recalls Hercules' capture of the Erymanthian boar, one of his twelve labours, and the killing of the Calydonian boar. Hippolyta and the Amazons are not connected with either legend, though the Calydonian boar was first wounded by a woman, Atalanta. But enough references to bear-hunts have been cited to support the original reading (see Var 185).

114 **chiding** angry noise, especially of hounds (*OED n.* 3, earliest citation)
    besides the groves i.e. not just the groves or woods but all nature

115 **fountains** Mountains are more commonly said to yield echoes; but Theobald notes classical passages, including *Aen.* 12.756–7 and *Met.* 3.495–501 (Golding, 3.625–8), where rivers, lakes etc. do the same.

---

107 SD] *Dyce; not in QF*   112 bear] boar *Hanmer (Theobald, Letter, 235)*   115 fountains] mountains *Ardⁱ (Theobald, dismissed conj.)*

Seemed all one mutual cry. I never heard
So musical a discord, such sweet thunder.

THESEUS

My hounds are bred out of the Spartan kind:
So flewed, so sanded, and their heads are hung
With ears that sweep away the morning dew;   120
Crook-kneed, and dewlapped like Thessalian bulls,
Slow in pursuit, but matched in mouth like bells,
Each under each. A cry more tunable
Was never holloed to nor cheered with horn

---

116 *Seemed The present-tense 'Seeme' in QF
   is hard to justify, though it conveys a sense
   of immediacy. F2 *Seem'd* is a plausible
   emendation; as Taylor ('Crux', 49) notes,
   confusion of final -*e* and -*d* is very common.
   mutual combined, but also reciprocal,
   echoing one another
   cry call of hounds
117 Two instances of oxymoron in one line,
   underscoring the theme of 'concord in
   discord'. This contradicts Theseus' jocular
   dismissal of such paradoxes in the
   description of *Pyramus and Thisbe*
   (5.1.56–60), using the very word *discord*.
   Duke Ellington named an album *Such
   Sweet Thunder*.
118 **kind** strain, breed (*OED n.* 10a)
119–20 Cf. Grattius' (63 BCE – 14 CE)
   Latin hunting-poem *Cynegeticon*, trans.
   Christopher Wase (1654), sig. B2ᵛ: 'their
   hairy ear's hung low, / Their mouth be deep,
   and flashing fervour blow / From open
   flews'. Grattius celebrates Sparta and Crete
   for hounds and Thessaly for horses (sigs
   A11ᵛ–12ʳ). Wase's commentary (sig. F10ᵛ)
   says a hound's long, hanging ears and upper
   lips indicate 'a merry deep mouth, and a
   loud ringer'. See also Baldwin, 'Pups'.
119 **flewed** with flews, a hound's pronounced
   lower jaws and cheeks. The word occurs in
   Golding (3.269).

sanded of a sandy colour
120 **sweep ... dew** Echoed in Heywood's
   description of 'fierce *Thessalian* hounds' in
   The Brazen Age (1613), 2.2 (sig. D1ᵛ), no
   doubt imitating this passage.
121 **Crook-kneed** with knees curving outward.
   Wase (see 109–10n.) describes the good
   hound as 'high knuckled' (sig. F10ᵛ).
   dewlapped See 2.1.50n.
   Thessalian bulls Fighting wild bulls was a
   sport in ancient Thessaly.
122–3 Continues the motif of music in hunting-
   dogs (see 105n.), and the general theme of
   'concord in discord'. Theseus seems to
   value the 'music' of his hounds no less than
   their speed or hunting skill. For sources
   of the idea, see *Shakespeare's England*,
   2.347. Brooks compares Kalander's
   hounds in Sidney's *New Arcadia* (54.22–4):
   'so well-sorted mouths that any man
   would perceive therein some kind of
   proportion, but the skilful woodmen did
   find a music'.
122 **matched in mouth** with their voices in
   harmony; but *matched* also = equal, on a
   par
123 **Each under each** each one a note lower
   than the last – i.e. literally musical
   cry (1) the hounds' call; (2) a pack of
   hounds (*OED n.* 13a, earliest citation)
124 **holloed to** urged on with hulloos

116 Seemed] *F2;* Seeme *QF*   124 holloed] *(*hollowd *Q); hallowed F*

235

In Crete, in Sparta, nor in Thessaly.   125
Judge when you hear. But soft: what nymphs are
  these?

EGEUS

My lord, this my daughter here asleep,
And this Lysander, this Demetrius is,
This Helena, old Nedar's Helena.
I wonder of their being here together.   130

THESEUS

No doubt they rose up early, to observe
The rite of May; and hearing our intent,
Came here in grace of our solemnity.
But speak, Egeus, is not this the day
That Hermia should give answer of her choice?   135

EGEUS

It is, my lord.

---

125 **Crete, Sparta** See 112–13n., 119–20n.
  Thessaly Julius Pollux's Greek thesaurus *Onomasticon* (second century CE, first printed in 1502) contains an epitaph attributed to Simonides for a Thessalian hound (Epigram 69), but it is doubtful whether Shakespeare could have known this. He may be mistakenly associating Thessaly with the Calydonian or the Erymanthian boar (see 112n.), as in *AC* 4.13.2. This subconscious association would support the reading 'boar' for *bear* in 112.

126 It seems unreal that Theseus should take so long to notice the sleeping lovers; but we may imagine the hunting party as moving through the woods all this time, and reaching the spot only now. They had occupied the forestage, while the lovers lay sleeping further back. (See 0.1n., 2.2.44n.)
  nymphs young women or girls, but Theseus may be jokingly suggesting actual nature-goddesses (contrasting with Egeus' matter-of-fact 'my daughter').

127 **this** In Q1, an *is* might have dropped out after *this* by haplography; but as the singular *is* in 128 covers *Lysander* and *Demetrius*, it can also cover *daughter*. The slight resultant irregularity of metre is common in the play, especially in Q1; see pp. 308–9.

132 ***rite of May** QF 'right' (prerogative, entitlement) is a different word, but conflated with *rite*: see *OED* right *n.* 15a, citing this passage as 'intentional wordplay'. On May Day vis-à-vis Midsummer, see pp. 88–9. Maying rites were observed throughout the month.
  our intent to come here

133 **in grace of** in honour or regard of (*OED* grace *n.* P3b, only citation in this sense)
  solemnity ceremony: presumably the hunt, seen as a festivity or celebration connected with Maying. (They return to Athens for their marriage ceremony, 179–85.) Chaucer uses the phrase 'great solemnity' four times, twice in *KnT* (870, 2702); cf. 184 and *solemnities*, 1.1.11.

---

127 this] this is *Q2, F*   130 their] this *Q2, F*   132 rite] *Pope;* right *QF*

THESEUS

Go, bid the huntsmen wake them with their horns.

[Exit an Attendant.] Shout within. Wind horns.
The lovers all start up.

THESEUS

Good morrow, friends. Saint Valentine is past.
Begin these wood-birds but to couple now?

LYSANDER

Pardon, my lord.   *[The lovers kneel.]*

THESEUS   I pray you all, stand up.   140

I know you two are rival enemies.
How comes this gentle concord in the world,
That hatred is so far from jealousy
To sleep by hate, and fear no enmity?

LYSANDER

My lord, I shall reply amazedly,   145
Half sleep, half waking; but as yet, I swear,

137.1–2 *SD F has two overlapping SDs, probably combining material from another manuscript with the Q SD.

138 **Saint Valentine** His day is 14 February, long before both May Day and Midsummer. Proverbially (Dent, S66), birds were said to choose their mates and start nesting on that day. Holland notes the Valentine's Day practices of 'a mock-betrothal, a marriage for a day with the partners chosen by lots' (Laroque, 106–7), and of 'a woman being obliged to take as her valentine the first man she sees, a practice with strong resonances' for *MND*.

139 **wood-birds** *OED wood n.¹* C1.b(a)(ii); perhaps punning on *wood*, mad, as in 2.1.192

140 *SD The lovers would kneel out of deference to the Duke, and still more as pleading for pardon. Theseus cannot

simply be asking them to rise from the ground where they are lying down; they would hardly ask his pardon from that position.

141 **you two** Lysander and Demetrius. Theseus is unaware that his words apply equally to Hermia and Helena; their sexual identities, though apparent at home, have been asserted in the wood in a way the patriarch cannot begin to imagine.

142 **concord** The general theme of concord and discord is explicitly touched upon; see 105n.

143 **jealousy** suspicion, mistrust

144 **by hate** next to someone who hates you

145 **amazedly** (amazèdly) in a confused or bewildered way

146 **waking** perhaps a noun (the state of being awake), to match *sleep*; but Lysander may not be capable of a rounded, balanced construction in his befuddled state.

137.1 SD *Exit an Attendant.*] Dyce; *not in QF*   137.1–2 *Shout . . . up.*] *Kittredge after Q (*Shoute within: they all start vp. Winde hornes.*); Hornes and they wake. (right margin) / Shout within, they all start vp. (centred, next line) F*   140 SD] *Ard² after Capell (*He [Lysander], and the rest, kneel to Theseus.*); not in QF*

237

I cannot truly say how I came here.
But as I think (for truly would I speak),
And now I do bethink me, so it is,
I came with Hermia hither. Our intent   150
Was to be gone from Athens, where we might
Without the peril of the Athenian law –

EGEUS

Enough, enough, my lord; you have enough.
I beg the law, the law, upon his head.
They would have stolen away, they would,
       Demetrius,   155
Thereby to have defeated you and me:
You of your wife, and me of my consent,
Of my consent that she should be your wife.

DEMETRIUS

My lord, fair Helen told me of their stealth,
Of this their purpose hither to this wood,   160
And I in fury hither followed them,
Fair Helena in fancy following me.
But my good lord, I wot not by what power
(But by some power it is) my love to Hermia,
Melted as the snow, seems to me now   165
As the remembrance of an idle gaud,

---

152 **Without** (1) free of, unencumbered by; (2)
   outside, beyond
   *The comma after *law* in Q1 indicates that
   Egeus breaks in angrily before Lysander
   can finish (Dyce). The full stop in Q2 and
   F, with 'be' (151) to fill out the sentence,
   misses this dramatic point.
153–8 On Egeus' tendency to repeat words
   when excited, see 1.1.28n.
155 **stolen** one syllable (QF 'stolne'); cf.
   1.1.32n.

156 **defeated** defrauded, hoodwinked (*OED v.* 7a)
158 Egeus' ploy to enlist Demetrius' support is
   undermined by this giveaway that he regards
   the latter's wishes as subject to Egeus' own.
159 **stealth** See 3.2.310n.
161 **fury** (1) anger; (2) madness
162 **in fancy** out of love (opposed to *in fury*,
   161: Johnson), but also implying 'on an
   impulse or whim'
163 **wot not** do not know
166 **gaud** toy, trifle; cf. 1.1.33.

---

151 might] might be *Q2, F*   152 law –] *Collier;* lawe, *Q1;* Law. *Q2, F*   155 stolen] *(*stolne
QF)   162 following] followed *Q2, F*   164–6] *so lined, Pope; QF line* loue, / snowe) / gaude, /

238

Which in my childhood I did dote upon;
And all the faith, the virtue of my heart,
The object and the pleasure of mine eye,
Is only Helena. To her, my lord,   170
Was I betrothed ere I see Hermia;
But like in sickness did I loathe this food.
But as in health, come to my natural taste,
Now I do wish it, love it, long for it,
And will for evermore be true to it.   175

THESEUS

Fair lovers, you are fortunately met.
Of this discourse we more will hear anon.
Egeus, I will overbear your will;
For in the temple, by and by, with us,
These couples shall eternally be knit.   180
And for the morning now is something worn,
Our purposed hunting shall be set aside.
Away with us to Athens. Three and three,
We'll hold a feast in great solemnity.
Come, Hippolyta.   185

Exeunt Theseus, [Hippolyta, Egeus and train.]

168 **virtue** strength or energy, perhaps with an added sense of higher impulses, 'the best part of my being'

170 **Is** rests in, is identified with

171 **see** *See* in the past tense was a recognized form; cf. *LLL* 4.1.69–70, *2H4* 3.2.29 (Q text), and see Blake, 4.2.4.1(c). But here it may be in the present tense, to convey immediacy.

172 ***in sickness** Farmer's emendation makes ready sense, and agrees with 'in health', 173.

176 **fortunately met** (1) with each other, in true partnership at last; (2) with Theseus, as he can approve their union

177 **anon** presently, by and by; cf. 3.2.18n.

178 Theseus reverses his earlier stand that he cannot 'extenuate' the law (1.1.120). Rather than seek factual or psychological explanations, this change may be attributed to the customary looseness of romantic plot-construction, in Shakespeare and elsewhere.
overbear overrule

181 **something worn** well advanced

184 **feast** probably not just a banquet but a celebration or festivity generally (*OED n.* 5)
solemnity ceremony. See 133n., 1.1.11n.

185 ***SD** Noble made Egeus leave separately from the others and not reappear in Act 5, implicitly following the Q text.

171 see Hermia] did see *Hermia / Rowe; Hermia* saw *Rowe²*   172 in] *Var 1793 (Farmer);* a *QF*   174 I do] do I *Q2, F*   177 more will hear] *(*more will here*);* will heare more *Q2;* shall heare more *F*   184–5] *so lined, Q2, F; one line, Q1*   185 SD] *Capell; Exit. Q2; Exit Duke and Lords. F; not in Q1*

DEMETRIUS

These things seem small and undistinguishable,
Like far-off mountains turned into clouds.

HERMIA

Methinks I see these things with parted eye,
When everything seems double.

HELENA   So methinks;
And I have found Demetrius, like a jewel   190
Mine own, and not mine own.

DEMETRIUS   Are you sure
That we are awake? It seems to me
That yet we sleep, we dream. Do not you think
The duke was here, and bid us follow him?

HERMIA

Yea, and my father.

HELENA   And Hippolyta.   195

LYSANDER

And he did bid us follow to the temple.

DEMETRIUS

Why then, we are awake. Let's follow him,

---

186 **undistinguishable** See 2.1.100.

187 **turned** turnèd

188 **parted** divided or unfocused, looking in
different directions at once

189 **everything ... double** perhaps because
they now constitute two happy couples; but
perhaps, more depressingly, because their
union still seems uncertain (191–3). The
lovers express doubt and bewilderment all
through this dialogue, rather than joy at
having found their partners at last.

190–1 **like ... ²own** like a jewel found by
chance and kept without secure title
(Malone, comparing *AC* 4.12.8–9: 'hope

and fear / Of what he has and has not').
Helena is still unsure of Demetrius' firm
love.

191–2 **Are ... awake?** not in F. The verse
scans more smoothly as a result, but the
metrical irregularity in the Q text of 191
can be explained by a wondering pause
before Demetrius begins to speak.

196 Q1 *did* was probably deleted mistakenly in
Q2, F as a duplication of *bid*.

197–8 *The lovers speak in verse throughout
this scene, justifying Rowe's line-division.

197 **Why then** i.e. seeing that all their accounts
tally; cf. 5.1.23–7.

191–2 Are . . . awake?] *not in F*   196 did] *not in Q2, F*   197–8] *so lined, Rowe²; prose QF*

And by the way let us recount our dreams.

                           [Exeunt] lovers.

Bottom wakes.

BOTTOM When my cue comes, call me, and I will
answer. My next is, 'Most fair Pyramus'. Heigh-ho! 200
Peter Quince? Flute the bellows-mender? Snout the
tinker? Starveling? Gods my life! Stolen hence, and
left me asleep? I have had a most rare vision. I have
had a dream, past the wit of man to say what dream it
was. Man is but an ass if he go about to expound this 205
dream. Methought I was – there is no man can tell
what. Methought I was – and methought I had – but
man is but a patched fool if he will offer to say what

---

198 **by the way** as we go
    *let us Q2, F let us is metrically better.
    Eye-skip from 197 could account for a
    second 'lets' in Q1.
198 *SD1, SD2 F has '*Exit Louers*' in the right
    hand margin, with 'Bottome wakes'
    centred on the same line, suggesting the
    latter is the later action. See 101.1n.,
    2.2.69.1n.
199 Bottom returns to the point of time where
    he left off at the rehearsal (Foakes); the
    interim has taken on the nature of a dream.
200 **Heigh-ho** The QF spelling 'Hey ho'
    heightens the possibility of a play on 'hay',
    and also the imitation of an ass's bray.
202 **Gods my life** God save my life: *OED* god
    n. P.1.c(b)(ii), earliest citation
203–4 **vision ... dream** On the lack of

distinction between these two words, see
p. 78, n.2.
205 **go about** set about, undertake to
206 **'I was ... I had** Bottom hesitates before
    continuing with 'an ass' and 'ass's ears'
    respectively. In many productions (at least
    since Phelps; Sprague, 53), he feels his ears
    at this point, or even finds hay in his pouch
    (Griffiths, 185–6). He may also find
    Titania's flowers, or otherwise think of her
    – movingly at the end of Hoffman's film,
    where he looks out at a swarm of fairy
    lights that might be fireflies, and recalls the
    fairy world. *I had* might even refer to
    Titania.
208 ***patched fool** a clown in patched or
    motley dress; cf. *patches*, 3.2.9n.

---

198 let us] *Q2, F;* lets *Q1* SD1] *F (Exit Louers.), in right margin; Exit. Q2; not in Q1; Exeunt.*
Rowe SD2] *F (before Exit Louers. / centred on same line); not in Q* 200 Heigh-ho] *(Hey ho QF)*
203–4 ²have ... dream] had a dreame *F* 205 to expound] *Q2, F;* expound *Q1* 208 a patched] *F;*
patcht a *Q*

methought I had. The eye of man hath not heard, the
ear of man hath not seen, man's hand is not able to   210
taste, his tongue to conceive, nor his heart to report
what my dream was. I will get Peter Quince to write a
ballad of this dream. It shall be called 'Bottom's
Dream', because it hath no bottom; and I will sing it
in the latter end of a play, before the duke.   215
Peradventure, to make it the more gracious, I shall
sing it at her death.   *Exit.*

209–11 **The . . . report** A garbled echo of 1 Cor.
2.9: 'The eye hath not seene, and the eare
hath not heard, neither haue entred into the
heart of man, the things which God hath
prepared for them that loue him.' Taylor
('Gower', 282) notes that this passage is
worked into Gower's tale of Pyramus and
Thisbe (*Confessio Amantis*, 3.1420–3). For
more analysis of the biblical echo, see
pp. 90–1. Stroup points out that in Tyndale
and the Geneva Bible (first version), the
next verse reads 'for the sprete [spirit]
searcheth all thynges ye [yea] the botome
of Goddes secretes', the last phrase later
refined to 'the deepe things of God'. The
earlier reading may underlie Bottom's play
on *bottom* here (though not his name as
Stroup argues).
   Bottom, like Quince, habitually confuses
the senses (*eye/heard, ear/seen* etc.); see
3.1.86n., 5.1.344–5n. This is obviously
comic, but Watson (55) points out a later
passage in 1 Cor. 12.17: 'If al the body *were*
an eye, where were then the hearing? If al
were hearing, where were the smelling?'
This association might link Bottom's dream
with 'the deepe things of God'.
213 **ballad** Ballads commonly reported
sensational events, and were sold cheaply

for a popular readership; see 3.1.22n. Hale
notes a broad parallel with Chaucer, *The
Book of the Duchess*, 276–9, 1330–3: the
dreamer thinks 'no man had the wyt' to
interpret his dream, and therefore decides
to put it in a poem.
214 **no bottom** (1) no conclusive meaning: it is
unfathomable; (2) no solid base: it is
illusory. Hence one can only dream of
fathoming the meaning. This provides a
rationale for the title 'Bottom's Dream';
but it better fits the speaker to take his
words as an inept *lucus a non lucendo*,
nomenclature by opposites.
215–17 **a . . . death** Editors have puzzled
unnecessarily over the mild inconsistencies
in Bottom's befuddled words: *a play* for
'the' or 'our play', *her* without explicit
reference to Thisbe. In 3.1.9–66, he shows
knowledge of the play's plot (though
perhaps only from his 'part', which
would contain Pyramus' death-scene but
not Thisbe's). Hence Theobald's
emendation 'after death' is attractive,
whether referring to Bottom's actual death
or Pyramus' in the play. The absurdity of a
dead man singing makes it appropriate to
Bottom.
216 **gracious** pleasing, attractive (*OED adj.* 1a)

213 ballad] (Ballet *QF*)   215 a play] the play *Hanmer;* our play *Dyce² (Walker, 2.321)*   217 at her] after
Theobald   217 SD] *Q2, F; not in Q1*

[4.2]   *Enter* QUINCE, FLUTE, SNOUT *and* STARVELING.

QUINCE   Have you sent to Bottom's house? Is he come
    home yet?
STARVELING   He cannot be heard of. Out of doubt he is
    transported.
FLUTE   If he come not, then the play is marred. It goes   5
    not forward. Doth it?
QUINCE   It is not possible. You have not a man in all
    Athens able to discharge Pyramus but he.
FLUTE   No, he hath simply the best wit of any
    handicraftman in Athens.   10
QUINCE   Yea, and the best person too, and he is a very
    paramour for a sweet voice.
FLUTE   You must say paragon. A paramour is (God bless
    us) a thing of naught.

[4.2] There is a brief return to the setting of 1.2 before proceeding to the court. This makes for exact 'scenic symmetry' (Griffiths, 187), as also a perfect 'pastoral cycle': from court through a proletarian setting to the 'green' fairy world, then back the same way; see pp. 71–2.

0.1 *SD QF mention 'Flute, Thisby' separately, though Flute plays Thisbe. Recurrent confusion on this point in Q SDs indicates they go back to authorial copy. At this point, F repeats the Q error, while correcting it at 3 SP and 5.1.155. The generic '*and the rabble*' in the Q SD is another recognized sign of authorial copy. See pp. 297, 304.

4 **transported** carried off by supernatural forces; also possibly (1) killed, dead

(Schmidt; *OED v.* 1e, citing only this passage and *MM* 4.3.67); (2) 'transformed, transfigured' (Wright; not in *OED*). The unintended meaning 'enraptured', inspired (*OED* transported 2) is also relevant in the light of Bottom's words in 4.1.203–12.

8 **discharge** See 1.2.86n.

11 **person** appearance (*OED n.* 4a, b); cf. *personage*, 3.2.292.

13 Flute corrects Quince's malapropism as Quince had earlier corrected Bottom's (3.1.77–8).

14 *naught QF 'nought' and F2 'naught' are cognate and overlapping words; but while both denote emptiness or worthlessness, 'naught' also suggests wickedness. Flute wrongly takes *paramour* as applying only to illicit partners.

[4.2] *Capell (SCENE* II.*); not in QF* 0.1 SD] *Rowe²; Enter* Quince, Flute, Thisby *and the rabble. Q; Enter* Quince, Flute, Thisbie, Snout, *and* Starueling. *F* 3 SP STARVELING] *F; Flut. Q* 5+ SP FLUTE] *Rowe²;* Thisbe *(subst.) QF* 14 naught] *F2;* nought *QF*

Enter SNUG.

SNUG   Masters, the duke is coming from the temple, and   15
there is two or three lords and ladies more married. If
our sport had gone forward, we had all been made
men.

FLUTE   O sweet bully Bottom! Thus hath he lost sixpence
a day during his life: he could not have scaped   20
sixpence a day. And the duke had not given him
sixpence a day for playing Pyramus, I'll be hanged.
He would have deserved it. Sixpence a day in
Pyramus, or nothing.

Enter BOTTOM.

BOTTOM   Where are these lads? Where are these hearts?   25
QUINCE   Bottom! O most courageous day! O most happy
hour!
BOTTOM   Masters, I am to discourse wonders; but ask me
not what. For if I tell you, I am not true Athenian. I
will tell you everything right as it fell out.   30
QUINCE   Let us hear, sweet Bottom.

---

16 **is** Singular verb-forms could be used with
plural subjects (see 3.1.77n.), especially if
the latter can be taken as a single entity
(here, the *lords and ladies* at their multiple
wedding. On such 'co-ordinate subjects',
see Blake, 6.1.1.1.
17 **sport** theatrical performance; see 3.2.14n.
made provided for, with their fortunes
made
19 **bully** See 3.1.7n.
19–20 **sixpence a day** At the time, many
skilled workmen got no more (along with
food) in London, and most rural craftsmen
and labourers (including weavers)
considerably less (*Shakespeare's England*,
1.331). There may be a hit at Thomas

Preston, author of the 'lamentable tragedy'
of *Cambises*, who received a Queen's
pension of £20 a year, over double that
envisaged for Bottom.
20 **scaped** escaped; obviously inappropriate
in the context of a gain
21 **And** 'an', if; cf. 'and if', 2.2.157.
23 **in** 'on account of, by means of' (Schmidt);
cf. 'conserve a life / In base appliances'
(*MM* 3.1.87–8).
25 **hearts** a comradely address, 'my hearties'
26 **courageous** 'brave', in a general sense of
'heartening, joyful'
happy perhaps also implying 'lucky'
(*OED adj.* 2), because of Bottom's return
28 **I am to** I must; cf. *we are to* (40), 1.2.92n.

14.1 SD] *(Enter* Snug, *the Ioyner. QF)*   29 not true] no true *F*   30 right] *not in F*

BOTTOM Not a word of me. All that I will tell you is
that the duke hath dined. Get your apparel together:
good strings to your beards, new ribands to your
pumps. Meet presently at the palace, every man look   35
o'er his part; for the short and the long is, our play is
preferred. In any case let Thisbe have clean linen; and
let not him that plays the Lion pare his nails, for they
shall hang out for the Lion's claws. And most dear
actors, eat no onions nor garlic, for we are to utter   40
sweet breath; and I do not doubt but to hear them
say, it is a sweet comedy. No more words. Away,
go away.   *Exeunt.*

---

33 **duke hath dined** We cannot tell how
Bottom obtained this information, and
maybe should not ask for such consistency
from the dramatist.

34 **strings** Stage beards could be either stuck
on or fastened with strings (Dessen and
Thomson, 23). This may be a glance at
Kyd's *Spanish Tragedy* 4.3.17–18, where
Balthazar enters before the play-within-a-
play with his stage beard half on and half
off. Cf. 1.2.25n., 3.1.125n., 5.1.286n.

35 **pumps** a light shoe closely fitting the foot,
but from the late sixteenth century, with
fastenings added (Linthicum, 253). They
were worn by both higher and lower
orders, so the artisans might simply have
tarted up their usual footwear with new
ribbons. Pumps were also worn by comic
actors; they heighten the anomaly of a
lamentable comedy (Foakes).
presently immediately

36 **part** See 1.2.92n.
short ... long For this version of the
proverbial phrase (Dent, L419) cf. *MW*
2.1.120.

37 **preferred** submitted for approval (*OED v.*
7); cf. 'prefer his suit to Caesar' (*JC* 3.1.28).
The final choice comes later (5.1.81).
'Characteristically, Bottom considers [the
play] as good as chosen' (Brooks).
In any case whatever happens, at all
events (*OED* case *n.¹* P4b)

41 **breath** literally, but also the words uttered
(*OED* 9)

43 SD] *F; not in Q*

[5.1]   *Enter* THESEUS, HIPPOLYTA, PHILOSTRATE *and Lords.*

HIPPOLYTA
'Tis strange, my Theseus, that these lovers speak of.
THESEUS
More strange than true. I never may believe
These antique fables, nor these fairy toys.
Lovers and madmen have such seething brains,
Such shaping fantasies, that apprehend   5

[5.1]   As in 1.1, this may be either a court scene
with attendant lords, as in F, or an informal
setting as in Q with only Theseus, Hippolyta,
Philostrate and, a little later, the lovers. As
Treadwell (23–4) notes, the *manager of
mirth* (35) must have been present from the
start, going not only by the opening SD in Q
but his ready response when summoned by
Theseus (38). But the way Theseus calls
him (unlike in 1.1.11) suggests a gathering
of some size, like a formal court.

0.1   *The Q and F SDs might relate respectively
to a private performance of *MND* (perhaps
at a wedding) with fewer actors in limited
space, and a full-fledged public
performance. This may or may not be
related to the substitution in F of Egeus for
Q's Philostrate, often explained by casting
requirements; but Appendix 1 indicates
how the number of actors would remain the
same, provided someone not otherwise onstage doubled as F's mute Philostrate in 1.1.
This suggests a thematic purpose behind
Egeus' return, as argued by Hodgdon
('Gaining'), McGuire ('Intentions',
'Egeus') and Holland (265–8). Egeus even
acts as Master of the Revels, a role assigned
to Philostrate in 1.1. He thus finds a place in
the happy ending from which he is excluded
in Q; but only a qualified place, for in F, it is
Lysander who reads the titles of the
entertainments on offer (44–57 and n.).

1   **my Theseus** The *my* indicates that,
whatever their earlier equation, Hippolyta
now actively returns Theseus' love
(MacDonald, 124); cf. 4.1.74–5n.

2   **More . . . true** reversing the proverbial 'no
more strange than true' (Dent, S914)

3   **antique** The Q2, F spelling 'anticke' was
used for both *antic* ('grotesque, bizarre':
OED adj. 2) and the cognate but distinct
antique (old, hence outworn). Theseus'
comment combines both senses: 'old and
quaintly figured' (Schmidt). The spelling
antique has been used here, as the sense
'ancient, legendary' seems most important.
Barkan (*Gods*, 234, 252) compares 'wilde
Antickes' (*FQ* 3.11.51.5), images from
metamorphic myths designated *grotteschi*
(whence 'grotesque').
   toys idle tales or fancies. The *fables* might
be classical legends, *toys* fairy lore. Floyd-
Wilson (188) notes how Theseus' dismissal
of 'fairy toys' is at odds with his alleged
relations with Titania (2.1.74–80).

4   **seething**   restless,   agitated;   literally
'boiling', opposed to *cool reason* (6). See
1.1.56–7n. Passion or madness was
thought to heat the brain; cf. *Mac* 2.1.39,
'the heat-oppressed brain'. Love was
proverbially considered a madness (Dent,
L505.2).

5–8   *Wilson (80–6) interpreted the patches
of mislined verse (corresponding to 5–8,
12–18, 29–31, 33–6, 58–60, 66–70, 76–8,
81–3) as later additions crammed into the
margin of the manuscript copy for Q1 (see
pp. 298–9, 310–12). The additions include
all references to the poet in 7–17.

5   **shaping fantasies** fancies that shape or
create images. On the faculty of fantasy,
see 1.1.32n.

[5.1] *Rowe (*ACT V. SCENE I.*); *Actus Quintus F; not in Q*   0.1 SD] *Yale; Enter* Theseus, Hyppolita,
and Philostrate. *Q; Enter Theseus, Hippolita, Egeus and his Lords. F*   3   antique] anticke *Q2, F*   5–8] *so
lined, Theobald; Q1 lines* more, / lunatick, / compact. *I; Q2, F line* more / comprehends. / Poet, / compact. /
5 fantasies] *(phantasies QF)*

More than cool reason ever comprehends.
The lunatic, the lover, and the poet
Are of imagination all compact.
One sees more devils than vast hell can hold:
That is the madman. The lover, all as frantic,   10
Sees Helen's beauty in a brow of Egypt.
The poet's eye, in a fine frenzy rolling,
Doth glance from heaven to earth, from earth to
    heaven;
And as imagination bodies forth
The forms of things unknown, the poet's pen   15
Turns them to shapes, and gives to airy nothing
A local habitation and a name.

---

apprehend visualize or form an impression of something, whether or not correctly

6 **comprehends** validates as actual or concrete: 'sense experience apprehends and reason comprehends' (Frye, *Deliverance*, 76; cf. Hankins, 92–4). Being guided by *cool reason*, *comprehension* might be thought more correct and reliable; but 19–20 finds it equally fallible. On the theme of illusion and reality, see pp. 99–104.

7–17 These lines carry marked echoes of Plutarch, *Moralia*, 'Of Love', 16. Plutarch compares clinical madness with (among others) poetic furor and the madness of love (Reinhold Sigismund: see Var).

8 **imagination** in the old sense: the faculty of recalling and reordering visual impressions or images planted in the mind, perhaps to create unreal creatures and objects; cf. *Ham* 1.4.87, 3.1.125, *Tem* 3.1.56. On imagination in madmen, cf. *2H4* 1.3.31–3. Theseus is deriding imagination in this sense, not celebrating it in the later philosophic sense formulated by Coleridge. On the implications for poetic theory, especially the Platonic theories of the time, see pp. 100–2. For the pronunciation, see 18n.

compact composed (*OED adj.*¹ 2), but perhaps 'Joined in compact, leagued' (*OED adj.*²), hence 'similar'

10 **all as frantic** quite as mad or delirious

11 **Helen's** of Troy; perhaps also suggesting Helena (see next note)
    brow of Egypt The common European misconception of the time (running through *AC*) held that Egyptians were dark or negroid, hence necessarily unbeautiful. The reference might also be to the gypsy or Romany race, thought to have come from Egypt. The line recalls the dark Hermia, set against *Helen* or Helena, see 2.2.117n.

12 **fine** 'sheer, absolute' (*OED adj.* 3), but also sarcastically 'good, excellent' in a general way
    frenzy insane or delirious fit, but also used of divine inspiration or furor

13 **heaven** slurred as one syllable both times

14 **bodies forth** 'give[s] mental shape to', conceives a form for something immaterial or non-existent (*OED* body *v.*: to body forth 1, 2: only example till 1759)

16 **shapes** forms that seem externally valid, authenticated in terms of the poet's narrative and not simply mental constructs

---

12–18] *so lined, Rowe²*; *Q1 lines* glance / as / things / shapes, / habitation, / imagination, /; *Q2, F line* glance / heauen. / things / shapes, / habitation, / imagination, /

Such tricks hath strong imagination
That if it would but apprehend some joy,
It comprehends some bringer of that joy;　　　　　20
Or in the night, imagining some fear,
How easy is a bush supposed a bear!

HIPPOLYTA
But all the story of the night told over,
And all their minds transfigured so together,
More witnesseth than fancy's images　　　　　25
And grows to something of great constancy,
But howsoever strange and admirable.

Enter LYSANDER, DEMETRIUS, HERMIA *and* HELENA.

THESEUS
Here come the lovers, full of joy and mirth.
Joy, gentle friends, joy and fresh days of love

---

18 **tricks** perhaps 'contrivances' (to work the process described in 19–20: *OED n.* 3); but 'illusory or deceptive appearance[s]' (*OED n.* 1c, first cited from 1602) exactly suits the context.
strong imagination Cf. Lyly, *Campaspe*, 4.4.12: the 'shadow' of the beloved in her picture will become 'by strong imagination . . . a substaunce'.
imagination six syllables, ending *ti-on*. At 8 and 14, the last two syllables are slurred to give something like the modern five-syllable form.
19–20 **apprehend . . . comprehends** See 5–6 and nn.; but here *apprehend* seems rather to mean 'conceptualize, think of'. Cf. *apprehension, R2* 1.3.300, alongside *imagination,* 297.
21 **imagining** endowing with an image or visible shape; but the *fear* is itself imaginary.
22 **bush . . . bear** proverbial (Dent, B738). *Bear* originally meant a bugbear or hobgoblin.

23 **told over** told in full (*OED* tell *v.* PV1: to tell over 2, first cited in this sense from *c.*1595)
24–7 'That so many accounts should agree suggests that their subject is not imaginary but stable and concrete, though certainly strange and wonderful.'
24 **transfigured** an unusual use, not in *OED*; perhaps 'transformed', i.e. 'conditioned, influenced' (so as to credit these abnormal events), or 'configured', shaped
25 **witnesseth** testifies to
fancy's images 'delusions of imagination' (Treadwell)
26 **something** answering Theseus' 'nothing', 16 (Holland)
great constancy suggests something permanent and therefore true. It also suggests that the lovers' relations have progressed beyond 'fancy' or casual attraction to firm love.
27 **But howsoever** even if, albeit
admirable something to 'admire' or wonder at

27.1] *Rowe; Enter Louers;* Lysander, . . . Helena. *QF*

Accompany your hearts.

LYSANDER   More than to us   30
Wait in your royal walks, your board, your bed.

THESEUS

Come now, what masques, what dances shall we have
To wear away this long age of three hours
Between our after-supper and bed-time?
Where is our usual manager of mirth?   35
What revels are in hand? Is there no play
To ease the anguish of a torturing hour?
Call Philostrate.

PHILOSTRATE   Here, mighty Theseus.

THESEUS

Say, what abridgement have you for this evening?
What masque, what music? How shall we beguile   40

---

30 **More ... us** i.e. May joy and love attend upon you more than upon us.

31 **walks** places of resort or habit (*OED n.¹* 11a); cf. 3.1.159.

33–7 [*T*]*hree hours* in what seems an added passage contradicts *a ... hour* (37) in what is probably the original text (unless the latter simply means 'a span of time'). The play-within-the-play may notionally last an hour, as expected of an after-supper entertainment. Later, as Shakespeare ponders the philosophical implications of his art, he thinks in terms of *three hours*, the approximate duration of a full professional production.

34 *****our** Wilson suggests Q 'or' is a misreading of contracted 'o'' for *our*.
after-supper perhaps the 'dessert' or collation immediately following a formal dinner or banquet (Wilson), but more likely the 'rere-supper' some hours after it (*OED*,

earliest citation in this sense), as everyone goes to bed immediately after the entertainment.

35–6 **manager ... revels** Philostrate is modelled on the Master of the Revels at the Elizabethan court, who organized court entertainments and previewed and censored plays.

37 **anguish** presumably in impatience for the marriage bed; cf. 'wear away this long age', 33.

38 On the style of the summons and response, see opening note to this Act.
SP See 0.1n. on the change from Philostrate in Q to Egeus in F.

39 **abridgement** 'Means of shortening time, pastime' (Onions; *OED* 4, citing only this passage and *Ham* 2.2.358); '(perh[aps]) shortened play for an evening's entertainment' (Onions)

40 **beguile** divert, charm away

29–30 Joy ... hearts] *so lined, Rowe; QF line* daies / hearts. / 30–1 More ... bed] *so lined, F2; one line, QF* 33–8] *so lined, Q2, F; Q1 lines* betweene / manager / play, / *Philostrate.* / *Theseus.* / 34 our] *F;* Or *Q* 38 Philostrate] *Egeus F* 38+ (to 72) SP] *Egeus (subst.) F*

The lazy time, if not with some delight?
PHILOSTRATE [*Gives him a paper.*]
There is a brief how many sports are ripe.
Make choice of which your highness will see first.
THESEUS [*Reads.*]
'The battle with the Centaurs, to be sung
By an Athenian eunuch to the harp'?   45
We'll none of that. That have I told my love
In glory of my kinsman Hercules.
'The riot of the tipsy Bacchanals
Tearing the Thracian singer in their rage'?
That is an old device, and it was played   50

41 **lazy** (1) sluggish; (2) unproductive, idle
42 **brief** list (*OED n.¹* 6, first citation)
    sports probably in the general sense
    'entertainments, recreations'; at least the
    first item is not a theatrical performance.
    Cf. 2.1.87n.
    ripe ready. Q2, F 'rife' (ready: *OED adj.*
    6a) makes equal sense, but there seems no
    reason to emend.
44–58 SP In F, Lysander reads out the titles
    and Theseus comments on them. Hence
    F has SP *Lis.* at 44, 48, 52, 56, and SP
    The at 46, 50, 54, 58. This arrangement
    presumably stems from the theatrical
    manuscript consulted by the F editors,
    indicating later dramatic practice (see
    pp. 303, 304n.). To divide the lines in this
    way makes for livelier presentation.
    McGuire ('Egeus', 110–11) and Holland
    (268) also make a thematic point: though
    Egeus is the 'manager of mirth' in F, it
    is Lysander who announces the
    entertainments on offer. The son-in-law
    has supplanted the father-in-law, the
    new generation the old. In F, Egeus 'presides
    over his own defeat' (Orgel, 95).
44 **Centaurs** mythical creatures, half human,
    half horse. They drunkenly fought the

Lapiths, a human tribe, for possession of
the latter's women at the wedding of the
Lapith king Pirithous, Theseus' friend.
Theseus played a leading part in quelling
the centaurs: see *Met.* 12.227–40, 341–62
(Golding, 12.256–68, 371–94), Plutarch
(29.3; North, 16, sig. B2ᵛ). Here Theseus
self-effacingly phrases his reference as a
tribute to Hercules. For his reverence for
Hercules and their kinship, see 4.1.111n.

45 **Athenian eunuch** presumably with a high
    or effeminate voice, inappropriate to such a
    theme. As with the lovers' garments (see
    2.1.264n.), *Athenian* seems superfluous.
48 **tipsy Bacchanals** drunken followers of the
    wine-god Bacchus: see 49n.
49 **Thracian singer** Orpheus the legendary
    singer, hailing from Thrace. After losing
    his wife Eurydice and failing to rescue her
    from the underworld, he was so demented
    with grief that he ignored the attentions of
    a band of frenzied women Bacchanals.
    They thereupon tore him to pieces in anger
    (*Met.* 11.1–66; Golding, 11.1–75).
50 **device** dramatic invention or composition,
    perhaps of an amateur or informal nature
    (*OED* 11, first cited from this passage, *LLL*
    5.2.660 and *Tim* 1.2.149)

42 SD] *Theobald (Giving a Paper), after 43; not in QF*   ripe] rife *Q2, F*   44 SP] *Lis. F*   SD] *Theobald;
not in QF*   46, 50, 54, 58 SP] *The. F*   48, 52, 56 SP] *Lis. F*

When I from Thebes came last a conqueror.
'The thrice three Muses mourning for the death
Of learning, late deceased in beggary'?
That is some satire keen and critical,
Not sorting with a nuptial ceremony.   55
'A tedious brief scene of young Pyramus
And his love Thisbe; very tragical mirth'?
Merry and tragical? Tedious and brief?
That is hot ice and wondrous swarthy snow.
How shall we find the concord of this discord?   60

PHILOSTRATE

A play there is, my lord, some ten words long,
Which is as brief as I have known a play.
But by ten words, my lord, it is too long,
Which makes it tedious; for in all the play
There is not one word apt, one player fitted.   65

---

51 After the death of Oedipus' sons, Cleon, ruler of Thebes, denied burial to the rebel son Polynices. Urged by the widows of Polynices' allies, Theseus undertook an expedition to Thebes and forced Cleon to grant them burial. For the various versions of this story, and its place in the history of Theseus, see p. 68.

52–3 For the supposed allusion in these lines, see pp. 289–90. The proverbial theme (Tilley, M1316) is too commonplace to support any specific allusion.

55 **sorting with** suitable for

56–7 See 1.2.11n. on such oxymoron in the titles of earlier plays.

59 *****swarthy** black. Though QF 'strange snow' makes sense, an oxymoron matching *hot ice* seems called for. (Cf. 'a num-cold fire': John Taylor, *Sir Gregory Nonsense* (1622), sig. B6ᵛ, which quotes from this scene.) Most proposed emendations are palaeographically improbable, but

'swarthe' (so spelt) could resemble 'strange' in the secretary hand, *h* taking a descender instead of an ascender and easily misread as *g*. The first minim in *w* could also extend upward and be confused with *t*. This is especially likely if (as the mislining in Q1 suggests) the line was a later addition cramped into the margin of the manuscript copy. 'Swarthe' could equally be modern 'swarth', but the two-syllable form is favoured by 'swarthy', *TGV* 2.6.26 and 'swartie', *Tit* 2.2.72, Q1 (F 'swarth'). *Tit* is only slightly earlier than *MND*, and its Q1, like *MND*'s, seems to have been set from Shakespeare's working manuscript.

60 **concord ... discord** a general theme of the play, reflecting the relations between Theseus and his defeated bride-adversary no less than between Oberon and Titania; cf. 4.1.111–17n.

65 **fitted** suitable, adequate

58–60] *so lined, Theobald; Q1 lines* Ise, / concord / discord? /; *Q2 lines* Ice, / discord? /; *prose F*   59 swarthy] *Dyce² (Staunton);* strange *QF;* scorching *Hanmer;* strange black *Capell*

And tragical, my noble lord, it is,
For Pyramus therein doth kill himself;
Which when I saw rehearsed, I must confess,
Made mine eyes water, but more merry tears
The passion of loud laughter never shed.   70

THESEUS
What are they that do play it?

PHILOSTRATE
Hard-handed men that work in Athens here,
Which never laboured in their minds till now,
And now have toiled their unbreathed memories
With this same play, against your nuptial.   75

THESEUS
And we will hear it.

PHILOSTRATE   No, my noble lord,
It is not for you. I have heard it over,
And it is nothing, nothing in the world,
Unless you can find sport in their intents,
Extremely stretched and conned with cruel pain   80
To do you service.

THESEUS   I will hear that play;
For never anything can be amiss

---

68 **saw rehearsed** The Master of the Revels
    would preview any play considered for
    performance at court. When this preview
    happened in the present case is a mystery,
    but 'the problem . . . would never occur to
    an audience' (Kittredge).
70 **passion** fit, outburst (*OED n.* 6c)
74 **toiled** strained, taxed
    unbreathed unpractised
75 **against** See 1.1.125n.
    nuptial three syllables, unlike in all earlier
    occurrences in the play

76 SP   The only speech allotted to Philostrate
    in F, probably by an oversight when
    revising the Q2 copy used to set F.
78 **nothing . . . world** of no worth at all (this
    sense not in *OED*)
79 **intents** (good) intentions, the desire rather
    than the ability to please; but *find sport*
    suggests the kind of unfeeling jests directed
    at the actors during the performance.
80 **Extremely stretched** strained to the
    utmost
    conned memorized

66–70] *so lined, F2; QF line Pyramus,* / saw / water: / laughter / shed. /   76–8 No . . . world] *so lined,*
Rowe²; QF line heare it. / heard / world; /   81–3] *so lined, Rowe²; QF line* seruice. / thing / it. /
82 anything] *(any thing QF)*

When simpleness and duty tender it.
Go bring them in, and take your places, ladies.

[*Exit Philostrate.*]

HIPPOLYTA

I love not to see wretchedness o'ercharged,   85
And duty in his service perishing.

THESEUS

Why, gentle sweet, you shall see no such thing.

HIPPOLYTA

He says they can do nothing in this kind.

THESEUS

The kinder we, to give them thanks for nothing.
Our sport shall be to take what they mistake.   90
And what poor duty cannot do,
Noble respect takes it in might, not merit.
Where I have come, great clerks have purposed

---

85 **wretchedness** probably misery or
discomfiture, as displayed most pitiably by
Starveling (234–53). The sense 'inferiority,
worthlessness' (*OED* 4) is not recorded
before 1810.
o'ercharged overburdened, taxed beyond
its powers

86 **in his service** in discharge of its task: the
actors fail in the very task they are
attempting, to entertain Theseus. *His* was
the usual possessive of *it* at this time, but
the man discharging the task seems implicit
here.

88 **in this kind** i.e. by way of acting

89 **The kinder we** Wilson compares the
Princess's words in *LLL* 5.2.513–18.

90 **take ... mistake** a play on words, linked
to another in *mis-take*: to err, but also to
misapply or perform ineptly. Theseus
means that he 'will accept with pleasure
even their blundering attempt' (Steevens,
Var 1821). But the courtiers' actual
behaviour suggests a harsher ironic
nuance: 'We will be entertained by their

mistakes.' For *sport* as entertainment at
another's expense, cf. 3.2.119, 161, 194.

91 Theobald first re-lined 91–2, hence
suggested 'poor willing duty' to fill out the
now short line 91.

92 **Noble** (1) virtuous, high-minded; (2)
appropriate to noblemen or rulers
respect 'Consideration, regard' (*OED n.* 3a)
in ... merit judged by the actors' powers,
not their achievement. Foakes compares
the proverbs 'To take the will for the deed'
(Dent, W393) and 'Everything is as it is
taken' (Tilley, T31).

93 **great clerks** eminent scholars. The local
schoolmaster or priest customarily read an
address or verses of welcome to the Queen
on her progresses; but Theseus' words
would better suit her visits to Oxford and
Cambridge. At Warwick in 1572, the
Queen told the Recorder performing this
function, 'It was told me that youe wold be
afraid to look vpon me or to speake boldly'
(Nichols, *Progresses*, 2.35).
purposed (purposèd) intended, prepared

---

84 SD] *Pope; not in QF*   91–2] *so lined, Theobald; QF line* respect / merit. /   91 poor duty] poor
willing duty *Theobald*

To greet me with premeditated welcomes
Where I have seen them shiver and look pale,   95
Make periods in the midst of sentences,
Throttle their practised accent in their fears,
And in conclusion dumbly have broke off,
Not paying me a welcome. Trust me, sweet,
Out of this silence, yet I picked a welcome;   100
And in the modesty of fearful duty,
I read as much as from the rattling tongue
Of saucy and audacious eloquence.
Love, therefore, and tongue-tied simplicity
In least speak most, to my capacity.   105

[*Enter* PHILOSTRATE.]

PHILOSTRATE
So please your grace, the Prologue is addressed.
THESEUS
Let him approach.

Flourish of trumpets. Enter [QUINCE *as*] *the* Prologue.

96 **periods** pauses (literally, full stops), anticipating Quince's problem while delivering the prologue (108–17)
97 **practised** (1) accustomed; (2) rehearsed
98 **in conclusion** (1) at the end of their speech; (2) (on Theseus' part) to sum up or put briefly
   dumbly silently, speechlessly; perhaps also stupidly (*OED* dumb *adj*. 7a)
101 **modesty** bashfulness
   fearful full of fear, nervous
102 **rattling** 'chattering, prattling' (*OED adj*. 2a, earliest citation)
104–5 This charitable sentiment seems touched with gratification at the speakers' failure, as proving Theseus' own patronizing

superiority. Dent (L165) compares the proverbial idea that love is silent.
105 **capacity** understanding, judgement
106 **addressed** ready (*OED v.* 12a)
107 *SP   the only occurrence of QF SP '*Duk.*' instead of *Theseus* in this part of the scene, perhaps added at the time of the '*Du*[*ke*]' SPs from 205 onward.
107.1 ***Flourish of trumpets** used to announce the start of a play. Steevens (Var 1778) cites Dekker, *The Gull's Hornbook* (1609): 'the quaking prologue . . . ready to giue the trumpets their Cue, that hees vpon point to enter' (Dekker, *Non-Dramatic*, 2.250).
   ***QUINCE ... Prologue** F 'Quince' in the right margin is clearly a theatrical note

105.1] *Capell (Re-enter* PHILOSTRATE.*); Enter* Philomon. *Pope; not in QF*   107 SP] *Rowe; Duke (subst.) QF*   107.1 *Flourish of Trumpets*] *(Flor. Trum.)* F *(opp. 107, right margin); not in Q*   QUINCE *as*] *Rowe (*Quince *for); Quince.* F *(separately, same line, right margin); not in Q*

QUINCE

> *If we offend, it is with our good will.*
>   *That you should think, we come not to offend,*
> *But with good will. To show our simple skill,*   110
>   *That is the true beginning of our end.*
> *Consider then, we come but in despite.*
>   *We do not come, as minding to content you,*
> *Our true intent is. All for your delight,*
>   *We are not here. That you should here repent you,*   115
> *The actors are at hand; and, by their show,*
>   *You shall know all, that you are like to know.*

identifying him with the Prologue. His role is not indicated in the text, but seems obvious: there is no-one else to serve as Prologue, and no other role for Quince.

108–17 a celebrated instance of wrong pauses and punctuation, reversing the intended meaning. The only sentence-breaks should come after *will* (110), *end* (111), *come* (113), *delight* (114) and *repent you* (115), with commas after *skill* (110), *come* (112) and *you* (113). Foakes suggests Quince may be reading from a script and failing to spot the punctuation correctly. Nicholas Udall's play *Ralph Roister Doister* (?1552; printed ?1566) offers a precedent (cited in Wilson, *Rule*, fols 67ʳ–68ʳ, sigs S3ʳ–4ʳ) where a mischievous servant deliberately garbles his master's love-letter.

108 *If we offend* echoed at the start of Robin's Epilogue (413): a piquant parallel between the main play and the play within it

110 *But* with the unintended suggestion that their good will might lead them to offend

111 *beginning ... end* our primary purpose (*end* = purpose, but also 'conclusion',

clumsily clashing with *beginning*)

112 *despite* scorn, malice

113 *as* Quince's garbled delivery makes this mean 'as though'. 'We have not come as though intending to please you.'
   minding intending
   content please

115 *repent you* regret (seeing the play)

116 *show* performance, but also appearance. Lines 116–17 thus bear two unfortunate implications: (1) 'You will have learnt nothing from the prologue itself.' (2) 'The very appearance of the actors tells you what to expect.'

Mehl (109–10) and Wells suggest this *show* (as also in 126) might have been a prefatory dumb-show outlining the action, presumably implicit in 125.1–3 or accompanying the 'Argument' that follows (126–50), as in Brook's production. Pearn (386) points out that dumb-shows, chiefly expository rather than allegorical, abound between 1591 and 1620. Of the nine examples where they serve as prologue, eight have a presenter explaining the action.

108–17] *italicized, Malone*   108+ SP QUINCE] *Wells; Prologue (subst.) QF*

THESEUS   This fellow doth not stand upon points.

LYSANDER   He hath rid his prologue like a rough colt: he
knows not the stop. A good moral, my lord. It is not   120
enough to speak, but to speak true.

HIPPOLYTA   Indeed, he hath played on this prologue like
a child on a recorder: a sound, but not in government.

THESEUS   His speech was like a tangled chain: nothing
impaired, but all disordered. Who is next?   125

Enter [BOTTOM *as*] *Pyramus,* [FLUTE *as*] *Thisbe,* [SNOUT
as] *Wall,* [STARVELING *as*] *Moonshine, and* [SNUG *as*]
Lion; [*a trumpeter*] *before them.*

QUINCE

Gentles, perchance you wonder at this show;
But wonder on, till truth make all things plain.

118 From this point, untypically in such a play,
the patricians speak prose and the artisans
verse – the latter, of course, only in the
clumsy dialogue of their play, so that the
rulers' prose gives a contrasting effect of
reason and good sense, as well as relaxed
diversion. Their witty, satiric commentary
on the players recalls that of the courtiers at
the pageant of the Nine Worthies, *LLL*
5.2.484–719.
fellow then used only of social inferiors
points punning on (1) niceties; (2)
punctuation marks
119 **rid** (1) rid himself of, somehow got
through; (2) ridden like a horse
rough (of a horse) untrained, unbroken
(*OED adj.* 12b)
120 **stop** (of a horse) stopping suddenly, which it
only learns to do by training (*OED n.*² 21a,
b); also a full stop or other punctuation mark
moral lesson, observation
123 **recorder** a simple wind instrument, used
to train children in music
government control, perhaps in a special
musical application (cf. *OED* govern *v.*
14); cf. 'govern', *Ham* 3.2.349, also with
reference to recorders.

124–5 **nothing ... disordered** not broken but
entangled
125.3 *The F SD mentions the actor William
Tawyer or Toyer of the King's Men. It
indicates the theatrical provenance of the
manuscript consulted by F, no doubt
reflecting a production long after the first.
Tawyer (d. 1625) was apprenticed to John
Heminges. The only record of his
employment occurs in a licence issued to
the company in December 1624 (Herbert,
Records, 158). See 126 SPn.
126 SP   Collier² observed that the inept
Quince would have mispunctuated this
summary no less than the prologue; hence
(*Collier MS*, 108–9) he cast Tawyer (see
125.3n.) as 'Presenter' of these lines.
126 *Gentles* 'gentlefolk', worthy or respectable
people: a customary address by actors to a
public audience (cf. 419), but inappropriate
for a courtly one
127 *truth ... plain* perhaps alluding to the
proverb 'Truth will come to light', Tilley,
T591 (Holland)
truth ironic when applied to a stage play,
especially given Theseus' remarks before
(12–17) and after (210–11)

122 this] his *F*   125.1–3 *Enter ... Lion] Wells; Enter* Pyramus, *and* Thisby, *[and Q1]* Wall, *[and Q1]* Moone-
shine, *and* Lyon. *QF*   125.3 *a ... them] Wells; Tawyer with a Trumpet before them. F (before Enter ... Lyon);
not in Q*   126+ *all subsequent lines of play-within-the-play] italicized, Craig; indicated in margin, Capell*

This man is Pyramus, if you would know.
This beauteous lady Thisbe is certain.
This man, with lime and roughcast, doth present   130
Wall, that vile Wall which did these lovers sunder,
And through Wall's chink, poor souls, they are content
To whisper; at the which, let no man wonder.
This man, with lantern, dog and bush of thorn,
Presenteth Moonshine. For if you will know,   135
By moonshine did these lovers think no scorn
To meet at Ninus' tomb, there, there to woo.
This grisly beast, which Lion hight by name,
The trusty Thisbe, coming first by night,
Did scare away, or rather did affright;   140
And as she fled, her mantle she did fall,
Which Lion vile with bloody mouth did stain.
Anon comes Pyramus, sweet youth and tall,
And finds his trusty Thisbe's mantle slain;

129 **certain** accented on the second syllable in a stilted and archaic way, to force the rhyme with *plain*. Steevens (Var 1821) cites earlier examples.

130–5 The addition of Wall and Moonshine shows that Quince has incorporated the suggestions made at the rehearsal (3.1.54–66). Perhaps to accommodate these new characters, and also himself as Prologue, he has left out Pyramus and Thisbe's parents. On their omission, and of the dialogue from 3.1, see 1.2.56–9n.

130 **roughcast** See 3.1.64n.

134 **lantern** indicating moonlight. On the form, see 3.1.55n. Q1 has 'lanterne' here, Quince being the speaker; cf. 234–54 and 234n.
dog and bush See 3.1.54–5n. A live dog may have been brought onstage, as in *TGV* 2.3 and 4.4.

137 **Ninus'** See 3.1.93n.

138 There is no rhyming line. It may have dropped out, or been deliberately omitted to heighten the crudity of the verse.
grisly F 'grizy' (grisy, *OED adj.¹*), cognate with *grisly*, was also current at this time.
hight is called; *by name* is tautological

139 **trusty** faithful (*OED adj.* 2a)

141 **mantle** Golding's word (4.125); also found in Thomson's poem in *Handful*, which is closer to Shakespeare in naming a lion in place of Ovid's (hence Golding's) lioness.
fall drop, let fall (*OED v.* 49)

143 **tall** (1) handsome (*OED adj.* 2b); (2) valiant (*adj.* 3)

144 F2 'gentle' was no doubt introduced to fill up the omission of *trusty* in F.
slain comically applied to the mantle and not to Thisbe herself

134 *lantern*] Lanthorne *Q2, F*   138 *grisly*] (grizly *Q*); grizy *F*   144 *trusty*] *not in F*; gentle *F2*

Whereat, with blade, with bloody blameful blade,　　145
　He bravely broached his boiling bloody breast,
And Thisbe, tarrying in mulberry shade,
　His dagger drew, and died. For all the rest,
Let Lion, Moonshine, Wall and lovers twain
At large discourse, while here they do remain.　　150
　　　　　　　　　　　　　　　[Exeunt] all but Wall.

THESEUS　I wonder if the lion be to speak.

DEMETRIUS　No wonder, my lord. One lion may, when
many asses do.

SNOUT

In this same interlude it doth befall
That I, one Snout by name, present a Wall;　　155
And such a Wall, as I would have you think,
That had in it a crannied hole or chink,

145–6 On the alliteration, see 1.2.27–34n.

146 **broached** pierced, stabbed; often applied to
a cask of liquid, but here perhaps recalling
Chaucer's description of blood flowing 'As
water whan the condit broken is' (*Legend
of Thisbe, LGW*, 852)
　boiling agitated: a jocularly literal
rendering of Ovid's *ferventi . . . vulnere
(Met.* 4.120), perhaps satirizing Golding's
phrase 'boyling brest' (8.478) elsewhere
(Burrow, 120)

147 **mulberry shade** so in *Met.* 4.88–90
(Golding, 4.110). Pyramus' blood turns the
white mulberry fruit to deep red; see
2.1.167n. Abbott (82) considers the omission
of 'the' before *mulberry* an archaism.

150 **At large** fully, expanding this summary
　here . . . remain contradicted by F exit at
150 and QF at 153. The actors probably
remain onstage throughout, and step
forward to speak their lines in the play-
within-the-play. Q and/or F enter and exit
SDs at 150, 153, 167.1, 185–6, 204, 216.1,
255.1, 257, 262.1, 308.1 are best taken as

referring only to the characters in Quince's
play (hence their names are used in SDs in
this edn); cf. F SDs at 3.2.344 and 4.1.44.1,
where characters already onstage simply
step forward. SPs in this edition name the
characters in the main play speaking the
lines, but the dialogue of the play-within-
the-play is italicized.

*SD QF have a similar SD after 153. It
seems better to adopt the F SD here, as
probably closer to stage practice, and
because the later SD omits Pyramus.

154–63 Pettitt (230–1) notes that such self-
introduction is common in medieval
miracle and mystery plays.

154 *interlude* See 1.2.5n. An interlude was
usually comic, making the term
inappropriate for a *lamentable tragedy.*

155 *As at 4.2.0.1 (see n.), in Q Shakespeare
has forgotten that Flute is playing Thisbe. F
corrects the confusion here though not at
4.2.0.1.

157 *crannied* Golding has 'crany' (4.83) for
Ovid's *fissus (Met.* 4.65); cf. *cranny*, 162.

---

150 SD] *F (Exit all but Wall.); not in Q*　153] *Here QF have SD Exit* Lyon, Thysby, *and*
Mooneshine.　154+ SP SNOUT] *this edn; Wall (subst.) QF;* SNOUT *as Wall / Wells*　155 *Snout*] F; *Flute Q*

Through which the lovers Pyramus and Thisbe
Did whisper often, very secretly.
This loam, this roughcast and this stone doth show   160
That I am that same Wall: the truth is so.
And this the cranny is, right and sinister,
Through which the fearful lovers are to whisper.

THESEUS   Would you desire lime and hair to speak
better?   165

DEMETRIUS   It is the wittiest partition that ever I heard
discourse, my lord.

Enter Pyramus.

THESEUS   Pyramus draws near the wall: silence.
BOTTOM

O grim-looked night, O night, with hue so black,
O night, which ever art when day is not,   170
O night, O night, alack, alack, alack,
I fear my Thisbe's promise is forgot.
And thou, O Wall, O sweet, O lovely Wall,

158–9 **Thisbe ... secretly** another clumsy
rhyme by wrong stress; cf. 129n. But it
indicates (as does the near-consistent
spelling 'Thisby' in the early editions,
sometimes varied by 'Thisbie', especially
in F) that the name was pronounced with
a clear final *-ee* sound (see Cercignani,
300).
160 **stone** an addition to the materials in 130
and 3.1.63–4, perhaps to make the point in
180. See also 176 SDn.
    doth For a singular verb with plural (or, as
here, multiple) subject, see 3.1.77n.
162 **sinister** literally 'left', hence clashing with
'right': a joke for the Latinate among the
audience. On Shakespeare's position vis-à-
vis the elite audience and the humble
actors, in his own theatre as well as
Pyramus and Thisbe, see pp. 97–9.

163 **fearful** see 101n.
164 **hair** Animal hair (especially horsehair)
was used to add tensile strength to mortar.
166 **wittiest** wisest, most intelligent; the
original sense
    partition punning on the meanings (1) a
wall; (2) a section of an academic treatise.
Demetrius may imply that even Snout's
lines are more intelligent than such learned
treatises. The phrase 'particion wall'
occurs in Eph. 2.14 in the popular Geneva
Bible; cf. 343n.
169–75 For the repeated 'O's, cf. the Nurse's
exclamations in *RJ* 4.5.49–54. Greenblatt
(Norton[3], 1038) notes that Puttenham, in
The Art of English Poesie, characterizes
epizeuxis or the repetition of words as 'a
very foolish impertinency of speech'.
169 **grim-looked** grim-faced

167.1] *F, after 168; not in Q*   169+ SP (to 284)] *this edn; Pyramus (subst.) QF;* BOTTOM *as Pyramus /
Wells*   173   *O sweet, O*] thou sweet and *F*

> That stand'st between her father's ground and
>   mine,
> Thou Wall, O Wall, O sweet and lovely Wall,   175
>   Show me thy chink, to blink through with mine eyne.
> [*Wall parts his fingers.*]
> Thanks, courteous Wall. Jove shield thee well for this.
> But what see I? No Thisbe do I see.
> O wicked Wall, through whom I see no bliss,
>   Curst be thy stones for thus deceiving me.   180

THESEUS   The wall, methinks, being sensible, should curse again.

BOTTOM   No, in truth, sir, he should not. 'Deceiving me' is Thisbe's cue. She is to enter now, and I am to spy her through the wall. You shall see it will fall. *(Enter*   185 *Thisbe.)* Pat as I told you: yonder she comes.

FLUTE

> O Wall, full often hast thou heard my moans
> For parting my fair Pyramus and me.

176 **blink** peep, glance (*OED v.* 4a)
   eyne See 1.1.242n.
   *SD   This is the customary SD, following Bottom's suggestion at 3.1.64–6; but *stones* (testicles, 180) and *hole* (199–200) suggest (and some recent productions present) a bawdy enactment of the lovers bending to speak between Snout's parted legs (Leech and Shand; Clayton, 'Fie'). *Wall* could mean the buttocks, as also a woman's private parts (Rubinstein, 298). Parker ('Murals', 195) links the breach in the wall to Thisbe's symbolic loss of virginity.
177 ***Jove shield thee*** God save you. *Jove* for 'God' satisfies the law against stage blasphemy. But oaths are left standing elsewhere (see 312–13n.), so this avoidance in Quince's crude verses may carry a satiric dig at the law.
179 **wicked Wall** The phrase occurs in

Chaucer's *Legend of Thisbe, LGW*, 756.
181 **sensible** animate
182 **again** in reply
183–6 *Except in the play-within-the-play, all dialogue (including the courtiers') during the performance is clearly in prose. Attempts in QF to divide as verse are unconvincing. On actors addressing the audience directly, see 1.2.47n.
183 **he should not** Another instance of the artisans' literalism. Bottom thinks Theseus is suggesting an actual speech by Wall.
185 *The F sentence division after 'fall' produces a telling comic effect, Thisbe entering 'pat' as Bottom says she will. This confirms the theatrical origin of the new copy used for F.
   fall befall, happen, but with a comic suggestion of the wall tumbling down
186 **Pat** exactly; cf. 3.1.2n.

174 *stand'st*] (standst); stands Q2, F   176 SD] *Cam²* after Capell (Wall *holds up his Fingers.*); *not in QF*   183–6] *prose* Pope; Q1 *lines* is / spy / fall / comes. /; Q2, F *line me,* / spy / fall / comes. /   184 now] *not in F*   185–6 fall.... comes.] F; fall / Pat ... comes. *Enter Thisby.* Q   187+ SP FLUTE] *this edn; Thisbe (subst.) QF;* FLUTE *as Thisbe* / Wells

> *My cherry lips have often kissed thy stones,*
> *Thy stones with lime and hair knit up in thee.*   190

BOTTOM
> *I see a voice. Now will I to the chink,*
> *To spy and I can hear my Thisbe's face.*
> *Thisbe?*

FLUTE   *My love thou art, my love I think.*

BOTTOM
> *Think what thou wilt, I am thy lover's grace;*
> *And like Limander, am I trusty still.*   195

FLUTE
> *And I, like Helen, till the Fates me kill.*

BOTTOM
> *Not Shafalus to Procrus was so true.*

FLUTE
> *As Shafalus to Procrus, I to you.*

190 *up in thee* Rhyme calls for the F reading. This is the only case where F rectifies a Q non-rhyme; cf. 1.1.216, 219; 3.2.80. Q 'now againe' might mean that the gap in the wall has been 'knit up' again by Snout bringing his fingers (or legs) together.

191–2 Quince, like Bottom, confuses the senses. see 3.1.86n.

192 *and* if, whether. See 4.2.21n.

193 *My ... think* Theobald's repunctuation improves the sense. The QF punctuation seems preferable for that very reason.

194 *lover's grace* perhaps 'the graceful form of your lover', or simply a 'complimentary periphras[i]s; (used ludicrously)' (Onions)

195 *Limander* for Leander, whose love of Hero led him to swim the Hellespont to his death. Shakespeare alludes to the story in *TGV* (1.1.22, 3.1.119–20), *RJ* (2.4.42) and later plays. (Marlowe and Chapman's *Hero and Leander* appeared in 1598.) Cf. the

distorted form *Phibbus* (1.2.31).

196 *Helen* probably in mistake for Hero, Leander's beloved, named alongside Thisbe in *RJ* 2.4.42. Helen of Troy was not attached to any single lover.

197–202 These lines were sung in Brook's production, providing a parallel (maybe not wholly ironic) to earlier sung lines in the lovers' dialogue.

197 *Shafalus ... Procrus* for Cephalus and Procris. Cephalus was abducted by the dawn-goddess Aurora but remained loyal to Procris; see 3.2.389n. Procris, however, faltered when Cephalus himself, in changed form, tempted her in an unfair trial of her chastity (*Met.* 7.700–52, Golding, 7.900–78). This may be why Thisbe compares herself to Cephalus rather than Procris (198), always assuming Quince the playwright knew the myth correctly.

190 *up in thee*] F; now againe *Q*   191–2 *see ... hear*] heare ... see *F2*   192–3 *To ... Thisbe?*] *so lined, Rowe²; one line, QF*   193] My love! thou art, my love, I think. *Theobald*   196 *I*] *not in F*

BOTTOM

O kiss me through the hole of this vile Wall.

FLUTE

I kiss the Wall's hole, not your lips at all.   200

BOTTOM

Wilt thou at Ninny's tomb meet me straightway?

FLUTE

Tide life, tide death, I come without delay.

SNOUT

Thus have I, Wall, my part discharged so;
And being done, thus Wall away doth go.

[Exeunt Wall, Pyramus and Thisbe.]

THESEUS Now is the more use between the two 205
neighbours.

---

199 **kiss ... hole** a double entendre suggesting (Snout's) arse-hole. See 176 SDn.
    vile Q1 spells 'vilde' only at this point, and QF at 285. This already old-fashioned dialectal form might be meant as peculiar to Bottom.
201 **Ninny's** see 3.1.92n.
    straightway directly, immediately
202 **Tide ... death** whether I live or die (though in the latter event, he obviously could not come)
    Tide happen
203 **discharged** dischargèd. See 1.2.86n.
204 *SD F '*Exit Clow.*' probably refers to 'Clowns' (*TxC*), indicating that Snout, Bottom and Flute – i.e. Wall, Pyramus and Thisbe – all leave. F constantly confuses singular 'Exit' and plural 'Exeunt'.
205 *SP In QF, always '*Du[ke]*' from this point, probably to avoid confusion between

'Th[eseus]' and 'Th[isbe]'. '*Dut[chess]*' henceforth is no doubt to match, in place of earlier 'Hip.' or 'Hyp[polita]' (1, 23). There is a stray '*Duk.*' earlier: see 107 SPn.
*more use As in 190, different readings in Q and F, but here neither makes ready sense. In secretary hand, 'mor use' is easily misread as 'mon usd', leading to Q 'Moon vsed'. *Use* might mean familiarity, customary exchanges (cf. *OED v.* 18, 19, P1), or even sexual exchanges or promiscuity, as in *MM* 1.4.62 (*OED n.* 1c; *v.* 14b, P1; Partridge, *Bawdy*, 210) – both possible now that the wall is breached. F may be an attempt to make sense of the garbled Q reading, but is itself garbled. It is best explained by some variant of 'mure' (wall; Theobald compares 'the wall is down', 343) or 'mural' (seldom meaning a wall, and never, it seems, in Shakespeare's day).

199 *vile*] (*vilde Q1*)   204 SD] *Capell; Exit Clow. F; not in Q*   205+ SP THESEUS] *Rowe; Duke (subst.)* *QF*   205 more use] *this edn; Moon vsed Q; morall downe F; mural down (Pope); wall down Collier MS, 109; mure rased Ard²*

DEMETRIUS   No remedy, my lord, when walls are so
   wilful, to hear without warning.

HIPPOLYTA   This is the silliest stuff that ever I heard.

THESEUS   The best in this kind are but shadows; and the   210
   worst are no worse, if imagination amend them.

HIPPOLYTA   It must be your imagination, then, and not
   theirs.

THESEUS   If we imagine no worse of them than they of
   themselves, they may pass for excellent men. Here   215
   come two noble beasts, in a man and a lion.

Enter Lion.

208 **wilful** willing, obliging (*OED adj.*[1] 3)
   hear probably alluding to the proverb
   'Walls have ears' (Dent, W19). Wall has
   been so obliging as to hear Pyramus' plea
   to part itself and then depart altogether,
   'aid(ing) and abet(ting) its own breaching'
   (Hawkes, 29) to allow *more use* (205n.)
   between the lovers.
   warning notice, signal (*OED n.*[1] 8c); cf.
   2H4 4.2.106–7, 'warning . . . to arm'.
   Warning = refusal, denial (*OED n.*[2]) suits
   the sense admirably, but is not recorded
   after 1487.
210 **in this kind** of this sort   i.e. stage
   performances
   shadows mere reflections or imitations of
   reality, illusions; see 413n., 3.2.347n. and
   pp. 99–104. Smith ('Forces', 6) observes
   that this is probably the first time
   Shakespeare comments on the art of the
   theatre in a play. Robin calls Oberon 'king
   of shadows' (3.2.347), and mentions
   'shadows' again in his last speech (413).
   Theseus' casual philosophizing draws
   together various strands of the play.
211 **imagination** See 8n.; here specifically the
   power to recreate mentally the reality

behind   an   inadequate   (stage)
representation. Cf. *Per* 3.0.58–9: 'In your
imagination hold / This stage the ship'.
Johnson calls this power 'supposition': it
does not mistake imitations for realities,
but uses them to bring realities to mind
(*Preface to Shakespeare*: Johnson, 1.
xxvii). Holland cites *The True Tragedy of
Richard the Third* (1594), sig. A3[r]:
'*Truth*. . . . what makes thou vpon a stage?
/ *Poet[ry]*. Shadowes. / *Truth*. Then will I
adde bodies to the shadowes.'
216 **two noble beasts** These are best taken as
conjoint in Snug, *a man and a lion*, as
suggested by the QF punctuation (as here)
and spelt out in a manuscript emendation in
the prompt-book of the late seventeenth-
century Smock Alley Theatre, Dublin, for
a performance that probably never took
place: 'Here comes two noble beasts, a
Man and a Lion in one' (*Promptbooks*,
7.1.51). Moonshine need not enter till 233:
all other characters in the play-within-the-
play 'enter' just before they speak. On the
class implications of the man–beast jibe,
see Arab, 110–11, 120.

209+ SP HIPPOLYTA] Rowe; *Duchess (subst.) QF*   ever] ere *Q2, F*   216 man] moon *Theobald*
216.1] *this edn; Enter* Lyon, *and* Moone-shine. *QF*

SNUG

> *You ladies, you whose gentle hearts do fear*
>   *The smallest monstrous mouse that creeps on floor,*
> *May now perchance both quake and tremble here,*
>   *When Lion rough in wildest rage doth roar.*   220
> *Then know that I, as Snug the joiner, am*
> *No lion fell, nor else no lion's dam.*
> *For if I should, as Lion, come in strife*
> *Into this place, 'twere pity on my life.*

THESEUS   A very gentle beast, and of a good conscience.   225

DEMETRIUS   The very best at a beast, my lord, that e'er I saw.

LYSANDER   This Lion is a very fox for his valour.

THESEUS   True, and a goose for his discretion.

DEMETRIUS   Not so, my lord. For his valour cannot carry
his discretion, and the fox carries the goose.   230

THESEUS   His discretion, I am sure, cannot carry his valour,
for the goose carries not the fox. It is well. Leave it to
his discretion, and let us listen to the Moon.

[Enter Moonshine.]

217–24 This speech accords with Bottom's advice in 3.1.33–42.

217 *whose . . . fear* See 3.1.25n.

218 *smallest monstrous* Cf. *monstrous little*, 1.2.48 and n.

222 **No . . . dam* Neither a fierce lion nor its mother, i.e. neither a male nor a female lion. The two are perhaps mentioned separately as Ovid (hence Golding) and Chaucer talk of a lioness, and Gower, Lydgate and Thomson of a lion; but the most likely reason seems 'the desperation for a rhyme' (van Emden, 201). The QF construction 'A . . . nor' is possible, but Rowe's emendation is simple and plausible. The phrase 'lions [*sic*] fell' occurs in *La Conusaunce damours*, sig. B2ᵛ. (See p. 61.) For allusions to this

passage by later political commentators, see p. 95.

223 *in strife* belligerently, fiercely

225 *gentle* (1) noble (as king of beasts); (2) mild, soft-hearted (because of its consideration for the ladies)

226 *best . . . beast* probably a pun, the two words being pronounced alike (White). Cf. *rest / beast* rhyming in *CE* 5.1.83–4.

227–33 drawing on the proverb 'Discretion is the better part of valour' (Dent, D354). The lion was marked by its valour and the fox by its wiles (discretion), while the goose is proverbially foolish, hence the ironic expression 'as wise as a goose' (Dent, G348).

229–30 *his . . . discretion* He has even less boldness than wit.

217+ SP SNUG] *this edn; Lyon. QF;* SNUG *as Lion / Wells*   221 *as*] one *F*   222 *No*] *Rowe;* A *QF*   224 *on*] of *F*   226 e'er] *Rowe;* ere *QF1–3;* e're *F4*   233 listen] hearken *Q2, F*   233.1] *this edn; not in QF*

STARVELING

This lanthorn doth the horned moon present.

DEMETRIUS   He should have worn the horns on his head.   235

THESEUS   He is no crescent, and his horns are invisible, within the circumference.

STARVELING

This lanthorn doth the horned moon present.
Myself, the man i'th' moon do seem to be.

THESEUS   This is the greatest error of all the rest. The   240
man should be put into the lanthorn; how is it else the
man i'th' moon?

DEMETRIUS   He dares not come there for the candle; for
you see, it is already in snuff.

HIPPOLYTA   I am aweary of this moon. Would he would   245
change.

THESEUS   It appears, by his small light of discretion, that

---

234 *lanthorn* This spelling and pronunciation are confirmed by the punning echo in *horned* (Wright, note on 3.1.55); cf. the pun in *2H4* 1.2.46–50 on *horne* and *lanthorne* (so spelt in both Q and F). From this point, QF consistently read *lanthorne*, reflecting the artisans' unlearned speech and the aristocrats' parody of it; see 3.1.55n. Wells and Taylor (*Modernizing*, 14, 16) support 'lanthorn' here and in *MA* 3.3.24. The form also supports a play on *lant*, stale urine and *horn*, (erect) penis; see 244n.

234, 238 *horned* (hornèd) crescent; but any hint of a cuckold's horns was always good for a laugh (see 235).

236 *crescent* literally 'growing', i.e. large or plump; like *circumference*, an ironic reference to Starveling's thinness

238–9 If there is any need felt to reconcile Starveling's account with Quince's (134–5),

Starveling by himself may be taken as the man in the moon, and together with his appurtenances, Moonshine.

244 *in snuff* about to be extinguished: Starveling is afraid of putting the candle out altogether. (There may be an underlying jibe at his alleged impotence; cf. *dares not come,*) To take *in snuff* could also mean to be vexed or offended (*OED* snuff *n.¹* 4a, Tilley, S598), as Starveling's next lines show him to be. The same pun occurs in *LLL* 5.2.22.

245–6 Hippolyta's words echo Theseus' in 1.1.3–4. They may hint at her impatience for the marriage bed, again showing that she now welcomes her marriage; cf. 1n., and see pp. 65–7, 80–1.

247 *small ... discretion* like the dwindling candle
discretion continuing the jibes against Lion on the same count (225–33)

234+ SP STARVELING] *this edn; Moon (subst.) QF;* STARVELING *as Moonshine / Wells*   234 (+238, 241, 252, 254) *lanthorn*] lantern *Malone (also in 238, 241), Var 1793 (Steevens: also in 238, 241, 252, 254)*   238–9] *prose F*   239 *do*] doth *F*   243–4] *Q2, F line* candle. / snuffe. /   245 aweary] weary *Q2, F*

he is in the wane; but yet in courtesy, in all reason, we
must stay the time.

LYSANDER   Proceed, moon.   250

STARVELING   All that I have to say is to tell you that the
lanthorn is the moon, I the man i'th' moon, this thorn-
bush my thorn-bush, and this dog my dog.

DEMETRIUS   Why, all these should be in the lanthorn; for all
these are in the moon. But silence: here comes Thisbe.   255

Enter Thisbe.

FLUTE

This is old Ninny's tomb. Where is my love?

SNUG

*O. (The Lion roars. Thisbe runs off [, dropping her
mantle].)*

DEMETRIUS   Well roared, Lion.

THESEUS   Well run, Thisbe.

HIPPOLYTA   Well shone, Moon. Truly, the Moon shines   260
with a good grace.

[Lion shakes Thisbe's mantle.]

THESEUS   Well moused, Lion.

Enter Pyramus.

DEMETRIUS   And then came Pyramus.   *[Exit Lion.]*

---

248 **in the wane** 'His wit is in the wane' was a
proverbial expression (Dent, W555).

249 **stay the time** stay till the play ends (when
the waning Moon will disappear – perhaps
recalling that their wedding night will
begin at the new moon)

251–3 The nervous and bewildered Starveling
now abandons his lines and speaks in his
own person.

256 ***Ninny's*** See 3.1.92n. Quince's attempt at
correction has clearly failed.

257 ***O*** presumably the lion's roar

260–1 Hippolyta might be making up for her
earlier jibe at Moonshine. Brook's
production brought out this possibility.

262 Theseus' comment sarcastically reverses
Demetrius' at 258.

moused shaken (the mantle) as a cat
shakes a mouse (*OED v.* 2a), itself a
derogatory comparison for a lion; but also
'acted like a mouse'

263 *SD   The Lion needs an exit line. It is
best placed here, as the Lion seems to flee
at Pyramus' entry (see 264).

---

251 SP] *Wells; Moon QF*   252 i'th'] *(*ith*)*; in the *Q2, F*   254–5 ²all these] they *Q2, F*   256–7] *so lined,
F; one line, Q*   256 *tomb*] *(*tumbe *Q1)*   *Where is*] *Q1, F*; wher's *Q2*   257 SD *The . . . off*] *F; not in Q*
dropping her mantle] *Cam²; not in QF*   260–1] *F lines* Moone. / grace. /   261 SD] *Riv after Capell
(*Lion *shakes* Thisbe's *Mantle, and Exit.*), after 262; not in QF*   262.1] *after 264, QF*   263 SD] *Riv
after Capell's SD at 262; not in QF*

LYSANDER   And so the Lion vanished.

BOTTOM

    Sweet Moon, I thank thee for thy sunny beams.   265
    I thank thee, Moon, for shining now so bright.
    For by thy gracious, golden, glittering gleams,
    I trust to take of truest Thisbe sight.
        But stay: O spite!
        But mark, poor knight,   270
            What dreadful dole is here?
    Eyes, do you see?
    How can it be?
        O dainty duck, O dear!
    Thy mantle good,   275
    What, stained with blood?
        Approach, ye Furies fell.
    O Fates, come, come,
    Cut thread and thrum,

265–340 Taylor ('Heart') demonstrates how in Pyramus and Thisbe's last speeches, Shakespeare echoes various contemporary translations of the classics

265 Moon ... sunny obvious comic contradiction

267 *gleams It is unlikely that *beams* would be made to rhyme with itself, even in designedly bad verse. *Gleams* is an attractive possibility as enhancing the comically overdone alliteration.

268 take There is no firm warrant for changing the Q reading, but F 'taste' is a plausible option. To 'taste' the *sight* of something would add to Bottom's comic confusion of the senses.

271 dole (cause for) lament or sorrow

274 duck a term of affection. 'As dainty as a duck' was proverbial (Dent, D630.1).
O dear either an affectionate address to Thisbe or an exclamation of concern

277 Furies the Erinyes or avenging goddesses of Greek mythology, presumably invoked to avenge Thisbe's supposed death

278 Fates the Parcae, goddesses who spun, measured and cut the thread of human lives; cf. 329. The Pyramus poem in *Handful* mentions Atropos, who cuts the thread (sig. C3^r).

279 thread and thrum respectively, the warp-yarn in woven cloth and the tuft where this yarn is joined to the loom (see *OED* thread *n.* 2c). The terms reflect Bottom's profession of weaver; but having been introduced by Quince, they are presumably a simple reference to the Fates' occupation.

---

267 *gleams*] Singer^3 (Knight); beames *QF*; streames *F2*   268 *take*] taste *F*   *Thisbe*] Thisbies *F*   269–80] *so lined and indented*, Pope; *QF line* knight, / here? / bee! / deare! / blood? / fell, / thrumme, / quell. /   277 *ye*] you *F*

> *Quail, crush, conclude, and quell.*   280
> THESEUS   This passion, and the death of a dear friend,
> would go near to make a man look sad.
> HIPPOLYTA   Beshrew my heart, but I pity the man.
> BOTTOM
>
> *O wherefore, Nature, didst thou lions frame?*
> *Since Lion vile hath here deflowered my dear.*   285
> *Which is – no, no, which was – the fairest dame*
> *That lived, that loved, that liked, that looked with*
> *cheer.*
> *Come, tears, confound;*
> *Out, sword, and wound*
> *The pap of Pyramus:*   290
> *Ay, that left pap,*
> *Where heart doth hop.*
> *Thus die I, thus, thus, thus.* [*Stabs himself.*]
> *Now am I dead,*
> *Now am I fled;*   295
> *My soul is in the sky.*
> *Tongue, lose thy light.*

280 Kittredge distinguishes *Quail*, subdue, from *quell*, slay, placing the four verbs in the line in a logical (and alliterative) sequence.

281 **passion** (1) strong emotion; (2) suffering (*OED n.* 3)

283 **Beshrew** See 2.2.58n.

285 *vile* QF 'vilde'; see 199n.
    deflowered malapropism for 'devoured'; but in conjunction with *mantle . . . stained with blood* (275–6), deepens the sexual undertones of the play-within-the-play.

286 *Which . . . was* Cf. Kyd's *Spanish Tragedy* 2.5.14–15: 'Alas, it is Horatio, my sweet son! / Oh, no, but he that whilom was my son!' This may be another jibe against Shakespeare's rival company, the

Admiral's Men, which produced Kyd's play; see 1.2.25n., 3.1.125n., 4.2.34n.

287 **with cheer** (1) happily, cheerfully; (2) with her face, i.e. eyes – empty words to provide a rhyme

288 *confound* destroy (me)

290 *pap* applied in the *Gallery* poem (116.2) to Thisbe's breast, here more ineptly to a man's

292 **heart doth hop** perhaps a parody of Thomas Phaer's translation of *Aen.* 5.137–8, where hearts are said to 'hop' (Taylor, 'Phaer', 'Heart')

297 *Tongue . . . light* another confusion of the senses (*tongue* for 'eye'), again presumably Quince's error of composition; cf. 191–2n., 344–5n., 3.1.86n.

281–2] F lines friend / sad. /   285 *vile*] *(vilde QF)* 288–99] *so lined and indented, Johnson; QF line*
wound / *Pyramus:* / hoppe. / thus. / sky. / flight, / dy. /   293 SD] *Dyce (opp. 292); not in QF*

> *Moon, take thy flight.*   [*Exit Moonshine.*]
> *Now die, die, die, die, die.*   [*Dies.*]

DEMETRIUS No die but an ace for him; for he is but one. 300

LYSANDER Less than an ace, man; for he is dead, he is nothing.

THESEUS With the help of a surgeon, he might yet recover, and yet prove an ass.

HIPPOLYTA How chance Moonshine is gone before 305 Thisbe comes back and finds her lover?

THESEUS She will find him by starlight. Here she comes, and her passion ends the play.

Enter Thisbe.

HIPPOLYTA Methinks she should not use a long one for such a Pyramus. I hope she will be brief. 310

DEMETRIUS A mote will turn the balance, which Pyramus, which Thisbe is the better: he for a man, God warrant us; she for a woman, God bless us.

298 *SD This is the traditional exit-point for Moonshine, as a comically literal response to Pyramus' outcry.

300 **ace** the face of a die with a single spot **but one** no better than the lowest score at dice; of little worth. Kökeritz (*Pronunciation*, 89) suggests *ace* was pronounced like 'ass'; Cercignani (179) demurs, arguing that the humour turns on 'antithesis rather than identity'.

302 **nothing** zero, less than one

304 **ass** See 300n. There is dramatic irony in this reminder to the audience of Bottom's transformation, which Theseus would not know of.

305–6 *Rowe's punctuation (as here) makes the meaning clearer. On line-division, see 183–6n.

305 **How chance** how does it chance, how come

308 **passion** a passionate speech (*OED n.* 6d),

as *a long one* (309) suggests; but perhaps more broadly 'suffering' (*OED* 3)

311 **A . . . balance** A speck of dust will tip the scales one way or the other – i.e. it is an open question.
*mote For the spelling, see 3.1.156n.

311–12 '**which . . . Thisbe** whether Pyramus or Thisbe

312–13 **he . . . bless us** As this Thisbe is not really a woman, Demetrius is disparaging the authenticity of Bottom's rendition of Pyramus (Arab, 110). These words are omitted in F. The omission is often explained by a 1606 statute banning oaths on stage (see 177n.), but other oaths are left standing (3.1.28, 4.1.202, 4.2.13). Taylor and Jowett (53, 89) suggest this was owing to haphazard consultation of the theatrical copy (where all profanities would have been omitted) used when preparing the F text.

313 **warrant** protect (*OED v.* 1)

298 SD] *Dyce (Capell, after 299); not in QF*   299 SD] *Warburton; not in QF*   304 yet] *not in Q2, F*   305–6] *Q2, F line* before? / Louer. /   305 before] *Rowe;* before? *QF*   306 lover?] *Rowe;* louer. *QF*   307–8] *F lines* starre-light. / play. /   308.1] *F, after 306; not in Q*   311 mote] *Var 1793 (Malone; conj. Heath, 59);* moth *QF*   312–13 he . . . ²us] *not in F*   313 warrant] *(warnd Q); not in F*

LYSANDER   She hath spied him already, with those
    sweet eyes.   315

DEMETRIUS   And thus she means, *videlicet.*

FLUTE

      Asleep, my love?
      What, dead, my dove?
        O Pyramus, arise.
      Speak, speak. Quite dumb?   320
      Dead, dead? A tomb
        Must cover thy sweet eyes.
      These lily lips,
      This cherry nose,
        These yellow cowslip cheeks   325
      Are gone, are gone:
      Lovers make moan.
        His eyes were green as leeks.
      O sisters three,
      Come, come to me,   330
        With hands as pale as milk;
      Lay them in gore,

---

316 **means** laments (especially for the dead:
OED mean *v.²* 2a); also used of a formal or
legal complaint (*v.²* 4a, b), hence *videlicet*
(see next note)
    videlicet as you may see, as follows. This
Latin legal term seems to have entered
ordinary English in the late sixteenth century.
321 **tomb** variously spelt in Q1; 'tumbe' at 256
and here, perhaps marking a comic
pronunciation rhyming with *dumb*
323–4 **lily ... nose** comically garbling the
mingled red and white of the ideal
complexion by confusing the usual phrases
'lily(-white) cheeks' and 'cherry lips'; cf.
189, 3.1.88–9n.
325 **cowslip cheeks** depriving the flower of its
fairy aura (2.1.10, 15); cf. 4.1.3n.

327 **make moan** The Pyramus poem in *Handful*
has the phrase 'made . . . mone' (sig. C3ʳ).
328 **green as leeks** proverbial (Dent, L176).
The comic effect of the comparison seems
preferable to taking *green* to mean 'fresh,
youthful' as in *RJ* 3.5.221, 'so green, so
quick, so fair an eye'.
329 **sisters three** the Parcae or Fates; see 278n.
331–2 Milk-white hands were ascribed to
heroines in romance and love-poetry.
Thisbe ascribes them ineptly to fatal or
avenging powers, apparently conflating the
Furies (hence *gore*) with the Fates (*shore
. . . his thread*); see 277n., 278n.
332 **Lay** place, put down; or perhaps cover, coat
(*OED* *v.¹* 42). Theobald's emendation
'lave' (wash, bathe) is worth considering.

316 means] moans *Theobald*   317–40] *so lined, Pope (323–4 as one line, divided by Theobald); QF line*
doue? / arise, / tumbe / eyes. / nose, / cheekes / mone: / leekes. / mee, / milke, / shore / silke. / sword, /
imbrew: / ends: / adieu. /   321 tomb] *(tumbe Q1)*   323 lips] brows *Theobald*   332 Lay] Laue *Theobald*

> *Since you have shore*
> > *With shears his thread of silk.*
> *Tongue, not a word.*   335
> *Come, trusty sword,*
> > *Come, blade, my breast imbrue.*
> *[Stabs herself.]*
> *And farewell, friends;*
> *Thus Thisbe ends.*
> > *Adieu, adieu, adieu.*   *[Dies.]*   340

THESEUS   Moonshine and Lion are left to bury the dead.

DEMETRIUS   Ay, and Wall too.

BOTTOM   No, I assure you, the wall is down that parted
their fathers. Will it please you to see the epilogue, or to
hear a Bergomask dance between two of our company?   345

THESEUS   No epilogue, I pray you; for your play needs
no excuse. Never excuse; for when the players are all
dead, there need none to be blamed. Marry, if he that

---

333 *shore* sheared: the 'strong' past tense was
still current.

337 An old stage convention had Thisbe kill
herself with the scabbard of Pyramus'
sword (see p. 4).
   imbrue stain, soak; perhaps also pierce
(*OED* 3b, citing two doubtful passages of
which this is one)

343 *SP   The officious Bottom would be more
likely than Snug (Lion), the speaker in Q,
to deviate from his theatrical part to
contradict Theseus (cf. 183–6); the 'dead'
Pyramus springing up in this way would
also create a comic effect. The theatrically
oriented F allots him the speech.
   wall is down Groves (279–80) points out
the biblical echo, 'hath broken downe the
middle wall that was a stop betweene vs'
(Eph. 2.14), alluding to the reconciliation
of Jews and Gentiles. This reinforces the
echo from 1 Cor. in 4.1.209.

343–4 **parted their fathers** Cf. *RJ* Prologue 8,
'Doth with their death bury their parents'
strife'.

344–5 **see . . . dance** Bottom's final confusion
of the senses

345 **Bergomask dance** a rustic dance
associated with the supposedly clownish
inhabitants of Bergamo, Italy (only citation
in *OED*). A clownish folk dance would
provide a contrasting prelude, like an
antimasque (Wilson), to the subsequent
dance by the fairies; cf. 'rural music'
followed by the fairy music of concord in
4.1.29, 82. On dance as a symbol of marital
harmony, see 4.1.84–91n.

347 **excuse** Epilogues were commonly phrased
as appeals to the audience to overlook the
defects of the play. Robin makes this very
plea in his final speech, an epilogue in all
but name.

337 SD] *Dyce; not in QF*   340 SD] *Warburton; not in QF*   343 SP BOTTOM] *F; Lyon. Q*

271

writ it had played Pyramus and hanged himself in
Thisbe's garter, it would have been a fine tragedy; and 350
so it is truly, and very notably discharged. But come,
your Bergomask; let your epilogue alone.
   [*Dance, and exeunt actors.*]
The iron tongue of midnight hath told twelve.
Lovers, to bed; 'tis almost fairy time.
I fear we shall outsleep the coming morn,   355
As much as we this night have overwatched.
This palpable gross play hath well beguiled
The heavy gait of night. Sweet friends, to bed.
A fortnight hold we this solemnity,   359
In nightly revels and new jollity.   *Exeunt.*

349–50 hanged . . . garter Proverbially, people hang themselves in their own garters (Dent, G42). Cf. *1H4* 2.2.42–3: 'Hang thyself in thine own heir-apparent garters!'

351 so . . . truly the apparent praise hides cruel disparagement: the play is no better than if Pyramus had hanged himself as suggested.
discharged performed, executed. Theseus may be sarcastically echoing Wall's use of this unnecessarily grand word (see 203, 1.2.83n., 86n.).

352 *SD *TxC* suggests the dance is between Bottom and Flute, the only two actors left onstage in the play-within-the-play. The two dead characters springing up to dance (as Bottom already has, to speak) adds to the comedy. It also solves the problem of removing the dead from the curtainless Elizabethan stage.

353 iron tongue like the clapper of a bell tolling the hours; cf. *KJ* 3.3.47–8, 'the midnight bell / . . . with his iron tongue'.
told counted (*OED* tell *v.* 17a), but also suggesting 'tolled'. Q 'tolde' combines both senses.

354 fairy time the time when fairies roam and

rule: 'begins after midnight, and closes at the rising of the morning star' (*Shakespeare's England*, 1.536: see 3.2.378–82). The phrase also suggests the pleasures of the marriage bed, perhaps implying that they are illusory.

356 overwatched stayed up late. 'Watch' originally meant 'remain awake' (*OED v.* 1).

357 palpable palpably, glaringly (intensified in Capell's compound 'palpable-gross'). For 'intensive adverbs' without a final -*ly*, see 1.2.20n., but here the word may be an adjective ('palpable and gross'). Cf. *E3*, printed 1596 and at least partly attributed to Shakespeare: 'That line hath two faults gross and palpable' (2.1.142: text as in Norton[3]).
beguiled See 40n.

358 *gait manner of moving, hence passage, progress, which suits *heavy* – slow and ponderous to lovers eager for the marriage bed. See *OED* gate *n.*[2] 7a; cf. (though a different word) *gate*, 406n.

359 fortnight This exact reference may indicate a particular wedding, perhaps the Stanley–de Vere one (see pp. 284–6).

---

349 hanged] hung *F*   352 SD] *this edn after Capell (Dance: and Exeunt Clowns.); not in QF*   358 gait] *Rowe*[2] *(*Gaite*); gate QF*

Enter [ROBIN GOODFELLOW *with a broom.*]

ROBIN

> Now the hungry lion roars
>   And the wolf behowls the moon,
> Whilst the heavy ploughman snores,
>   All with weary task fordone.
> Now the wasted brands do glow,   365
>   Whilst the screech-owl, screeching loud,
> Puts the wretch that lies in woe
>   In remembrance of a shroud.
> Now it is the time of night

361–428 There are many questions about the play's close. It may amalgamate two separate endings: one for the public stage, another for a private (wedding-night?) performance (see pp. 291–4). Again, 391–412 might be the original song to which the F heading refers, or that may have been lost (perhaps with a second one), as scholars since Johnson and producers at least since Granville-Barker (1914, 39) have conjectured. F prints 391–412 as a distinct 'Song', indented and italicized. If so, Oberon alone might sing it as the Q SP at 391 indicates, or the fairies *by rote*, as Titania enjoins (387). Noble (55–7) suggests that Oberon leads the song with all the fairies joining in. While all these are open issues, the text common to all early editions (differing only in an SD/SP at 391) provides a consistent construct that can be performed in its entirety even if, perhaps, of multiple origin. Gooch and Thatcher list 16 settings for the fairy speeches, and another 11 for Robin's preceding speech.

361–4 As Foakes observes, these lines combine a wild forest with a pastoral landscape; cf. 2.1.180–1n., 228n.; 2.2.35n.

361 *lion roars* perhaps reflecting Psalms 104.21, 'The lions roaring after their pray'. This would justify QF 'Lyons' (compatible

with the verb ending in -*s*; see 3.1.77n.), but the next line has singular *wolf.*

362 *behowls* QF 'beholds' makes sense as 'gazes at' (and howls), but seems a somewhat indirect way to describe the wolf's behaviour. *Behowls* (though not otherwise recorded till the nineteenth century) is supported by 'the howling of Irish wolves against the moon' (*AYL* 5.2.105–6) and 'Bemock the modest moon' (*Cor* 1.1.252). Shakespeare has many coinages starting with *be-*, including *Beteem* (1.1.131) and *Bedabbled* (3.2.443). The unusual transitive use of 'howl' may be accepted in a coinage.

363 **heavy** weary, sleepy (*OED adj* [1] 28)

364 **fordone** exhausted

365 **wasted brands** burnt-down torches or logs

366–8 The owl's screech was thought to presage death; cf. *Mac* 2.2.3–4. Wolf and owl had appeared in a similar context in *FQ* 1.5.30.6–9.

369–72 Cf. Robin's account in 3.2.381–2, and *Ham* 3.2.378–80 on the 'witching time of night' when 'churchyards yawn'. All in all, 361–80 paints a surprisingly sinister picture of the night in the context of a wedding, whether real or fictitious. The fairy blessing that follows is placed in this sombre setting. On churchyards in ancient pagan Greece, cf. 1.1.70–8n., 3.2.382n.

360.1] *Oxf; Enter Pucke. QF*   361 SP] *Oxf; Puck QF*   lion] *Rowe;* Lyons *QF*   362 behowls] *Theobald (Warburton);* beholds *QF*

That the graves, all gaping wide,   370
    Every one lets forth his sprite
        In the churchway paths to glide.
And we fairies, that do run
    By the triple Hecate's team
From the presence of the sun,   375
    Following darkness like a dream,
Now are frolic. Not a mouse
Shall disturb this hallowed house.
I am sent with broom before,
To sweep the dust behind the door.   380

Enter [OBERON] *and* [TITANIA], *with all their train.*

OBERON

Through the house give glimmering light
    By the dead and drowsy fire.
Every elf and fairy sprite

---

371 **sprite** the ghost of the buried person

373 **we** Q1 'wee' is best taken as a variant of *we*. 'Wee' (small) was hardly current in southern English at the time, though one contemporary citation (*OED adj.* a) is a variant of *MW* 1.4.20.

374 **triple Hecate's team** The same goddess was Cynthia in the heavens, Diana on earth and Hecate or Proserpina in the underworld. Her chariot (the moon's, often conflated with the night's) was drawn by a team of dragons (see 3.2.379n.). Golding uses 'triple Hecate' twice (7.136, 318; see Baldwin, *Small Latine*, 2.436–9).

   Hecate two syllables, as always in Shakespeare

376 **like a dream** This might refer to darkness or to the fairies. Either way, it suggests an illusory or ephemeral condition rather than

the happy, ideal state conveyed by the modern use of the phrase.

377 **frolic** playful, active

379 **broom** This detail allies Robin with the brownie that performs household chores at night. Bruster (*Culture*, 54) notes how at the end of mummers' plays, an actor playing a devil swept up coins thrown by the audience. The action may also have symbolized a cleansing function.

380 **sweep ... door** presumably not shove the dust out of sight, but remove what was left there by negligent servants

381 **glimmering light** perhaps the last light of a *drowsy fire* (382), or a light emanating from the fairies. For *glimmering* in a 'fairy' context, cf. 2.1.77n. The actors might have carried tapers on their heads, as in *MW* 4.4.49.

373 we] *Q2, F;* wee *Q1*   380.1 OBERON *and* TITANIA] *Malone; King and Queene of Fairies QF*   all] *not in Q2, F*

Hop as light as bird from brier,
And this ditty after me   385
Sing, and dance it trippingly.

TITANIA

First rehearse your song by rote,
To each word a warbling note.
Hand in hand, with fairy grace,
Will we sing and bless this place.   390

OBERON

THE SONG

Now, until the break of day,
Through this house each fairy stray.
To the best bride-bed will we,
Which by us shall blessed be,
And the issue there create   395
Ever shall be fortunate.
So shall all the couples three
Ever true in loving be,
And the blots of nature's hand
Shall not in their issue stand.   400

384 brier bush. 'As blithe as bird (on) brier'
   was a proverbial phrase (Dent, B359),
   common in poem and song.
386 trippingly in a nimble or frolicsome
   manner: earliest *OED* citation
387 rehearse recite, render, perhaps by way of
   practice or memorization (*OED v.* 7a); cf.
   3.1.68n.
   by rote (1) with precision, by heart (*OED*
   rote *n.*[1] 1a); (2) in turn in a circle, perhaps
   accompanying a round dance (from Latin
   rota, wheel; not in *OED*). See 361–428n.
389 grace favour, blessing, but also suggesting
   elegance and delicate movement
391–2 In the Folio text of *MW*, the 'fairies' –
   there human children led by Mistress
   Quickly – similarly make their way

through Windsor Castle.
391 SP, *SD The SP occurs only in Q, the SD
   only in F. See 361–428n.
393–4 bride-bed ... blessed Blessing the
   marriage bed was a general custom, but see
   Hattaway (30) on its equivocal religious
   implications in that age. Moreover, houses
   were generally blessed to keep fairies away
   (Young, 22).
393 best bride-bed that of Theseus and
   Hippolyta, to be blessed in person by
   Oberon and Titania
394 blessed blessèd. See 1.1.74n.
395 create created, i.e. begotten in that
   marriage bed
399–400 Their children will have no physical
   defects.

385–6] *so lined, Rowe*[2]; *one line, QF*   387 your] *this Q2, F*   391–412] *indented and italicized, F*
391 SP OBERON] *not in F*   THE SONG] *F; not in Q*

Never mole, hare-lip, nor scar
Nor mark prodigious, such as are
Despised in nativity,
Shall upon their children be.
With this field-dew consecrate,   405
Every fairy take his gate
And each several chamber bless
Through this palace with sweet peace;
And the owner of it blest
Ever shall in safety rest.   410
Trip away, make no stay.
Meet me all, by break of day.   *Exeunt [all but Robin.]*

ROBIN

If we shadows have offended,
Think but this, and all is mended:
That you have but slumbered here   415
While these visions did appear.
And this weak and idle theme,

---

402 **prodigious** (1) ominous, portentous (*OED* 1); (2) abnormal (*OED* 3). The latter sense could imply the former.

403 **Despised** Despisèd

405 **field-dew** the final change on the 'dew' motif; see p. 73.
   consecrate consecrated. Oberon's action resembles the Catholic 'sacramental' where holy water was sprinkled on a marriage bed to promote fertility (Hattaway, 30). This may be Shakespeare's reversion to a pre-Reformation concept, or (more likely) its scaling-down to an unserious level in a notionally pagan setting (cf. 369–72n., 1.1.70–8n., 3.2.382n.).

406 **gate** route, course (*OED n.²*); cf. 358n.

407–10 *No emendation can rectify the irregular grammatical construction implicit in the QF order of 407–8, 410, 409. Interchanging 409 and 410 solves the

problem. An erroneous transposition would be perfectly possible if a whole line of type needed replacing.

407 **several** separate, individual

409 **blest** On the form, see 1.1.74n.

411 **stay** stop, pause

413 Robin's epilogue opens like Quince's prologue (108).
   shadows illusory appearances, applicable to both fairies and actors; see 210n. and 3.2.347n. Robin speaks both as the supernatural character and as the actor playing him, rounding off the play's story as well as its performance; the dramatic illusion aligns itself with the supernatural illusion. (See also Mandel, 67.)

417 **theme** unusually applied (perhaps merely to provide a rhyme) to the entire action or 'subject' of the play instead of a specific topic treated there

---

409–10] *so arranged, Staunton (Singer); 410 before 409, QF*   410] *Ever shall it Safely rest / Rowe² (before 409)*   412 SD *Exeunt] not in F*   *all but Robin] Alexander (*all but Puck*)*   416 these] *Q1, F; this Q2*

No more yielding but a dream,
Gentles, do not reprehend:
If you pardon, we will mend.   420
And as I am an honest puck,
If we have unearned luck
Now to scape the serpent's tongue,
We will make amends ere long;
Else the puck a liar call.   425
So, good night unto you all.
Give me your hands, if we be friends;
And Robin shall restore amends.   *[Exit.]*

---

418 **No more yielding** no better than (*yielding*, productive, beneficial: *OED adj.* 2)
419 **Gentles** an address appropriate to the audience at a public playhouse. Robin again echoes Quince's prologue: see 126n., 413n., and pp. 291–4.
420 **mend** improve, correct our faults
421 **honest puck** As the puck or pouka could be an evil spirit, even identified with the devil, this phrase is something of an oxymoron: 'I may be a devil, but an honest one.'

422 **unearned** (unearnèd) undeserved
423 **the serpent's tongue** i.e. the hisses of a hostile audience
424 **amends ere long** This suggests a new play in preparation.
427 **hands** metaphorically shaken in friendship, literally clapped in applause
428 **restore amends** make amends (for their poor performance by a better one to come, as promised in 424)

428 SD] *Capell; not in QF*

APPENDIX 1

Casting chart

The rationale for this tentative casting, with twelve adults and eight boys, is explained in the Introduction (see pp. 8–9). Ringler's proposed casting (132) conforms to his standard ceiling of sixteen actors in virtually all Shakespeare's pre-Globe plays and most later ones. He doubles Philostrate with Robin, Egeus with Quince and Theseus, curiously, with the fairy at the start of 2.1. King (83) more plausibly doubles the fairy with Hippolyta. Ringler also doubles four adult actors as artisans and Titania's attendant fairies, making a total of eleven adults and four boys in female roles. King (83–4, 179–82), eschewing all doubling (except of Hippolyta with a fairy), calculates nine adults and four boys in principal roles, besides some small speaking parts (among which he counts Philostrate in Q, Snout, Snug and Starveling) and mutes, in both Q and F versions. Grote (28–30, 228–33) proposes a more specific cast of twelve adults and eight boys, on the assumed membership of the Chamberlain's Men at the time. I have noted Grote's suggestions, but they are entirely conjectural.

	Character	Actor (all conjectural)	Grote's casting	1.1	1.2	2.1	2.2	3.1	3.2	4.1	4.2	5.1
	ADULTS											
1	Theseus	Richard Burbage	George Bryan	X						X		X
2	Oberon		John Heminges			X	X			X	X	X
3	Bottom	William Kemp	William Kemp		X			X	Asleep: hidden	X	X	X
4	Robin		Augustine Phillips			X	X	X	X	X		X
5	Lysander	John Heminges	Richard Burbage	X		X	X		X	X		X
6	Demetrius	Henry Condell	Henry Condell	X		X	X		X	X		X
7	Flute		Kemp's apprentice (William Bee?)		X			X			X	X
8	Starveling	John Sincklo	John Sincklo		X			X			X	X
9	Snout		Richard Cowley (or Robert Pallant)		X			X			X	X
10	Snug		John Duke		X			X			X	X
11Q	Philostrate (Q)			X (mute)								X
12Q	Egeus + Quince (Q)	William Shakespeare		X	X			X		X	X	X
11F	Egeus (F)	Shakespeare (if not Quince)	Thomas Pope	X						X		X
12 F	Quince (F)	Shakespeare (if not Egeus)	William Shakespeare		X			X			X	X
	Philostrate (F)		Thomas Pope[1]	X (mute)								

	Character	Actor (all conjectural)	Grote's casting	1.1	1.2	2.1	2.2	3.1	3.2	4.1	4.2	5.1
	BOYS											
1	Hippolyta + Fairy		Hippolyta: Bryan's apprentice (Thomas Belt?) Fairy: William Rowley?	X		X				X		X
2	Titania	Alexander Cooke				X	X	X	Asleep: hidden	X		X
3	Hermia	Nicholas Tooley?	'Saunder'	X		X	X		X	X		X
4	Helena	Robert Gough	Robert Beeston?	X		X	X		X	X		X
5	Cobweb	[Casual]	'Shakespeare's boy' (Fairy)					X		X		X
6	Pease-blossom	[Casual]	Christopher Beeston (Fairy)					X		X		X
7	Mote	[Casual]	Robert Gough? ('Boy')					X		X		X
8	Mustardseed	[Casual]	'Ned'? ('Boy')					X		X		X

[1] Grote (29) assigns the mute Philostrate of F 1.1 and the speaking Egeus of F 1.1, 4.1 and 5.1 to the same actor, citing the 'confusion' of SPs at 5.1.76. But it seems much more likely that some other actor – probably from the fairy scenes – played Philostrate in the F text, avoiding a lightning costume-change, however slight, by the same actor between 1.1.15 and 1.1.20.

[2] Dusinberre (362) suggests Alexander Cooke and Robert Gough as the contrasting pair of boy actors in later comedies (see p. 9). Cooke was bound to Heminges in January 1597, probably too late for the first staging of *Dream*. Nicholas Tooley (with the company by that date, like Gough) is a likelier possibility, for *Dream* and thus perhaps the later plays.

APPENDIX 2

Date and occasion

The only firm evidence for the date of *Dream* is its mention in Francis Meres's *Palladis Tamia*, which appeared in 1598. It is fifth in order among the six comedies named, followed only by *The Merchant of Venice*. This need not reflect the order of composition or of public performance; the list of 'tragedies' clearly does not. Supposed allusions and references in the play's text have been taken as pointers to the date. The account below suggests how inconclusive they are.

WEDDING PLAY?

There is no firm evidence that *Dream* was written for an aristocratic wedding or even performed at one, yet readers have assumed this down the ages. The wedding motif is unusually clear from the start. It is rare for a comedy to open by announcing a marriage. Marriages are, of course, customary at the close; but the fairy pageant concluding the *Dream*, with its elaborate blessing bestowed on the newlyweds, may be thought to exceed the demands of mere narrative or unforced stage spectacle. There are fault-lines in the final sequence suggesting that two endings have been amalgamated, one of them perhaps a customized wedding piece (see pp. 291–4). In fact, it is unusual for the love-plot of a comedy to be resolved by the end of Act 4, and the entire last act devoted to wedding celebrations. Even today, sober Shakespeareans readily speak of *Dream* as performed at a wedding if not actually written for one.[1]

---

1 See Honigmann, 150–3; Thomson, 46; Weis, 42. Duncan-Jones (*Ungentle*, 100–2; *Upstart*, 203–7) links *Dream* categorically with the Berkeley–Carey wedding (see below). Gurr, as categorically, says any wedding link is 'nonsense' (*Company*, 129).

Others would not agree. Past scholars have proposed many possible weddings, often on slender evidence.[1] Perhaps in reaction, some of their successors have tried to resolve the issue by dismissing it.[2] We need to revisit the idea of a wedding as the venue of one (not necessarily the first) performance, even if we cannot identify the occasion. We may be unable to put a name to the Friend or the Dark Lady of the Sonnets; it does not follow that the Sonnets have no relation to Shakespeare's life, loves or patronage.

As Chambers observed long ago (*Shakespeare*, 1.359), only two weddings offer plausible fits. One is that of William Stanley, sixth Earl of Derby, to Elizabeth de Vere, daughter of Edward de Vere, Earl of Oxford, on 26 January 1595 (or 30 January as argued by Wiles, *Almanac*, 145–6). Stanley, like his brother the previous earl Ferdinando, was a poet and patron of the theatre. Ferdinando had been patron of Lord Derby's Men, probably Shakespeare's earlier company (and predecessor of his principal one, the Chamberlain's Men). At the turn of the century, William Stanley was patronizing the boys' company of the Children of St Paul's and even writing plays for them (Gair, 116, 118). He also continued his brother's patronage of Lord Strange's Men, named after the other title the brothers bore. This makes it more likely that, untypically at this date, his wedding entertainment should have taken the form of a full-length play (not necessarily written for the purpose) rather than a masque or pageant.

Other factors are compatible with this wedding. Like most of the others named in this connection, it took place in the winter, anomalously for a work with such a title.[3] But the Stanley–de

---

1 Chambers (*Shakespeare*, 1.358) cites six suggested weddings; Williams (*Revels*, 263–5) eleven; Gurr ('Patronage', 398), without giving details, fourteen.
2 Wells (12–14; 'Revisited', 14–17) strongly questions a wedding performance; Holland (111–12) and Williams (*Revels*, ch. 1) are openly sceptical. Hackett (*Elizabeth*, 120–4) balances the opposite views.
3 Winter weddings could occasion springtime masques, like Thomas Campion's masque for Lord Hayes's marriage (6 January 1607) with its 'bower of Flora'.

Vere wedding had been in abeyance since a marriage agreement in June 1594, awaiting the outcome of Ferdinando's widow's proclaimed pregnancy, which jeopardized William Stanley's claim to the earldom. A date in June or shortly thereafter would have made a midsummer setting entirely appropriate. The specific reference to a fortnight's revels (5.1.359) suits the sumptuous celebrations for Stanley and de Vere, extending at least to 5 February (Ungerer, 2.397). Moreover, Theseus could be seen as a type of William Stanley, renowned for his exploits in Europe and perhaps further afield.[1] They became the stuff of legend, as witnessed by a ballad surviving from *c*.1790, *Sir William Stanley's Garland.*

The other marriage is of Thomas Berkeley, son of Henry, Lord Berkeley, to Elizabeth Carey, daughter of Sir George Carey and granddaughter of Lord Hunsdon, the Lord Chamberlain, on 19 February 1596. The Careys were the patrons of Shakespeare's company, the Lord Chamberlain's Men (briefly Lord Hunsdon's Men: Sir George succeeded to his father's title in 1596 and to the post of Chamberlain in 1597). This makes it likely that 'their' players would be commissioned for a wedding entertainment, and that it should consist of a full-length play. For his wedding entertainment, Theseus thinks of a 'play' (5.1.36), at least in a loose sense, besides masques, dances and music. If the choice was open to Theseus in an Elizabethan play, why not to an Elizabethan peer in his own time?

But this only suggests a general practice, not a specific date or occasion. The same may be said of a related factor. Oberon's unmissable compliment to Queen Elizabeth (2.1.155–64) has been taken to signal her presence in the audience. She seems to have attended the Stanley–de Vere wedding,[2] and quite possibly the other one as well,[3] Elizabeth Carey (like

---

1 Chambers, 'Occasion', 63; Honigmann, 150–1.
2 Chambers, 'Occasion', 61–2, *Stage*, 4.109 n.11.
3 Colthorpe argues strongly against the latter possibility.

Elizabeth de Vere) being her goddaughter. In any case, the playscript would be written in advance in anticipation of her presence.

These factors do not constitute proof, or even circumstantial evidence. The Stanley–de Vere wedding provides the best fit, the Berkeley–Carey wedding a passable one; the rest are doubtful in the extreme. Until we firmly identify the wedding, we cannot use it to date the play, let alone determine whether it was written for the occasion, revised, or merely restaged.

Yet the fact that we cannot identify the occasion does not negate its possibility. Rather, the substantial overlap with two weddings, and points of resemblance with several others, strengthen the case. The wedding motif in *Dream*, with its teasing hints of an actual event, helps us place the play in its social and cultural context. The implications for its general intent and design are more important than specific topical allusion. The possible context of an aristocratic wedding affects our understanding of *Dream* as an imaginative construct, not as stuff for a historical guessing-game.

THE FAIR VESTAL: POLITICS AND PAGEANTRY

There is rare unanimity among scholars that Oberon's account of a 'fair vestal' (2.1.155–64) is a tribute to Elizabeth. The passage cannot be a late addition: it describes the transformation of the flower central to the plot. Such tributes were endemic in that age. The Queen need not have been present in person to receive it, or even expected to be. Dover Wilson (Cam[1] 100) and Wiles (*Almanac*, 139) explicitly dismiss the possibility of her presence. The celebration of chastity in this passage is countered by the stress on its sterile and frustrating aspect elsewhere in the play; and it would have been politically dangerous to present the Fairy Queen as infatuated with an ass-headed yokel (see p. 96).

The 'fair vestal' passage testifies rather to the Queen's 'pervasive *cultural presence*' in the play (Montrose, 'Fantasies', 113: his italics). It illustrates a common vein of courtly compliment, often embodied in pageant and spectacle. As a boy, Shakespeare may or may not have seen the pageantry at the Queen's 1575 visit to Kenilworth in his native county of Warwickshire. The Kenilworth revels featured (though not together) a mermaid, a dolphin, music and fireworks (flying stars); the Queen's presence; and metaphorically, the Earl of Leicester allegedly shooting a love-dart at her in vain. The connection has been played down by most recent commentators but admitted by scholarly biographers.[1] Shakespeare must also have known of the Queen's visit to Elvetham, Hampshire in 1591.[2] Here the revels featured *inter alia* a Fairy Queen married to 'Auberon'.

A closer but less noted parallel occurs in Thomas Churchyard's entertainment for the Queen at Norwich in 1578. This had both water nymphs and fairies, with a dance by the latter and a speech by their Queen. There is also an episode of Cupid's futile challenge to Chastity. The latter's speech recalls Oberon's vision:

> [Chastity] quencheth sparkes and flames of fancies fire,
> . . . thy heart it is so cleane,
> Blind *Cupid's* boltes therein can take no roote.[3]

Books had appeared recounting all three progresses shortly after they took place. Other such instances may have gone unrecorded. There are points of contact with the Masque of Proteus in the *Gesta Grayorum* and the interlude of a ship at the baptismal feast of Prince Henry of Scotland, both in 1594.[4]

1 Greenblatt, 47–50; Duncan-Jones, *Ungentle*, 12–13, *Upstart*, 205–6.
2 Rickert (54–6) and Griffin (140–2) note the points of resemblance, though we need not accept the political allegory proposed by Rickert.
3 Nichols, *Progresses*, 2.731; see also 2.747–51.
4 Nichols, *Progresses*, 3.760–3, 3.852–4; *Reportarie*, C1ᵛ–3ᵛ. Henry's baptismal revels are a likely source for the 'lion among ladies' (3.1.28): see below.

Oberon's vision recalls the allegorical spectacle and fantasy in these pageants, and loosely overlaps with some details in them. Those arguing for closer links have not proved their case. We cannot posit any specific event, hence cannot use the passage to date the play. As for the topical allegories read into Oberon's speech, earlier scholars made fertile conjectures that fill seventeen pages of the New Variorum edition. They are discredited or forgotten, and I find no reason to urge any of them.

OTHER INDICATIONS OF DATE

Bad weather: Titania's powerful description of the disordered seasons (2.1.88–117) has been employed to date the play. The 'Little Ice Age', as the term is now understood, was well under way by the 1590s, causing such climatic upheavals (Ladurie, 67, 223–5, 299–300). Stow's *Annals* (1274–9, sigs 4O6^v–4P1^r) describes the exceptionally bad weather throughout the spring and summer of 1594: 'many great stormes of winde', 'great water flouds', 'sodaine showres of haile and raine'. Simon Forman also describes May–July 1594 as 'wonderfull cold like winter', with rain and floods (Halliwell, *Introduction*, 6–7). However, Camden (450, sig. 2P2^v) reports 'continuall raine in Summer' in 1595 as well;[1] Barlow (sig. A3^v) 'neuer ceasing raine' in 1596; and Stow (1298–9, sigs 4Q2^v–3^r), almost continuously bad weather till May 1597. Similarly, with reference to 2.1.93–5, Hoskins (32, 38) notes four years of bad harvests from 1594 to 1597 resulting in a 'Great Famine', with cattle-plague and sheep-rot specifically in 1594. Thomas ('Weather', 320–1) reports that only in 1596 did the corn rot on the ground (see 2.1.94–5), on Barlow's evidence (sig. A3^r) and, we may add, implicitly Stow's (1299, sig. 4Q3^r).The passage is of little use in dating the play.

---

1   Thomas Churchyard's poem *Churchyard's Charity* (1595) also describes such weather.

A lion among ladies: On 30 August 1594, at the baptismal feast of Prince Henry of Scotland in Stirling Castle, there was a plan to bring a chariot into the banquet hall, drawn by a real lion. The idea was dismissed 'because his presence might haue brought some feare to the neerest'; instead, the chariot was drawn by a 'Black-moore' (*Reportarie*, sig. C1^{r-v}; Nichols, *Progresses*, 3.758–60). The link with 3.1.28 seems too marked to be coincidental. It establishes August 1594 as the earliest possible date of composition.

The Indian boy: Buchanan (59–60) thinks the Indian boy, apparently a king's son, was suggested by Walter Ralegh's return from his Guiana expedition with the son of a tribal king from western 'India' or Indies. Ralegh returned home in August 1595, and published his *Discovery of Guiana* in March 1596. If we admit the allusion in an episode so basic to the plot, *Dream* could not have been written before August 1595.

The mourning Muses: Among the entertainments on offer at Theseus' wedding is 'The thrice three Muses mourning for the death / Of learning, late deceased in beggary' (5.1.52–3). The theme is virtually as old as poetry, but many scholars have linked it to Robert Greene's death in 1592 – too early for *Dream*, and improbable in the light of Greene's attacks on Shakespeare. It is specially misleading to cite *Greene's Funerals*, a 1594 collection of poems by 'R.B. Gent.' mourning Greene's death which says nothing about beggary, Greene's or any other poet's, and little about the Muses.[1] Others have found an allusion to 'The Tears of the Muses' in Spenser's *Complaints*

---

1 Daugherty takes 'R.B.' as Richard Barnfield, William Stanley's protégé and perhaps his lover. He casts Stanley as the Friend of Shakespeare's Sonnets and Barnfield as the Rival Poet – in which case the dig at *Greene's Funerals* would come easily to Shakespeare, targeting Barnfield as well as Greene. But it would imply that Shakespeare had no idea of the contents of *Funerals*. Duncan-Jones too detects 'some as yet unexplained connection between Shakespeare and Barnfield' (*Sonnets*, 46, 91).

of 1591. This can be neither proved nor disproved, but is of no help in dating the play. An epithalamion composed by Sir John Davies for the Stanley–de Vere wedding consists of songs by the nine Muses, but is devoid of satire or complaint. Common sense suggests it is impossible to link such an open-ended reference to a specific work or event.

Date of publication: Lukas Erne (*Dramatist*, 109–11) has traced an interesting pattern: Shakespeare's company seems to have released most of his earlier plays for publication about two years after their first performance. The one evident exception is *Dream*, for which Erne accepts the commonly assumed date of composition and production, 1595–6. He finds no compelling reason to bring it in line with the general pattern of a two-year gap. If we apply Erne's rule in reverse to *Dream* (first printed in 1600), a play first produced in 1598 could barely make it into Francis Meres's list. (*Palladis Tamia* was registered on 7 September 1598.) In any case, this is to give Erne's formula a blanket application that he himself wisely avoids. Rather, he accepts the common position that for *Dream*, 'there is nothing beyond style to suggest a particular date'.

To date a play by its style is an uncertain business. But *Dream* can be convincingly grouped with certain other plays as marking the first phase of Shakespeare's stylistic maturity (see pp. 108–9). This means it would have been composed sometime between 1594 and 1596. Many of the proposed topical links fit this date-span. They are the more likely to be valid, but to use them to confirm the date would imply circular logic. Grote (28) argues on circumstantial grounds that *Dream* was 'the first fully original work' that Shakespeare wrote for the Chamberlain's Men, a new and as yet small company, but with Richard Burbage and Will Kemp as sharers. Gurr, more cautiously, places *Dream* among the plays 'acquired by the Chamberlain's [Men] in 1594 or written for them afterwards' by 1598 (*Playing*, 281).

Proposing a date or date-bracket does not mean that every word was set down in one go; but in the absence of clear contrary evidence, and without engaging in fine-spun speculations, we may assume this to have been the case. Some variants, especially between Quarto and Folio, can be explained by later revision for theatrical needs. But there seems to be one case of substantial replacement, an alternative text with an alternative purpose. This is where the wedding performance enters the story again.

GENETICS AND TRANSMISSION

The ending of the play (5.1.353–428) has intrigued scholars. It suggests two endings joined up in one. The first (361–412), with Theseus' speech (353–60) as prelude, has a more intimate indoor setting, elaborate fairy spectacle, probably controlled lighting, and possibly local reference. It is compatible with a wedding-night performance, or an indoor private theatre like the Blackfriars. The other segment (413–28) is a simpler, more general address by Robin, asking for the audience's applause in the accustomed way of public playhouses.[1] The structural ambiguities preclude easy solutions. There is a play-within-the-play; the Bergomask is primarily the ending of that alone, yet it cannot but extend to the play encasing it, coming so near the latter's close. Performances in public playhouses commonly ended with a dance. Again, there are several weddings within the play; there is no need to postulate a real one to account for the nuptial blessings in the fairies' song, but were there one, this is exactly the kind of double reference that would lend body and relevance to the entertainment. We should not force the inadequate evidence at our disposal. Equally, we should not dismiss the possibility because we do not have the data to clinch it.

---

1 The contrast is most clearly defined by Wilson (87–8, 151, 153), though we need not share his conclusions about textual revision or 'Puck/Robin' variations. The double ending has found support from Chambers (*Shakespeare*, 1.360–1), Brooks (127) and Stern (*Making*, 40), but Wells ('Revisited', 17–18) explicitly argues against it.

There is a rough parallel in the last scene of a slightly later play, *The Merry Wives of Windsor.* In the Folio text of *Wives*, the Fairy Queen (played by Mistress Quickly) has a speech (5.5.55–76) blessing and extolling Windsor Castle, chiefly as home to the Order of the Garter. It celebrates the investiture of Lord Hunsdon with the Garter: he commissioned the performance by his own company on the occasion. The Quarto lacks this speech; the preceding lines (5.5.42–54) are also very different there, much more oriented to popular and city life. In other words, *Wives* certainly has alternative endings for two different occasions, and so, arguably, may *Dream*. In *Wives*, the two are too different to conflate; in *Dream*, they are close enough to combine without glaring anomaly in a single version.

As a minimal hypothesis, we can suggest two contexts of production for *Dream*: public staging, and a wedding performance broadly on the lines of indoor staging in a private playhouse. Except in the closing sequence, there are no lines clearly assignable to one or other version: in other words, nothing that really distinguishes two 'versions' at all. It is improbable in any case that the play was composed for a wedding. Virtually every Elizabethan play that reached the public stage was originally written for it.[1] The first full play undoubtedly composed for a wedding is Samuel Daniel's *Hymen's Triumph* (1614). If *Dream* was acted at a wedding, its original playhouse text would have been adapted to the bespoke performance. The variant SDs in Q and F at the start of 5.1 might reflect different staging conditions (see 5.1.0.1n.).

But a new strand now enters the story. The Q1 title-page testifies that *Dream* was 'sundry times publickely acted, by . . . the Lord Chamberlaine his seruants': no doubt at their original venue the Theatre and then the Globe, opened in 1599, a year before the printing of Q1. In much the same years, James Burbage, leading proprietor of the Chamberlain's Men,

---

1 See Gurr, *Company*, 129; Williams, *Revels*, 14–16.

ventured on a commercial gamble. In 1596, he bought the property of the old Blackfriars theatre, home to children's companies from 1576 to 1584. Failing to house their own troupe there (largely owing to objections from elite neighbours including their own patron the Lord Chamberlain), James's son Richard Burbage leased it to a new generation of children's companies; but in 1608, the Chamberlain's Men regained possession and started performances there. In course of time, the select, upmarket private theatre seriously challenged the primacy of the public Globe.

The children's companies acted all kinds of plays in both phases of their history. But there are features specially identified with their repertoire: a delicate mythological fancy, plots and sentiments geared to a feminine audience, and a general refinement of tone. These features are prominent in the work of John Lyly, the leading playwright for these companies in the 1580s. When Burbage contemplated reviving Blackfriars in 1596, the lyrical, fanciful, outwardly romantic *Dream* would be an obvious choice for its repertoire. This may have induced the company to review the play for an indoor stage with artificial lighting. If there had meanwhile been an indoor wedding performance, its staging conditions would have been somewhat similar: passages specially written for it (such as 5.1.361–412) would be sought out and dovetailed into the text for the public stage. This is exactly what we find at the end of *Dream*. Other local revisions could have been made in the same way, even such weighty ones as adding the poet to the lunatic and the lover in Theseus' speech (see pp. 298–9 and 5.1.5–8n.). As a stakeholder in the company's new venture, Shakespeare might himself have made the revisions in the margins of an earlier authorial copy. This would account for the rash of mislining in this scene. Of course, the revisions may have been made in one go during first composition. Taylor ('Cobham', 342) would have it so, arguing that it is difficult to explain why Shakespeare should have returned later to make changes in the foul papers rather than the prompt-book. The situation envisaged here suggests an explanation, if the prompt-book was being used in the public theatre and the revisions were for a planned future performance on the private stage. In such an event, the revisions were more likely to be made in the authorial manuscript preserved by the acting company (see pp. 303–7). We cannot tell. But the account above offers a plausible explanation for the state of the text. The play might even, though improbably, have been written *c.*1596 for the newly acquired private playhouse, and when that plan fell through, adapted for the public stage.

The revision, if any, served no end: the Chamberlain's Men could not use Blackfriars till 1608. Hence the copy was not filled out with the full array of stage directions and other theatrical mark-up: it remained 'foul papers' (as authorial drafts are often misleadingly termed), perhaps a little 'fouler' for the new insertions and revisions, and was made over to the printers in that state in 1600 (see pp. 306–7). Such a situation would also explain the delay in print publication, breaking Erne's otherwise consistent pattern of a two-year gap between performance and print. If the play dates from 1595–6, the company was planning a notably new launch for it in 1597–8: they may not have cared to publish it at that point. Conversely, if the print edition was planned as a publicity move for the stage production, it may have been eschewed when the new production was aborted. It is harder to explain why they did not sell this play, like several others, to a publisher in the 'cash-straitened years' (Gurr, *Playing*, 284) after their plan for a private theatre failed. But as Gurr adds, 'The company also made money in these years with their appearances at court and at private houses.' *Dream* would have been an ideal play for this purpose.

There is no direct evidence for this genetic history, but it meshes with the known facts about the play and the variations within its basically homogeneous style and design. At the same time, it provides a structural rationale for its varied and eventful performance history in later times.

APPENDIX 3

The text

THE EARLY EDITIONS AND THEIR COPY

In Appendix 2, I suggested a model for the genetic history of the play. I will now examine how this agrees with the state of the early texts and their printing history. *Dream* has the full Shakespearean complement of texts: two early quartos and the First Folio of 1623, the first collected edition of the plays. The three editions present hearteningly consistent versions of the text. There are only some half-dozen serious textual cruces. A few lines vary substantially and a few speeches are reallocated. Most other variants that are not clearly erroneous are minor in nature.

Publishers of the time established their claim to a title by entering it in the Register of the Stationers' Company. The First Quarto (Q1) was entered on 8 October 1600 in the name of Thomas Fisher and published by him the same year, 'to be soulde at his shoppe, at the Signe of the White Hart, in *Fleetestreete*'. Fisher's career as publisher is very brief: he brought out only three other titles, all between 1600 and 1602, including John Marston's companion plays *Antonio and Mellida* and *Antonio's Revenge*. These two were almost certainly, and the third title (Nicholas Breton's *Pasquil's Mistress*) was probably, printed by Richard Bradock, who may therefore have printed *Dream* as well. Bradock was an established printer, producing several playtexts among other titles.

On the whole, Q1 offers a good, clear text, apparently printed from an authorial draft or working manuscript (misleadingly termed 'foul papers'). It shows the traditionally accepted signs

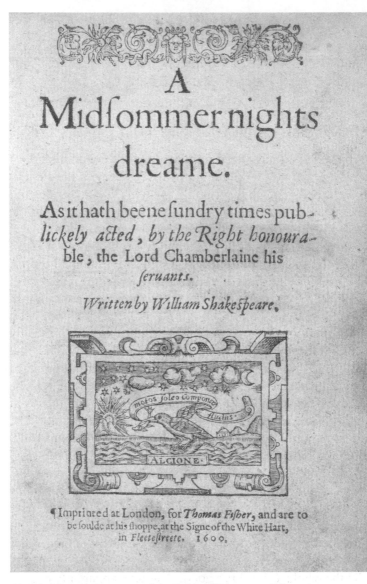

A
Midſommer nights
dreame.

As it hath beene ſundry times publickely *acted, by the Right honoura*-
ble, the Lord Chamberlaine his
ſeruants.

Written by William Shakeſpeare.

¶ Imprinted at London, for *Thomas Fiſher*, and are to
be ſoulde at his ſhoppe, at the Signe of the White Hart,
in *Fleeteſtreete.* 1600.

18 Q1 title-page (courtesy of the Folger Shakespeare Library)

of a working copy: gaps and inconsistencies in entries and exits, with other inadequate and imprecise stage directions;[1] varying designations for the same character (Duke/Theseus, Duchess/Hippolyta, King/Oberon, Queen/Titania, Clown/ Bottom, Puck/Robin), including generic names in speech prefixes and stage directions;[2] and descriptive stage directions.[3] There can be other anomalies: in the later scenes, Thisbe in the play-within-the-play is referred to separately from Flute, though Flute plays Thisbe.[4] These assumed hallmarks of so-called 'foul papers' have been vigorously challenged by Werstine ('Narratives', 'Suggestion', *Manuscripts*) and, with specific reference to *Dream*, by Long (33–7). They argue that these assumptions are largely speculative, and contradicted by the evidence of surviving playtexts. But Q1 carries other indicators of authorial provenance, chiefly twofold.

1   See the missing or misleading entry and exit SDs in Q1 at 1.1.19.1; 1.1.127; 2.1.237/244; 2.2.91; 3.1.98.1–2/107.1, 101; 3.2.101, 338, 441.1, 446, 447; 4.1.185, 198, 217; 4.2.43; 5.1.167.1, 204, 308.1. Some of these cases are rectified in Q2, and nearly all in F. There are two SDs (3.2.344, 5.1.412) present in both quartos but lacking in F. F confuses the correct Q SD at one point (3.1.156.1–2), and Q seems to reflect Oberon's presence more correctly than F at 4.1.44.1.
    Other key SDs (supplied in F) are missing in both quartos at 2.2.28, 69; 3.2.137, 416, 418, 463; 4.1.29, 82, besides SDs in the play-within-the-play. Note also the wrong Q SPs '*Quin(ce)*' for Puck/Robin, 3.1.83; '*Flut(e)*' for Starveling, 4.2.3; and (doubtfully) '*Lyon*' for Bottom, 5.1.343 – all corrected in F.
2   For instance, the frequent '*King of Fairies*' and '*Queen(e) of Fai(e)ries*'; '*the Clownes*', 3.1.0.1 etc.; '*Clowne*' for Bottom throughout 4.1; '*the rabble*', 4.2.0.1; and in a different category, SDs and SPs naming the characters in the play-within-the-play rather than the people acting them ('*Pyra(mus)*' for Bottom etc.). The SP '*Duk(e)*', hence also '*Dutch(ess)*', from 5.1.205 onwards is probably to avoid confusion between Theseus and Thisbe. Kennedy, with detailed reference to *Dream*, attributes many such variations to a shortage of type. At the other extreme, Wilder (42) sees the varying names for Bottom as deliberate variants reflecting different facets of the character.
3   Such as '*Egeus and his daughter* Hermia' (1.1.19); '*Quince, the Carpenter*; *and* Snugge, *the Ioyner*' etc. (1.2.0.1–2); and even later, '*Snug, the Ioyner*' (4.2.14.1); '*Louers*; Lysander, Demetrius, Hermia *and* Helena' (5.1.27.1).
4   F retains the error at 4.2.0.1 while correcting it at 4.2.3 and 5.1.155. In the rest of 4.2, F has the SP '*This(bie)*', though their actual names for the other artisans.

The first is Shakespeare's idiosyncratic spelling as deduced (Wilson, 'Spellings') from printed playtexts and three pages ascribed to Shakespeare in the manuscript play *Sir Thomas More*. This is obviously an inexact test. Besides the uncertain identification of 'Hand D' in *More* and the limitations of Wilson's methodology,[1] Shakespeare's practices were undoubtedly shared by many others in that age of supremely fluid spelling. But the *combination of practices* can be distinctive, and many of them (though not others) are clearly present in Q1. Most instances would be altered by scribes and compositors.[2] Hence a few cases, or even one, can carry weight.[3] By a rough count of this necessarily imprecise factor, Q1 has 127 such distinctive spellings, of which 59 were altered in Q2.[4] This shows how readily authorial spellings change in print, and how significant the large number in Q1 might be.

The second pointer lies in the many cases of wrong line-division, most strikingly near the start of 5.1, where 5.1.5–8, 12–18, 29–31, 33–6, 58–60, 66–70, 76–8, 81–3 are mislined. As Wilson (80–6) famously pointed out, if these lines are omitted, the rest (which are correctly lined) form a coherent structure of their own. This suggests that the wrongly divided lines (including everything about the poet in the famous 'lunatic, lover and poet' speech, 7–22) are later additions, crammed into the margins of the original manuscript and wrongly set by the Q1 printer. Q2 and F rectify a few mislinings

1 As noted, for instance, by Werstine ('Science', 121–2).
2 On the strong general tendency to do so, see Howard-Hill, 'Printers'.
3 For examples, see 'othes' (1.1.243), 'rore' (3.1.106), 'waigh' (3.2.131), 'hearbe' (3.2.366).
4 As counted by this editor on the basis of the Oxford Concordance. Major categories include *ea* for *e* (26), *ow* for *ou* (19), *oo* for *o* (17), *ore* for *o'er* (11), *to* for *too* (11), *o* for *oa* (10), *ai* for *ei* (7), *ew* for *ue* (6), plus contractions like *heele* and *weele*. Some of Wilson's categories, like the doubling or singling of consonants, were not taken into account, as likely to have been common practice. On the spelling changes between Q1 and Q2, and generally between the Pavier Quartos (see pp. 301–2) and their copy-texts, see Blayney, 'Pavier', 185–6.

but not the rest. Lines 37–8 are mislined, but Wilson places them in the original text, though 58 among the additions. Holland (259) reasonably restores 58 to the original text to provide a context for Philostrate's response (61–5). However we interpret the details, this evidence indicates that Q1 was set from an advanced stage of an authorial draft incorporating many deletions and insertions, sometimes in a confusing way.

We should revisit the field in the light of recent research, especially Werstine's detailed enquiry into manuscript playtexts. He takes *Dream* as a test case (*Manuscripts*, 130–3) to show how the features ascribed to 'foul papers' are also present in manuscripts, both authorial and scribal, of theatrical function and location.[1] Thus in effect, the evidence he painstakingly gathers supports the case for theatrical use of authorial manuscripts – or, if we prefer, the authorial source of theatrical manuscripts. Werstine's research significantly changes our view of the nature and provenance of the latter; but it does not negate the authorial basis of the textual features in question.[2] It simply suggests that manuscripts of authorial provenance, perhaps in worked-over or annotated form, were often used in the theatre instead of customized, 'fair' non-authorial copies. This was possible because the authorial copies were not literally 'foul' but could supply a clean, reasonably unambiguous text. They would retain the authorial features described above – perhaps modified, but still embedded in the text. These features seem manifestly present in Q1, with relatively little theatrical adaptation. Such a manuscript might still have been held or accessed by the theatrical company (see pp. 306–7).

---

1 In particular, he finds strong resemblance between the 'foul papers' postulated as copy for Q1 *Dream* and the presumed copy for F *Julius Caesar*, adjudged by Greg (but not all later editors) to be a theatrical manuscript.

2 This is implied by Werstine's use of phrases such as the prompter's 'not troubl[ing] to alter' (*Manuscripts*, 125) vague or inconsistent SDs in the manuscript he uses, or the 'persistence' of such features in theatrical copy (133). The ultimate source of such features can only be authorial.

A
Midſommer nights dreame.

As it hath beene ſundry times pub-
likely aĉted, *by the Right Honoura-*
ble, the Lord Chamberlaine his
ſeruants.

VVritten by VVilliam Shakeſpeare.

Printed by Iames Roberts, 1600.

19 Q2 title-page

The Second Quarto (Q2) has a curious history, recently redefined. Like Q1, its title-page is dated 1600, but names James Roberts as the printer. In fact, as shown by Greg ('Dates') and elaborated by later scholars, Q2 was printed by William Jaggard in 1619. It was part of a larger enterprise involving nine other plays (two wrongly ascribed to Shakespeare), masterminded by the publisher Thomas Pavier.[1] James Roberts had played a role in producing other Shakespeare titles: *The Merchant of Venice* Q1 (1600), *Titus Andronicus* Q2 (1600) and *Hamlet* Q2 (1604). *Troilus and Cressida* was registered in his name in 1603. Jaggard bought up his business around 1608.

A book with a false title-page does not inspire confidence. Q2 has been routinely dismissed by editors as a mere reprint of Q1, correcting some obvious errors but introducing others, with no fresh input worth note. Pavier's standing as a publisher has been questioned, but his plan seems clear: to issue a collected series of reprints to consolidate Shakespeare's standing as a 'readerly' author, not only a writer for the stage. Erne (*Dramatist*), Bruster ('Stationer') and others demonstrate how Shakespeare had already assumed such a role.[2] As deduced from the ornaments and stock of type, the printers of the Pavier Quartos were William Jaggard and his son Isaac, who played a major part in producing the First Folio in 1623. There is no evidence of a conflict between Pavier and Jaggard over this long-term goal. They may even be seen as jointly laying the ground for a collected folio edition – in Massai's perhaps overstated view (119), carrying out 'a pre-publicity strategy' for the Folio.[3]

---

1   See Johnson, 'Pavier'; Murphy, 38–41; Erne, *Dramatist*, 280–3, *Trade*, 175–9; Massai, ch. 4.
2   Bruster ('Stationer', 119–21) notes how 1600 marks the high point in Shakespearean publications in the dramatist's lifetime: *Dream* was among ten titles, including five new ones, appearing that year.
3   See also Murphy, 41, and Halasz's more nuanced account (24–7).

Also in 1619, a court order was issued prohibiting the publication of playtexts acted by the King's Men. This was long thought to be directed against Pavier, and the false dates of *Dream* Q2 and four other Pavier Quartos to constitute a token evasion of the order. But as Johnson ('Pavier', 36–40) argues and Murphy (40) and Massai (116) agree, the falsely dated quartos were hardly designed to defraud: the attempt at deception was perfunctory. Pavier held rights to five titles anyway, had probably negotiated three more, and the rights in the remaining two (*Dream* being one) were derelict or obscure. Massai even argues (106–8) that the court order was intended to *protect* Pavier and Jaggard's venture from rival publications. Her argument has not been universally accepted, but it reinforces the view that Q2 is no casual reprint. It was part of the most elaborate publishing programme till that date for Shakespeare's or any other contemporary playtexts, except for Ben Jonson's First Folio (1616). Besides correcting some obvious errors, the departures from Q1 seem the outcome of a considered review, in contrast to the casual quarto reprints of most contemporary plays. This is not to say the revisions are authorial; they often clearly are not. A few misconstrue the drift of the text; many introduce unnecessary changes, or changes contrary to the play's usual trends in metre and diction. None of them carries the stamp of theatrical practice. Even the seven added SDs can be deduced from the text: one is an entrance (3.2.441.1), the rest all exits,[1] signposted in the dialogue and in one case (4.1.217) concluding a scene. Hence even after its recent rehabilitation, Q2 does not provide any new lead for the modern editor. We may pay it more heed than before, especially where Q1 is clearly wrong or suspect, but we can hope for little beyond well-intentioned guesses by the 1619 reviewer.

The situation is somewhat different with the Folio (F) text. F starts with the comedies, fourteen in number. *Dream* is

---

1   2.1.244; 3.2.101, 338; 4.1.185, 198, 217.

placed eighth, preceded by *Much Ado about Nothing* and *Love's Labour's Lost* and followed by *The Merchant of Venice*. The F editors seem to have begun by using freshly prepared manuscript copies by the scrivener Ralph Crane, but discontinued the plan after the first four plays. (The later *Winter's Tale* and *Othello* are also thought to be set from Crane transcripts.) The four comedies named above were printed from previously published quartos, and the rest from manuscripts of varying nature and provenance. The F *Dream* seems to have been set from a copy of Q2, marked up both in the dialogue and, more particularly, in the SDs and SPs. It matches the tenth category of printer's copy defined by Bowers (11), 'a copy of an earlier printed edition annotated by comparison with some manuscript, usually assumed to be authorial or prompt, preserved in the theatre's archives'.[1] What are the grounds for this assumption?

There are substantive innovations in F like replacing Philostrate with Egeus in 5.1, and dividing between Theseus and Lysander the passage on the entertainments on offer (5.1.44–60). These are crucial to the case for a new theatrical manuscript behind F. At the level of detail, SPs and SDs in F are more numerous, elaborate and consistent (though not entirely so), and a minor actor, William Tawyer, is specifically named (see 5.1.125.3n.). As the first other mention of Tawyer (d.1625) dates from 1624, the manuscript consulted for F must have been in use long after the first performance. This is also indicated by a reference to intervals between the acts, perhaps with music (see p. 320 and 3.2.463 SDn.). Many stage actions are incorporated in SDs for the first time, most notably the lovers' sleeping on from 3.2 to 4.1. But Titania and Bottom, sleeping alongside them and indeed from the end of 3.1, find no mention – perhaps because they were hidden in the 'discovery

---

1 Mowat and Werstine (Folg, xlix) consider the theatrical use of this manuscript a 'conjecture rest[ing] on the most slender evidence'.

space' through the long intermediate 3.2 (see 4.1.0.1n. and pp. 6–8).

As this indicates, F ignores many loose ends and inconsistencies in the Quartos where they do not affect stage business. Virtually all SP variants from Q1 (Puck/Robin, Bottom/Clown, Theseus/Duke, Hippolyta/Duchess) continue into F, presumably because they do not affect performance.[1] This is general practice in theatrical copies derived from authors' manuscripts.[2] F overlooks Q's confusion over Flute's identity at 4.2.0.1 while correcting it at 4.2.3 and 5.1.155, and makes a few fresh errors in SDs (see p. 297 n. 1). F also makes certain changes in the dialogue, occasionally departing from both quartos for no apparent purpose. With a few striking exceptions, the variations are minor; but a production based on F would differ all through in detail, and thus ultimately in total effect, from one based on either of the quartos.[3] At many points, F agrees with Q2 in departing from Q1; at many others, it departs from a common reading in both quartos; at yet others, from different readings in Q1 and Q2. The first group is easily explained: a marked-up copy of Q2 provided the printer's copy for F. For the second

---

1 Only at 3.1.102 is Q '*Rob.*' changed to F '*Puk.*', perhaps influenced by two new 'Puck' additions in F (3.1.48.1; 3.1.83 SP). Even here, two other 'Robin' entries persist from Q (3.1.71 SD; 3.1.72 SP). Several times in 3.1, Q2 and F unnecessarily change Q1 '*Quin(ce)*' to '*Pet(er)*' or '*Peter quince*'. Kennedy (179–82) attributes this to a shortage of type while printing Q2.

2 'In actual surviving "Prompt-Books" the stage-revisers show little interest in the text itself . . . further than is necessary superficially to cut, shape and adapt it to the stage. [Hence] to prove that a play is from a "Prompt-Book" is not to prove that it has divested itself of all characteristics of the author's "foul papers"' (Baldwin, *Division*, 155–7). See also Werstine, *Manuscripts*, 124–7, 129 (citing Baldwin), ch. 4 *passim*, and the detailed evidence in his Appendix A.

3 Erne and Kidnie (3) go so far as to say 'Just what kind of comedy we think *A Midsummer Night's Dream* is has much to do with whether we [follow] the first quarto or the Folio', rather exaggeratedly premising 'a scapegoat ritual of expulsion' (of Egeus) in the last scene. See 5.1.0.1n., 44–58n.

and third groups, we must assume one or more independent sources.

Like the new readings in Q2, some unique F readings might stem from editorial conjecture, correcting what are rightly or wrongly seen as errors. But many F readings clearly derive from a theatrical manuscript. Two questions follow. Are these new readings confined to matters of staging (SDs and SPs) or do they extend to the dialogue? And could the latter changes be authorial? There can be no clear answer to these questions. F introduces some new readings that cannot be owing to compositor's error, in places where neither theatrical reviser nor publisher should feel the need for change, though the author conceivably might for stylistic reasons. The changes relate to one or a few words, and make little or no difference in meaning and impact except in a few cruces (1.1.139; 5.1.190, 205). Some new readings may be garbled or corrupt (see 1.1.139n., 3.2.386n., 5.1.205n.). There is no evidence that any of these variants is authorial, but we cannot dismiss the possibility. The theatrical manuscript newly consulted for F might go back to an authorial source, especially as this author was a partner in the theatrical company. Hence paradoxically, a variant found only in F might carry more weight than one found in both Q2 and F: the latter might have been introduced without warrant in Q2 and mechanically repeated in F. At the very least, F might provide authentic variants (even if not authorial) in the dialogue delivered on stage. Its SDs and SPs may also reflect stage practice more closely; but that practice may be of later date than the original production, as in the matter of intervals between the acts. They cannot be accepted uncritically except when (as often) they rectify obvious errors and omissions in Q.

On balancing the evidence, F cannot challenge the greater authorial standing of Q1 as a whole. There seems no reason to depart from Q1 where it provides a viable text, unless F (or rarely Q2) provides a manifestly preferable variant (or, of course, corrects an obvious error). I have redefined the relationship between Q1, Q2 and F in the light of recent research. But I follow all modern editors in adopting Q1 as my control text.

Authorial manuscripts, of the kind postulated as the copy for Q1, seem to have been at the disposal of the acting company alongside the theatrical copy used during production (the so-called 'prompt copy'). There is record of two such manuscripts, of John Fletcher's *Bonduca* (the original object of the term 'foul papers') and *The Honest Man's Fortune* by Fletcher and others. Both manuscripts, either held by or otherwise accessible to the company, were used to prepare scribal copies – one for a patron, the other for the censor – the theatrical copies being lost. Subsequent versions of the texts, whether or not indebted to the same source, provided the copy for both plays in the 1647 Beaumont and Fletcher Folio.[1] Erne (*Dramatist*, 207–13) suggests that the transmissional model of *The Honest Man's Fortune* can be applied to Shakespearean works such as *Hamlet*, *Othello*, *King Lear* and *Richard III*, 'of which two substantive, "good," texts have come down to us'. These plays present issues of abridgement and marked variation that do not occur in *Dream*. But I would suggest that *Dream* illustrates a simpler version of the same model. That assumption bears upon the publishing history that I will now propose.

Q1 was set from an authorial copy. This copy contained a working text of the play, still in a somewhat untidy state with many deletions and insertions, and many gaps and inconsistencies in the SPs and SDs. This manuscript, held or obtained by the Chamberlain's Men as described above, was made over to Thomas Fisher in 1600. In 1619, the Q1 text provided the basis for Q2, produced in the unusual circumstances related above. For this, the Q1 text was reviewed with some care but not always to good purpose, and without reference to

---

1   Erne, *Dramatist*, 206; Egan, 24–6; Werstine, *Manuscripts*, 13, 60–1, 73.

any new source. For F, a copy of Q2 was marked up as printer's copy after more editorial review, including reference to a theatrical manuscript (perhaps the bookkeeper's or 'prompt' copy). This theatrical copy may carry authorial weight. Such a model accounts for most of the differences between the three versions. It does not explain the markedly variant, uniformly unsatisfactory readings of a handful of textual cruces.

One might, of course, propose with Dover Wilson that the play was repeatedly revised. Wilson advanced a theory of threefold composition, based on the distribution of rhymed verse, blank verse and prose; the variation between 'Puck' and 'Robin' in SPs and SDs; and supposed topical references. No later scholar has endorsed this eventful history.[1] The variant names in SPs and SDs, especially the oscillation between 'Robin' and 'Puck',[2] are hard to relate to a cogent chronology of revision. Wilson even suggested (89) that the flower love-in-idleness was 'an afterthought on Shakespeare's part', replacing 'some other kind of charm'. If there was such radical revision, it is impossible to speculate what the original might have been like. Again, if the rhymed sections are survivals from the first phase, we can hardly imagine how the rest of the play looked in that version, or why those parts alone should be so drastically revised.

If anything, the interfusion of rhyme and blank verse tells *against* any theory of repeated revision. It is sufficiently explained by the general trajectory of Shakespeare's art. *Dream* belongs to a transitional phase of Shakespeare's creative development (see p. 109). This (and perhaps varying conditions of performance) would account for rewriting and readjustments to the very end of the original phase of composition, in the authorial manuscript used as copy for Q1 (see pp. 293–4 and

---

1   A partial exception is Hardin Craig (*Quartos*, 108–9). Craig takes an idiosyncratic view of the early texts whereby Q1 was set from the 'foul papers' of Shakespeare's revision of an earlier text, and F independently of the quartos from the 'official playbook' derived from the same 'foul papers'.

2   Brooks (xxiv–xxv) proposes a justification on dramatic and literary grounds.

5.1.0.1n.). Some local changes with structural implications, like Egeus' presence in Act 5 and the division of 5.1.44–60 between Theseus and Lysander, might have been made at a later stage for theatrical reasons (see p. 303) and incorporated in F. But there is nothing to suggest repeated stages of general revision.

Many changes between Q1 on the one hand, and Q2 and/or F on the other, seem intended to smooth out the metre or make for greater euphony.[1] Others aim at more elegant, formal or up-to-date diction.[2] Yet others simplify or distort the sense,[3] and a few mistake prose for verse and 'regularize' metrically.[4] The categories overlap, and a presumed 'improvement' to one end might impair another.[5] Most of these revisions generically resemble those made by eighteenth-century or later editors. In the absence of other factors, slight irregularity of metre, grammar or diction should not be grounds for dismissing a (usually Q1) reading; it might sometimes be an argument in its favour, as stressing a point or drawing out a nuance.[6] Supposed metrical irregularities might be regularized in delivery by prolonging or slurring a syllable, or introducing a median pause for dramatic effect. In songs or song-like passages, in particular,

1 For changes in both Q2 and F, see 1.1.200, 207; 2.1.3, 5, 34, 183; 2.2.117; 3.2.64, 68 (mistakenly), 172, 323; 4.1.95, 127, 174; 5.1.209, 245; for changes in F only, see 2.1.77; 2.2.108; 3.2.220; for graded changes from Q1 through Q2 to F, see 1.1.239; 3.2.164.

2 For changes in both Q2 and F, see 1.2.70; 2.1.33; 3.1.55 (change to a more popular form); 3.2.137; for changes in F only, see 1.2.20, 88, 101; 2.1.158; 3.1.27, 179; 3.2.19, 99, 145, 210, 346, 435; 4.2.29.

3 For changes in both Q2 and F, see 2.2.51; 3.2.264; 4.1.48, 152, 162; 5.1.42; for changes in F only, see 1.1.143; 2.1.91; 2.2.53, 144; 5.1.122.

4 For instance 'ever' to 'ere' [e'er], 5.1.209; 'aweary' to 'weary', 5.1.245.

5 Changing Q1 'sprite' to 'spirit' at 2.1.33 impairs both metre and rhyme. Omitting one 'tell true' at Q1 3.2.68 badly impairs the metre, as more subtly do the changes from Q1 'from off' to 'off from' at 2.1.183, or Q1 'all are' to 'are all' at 3.2.145.

6 For grammar and diction, see Bottom's use of singular 'your selfe' with plural 'Masters' (3.1.27), or Oberon's charge that Robin was working confusion 'wilfully' rather than F's 'willingly' (3.2.346). For metre or euphony, see 1.1.132, 207; 2.1.158; 2.2.108, 117; 3.2.323; 4.1.127.

apparent irregularities can be and no doubt were absorbed in the tune: we need not change Q1 'thorough' to Q2, F 'through' in the fairy's 'song' (2.1.3, 5). Accepting such expressive irregularities in Q1 might also deter us from endorsing later emendations that iron them out. We may agree, for instance, that Q 'nature shewes arte' (2.2.108) might be preferred to F 'nature her[e] shewes art' or Malone's 'Nature shews her art'; that Pope need not have emended 'Ty vp my louers tongue' (3.1.192) to '... love's tongue', or Theobald inserted an arbitrary 'willing' into 5.1.91; that we might read 'Moons' (QF) and not 'moones' at 2.1.7, like Q1 'nights' rather than Q2, F 'the nights' at 4.1.95; and that 1.1.219 might be emended to end 'strange companies' rather than 'stranger companies'.

THE PRINTING OF THE EARLY EDITIONS

The printing history of Q1 has some unusual features, although they never affect substantive readings.[1] In a quarto, the sheet is folded twice, making a quire of four leaves or eight pages. Arguing from the recurrence of distributed type and the use of wrong founts (chiefly italic or small capitals for regular roman capitals), Turner ('Printing') concludes that Q1 was set by formes:[2] that is, the 'forme' or four pages (not in sequence) on one side of a sheet was set before work on the other side was taken up. This involved casting off copy for the whole quire – i.e. estimating in advance the amount of text to fit on each page – and adjusting the text accordingly while printing. However, seriatim composition (following the sequence of the

---

1   The eight extant copies of Q1 have been collated by Berger (vii). The only press variants are routine corrections of minor errors and flaws. I agree with Berger (vi, nn.4, 5) against *TxC* (281, 287) that in the Bodleian copy, the 'comma' after 1.1.189 is an over-inked (indeed somewhat under-inked) full stop, and the comma after 2.2.47 a later insertion by hand.

2   Blayney (*Lear*, 92–3) contests the principles behind Turner's arguments without necessarily dismissing them in this particular case.

text) was attempted in part of quire C (Turner, 'Printing', 41). There are departures from usual practice elsewhere too. Turner also concludes that the outer forme (pages 1, 4, 5, 8) was printed before the inner (pages 2, 3, 6, 7), except in quire A.[1] Following common practice, quire A was the last to be set; but as it contains part of the main text as well as the preliminaries (here only the title-page), casting off must have begun from the very first page of the text.

The greatest deviation occurs in quire G. Sigs G1^r–G2^v contain 34 lines per page instead of the standard 35. On sig. G2^r, two of these are blank lines before SDs.[2] Together with the avoidance of a turnover in 4.2.4 (where only half a word spills over) this gives sig. G2^r an open, widely spaced appearance. The compositor seems to have stretched out an inadequate amount of text in order to fill the page. But on sig. G3^v of the same forme, he compresses into 35 lines what would normally have occupied 37, given two mid-line changes of speaker (in 5.1.76, 81). Sigs G2^v–G3^v contain the mislined passage (5.1.5–83) where virtually all editors accept Wilson's thesis of later insertions crammed into the margin of the manuscript copy (see pp. 298–9). The mislining seems due primarily to unclear marginal copy: many instances do not affect the number of lines.[3] But it may sometimes be owing to adjustments for incorrectly cast-off copy – for instance, by reducing 14 verses to 12 at 5.1.5–18 (sigs G2^v–G3^r). Why, even while compressing verses in this way, should the compositor have reduced the number of lines on sig. G2^v, or even earlier on sig. G1^r of this forme?

---

1   The inner forme of quire A might have been composed first to settle the layout and typography of the heading on sig. A2^r before tackling the join between sig. A4^v (in the outer forme) and the already set sig. B1^r (Henry Woudhuysen, personal communication).

2   Turner overlooks these, thus wrongly reporting 32 lines on sig. G2^r.

3   See 5.1.29–31 (sig. G3^r; but the mislining clears space for a turnover in 32), 58–60, 66–70 (sig. G3^v); also earlier at 4.1.164–6 (sig. G1^r).

Sig. G2^v ends mid-line in 5.1.15. Confused copy at that point could lead to wrong casting off all through sigs G1^r–G2^v, overestimating the material in a way that could later be tackled only by reducing a line per page. But it is curious that the compositor should have realized this already when setting sig. G1^r, the first page of the outer forme (hence of the entire quire), if the pages were set in the usual order. There is no evident source of confusion in sig. G1^r itself. All this suggests delay and departure from the normal sequence of composition in quire G. It is consistent with Turner's finding ('Printing', 37–8) that 'G (o[uter forme]) type ... is found only in H (i[nner forme]) rather than in both formes of that sheet', and 'G (i[nner forme]) type does not reappear before sheet A.' This implies that the outer and inner formes of quire G were printed (or at least their type distributed) after the outer and inner formes respectively of quire H had been set, contrary to the usual practice. But the copy for both formes of quire G must have been reviewed and recast as a whole (hence the delayed printing), resulting in the decision to have only 34 lines per page on sigs G1^r–G2^v.[1] This proved too radical, calling for some adjustment in the opposite direction by compressing verses on sigs G2^v–G3^v.[2]

Pace Turner, casting off might well be a factor in the mislining of 5.1.5 83 and possibly elsewhere,[3] as expected in a book set by formes. The chief cause, no doubt, was the unclear nature of the copy; but the one explanation does not preclude the other. Such persistent opposite-tending errors in casting off (especially with material entirely in verse) are hard to explain

---

1 Turner ('Printing', 53–4) explains this by piecemeal page-to-page adjustments.
2 See 5.1.5–8 (sig. G2^v), 5.1.12–18 (sigs G2^v–G3^r), 5.1.32–8 (sig. G3^r) and 5.1.76–83 (sig. G3^v: includes two verses divided between speakers). In all but the third case, the lines are near the foot of the page, where the need for compression would be most urgent.
3 For examples, see 2.1.175–6 (sig. C1^v), 3.2.48–9 (sig. D4^v), 4.1.184–5 (sig. G1^v), 5.1.385–6 (sig. H4^r).

except by an unclear and confusing text, perhaps owing to crowded marginal insertions. My account above questions Turner's general dismissal of inaccurately cast-off copy,[1] but upholds his basic conclusion that the copy for Q1 was a 'heavily revised manuscript' (55), which the compositor tackled to the best of his ability. This agrees with the general view of the copy for Q1 (see pp. 298–9).

Q2 seems to be a page-by-page reprint of Q1, taking advantage of the already cast-off copy. Hence two compositors might have been at work, as Blayney suggests ('Pavier', 202–5) by tentative analogy with the *Merchant of Venice* quarto.[2] The *Dream* Q1 page-division is exactly followed in Q2 except in quire G. To avoid disturbing the number of lines per page, where the last line of a prose speech barely fits the measure in Q1,[3] the Q2 compositor carefully follows the Q1 line division;[4] where there is room to spare, he allows himself more freedom. In the one case (3.1.54–9, sig. D2^r) where a tightly justified speech in Q1 is allowed an extra line, a line is reduced at 3.1.62–6 to compensate. This also eliminates the clumsy spillover in Q1 of a truncated syllable at the end of

---

1 Turner (55) grants this factor at only two points in the play, 1.2.53–4 (sig. B2^r) and 5.1.256–7 (sig. H2^r); but then why not at 1.1.53 (sig. A2^v) or 3.1.97–8 (sig. D2^v)? He observes (48) that in many cases, the printing of verse as prose could not be owing to this reason: above all in 1.2.27–34 (sig. B2^r), where the compositor could not have grossly miscalculated the space needed for eight lines of verse. This is not a foolproof argument. The verse might have occupied four lines in the manuscript copy, as Turner himself argues (47–8, 50) for 2.1.2–9 (sig. B3^r) and 3.2.396–9 (sig. F1^v), adding moreover that the Q1 printer divided 2.1.10–13 into shorter units to fill out the page. Also, Turner does not distinguish between the measures of octosyllabic verse and blank verse.

2 Kable had suggested that 'Compositor B' of F set the type for all the 1619 Pavier Quartos including *Dream* Q2. Blayney strongly contests the identification and suggests two compositors setting alternate sheets of *Merchant* but, from the inadequate evidence, less certainly so of *Dream*.

3 See 1.2.4–10 (sig. B1^v), 5.1.343–5 (sig. H3^r), or even a marginal case like 3.1.182–7 (sig. D3^v).

4 He even clears some elbow-room at 1.2.86–9 (sig. B2^v).

3.1.66.[1] Again, Q2 might reline verse, and change prose to verse or vice versa, correctly or incorrectly, but always keeping the number of lines intact.[2] On sig. F3^r, Q1 had lined 4.1.34–5 wrongly, in two lines plus a turnover. Q2 splits the two verses between three lines, balancing the reduction of a line in 4.1.10–17 to eliminate another spillover of a residual half-word. In other words, the Q2 compositor[3] is alive to refinements of detail, but will not lose the advantage of Q1's spadework.

The problem comes in sigs G1^r–G2^v, where Q1 has one line less than usual per page but Q2 reverts to the usual 35. Interestingly, no attempt is made to adjust this by sorting out the Q1 mislining of 5.1.2–22. Q2 adds an extra line at the foot of sig. G1^r; but then proceeds inconsistently,[4] so that sig. G2^v starts five lines ahead of Q1. This may be because the compositor had noticed that sigs G1^r–G2^v in Q1 had fewer lines per page, and cast off copy accordingly to set by formes; or it may reflect unplanned seriatim setting, adjusted only on sig. G3^r when the mismatch with Q1 became too glaring. Sig. G3^r restores the balance largely by spreading Theseus' speech in 5.1.32–8 over eight lines in place of five (plus a turnover) in Q1. Thereafter, the page-breaks follow Q1 again till the end.

The printing of F has been documented in unique detail by Hinman. It is a 'folio in sixes': three sheets folded together in a quire of six leaves or twelve pages, for which copy had to be

---

1 In Q1, this syllable could easily have been fitted in the previous line. The spillover seems an adjustment for wrong casting off.

2 See 3.1.93–6 (sig. D2^v), 3.2.257–8, 262–3 (sig. E3^v), 396–400 (sig. F1^v), 5.1.58–60 (sig. G3^v).

3 If two compositors set alternate sheets, the same man would have set quires D and F. He may also have had a preference for the spelling *hee*. Most cases of Q1 'hee', and the virtually default-mode 'mee', are standardized to 'he', 'me' in Q2. But in four cases, Q1 'he' is changed to 'hee' in Q2 (3.1.34, sig. D1^v; 3.2.414, sig. F2^r ('hee's'); 4.2.3, sig. G2^r; 5.1.312, sig. H3^r).

4 Sig. G1^v breaks up 4.1.184–5 (adding an SD), and brings forward nearly two lines of Bottom's speech (4.1.211–12) from sig. G2^r to fill out the page, thereby adding to the deficit on sig. G2^r. Sig. G2^r reduces another line at 4.2.19–24, and sig. G3^r in the SD at 5.1.27.1, though this is balanced by adding a blank line above.

cast off in one operation. Printing generally began with the innermost two-page forme of the quire and proceeded outwards. A pressman could print off a forme in roughly half the time taken to set it (Hinman, 2.379). Thus the ideal arrangement would be for two compositors to work simultaneously, each composing one page of a forme. This ideal order is most closely followed in the History plays, and in good measure in the Tragedies. The course of the Comedies is more complex, as exemplified in the 18 pages of F *Dream*: sigs N1^r to O3^v, pages 145 to 162. Three pages were wrongly numbered: 165 for 159 (sig. O2^r), corrected in proof; 151 for 153 and 163 for 161 (sigs N5^r and O3^r), left uncorrected, like 162 and 163 for 164 and 165 on sigs O4^v and O5^r carrying the next play, *The Merchant of Venice*. Sig. O5^v (page 166) was wrongly numbered 160 but corrected in proof.

Proof-reading progressed alongside the printing, so that formes can exist in uncorrected and corrected states. In these two quires, there are no corrections of substantive readings and (besides two page numbers) only three of inconsequential flaws (Hinman, 1.260–1). On sig. N2^v, F may have relined verse to fit cast-off copy: lines 2.1.59, 60 are each split in two, with a widely spaced SD in between, perhaps to fill out the column. The few other instances of fresh relining in F (i.e. not following Q2 copy) do not seem attributable to printers' needs. For all practical purposes, the printing history of F does not affect our reading of the play.

The first five quires of the First Folio were printed alongside another large volume, Thomas Wilson's *A Christian Dictionary*. Once this was completed, an extra case of type was available for the Folio from quire F onward. Moreover, two new compositors, C and D, now appear alongside A and B who composed most of the volume. Hinman's classic spelling-tests indicate that both C and D worked on *Dream*, as did B. Hinman (2.418, 424, 430) suggested the presence of A in sig. N6^v column b (carrying *Dream*) and four pages each of quires O and P (all carrying *Merchant*), but granted that these pages might equally have been set by D, who undoubtedly used the same type-case elsewhere in quire N. This seems more likely, as Hinman found A otherwise absent between quires I and T,[1] and later scholars do not bring him in again till much later, in quire Aa.[2] But at least three compositors were certainly involved: B, C and D.[3] Hinman (2.414–26, 514) concluded that B set sigs N2^v, N1^v, N1^r, O3^r; C, sigs N3^v, N3^r, N2^r, N5^v, O2^v, O3^v, O2^r, O1^v, O1^r; D, sigs N4^r, N4^v, N5^r, N6^r, N6^v – in all cases, in the order given.[4]

The presence of three compositors results in some noteworthy features. The same compositor, C, set both pages of a forme, sigs N2^r and N5^v. This is not unusual;[5] but it implies either a delay in printing; or – in an 'all but unique instance' (Hinman, 2.418) – that Compositors B and D, who set the obverse forme of the sheet (sigs N2^v and N5^r) from two other type-cases, worked simultaneously with C and with each other to obviate the delay. Similar compulsions of speed might have caused another rare situation, two different compositors setting the two columns on a page. Of only twenty instances in F, two occur in quire O (sigs O4^r and O4^v, in *Merchant* but with forme-mates from *Dream*, sigs O3^v and O3^r respectively). Here two compositors, B and C, each set roughly three columns of one forme and one column of the other. Also, the normal order of composition, from innermost to outermost forme, was disturbed in quire O, the first three formes being set in the order sigs O3^r/O4^v, O2^v/O5^r, O3^v/O4^r. This is the likeliest cause of the wrongly numbered pages, involving three

1 Hinman suggests A's presence in quire K, but again with Compositor C as an alternative (2.514).
2 See Howard-Hill, 'Compositors'; Blayney (Norton, xxxv).
3 Three (rarely four) compositors worked together on at most thirteen quires of F.
4 This is corroborated by Blayney (Norton, xxxv), and for sig. N6^v by Howard-Hill, 'Compositors', 83; O'Connor, 97, 117.
5 168 of 441 formes were so set (Blayney, Norton, xxxiii).

compositors.[1] There is the overall sense of an uncertainty of procedure, leading to delay and makeshift devices while setting quires N and O. The possibility must be borne in mind when assessing the F text.

EDITORIAL PROCEDURE

This section describes the challenges in editing a Shakespeare play from the old texts, and the strategies adopted in this edition to meet them. The images from Q1 and F, with overlapping text (5.1.186–221 in Q1, 5.1.199–337 in F), illustrate most of the points in question, except the broad issue of act and scene divisions. *All line numbers in this section refer to Act 5, scene 1 unless otherwise mentioned. Most references are to readings in the Q1 and/or F images.*

Variant readings and emendations

The F page, though numbered 163, is actually 161, which prefigures the pitfalls awaiting reader and editor. Most importantly, there are substantive textual variants in these pages. The Q1 page contains two, the F page one, of the few serious cruces in the play. Line 190 reads 'knit now againe' in Q, 'knit vp in thee' in F; line 205, 'Now is the Moon vsed' in Q, 'Now is the morall downe' in F. I have adopted the F reading at 190, and emended to 'Now is the more use' at 205, for reasons explained in the commentary. In choosing between variant texts or opting to emend, the editor must weigh the overall authority of the respective texts against the likelihood of a particular reading being corrupted, at the manuscript stage or in transition to print. At line 190, the need for a rhyming word justifies the F reading, though Q1 is the control text for this edition. The status of manuscript readings can only be conjectured, taking into

---

1   The three pages numbered 163 (sigs O3ʳ, O4ʳ, O5ʳ) were set by B, C (probably) and D respectively.

A Midſommer nightes dreame.

Pat as I told you : yonder ſhe comes.　　　*Enter* Thiſby.

Thiſ. O wall, full often haſt thou heard my mones,
For parting my faire *Pyramus,* and mee.
My cherry lips haue often kiſt thy ſtones;
Thy ſtones, with lime and hayire knit now againe.

　　Pyra. I ſee a voice : now will I to the chinke,
To ſpy and I can heare my *Thiſbyes* face. Thy ſby?
Thiſ. My loue thou art, my loue I thinke.

Py. Thinke what thou wilt, I am thy louers Grace:
And, like *Limander,* am I truſty ſtill.

　　Thiſ. And I, like *Helen,* till the fates me kill.

Pyra. Not *Shafalus,* to *Procrus,* was ſo true.

Thiſ. As *Shafalus* to *Procrus,* I to you.

Pyr. O kiſſe mee, through the hole of this vilde wall.

Thiſ. I kiſſe the walles hole; not your lips at all.

Pyr. Wilt thou, at *Ninnies* tombe, meete me ſtraight way?

Thy. Tide life, tyde death, I come without delay.

Wal. Thus haue I, *Wall,* my part diſcharged ſo;
And, being done, thus wall away doth goe.

Duk. Now is the Moon vſed betweene the two neighbors.

Deme. No remedy, my Lord, when wals are ſo wilfull, to
heare without warning.

Dutch. This is the ſillieſt ſtuffe, that euer I heard.

Duke. The beſt, in this kinde, are but ſhadowes : and
the worſt are no worſe, if imagination amend them.

Dutch. It muſt be your imagination, then; & not theirs.

Duke. If we imagine no worſe of them, then they of the-
ſelues, they may paſſe for excellent men. Here come two
noble beaſts, in a man and a Lyon.

　　　　Enter Lyon, *and* Moone-ſhine.

Lyon. You Ladies, you (whoſe gentle hearts do feare
The ſmalleſt monſtrous mouſe, that creepes on floore)
May now, perchance, both quake and tremble here,
When Lyon rough, in wildeſt rage, doth roare.
Then know that I, as *Snug* the Ioyner am

A

Pir. O kiſſe me through the hole of this vile wall.

Thiſ. I kiſſe the wals hole, not your lips at all.

Pir. Wilt thou at *Ninnies* tombe meete me ſtraight way?

Thiſ. Tide life, tide death, I come without delay.

Wall. Thus haue I *Wall*, my part diſcharged ſo; And being done, thus *Wall* away doth go.   *Exit Clow.*

Du. Now is the morall downe betweene the two Neighbors.

Dem. No remedie my Lord, when Wals are ſo wilfull, to heare without warning.

Dut. This is the ſillieſt ſtuffe that ere I heard.

Du. The beſt in this kind are but ſhadowes, and the worſt are no worſe, if imagination amend them.

Dut. It muſt be your imagination then, & not theirs.

Duk. If wee imagine no worſe of them then they of themſelues, they may paſſe for excellent men. Here com two noble beaſts, in a man and a Lion.

Enter Lyon and Moone-ſhine.

Lyon. You Ladies, you (whoſe gentle harts do feare The ſmalleſt monſtrous mouſe that creepes on floore) May now perchance, both quake and tremble heere, When Lion rough in wildeſt rage death roare. Then know that I, one *Snug* the Ioyner am A Lion fell, nor elſe no Lions dam: For if I ſhould as Lion come in ſtrife Into this place, 'twere pittie of my life.

Du. A verie gentle beaſt, and of a good conſcience.

Dem. The verie beſt at a beaſt, my Lord, ý ere I ſaw.

Liſ. This Lion is a verie Fox for his valor.

Du. True, and a Gooſe for his diſcretion.

Dem. Not ſo my Lord: for his valor cannot carrie his diſcretion, and the Fox carries the Gooſe.

Du. His diſcretion I am ſure cannot carrie his valor: for the Gooſe carries not the Fox. It is well; leaue it to his diſcretion, and let vs hearken to the Moone.

Moon. This Lanthorne doth the horned Moone preſent.

De. He ſhould haue worne the hornes on his head.

Du. Hee is no creſcent, and his hornes are inuiſible, within the circumference.

Moon. This lanthorne doth the horned Moone preſent: My ſelfe, the man i'th Moone doth ſeeme to be.

Du. This is the greateſt error of all the reſt; the man ſhould be put into the Lanthorne. How is it els the man i'th Moone?

Dem. He dares not come there for the candle. For you ſee, it is already in ſnuffe.

Dut. I am vvearie of this Moone; vvould he would change.

Du. It appeares by his ſmal light of diſcretion, that he is in the wane: but yet in courteſie, in all reaſon, vve muſt ſtay the time.

Liſ. Proceed Moone.

Moon. All that I haue to ſay, is to tell you, that the Lanthorne is the Moone; I, the man in the Moone; this thorne buſh, my thorne buſh; and this dog, my dog.

Dem. Why all theſe ſhould be in the Lanthorne: for they are in the Moone. But ſilence; heere comes *Thisby*.

Enter Thisby.

Thiſ. This is old *Ninnies* tombe : where is my loue? *Lyon.* Oh.

The Lion roares, Thisby runs off.

Dem. Well roar'd Lion.

Du. Well run *Thisby*.

Dut. Well ſhone Moone.

Truly the Moone ſhines with a good grace.

Du. Wel mouz'd Lion.

Dem. And then came *Piramus*.

Lyſ. And ſo the Lion vaniſht.

Enter Piramus.

Pyr. Sweet Moone, I thanke thee for thy ſunny beames, I thanke thee Moone, for ſhining now ſo bright: For by thy gracious, golden, glittering beames, I truſt to taſte of trueſt *Thisbies* ſight. But ſtay : O ſpight! but marke, poore Knight, What dreadful dole is heere? Eyes do you ſee! How can it be? O dainty Ducke : O Deere! Thy mantle good; what ſtaind with blood! Approch you Furies fell : O Fates! come, come : Cut thred and thrum, Quaile, cruſh, conclude, and quell.

Du. This paſſion, and the death of a deare friend, Would go neere to make a man looke ſad.

Dut. Beſhrew my heart, but I pittie the man.

Pir. O wherefore Nature, did ſt thou Lions frame? Since Lion vilde hath heere deflour'd my deere : Which is : no, no, which was the faireſt Dame That liu'd, that lou'd, that lik'd, that look'd with cheere. Come teares, confound : Out ſword, and wound The pap of *Piramus* : I, that left pap, where heart doth hop ; Thus dye I, thus, thus, thus. Now am I dead, now am I fled, my ſoule is in the sky, Tongue loſe thy light, Moone take thy flight, Now dye, dye, dye, dye, dye.

Dem. No Die, but an ace for him ; for he is but one.

Liſ. Leſſe then an ace man. For he is dead, he is nothing.

Du. With the helpe of a Surgeon, he might yet recouer, and proue an Aſſe.

Dut. How chance Moone-ſhine is gone before? *Thisby* comes backe, and findes her Louer.

Enter Thisby.

Duke. She wil finde him by ſtarre-light. Heere ſhe comes, and her paſſion ends the play.

Dut. Me thinkes ſhee ſhould not vſe a long one for ſuch a *Piramus* : I hope ſhe will be breefe.

Dem. A Moth wil turne the ballance, which *Piramus* which *Thisby* is the better.   (eyes.

Lyſ. She hath ſpyed him already, with thoſe ſweete

Dem. And thus ſhe meanes, videlicet.

This. Aſleepe my Loue? What, dead my Doue? O *Piramus* ariſe : Speake, ſpeake. Quite dumbe? Dead, dead? A tombe Muſt couer thy ſweet eyes. Theſe Lilly Lips, this cherry noſe, Theſe yellow Cowſlip cheekes Are gone, are gone : Louers make mone : His eyes were greene as Leekes. O ſiſters three, come, come to mee, With hands as pale as Milke, Lay them in gore, ſince you haue ſhore With ſheeres, his thred of ſilke. Tongue not a word : Come truſty ſword : Come blade, my breſt imbrue :

O 3   And

account not only the assumed nature of the manuscript (whether draft or fair copy, authorial or scribal) but the likely appearance of the text in the secretary or English hand used in Shakespeare's time. My emendation of 'strange' to 'swarthy' at 59 turns on this factor. Here, Q and F agree on a reading it seemed necessary to change, and the emendation was influenced by its likely appearance in secretary hand. There is a full justification in the commentary. All substantive variants in the early editions are recorded in the textual notes, along with all emendations introduced in this edition or adopted from earlier ones, and some notable earlier emendations even if not adopted.

Although most vital, these substantive issues cover only a fraction of editorial decisions and revisions, especially in a play like *Dream* which has few textual cruces. 'Accidentals' like spelling and punctuation, paratextual components like speech prefixes and stage directions, and issues of format and layout like act, scene and line divisions, call for continuous assessment and adjustment. Each of these factors contributes to our total reception of the play, often in imperceptible ways. It is the more necessary for the editor to sort out these details, as they may not consciously register on the reader.

Act and scene divisions

A glance at any modern edition of a Shakespeare play shows how irregular the act and scene divisions can be. *Dream* is no exception. It is unusual in that no act consists of more than two scenes in most modern editions, and Act 5 of only one. Scenes can vary in size from the very large (3.2 or 5.1) to the very short (4.2).

The Folio divides the play into acts; the Quartos have no divisions at all. The scene divisions are the work of later editors. Eighteenth-century editors from Pope onwards often divided the acts into scenes on the principle of French drama, beginning a new scene with every new combination of characters onstage. The scene divisions now commonly found derive from Edward

Capell's edition of 1767, except that Capell starts a new scene at 5.1.361.

Act-division in Elizabethan drama is thought to be modelled, somewhat mechanically, on the division of classical plays in humanist editions. The classically inclined Ben Jonson certainly adopted this model; his 1616 Folio might have specially influenced the Shakespeare Folio of 1623. Hirsh (227), arguing for act-division in the printing-house rather than the theatre, even suggests F divided the plays into five acts to make them 'look classical'. Hirsh also attributes the act-division of all Folio texts to two people working on different principles, both quite arbitrary. But Taylor and Jowett demonstrate how theatrical practice might be a major factor in such divisions. Plays for public playhouses printed before 1616 almost always lack act divisions, while those published later invariably have them. (This does not apply to plays for children's companies and private playhouses: see Greg, 'Divisions'.) Taylor and Jowett (12–15) also show how authors' manuscripts of the earlier period seldom if ever contain act divisions.[1] Hence they postulate a change in theatrical practice in the 1610s, whereby the performance was broken up by four intervals accompanied by music. Earlier plays were restructured to this end. The operative force was surely the example of private playhouses like Blackfriars, where the King's Men had been performing since 1608. Many plays were acted at both public and private playhouses; *Dream* would be specially suitable and popular in the latter.

Hence the *Dream* quartos, based on authorial copy and first published in 1600, lack act divisions; the Folio text, influenced by post-1610 theatrical practice, inserts them in a play not designed for the purpose. There is a single setting and a broad continuity of action from the start of 2.1 to the end of 4.1; any

---

1   This supersedes Baldwin's general conclusion (*Division*, 10–13) that authors' manuscripts usually carried act and scene divisions, irrespective of date.

division within this span is more or less arbitrary. The stage is indisputably cleared only once, at the end of 3.1:[1] this seems the best place for a half-way intermission if called for. But even there, Titania and Bottom are probably sleeping in an inner recess or 'discovery space', perhaps behind a curtain, like Titania at the end of 2.2. They remain there through 3.2 (though Titania seems to have emerged at least once: see 4.1.47–60), till we see them awake at the start of 4.1 (see 2.2.0.1n., 3.1.192n., 4.1.0.1n.). The lovers are explicitly said in F to lie onstage between 3.2 and 4.1 (see 3.2.463 SDn., 4.1.0.1n.). Also, Oberon may hide onstage between 2.1 and 2.2 (see 2.1.268 SDn., 2.2.0.1n.).

The best that can be said of Capell's scene-division is that, if we exclude sleeping and concealed characters, it clears the stage at the end of every scene. At several points, however, the only characters binding a scene together mid-way through its course are asleep: Titania at 2.2.38, Titania, Hermia and Lysander at 2.2.69, the lovers and Bottom at 4.1.101, Bottom at 4.1.198.[2] F provides a SD for sleeping characters not only at the end of an act at 3.2.463 but in the middle of one (and a scene as later demarcated by Capell) at 4.1.101, though not in other such instances. One explanation might be that there was originally no difference between these two cases: the break at the end of 3.2 was a late insertion when the play was divided into acts following the new theatrical practice. That seems to be Taylor and Jowett's conclusion (47), going by their explanation of a similar problem in *Titus Andronicus*. The new theatrical manuscript consulted for F but not for Q2 (see pp. 303–4) would contain this and the other act divisions, with SDs added inconsistently.

---

1   Dessen and Thomson (206) note how the term *solus* (alone), applied to Oberon at the start of 3.2 in F, is almost always used of a character walking on to an empty stage.
2   This also provides support for making Oberon and/or Robin lurk onstage rather than exit at 2.1.187, 3.2.40 and 3.2.121.

In this fluid situation, there seems no reason to deviate from the standard act and scene divisions based on F and Capell respectively. There is no obvious justification for any other divisions, which would only confuse readers and make it hard to compare this text with other editions.

Line divisions

Line divisions in the old editions can be erratic, as famously at 5–83. (See pp. 298–9 and 5.1.5–8n.) This seems to be chiefly owing to additional copy crammed into the margin in a confusing way. Less prominent instances elsewhere may be owing to less radical causes, perhaps simple misunderstanding. Lines 183–6, of which the last part appears at the top of the Q1 image, are wrongly printed as verse in both Q and F, though Bottom never speaks verse except when acting as Pyramus. F also converts the courtiers' prose dialogue (correctly printed as such in Q1) to verse at 281–2 and 305–8 (as Q2 had done at 305–6) wrongly but understandably, as courtiers are normally expected to speak in verse, in *Dream* and generally.

Elsewhere, mislining may be due to the need to adjust space. In the Q1 image, '*Thysby?*' (193) actually starts a new line. Tagging it to the previous line saves space on this tightly packed page: an important factor when adjusting cast-off copy.[1] In F, as in Q, 294–6 is printed as a single line, though all equivalent verses are split in two (and in this and most modern editions, in three). This too may have been to save a line. Casting off, rather than error, might cause verse to be printed as prose or vice versa. The F mislinings at 281–2 and 307–8, like that in Q2/F at 305–6, are probably owing to error, as no lines are saved thereby. But in F 238–9, conversion to prose was one way of fitting Starveling's speech into two lines.[2] (A turnover

---

1 For other examples, see the Q1 text of 1.1.53 (printing both parts of a divided verse on the same line); 1.2.53–4; 2.1.42–3, 175–6; 5.1.256–7.
2 Conversely, 2.1.59 and 60 are each split in two in F, perhaps to fill out a column.

would have been another.) In the old editions, lines can sometimes be divided by visual appearance. The editor must scan them mentally, though scansion may not be the only factor involved.

Speech prefixes and stage directions

Speech prefixes are often inconsistent. In the illustrated pages, SPs always refer to the 'Duke' and 'Duchess' (variously spelt and contracted), no doubt because 'Th' might refer to both Theseus and Thisbe. The two characters do not appear together in any earlier scene, hence the SPs there can spell and contract either name as space demands. The SPs in this scene illustrate another choice, to name the characters in the play-within-the-play rather than the people playing them: Pyramus not Bottom, Thisbe not Flute. This edition, like some earlier ones, names the actual people to avoid confusion where the character also speaks in his own person, as at 183: SPs in early texts name Pyramus here too. At 3.1.97–8 Flute speaks a single speech partly as himself and partly as Thisbe. The names Robin and Puck alternate intricately. All such cases call for decisions on the editor's part.

SDs can be irregular in every way. Q1 has no SD at all at 204; F has '*Exit Clow.*' '*Clow.*' might stand for 'Clown' or 'Clowns' – in other words, it might cover Pyramus and Thisbe besides Wall. F often uses singular 'Exit' for plural 'Exeunt', sometimes making it uncertain how many people leave (see 2.1.268n.). In any case, 'Clown(s)' refers to the characters' actual identity, not their assumed roles as in SPs and other SDs in both Q and F. Also, does '*Exit*' relate only to the play-within-the-play, or do the actors totally leave the stage? The solution adopted in this edition is explained at 5.1.150n. As in most early modern playtexts, entry and exit SDs are highly inconsistent (there is no exit for Lion in either Q or F), though entrances are marked more consistently than exits: in theatrical manuscripts ('prompt copies'), actors had to be alerted when to enter, but could be trusted to exit at the right point. This argument raises a more basic issue. Early texts often omit self-evident or 'embedded' SDs, where the dialogue implies the action. How far should a modern editor insert such SDs? In practice, most editors do so to varying degrees. In this edition, for instance, SDs involving Thisbe's mantle seemed necessary at 257 and 261, as readers (even those conversant with the story) might otherwise miss the point of 'Well moused' (262).

There can be subtler issues relating to SDs. The F image illustrates one such. At 216.1, all previous editions retained the QF SD '*Enter* Lyon, *and* Moone-shine.' This edition has only Lion enter at that point and Moonshine after 233, for reasons explained in the commentary. 'Enter' can signify a 'massed entry' covering later entrances, as for Helena at 1.1.19.1 in Q (if that is not simply an error, corrected in F); or it can signal emergence from hiding (see 3.1.71n., 3.2.344.1n., 463 SDn., 4.1.44.1n.). Both types of cases called for emended SDs in this edition. For other issues involving entries and exits, see 2.1.237 SDn., 246.1n.; 3.1.48.1n., 83 SD2n., 98.1–2n., 107.1n.; 3.2.338 SDn., 343–4n., 404 SDn.

Spelling

A glance at the illustrated pages confirms what is well known, that Early Modern English spelling is entirely fluid. The variants seem (and often are) quite arbitrary, but some possible factors governing them should be borne in mind. One is authorial practice: in Shakespeare, largely a matter of conjecture, as very little of his writing survives. Another is the practice of particular printing offices or compositors. Weighing the one against the other, we can assess the case for authorial provenance of the manuscript copy underlying the printed text – in the case of *Dream*, principally Q1 (see pp. 298–9). The idiosyncrasies of spelling (especially of *do*, *go* and *here*) of each F compositor is accepted as a major pointer to the printing history of F. There is a third factor to take into account. Spellings can be expanded or contracted to fit a line within the span of a page or column, or a section of text within a page where copy has been cast off. The spelling *com* at 216 in F, though *come* at thirteen other points on the page (*come* also in the F copy-text Q2 and the latter's own copy-text Q1), is surely to allow the compositor to fit that last word within the line. He could have moved it down to the next line, but that would have involved re-setting the whole line. Other expedients to fit a line within the column-span include contractions derived from scribal practice, as at F 212 (for 'and') and 226 (for 'that'), or a turnover, moving the last word into the line above or below, like 'eyes' in F 315. In Q1, 201 starts farther to the left than other SPs so that the whole speech can fit into a single line.

The issue of variant spellings is largely irrelevant to this edition, as the Arden Shakespeare modernizes fluid and obsolete spellings. But there is a tricky category of old spellings that might carry special nuances of sound or meaning, like *vilde* for *vile*. Q1 reads *vilde* and F *vile* (following Q2) at 199, but Q1, Q2 and F all read *vilde* at 285. In such cases, the modern form has been used in this edition, but variants that might affect the nuance or impact of the speech (*loffe*, *margent*, *swoune/swound/sound*, *apricocks*) or carry extra meaning (*loose*) are noted in the commentary and textual notes. Variants like *courtesie/curtsie* or *antique/anticke*, where both modern meanings are relevant, have also been noted. So have variants marking a difference in class identity (*perfit/perfect*, *lanthorne/lantern*), on the analogy of rustic or popular forms like *byrlakin* and *parlous* used by the same speakers. Rarely, modern variant forms (*feigning/faining*) have been introduced to bring out a play on words.[1] Judgement is also needed to distinguish different spellings of the same word from different words

---

1 For the examples above, see respectively 2.1.55–6n., 2.1.85n., 2.2.158, 3.1.160n., 2.1.206n., 4.1.20n., 5.1.3n., 1.2.88n., 101n., 3.1.55n., 5.1.134n., 234n., 3.1.12n. (twice), 1.1.31n.

covered by the same spelling. At 209, F *ere* is clearly the contraction 'e'er' for Q1 *euer*, like QF *ere* at 226; but in 3.1.83 and 3.2.170, the spelling *ere* in all early texts might stand for either 'e'er', ever, or 'ere', before.

Some other conventions, of typography rather than spelling, have also been brought into conformity with modern practice. Modern *i* and *j* were both commonly represented by *i*: thus 'Ioyner' for 'Joiner' (221). (As this and other examples show, *y* was freely used instead of *i* in mid-word.) *U* was commonly used in mid-word and *v* at the start: thus *haue* (189, 203), *loue* (193), but *vsed* (205). These are conventions like the (inconsistent) use of italics and initial capitals for proper names: contrast Q1 lower-case *f* with F upper-case *F* in *fates* at 196 and 278. There can also be anomalous fount, perhaps owing to shortage of type, as in Q1 'Procrus' (197–8) with roman small-capital P followed by larger italics.

In accord with Arden practice, verb endings in *-ed* are so spelt in this edition, even where the *e* is clearly elided. Departures are indicated in the notes. Where metre requires the final *-ed* to be pronounced, the word has been repeated in the notes with the ending as *-èd*. *Blessed/blest* is a special case, as the early texts use both spellings with clear intent to distinguish the pronunciation (see 1.1.74n.). *Curst*, by contrast, is always so spelt to indicate pronunciation in one syllable as the metre demands. Contractions in early texts (like QF *belou'd*, 1.1.104; F *lou'st*, 1.1.163; Q2, F *speak'st*, 2.1.42) have been retained.

Punctuation

The debate over early modern punctuation continues. Scribal and printing practice, especially in playtexts, may reflect nuances of speech. But it is hard to trace any consistency of use, or to ignore the demands of logical pointing according to current lights.

Q1, the control text of this edition, has unusually heavy pointing, particularly in the use of commas, contrary to what is commonly assumed of authorial drafts. Other plays thought to be set from authorial copy are consistently lighter in pointing, the three pages supposedly in Shakespeare's hand in the manuscript play *Sir Thomas More* even more so.[1] In the Q1 image, there is a specially thick cluster of commas in 209–16. In this edition, commas that might confuse or irk the modern reader have been removed. Others, compatible with modern usage or even guiding the sense, are retained. The colon was more widely used in early modern texts than today, especially so in Q1. In this edition, they have often been replaced by commas or semi-colons, or by no mark at all. Sometimes (though never contrary to modern usage) some light pointing is retained where a modern text might have none, to underpin a possibly meaningful sequence of pauses plotted by the Q1 punctuation. It may help to convey the feel of the text in the version closest to what Shakespeare wrote: in fact, to signal how the lines sounded to Shakespeare as he wrote them and how, therefore, he meant them to be delivered in performance.

The issues illustrated from these two images, and the principles arising from them, indicate how there is no routine or mechanical way of editing a Shakespeare play. Matters apparently unrelated to the substantive text need close attention and considered revision if they are not to irk or mislead the modern reader at every stage.

---

1   See Partridge, *Orthography*, 58–9. The Oxf editors (xxxvii) give no reasons for their view that Q1 is 'far more precisely punctuated than any Shakespearian manuscript is likely to have been'.

ABBREVIATIONS AND REFERENCES

The place of publication is London unless otherwise indicated.

Shakespeare plays not yet published in the third series of the Arden Shakespeare are cited from the second series.

Biblical references are to the 1588 edition of the 'Bishops' Bible' (*STC* 2149), whose chapter and verse divisions agree broadly with those of most later versions including the King James.

Oxford English Dictionary (*OED*) refers to the online (third) edition, checked on 23–24 August 2016. The *OED* headword has not been repeated in the commentary where the form in the *MND* text differs only in number, tense or degree, or in being the adverbial form of the root adjective.

References to Abbott, Blake and Hope cite paragraph numbers, not page numbers.

Works cited only once from a pre-1800 edition have usually not been listed. Their details have been stated at the point of citation. Subtitles of books and articles, where not directly necessary, have sometimes been omitted.

ABBREVIATIONS

ABBREVIATIONS USED IN NOTES

*	identifies commentary notes on readings different from the control text Q1
conj.	conjecture (by)
edn	edition
n.	commentary note
om.	omitted
opp.	opposite
rev.	revised
rpt.	reprinted
SD	stage direction

SP	speech prefix
subst.	substantively
this edn	a reading, SD or SP first adopted in this edition

WORKS BY AND PARTLY BY SHAKESPEARE

AC	*Antony and Cleopatra*
AW	*All's Well That Ends Well*
AYL	*As You Like It*
CE	*The Comedy of Errors*
Cor	*Coriolanus*
Cym	*Cymbeline*
E3	*King Edward III*
Ham	*Hamlet*
1H4	*King Henry IV, Part 1*
2H4	*King Henry IV, Part 2*
H5	*King Henry V*
1H6	*King Henry VI, Part 1*
2H6	*King Henry VI, Part 2*
3H6	*King Henry VI, Part 3*
H8	*King Henry VIII*
JC	*Julius Caesar*
KJ	*King John*
KL	*King Lear*
LC	*A Lover's Complaint*
LLL	*Love's Labour's Lost*
Luc	*The Rape of Lucrece*
MA	*Much Ado about Nothing*
Mac	*Macbeth*
MM	*Measure for Measure*
MND	*A Midsummer Night's Dream*
MV	*The Merchant of Venice*
MW	*The Merry Wives of Windsor*
Oth	*Othello*
Per	*Pericles*
PP	*The Passionate Pilgrim*
PT	*The Phoenix and Turtle*
R2	*King Richard II*
R3	*King Richard III*
RJ	*Romeo and Juliet*
Son	*Sonnets*
STM	*Sir Thomas More*
TC	*Troilus and Cressida*
Tem	*The Tempest*

330

TGV	*The Two Gentlemen of Verona*
Tim	*Timon of Athens*
Tit	*Titus Andronicus*
TN	*Twelfth Night*
TNK	*The Two Noble Kinsmen*
TS	*The Taming of the Shrew*
VA	*Venus and Adonis*
WT	*The Winter's Tale*

REFERENCES

EDITIONS OF SHAKESPEARE COLLATED

Alexander	William Shakespeare, *The Complete Works*, ed. Peter Alexander (1951)
Ard[1]	*A Midsummer Night's Dream*, Arden Shakespeare, ed. Henry Cuningham, 4th edn (1938)
Ard[2]	*A Midsummer Night's Dream*, New Arden Shakespeare, ed. Harold F. Brooks (1979)
Berger	*A Midsummer Night's Dream 1600* (Q1 facsimile), ed. Thomas L. Berger, Malone Society Reprints, vol. 157 (Oxford, 1995)
Bevington	*The Complete Works of Shakespeare*, ed. David Bevington, 6th edn (New York, 2008)
Brook, *Acting*	*Peter Brook's ... A Midsummer Night's Dream*, Authorized Acting Edition (Stratford-upon-Avon, 1974)
Brooks	See Ard[1]
Cam	*The Works of William Shakespeare*, ed. William George Clark, John Glover and William Aldis Wright, 9 vols (Cambridge, 1863–6), vol. 2
Cam[1]	*A Midsummer Night's Dream*, the New [Cambridge] Shakespeare, ed. Arthur Quiller-Couch and John Dover Wilson (Cambridge, 1924)
Cam[2]	*A Midsummer Night's Dream*, ed. R.A. Foakes, New Cambridge Shakespeare (Cambridge, 1984; rev. edn, 2003)
Capell	*The Works of Shakespeare*, ed. Edward Capell, 10 vols (1767–8), vol. 3
Chambers	*A Midsummer Night's Dream*, The Warwick Shakespeare, ed. Edmund K. Chambers (1897)

Clemen	*A Midsummer Night's Dream*, Signet Classic Shakespeare, ed. Wolfgang Clemen, rev. edn (New York, 1998)
Collier	*The Works of William Shakespeare*, ed. J. Payne Collier, 8 vols (1842–4), vol. 2
Collier²	*The Works of William Shakespeare*, ed. J. Payne Collier, 6 vols (1858), vol. 2
Collier MS	J. Payne Collier, *Notes and Emendations to the Text of Shakespeare's Plays, from Early Manuscript Corrections in a Copy of the Folio, 1632*, rev. and enlarged edn (1853)
Craig	*The Complete Works of William Shakespeare*, Oxford Shakespeare, ed. W.J. Craig (Oxford, [1892])
Daly	*A Midsummer Night's Dream*, privately printed by Augustin Daly for his production at Daly's Theatre, New York, 31 January 1888
Deighton	*A Midsummer Night's Dream*, ed. Kenneth Deighton (1891)
Doran	*A Midsummer Night's Dream*, Pelican Shakespeare, ed. Madeleine Doran (Harmondsworth, 1959)
Durham	See Yale
Dyce	*The Works of William Shakespeare*, ed. Alexander Dyce, 6 vols (1857), vol. 2
Dyce²	*The Works of William Shakespeare*, ed. Alexander Dyce, 2nd edn, 8 vols (1864–7), vol. 2
Evans	See *Riv, Riv²*
F	*Mr. William Shakespeares Comedies, Histories, and Tragedies*, The First Folio, 1623
F2	*Mr. William Shakespeares Comedies, Histories, and Tragedies*, The Second Folio, 1632
F3	*Mr. William Shakespeares Comedies, Histories, and Tragedies*, The Third Folio, 1663
F4	*Mr. William Shakespear's Comedies, Histories, and Tragedies*, The Fourth Folio, 1685
Foakes	See Cam²
Folg	*A Midsummer Night's Dream*, Folger Shakespeare Library, ed. Barbara A. Mowat and Paul Werstine (New York, 1993)
Furness	See Var
Globe	*The Works of William Shakespeare*, Globe edn, ed. William George Clark and William Aldis Wright (1864)
Griffiths	*A Midsummer Night's Dream*, Shakespeare in Production, ed. Trevor R. Griffiths (Cambridge, 1996)

Halliwell	*The Complete Works of Shakespere*, ed. J.O. Halliwell, [*c.*1855], Comedies volume
Hanmer	*The Works of Shakespear*, ed. Thomas Hanmer, 6 vols (Oxford, 1743–4), vol. 1
Harrison	*A Midsummer Night's Dream*, Penguin Shakespeare, ed. G.B. Harrison, rev. edn (Harmondsworth, 1953)
Holland	See Oxf[1]
Hudson	*A Midsummer Night's Dream*, ed. Henry Norman Hudson (Boston, MA, 1880)
Johnson	*The Plays of William Shakespeare*, ed. Samuel Johnson, 8 vols (1765), vol. 1
Keightley	*The Plays of William Shakespeare*, ed. Thomas Keightley, 6 vols (1864), vol. 1
Kittredge	*A Midsummer Night's Dream*, ed. G.L. Kittredge (Boston, MA, 1939)
Knight	*The Pictorial Edition of the Works of Shakspere*, ed. Charles Knight, 8 vols ([1838]–43), *Comedies*, vol. 1
Malone	*The Plays and Poems of William Shakspeare*, ed. Edmond Malone, 10 vols (1790), vol. 2
Norton	*The Norton Facsimile. The First Folio of Shakespeare*, prepared by Charlton Hinman, 2nd edn with a new Introduction by Peter Blayney (New York, 1996)
Norton[3]	*The Norton Shakespeare*, 3rd edn, ed. Stephen Greenblatt et al. (New York, 2016)
Oxf	William Shakespeare, *The Complete Works*, Oxford Shakespeare, gen. ed. Stanley Wells and Gary Taylor (Oxford, 1986)
Oxf[1]	*A Midsummer Night's Dream*, Oxford Shakespeare, ed. Peter Holland (Oxford, 1994)
Oxf[2]	William Shakespeare, *The Complete Works: Modern Critical Edition*, New Oxford Shakespeare, gen. ed. Gary Taylor et al. (Oxford, 2016); *MND* ed. Terri Bourus
Pope	*The Works of Shakespear*, ed. Alexander Pope, 6 vols (1723–5), vol. 1
Q1	*A Midsommer nights dreame*, The First Quarto (1600)
Q2	*A Midsommer nights dreame*, The Second Quarto (1619)
Rann	*The Dramatic Works of Shakspeare*, ed. Joseph Rann, 6 vols (Oxford, 1786–?93), vol. 2
Riv	*The Riverside Shakespeare*, ed. G. Blakemore Evans et al. (Boston, MA, 1974)
Riv²	*The Riverside Shakespeare*, 2nd edn, ed. G. Blakemore Evans et al. (Boston, MA, 1997)

Rowe	*The Works of Mr William Shakespear*, ed. Nicholas Rowe, 6 vols (1709), vol. 2
Rowe[2]	*The Works of Mr William Shakespear*, ed. Nicholas Rowe, 2nd edn, 8 vols (1714), vol. 2
RSC	William Shakespeare, *The Complete Works*, The RSC Shakespeare, ed. Jonathan Bate and Eric Rasmussen (Basingstoke, 2007)
Singer	*The Dramatic Works of William Shakespeare*, ed. Samuel Weller Singer, 10 vols (Chiswick, 1826), vol. 2
Singer[3]	*The Dramatic Works of William Shakespeare*, ed. Samuel Weller Singer, 3rd edn, 10 vols (1856), vol. 2
Sisson	William Shakespeare, *The Complete Works*, ed. Charles Jasper Sisson (1953)
Staunton	*The Plays of Shakespeare*, ed. Howard Staunton, 3 vols (1858–60), vol. 1
Steevens	*Twenty of the Plays of Shakespeare*, ed. George Steevens, 4 vols (1766), vol. 1
	See also Var 1778, Var 1793, Var 1821
Taylor	See Oxf
Theobald	*The Works of Shakespeare*, ed. Lewis Theobald, 7 vols (1733), vol. 1
Treadwell	*A Midsommer nights dreame*, ed. T.O. Treadwell, Shakespearean Originals (1996)
Var	*A Midsommer Nights Dreame*, New Variorum, ed. Horace Howard Furness (Philadelphia, PA, 1895)
Var 1778	*The Plays of William Shakspeare*, ed. Samuel Johnson and George Steevens, 2nd edn, 10 vols (1778), vol. 3
Var 1785	*The Plays of William Shakspeare*, ed. Samuel Johnson, George Steevens and Isaac Reed, 3rd edn, 10 vols (1785), vol. 3
Var 1793	*The Plays of William Shakspeare*, ed. Samuel Johnson, George Steevens and Isaac Reed, 4th edn, 15 vols (1793), vol. 5
Var 1803	*The Plays of William Shakspeare*, ed. Samuel Johnson, George Steevens and Isaac Reed, 5th edn, 21 vols (1803), vol. 4
Var 1821	*The Plays and Poems of William Shakspeare*, ed. Edmond Malone and James Boswell the younger, 21 vols (1821), vol. 5
Warburton	*The Works of Shakespear*, ed. William Warburton, 8 vols (1747), vol. 1
Wells	*A Midsummer Night's Dream*, New Penguin Shakespeare, ed. Stanley Wells (Harmondsworth, 1967)

White	*The Works of William Shakespeare*, ed. Richard Grant White, 12 vols (Boston, MA, 1857–66), vol. 4
Wilson	See Cam[1]
Wright	*A Midsummer Night's Dream*, ed. William Aldis Wright (Oxford, 1877) See also Cam
Yale	*A Midsummer Night's Dream*, Yale Shakespeare, ed. Willard Higley Durham (New Haven, CT, 1918)

OTHER WORKS CITED OR USED

Abbott	E.A. Abbott, *A Shakespearian Grammar*, 3rd edn (1878)
Aen.	*Aeneid*: see Virgil
Agrippa	Henry Cornelius Agrippa, *Three Books of Occult Philosophy* (1651 for 1650)
Allen	John A. Allen, 'Bottom and Titania', *SQ* 18 (1967), 107–17
Allusion-Book	*The Shakspere Allusion-Book*, compiled by C.M. Ingleby, L. Toulmin Smith and F.J. Furnivall, rev. John Munro, preface by E.K. Chambers, 2 vols (1932)
Andrews	Michael Cameron Andrews, 'Titania on "Enforced Chastity"', *N&Q* 31 (229, 1984), 188
Apuleius	Apuleius, *The Golden Ass*, trans. W. Adlington, Loeb Classical Library (Cambridge, MA, 1915)
Arab	Ronda Arab, *Manly Mechanicals on the Early Modern English Stage* (Selinsgrove, PA, 2011)
Arbor	*The Arbor of Amorous Devices 1597*, ed. Hyder Edward Rollins (Cambridge, MA, 1936)
Arcadia	See *New Arcadia*, *Old Arcadia*
Arrell	Douglas H. Arrell, 'John a Kent, the Wise Man of Winchester', *Early Theatre*, 17 (2014), 75–92
Auden	W.H. Auden, *Lectures on Shakespeare*, ed. Arthur Kirsch (Princeton, NJ, 2000)
Aydelotte	Laura Aydelotte, '"A local habitation and a name": The Origins of Shakespeare's Oberon', *SS 65* (2012), 1–11
Bakhtin	Mikhael Bakhtin, *Rabelais and His World*, trans. Hélène Iswolsky (1968; Bloomington, IN, 1984)

Baldwin, *Division*   T.W. Baldwin, *On Act and Scene Division in the Shakspere First Folio* (Carbondale, IL, 1965)

Baldwin, 'Pups'   T.W. Baldwin, 'The Pedigree of Theseus' Pups', *Shakespeare Jahrbuch West*, 104 (1968), 109–20

Baldwin, *Small Latine*   T.W. Baldwin, *William Shakspere's Small Latine & Lesse Greeke*, 2 vols (Urbana, IL, 1944)

Ball   Robert Hamilton Ball, *Shakespeare on Silent Film* (1968)

Barber   C.L. Barber, *Shakespeare's Festive Comedy* (Princeton, NJ, 1959)

Barkan, 'Diana'   Leonard Barkan, 'Diana and Actaeon: The Myth as Synthesis', *ELR* 10 (1980), 317–59

Barkan, *Gods*   Leonard Barkan, *The Gods Made Flesh* (New Haven, CT, 1986)

Barlow   William Barlow, *Three Christian Sermons, made by Lodouike Lauatere* (1596)

Barr   Helen Barr, '"Wrinkled deep in time": Emily and Arcite in *A Midsummer Night's Dream*', *SS* 65 (2012), 12–25

Bate   Jonathan Bate, *Shakespeare and Ovid* (Oxford, 1993)

Baumbach   Sibylle Baumbach, 'Voice, Face and Fascination: The Art of Physiognomy in *A Midsummer Night's Dream*', *SS* 65 (2012), 77–91

Baxter   John Baxter, 'Growing to a Point: Mimesis in *A Midsummer Night's Dream*', *English Studies in Canada*, 22 (1996), 17–33

Beaumont and Fletcher   Francis Beaumont and John Fletcher, *The Dramatic Works in the Beaumont and Fletcher Canon*, gen. ed. Fredson Bowers, 10 vols (Cambridge, 1966–96)

Beckerman   Bernard Beckerman, *Shakespeare at the Globe, 1599–1609* (New York, 1962)

Bentley   Gerald Eades Bentley, *The Jacobean and Caroline Stage*, 7 vols (Oxford, 1941–68)

Berry   Edward Berry, *Shakespeare's Comic Rites* (Cambridge, 1984)

Bevington, 'Dark Side'   David Bevington, '"But We are Spirits of Another Sort": The Dark Side of Love and Magic in *A Midsummer Night's Dream*' in

	Medieval and Renaissance Studies, ed. Siegfried Wenzel (Chapel Hill, NC, 1978)
Bevington, 'Hearing'	David Bevington, 'Hearing and Overhearing in *The Tempest*' in *Who Hears in Shakespeare?*, ed. Laury Magnus and Walter W. Cannon (Madison, WI, 2012), 101–12
Blake	N.F. Blake, *A Grammar of Shakespeare's Language* (Basingstoke, 2002)
Blayney, *Lear*	Peter W.M. Blayney, *The Texts of* King Lear *and Their Origins*, vol. 1 (Cambridge, 1982)
Blayney, 'Pavier'	Peter W.M. Blayney, '"Compositor B" and the Pavier Quartos', *The Library*, 5th series, 27 (1972), 179–206
Boccaccio	Giovanni Boccaccio, *Teseida*, ed. Salvatore Battaglia (Florence, 1938)
Booth	Stephen Booth, 'Speculations on Doubling in Shakespeare's Plays' in *Shakespeare: The Theatrical Dimension*, ed. Philip C. McGuire and David A. Samuelson (New York, 1979), 103–31
Bourdieu	Pierre Bourdieu, *Distinction: A Social Critique of the Judgement of Taste*, trans. Richard Nice (1984)
Bowers	Fredson Bowers, *On Editing Shakespeare and the Elizabethan Dramatists* (Philadelphia, PA, 1955)
Bradley	David Bradley, *From Text to Performance in the Elizabethan Theatre* (Cambridge, 1991)
Briggs, *Anatomy*	Katharine Briggs, *The Anatomy of Puck* (1959; Abingdon, 2003)
Briggs, *Dictionary*	Katharine Mary Briggs, *A Dictionary of Fairies* (1976)
Briggs, *Fairies*	K.M. Briggs, *The Fairies in Tradition and Literature* (1967)
Briggs, *Vanishing*	Katharine Briggs, *The Vanishing People* (1978)
Brissenden	Alan Brissenden, 'Shakespeare in Adelaide' in *O Brave New World: Two Centuries of Shakespeare on the Australian Stage*, ed. John Golder and Richard Madelaine (Sydney, 2001), 143–62
Britten	Benjamin Britten, *A Midsummer Night's Dream: An Opera in Three Acts* (1960)
Brook, *Threads*	Peter Brook, *Threads of Time* (1998)

Bruster, *Culture*	Douglas Bruster, *Shakespeare and the Question of Culture* (New York, 2003)
Bruster, 'Stationer'	Douglas Bruster, 'Shakespeare the Stationer' in Straznicky, 112–31
Buchanan	Henry Buchanan, '"India" and the Golden Age in *A Midsummer Night's Dream*', *SS 65* (2012), 58–68
Bullough	Geoffrey Bullough, *Narrative and Dramatic Sources of Shakespeare*, 8 vols (1957–75); sources for *MND* in vol. 1.
Burrow	Colin Burrow, *Shakespeare and Classical Antiquity* (Oxford, 2013)
Burton	Robert Burton, *The Anatomy of Melancholy*, ed. Thomas C. Faulkner et al., 6 vols (1989–2000)
Calderwood	James L. Calderwood, '*A Midsummer Night's Dream:* Anamorphism and Theseus' Dream', *SQ* 42 (1991), 409–30
Camden	William Camden, *Annales*, 3rd edn (1635)
Capell, *Notes*	Edward Capell, *Notes and Various Readings to Shakespeare, Part the third*, vol. 2 (1779–80)
Caracalla	Alissar Caracalla, *Midsummer Night's Djinn* in *The Living Shakespeare*, British Council (2016)
Carroll	William C. Carroll, *The Metamorphoses of Shakespearean Comedy* (Princeton, NJ, 1985)
Carter	Angela Carter, 'Overture and Incidental Music for *A Midsummer Night's Dream*' in *Black Venus* (1985; 1996), 43–53
Carver	Robert H.F. Carver, *The Protean Ass: The Metamorphoses of Apuleius* (Oxford, 2007)
Catullus	*Catullus*, ed. F.W. Cornish in *Catullus, Tibullus and Pervigilium Veneris*, Loeb Classical Library rev. edn (Cambridge, MA, 1962)
Cercignani	Fausto Cercignani, *Shakespeare's Works and Elizabethan Pronunciation* (Oxford, 1981)
Chambers, 'Occasion'	E.K. Chambers, 'The Occasion of *A Midsummer-Night's Dream*' in *Shakespearean Gleanings* (Oxford, 1944), 61–7; first published in *Shakespeare: A Book of Homage*, ed. I. Gollancz (Oxford, 1916)
Chambers, *Shakespeare*	E.K. Chambers, *William Shakespeare: A Study of Facts and Problems*, 2 vols (Oxford, 1930)
Chambers, *Stage*	E.K. Chambers, *The Elizabethan Stage*, 4 vols (Oxford, 1923)

Chapman
George Chapman, *Bussy d'Ambois*, ed. Nicholas Brooke, Revels Plays (1964)

Chaucer
The Riverside Chaucer, 3rd edn, gen. ed. Larry D. Benson (Oxford, 1988)
See also *CT, KnT, LGW*

Chaudhuri, 'India'
Sukanta Chaudhuri, 'Shakespeare's India' in *India's Shakespeare*, ed. Poonam Trivedi and Dennis Bartholomeusz (Newark, DE, 2005), 158–67

Chaudhuri, 'Venus'
Supriya Chaudhuri, 'The Chariot of Venus', *Journal of the Warburg and Courtauld Institutes*, 44 (1981), 211–13

Chesterton
G.K. Chesterton, 'A Midsummer Night's Dream', *Good Words*, 45 (1904), 621–6: as in *Tradition*, 360–4

Clare
Janet Clare, *Shakespeare's Stage Traffic* (Cambridge, 2014)

Clayton, 'Fie'
Thomas Clayton, '"Fie What a Question's That If Thou Wert Near a Lewd Interpreter"' The Wall Scene in *A Midsummer Night's Dream*', *SSt* 7 (1974), 101–13

Clayton, *Hole*
F.W. Clayton, *The Hole in the Wall* (Exeter, 1979)

Clemen, *Tragedy*
Wolfgang Clemen, *English Tragedy before Shakespeare*, trans. T.S. Dorsch (1961)

Cody
Richard Cody, *The Landscape of the Mind* (Oxford, 1969)

Coghill
Nevill Coghill, *Shakespeare's Professional Skills* (Cambridge, 1964)

Colthorpe
Marion Colthorpe, 'Queen Elizabeth I and *A Midsummer Night's Dream*', *N&Q* 34 (232, 1987), 205–7

Concordance
A Midsummer Night's Dream, Oxford Shakespeare Concordances (Oxford, 1970)

Connolly
Annaliese Connolly, 'Evaluating Virginity: *A Midsummer Night's Dream* and the Iconography of Marriage' in *Goddesses and Queens: The Iconography of Elizabeth I*, ed. Annaliese Connolly and Lisa Hopkins (Manchester, 2007), 136–53

Conusaunce
La Conusaunce damours [1528]

Cooper, 'Anomalies'
Helen Cooper, 'Editorial Anomalies and Stage Practice: *A Midsummer Night's Dream* 3.2–4.1', *Early Modern Culture Online*, 6 (2015), 1–10,

	http://journal.uia.no/index.php/EMCO/article/view/326/261, accessed 16 August 2016
Cooper, 'Guy'	Helen Cooper, 'Guy as Early Modern English Hero' in *Guy of Warwick: Icon and Ancestor*, ed. Alison Wiggins and Rosalind Field (Cambridge, 2007), 185–99
Cooper, *Medieval*	Helen Cooper, *Shakespeare and the Medieval World* (2010)
Cox	Roger L. Cox, *Shakespeare's Comic Changes* (Athens, GA, 1991)
Craig, *Quartos*	Hardin Craig, *A New Look at Shakespeare's Quartos* (Stanford, CA, 1961)
Cressy	David Cressy, *Birth, Marriage, and Death: Ritual, Religion, and the Life-Cycle in Tudor and Stuart England* (Oxford, 1997)
Crystal	David and Ben Crystal, *Shakespeare's Words: A Glossary and Language Companion* (2002)
CT	*The Canterbury Tales*: see Chaucer
Daugherty	Leo Daugherty, *William Shakespeare, Richard Barnfield, and the Sixth Earl of Derby* (Amherst, MA, 2010)
Dekker	*The Dramatic Works of Thomas Dekker*, ed. Fredson Bowers, 4 vols (Cambridge, 1953–61)
Dekker, *Non-Dramatic*	*The Non-Dramatic Works of Thomas Dekker*, ed. A.B. Grosart, 5 vols (1884–6)
della Porta	Giambattista della Porta, *De Humana Physiognomia* (Naples, 1586)
Demetz	Peter Demetz, 'The Elm and the Vine: Notes toward the History of a Marriage Topos', *PMLA* 73 (1958), 521–32
Dent	R.W. Dent, *Shakespeare's Proverbial Language: An Index* (Berkeley, CA, 1981)
Dessen	Alan C. Dessen, *Elizabethan Stage Conventions and Modern Interpreters* (Cambridge, 1984)
Dessen and Thomson	Alan C. Dessen and Leslie Thomson, *A Dictionary of Stage Directions in English Drama, 1580–1642* (Cambridge, 1999)
Diana	*George of Montemayor's Diana and Gil Polo's Enamoured Diana*, trans. Bartholomew Yong, ed. Judith M. Kennedy (Oxford, 1968)
Dobson, *Amateur*	Michael Dobson, *Shakespeare and Amateur Performance* (Cambridge, 2011)

Dobson, 'Joke'	Michael Dobson, 'Shakespeare as a Joke: The English Comic Tradition, *A Midsummer Night's Dream* and Amateur Performance', *SS* 56 (2003), 117–25
Dodypoll	*The Wisdom of Doctor Dodypoll, 1600*, ed. M.N. Manton and Arthur Brown, Malone Society Reprints (1965)
Donaldson	E. Talbot Donaldson, *The Swan at the Well: Shakespeare Reading Chaucer* (New Haven, CT, 1985)
Doran, *Language*	Madeleine Doran, *Shakespeare's Dramatic Language* (Madison, WI, 1976)
Douglas	Gavin Douglas, *The Aeneid (1513)*, ed. Gordon Kendal, 2 vols (2011)
Duncan-Jones, 'Pyramus'	Katherine Duncan-Jones, 'Pyramus and Thisbe: Shakespeare's Debt to Moffett Cancelled', *RES* ns 32 (1981), 296–301
Duncan-Jones, *Sonnets*	*Shakespeare's Sonnets*, ed. Katherine Duncan-Jones, rev. edn, Arden Shakespeare, 3rd series (2010)
Duncan-Jones, *Ungentle*	Katherine Duncan-Jones, *Shakespeare: An Ungentle Life* (2010)
Duncan-Jones, *Upstart*	Katherine Duncan-Jones, *Shakespeare: Upstart Crow to Sweet Swan 1592–1623* (2011)
Dunn	Allen Dunn, 'The Indian Boy's Dream Wherein Every Mother's Son Rehearses His Part', *SSt* 20 (1988), 15–32
Dusinberre	William Shakespeare, *As You Like It*, ed. Juliet Dusinberre, Arden Shakespeare, 3rd series (2006)
Eccles	Mark Eccles, 'Shakespeare's Use of *Look How* and Similar Idioms', *Journal of English and Germanic Philology*, 42 (1943), 386–400
Edgecombe	Rodney Stenning Edgecombe, 'Shakespeare's *A Midsummer Night's Dream*', *Explicator*, 58 (2000), 181–4
EETS	Early English Text Society
Egan	Gabriel Egan, *The Struggle for Shakespeare's Text* (Cambridge, 2010)
ELH	*English Literary History*
ELR	*English Literary Renaissance*
Empson, *Pastoral*	William Empson, *Some Versions of Pastoral* (1935; Harmondsworth, NY, 1966)

Empson, 'Spirits'   William Empson, 'The Spirits of the "Dream"', *Essays on Renaissance Literature*, ed. John Haffenden, vol. 2 (Cambridge, 1994)

Erlich   Bruce Erlich, 'Queenly Shadows: On Mediation in Two Comedies', *SS 35* (1982), 65–77

Erne, *Dramatist*   Lukas Erne, *Shakespeare as Literary Dramatist*, 2nd edn (Cambridge, 2013)

Erne, *Trade*   Lukas Erne, *Shakespeare and the Book Trade* (Cambridge, 2013)

Erne and Kidnie   *Textual Performances: The Modern Reproduction of Shakespeare's Drama*, ed. Lukas Erne and Margaret Jane Kidnie (Cambridge, 2004)

Evans   Bertrand Evans, *Shakespeare's Comedies* (Oxford, 1960)

Fairies   [?]David Garrick and [?]J.C. Smith, *The Fairies. An Opera. Taken from A Midsummer Night's Dream*, 2nd edn (1755)

Fayard   Nicole Fayard, *The Performance of Shakespeare in France since the Second World War* (Lewiston, NY, 2006)

Fisher   Will Fisher, 'The Renaissance Beard', *RQ* 54 (2001), 155–87

Fleay   F.G. Fleay, 'On "A Midsummer Night's Dream"', *Robinson's Epitome of Literature* (April 1876), 56–7

Fletcher   See Beaumont and Fletcher

Flower and Leaf   *The Flower and the Leaf* in *Chaucerian and Other Pieces*, ed. Walter W. Skeat (Oxford, 1897)

Floyd-Wilson   Mary Floyd-Wilson, 'Potions, Passion, and Fairy Knowledge in *A Midsummer Night's Dream*' in *Shakespeare in Our Time*, ed. Dympna Callaghan and Suzanne Gossett (2016), 184–8

Folkerth   Wes Folkerth, *The Sound of Shakespeare* (2002)

Foreign   *Foreign Shakespeare*, ed. Dennis Kennedy (Cambridge, 1993)

FQ   *The Faerie Queene*: see Spenser

Freedman   Barbara Freedman, *Staging the Gaze: Postmodernism, Psychoanalysis, and Shakespearean Comedy* (Ithaca, NY, 1991)

Frye, *Deliverance*	Northrop Frye, *The Myth of Deliverance: Reflections on Shakespeare's Problem Comedies* (Toronto, 1983)
Frye, *Perspective*	Northrop Frye, *A Natural Perspective: The Development of Shakespearean Comedy and Romance* (New York, 1965)
Gair	Reavley Gair, *The Children of Paul's* (Cambridge, 1982)
Gallery	*A Gorgeous Gallery of Gallant Inventions*, ed. Hyder E. Rollins (Cambridge, MA, 1926)
Garber, *Dream*	Marjorie B. Garber, *Dream in Shakespeare* (New Haven, CT, 1974)
Garber, *Shakespeare*	Marjorie Garber, *Shakespeare after All* (New York, 2004)
Gaw	Allison Gaw, 'John Sincklo as One of Shakespeare's Actors', *Anglia*, 37 (49: 1925), 289–303
Gehring	Wes D. Gehring, *Joe E. Brown, Film Comedian and Baseball Buffoon* (Jefferson, NC, 2006)
Gervase	Gervase of Tilbury, *Otia Imperialia*, ed. and trans. S.E. Banks and J.W. Binns (Oxford, 2002)
Gil Polo	See *Diana*
Giraldus	Giraldus Cambrensis, *Itinerarium Cambriae*, trans. Richard Colt Hoare, in *Historical Works*, ed. Thomas Wright (1863)
Girard, *Envy*	René Girard, *A Theatre of Envy: William Shakespeare* (New York, 1991)
Girard, 'Myth'	René Girard, 'Myth and Ritual in Shakespeare: *A Midsummer Night's Dream*' in *Textual Strategies*, ed. Josué V. Harari (Ithaca, NY, 1979), 189–212
Godsalve	William H.L. Godsalve, *Britten's A Midsummer Night's Dream: Making an Opera from Shakespeare's Comedy* (Cranberry, NJ, 1995)
Godshalk	W.L. Godshalk, 'Bottom's "Hold or Cut Bowstrings"', *N&Q* 42 (240, 1995), 315–16
Golding	*Ovid's Metamorphoses: The Arthur Golding Translation*, ed. John Frederick Nims (New York, 1965)
Gooch and Thatcher	Bryan N.S. Gooch, David Thatcher et al., *A Shakespeare Music Catalogue*, 5 vols (Oxford, 1991)

Gower	*The English Works of John Gower*, ed. G.C. Macaulay, 2 vols, EETS extra ser. 81–2 (1900–1)
Grady	Hugh Grady, 'Shakespeare and Impure Aesthetics: The Case of *A Midsummer Night's Dream*', *SQ* 59 (2008), 274–302
Granville-Barker	Harley Granville-Barker, *Prefaces to Shakespeare*, vol. 6 (1974), with two prefaces to *MND*: of 1914, and the Introduction to *The Players' Shakespeare* (1924)
Greaves	Richard L. Greaves, *Society and Religion in Elizabethan England* (Minneapolis, MN, 1981)
Greenblatt	Stephen Greenblatt, *Will in the World* (2004)
Greene	*The Life and Complete Works in Prose and Verse of Robert Greene*, ed. Alexander B. Grosart, 15 vols (1881–6) See also *James IV*
Greenfield, 'Delight'	Peter H. Greenfield, '"All for your delight / We are not here": Amateur Players and the Nobility', *Research Opportunities in Renaissance Drama*, 28 (1985), 173–80
Greenfield, 'Madness'	Thelma N. Greenfield, 'Our Nightly Madness: Shakespeare's *Dream* without *The Interpretation of Dreams*' in *A Midsummer Night's Dream: Critical Essays*, ed. Dorothea Kehler (1998; New York, 2001), 331–44
Greenham	Richard Greenham, *Grave Covnsels, and Godlie Observations* in *Works*, compiled by Henry Holland, 2nd edn (1599)
Greg, 'Dates'	W.W. Greg, 'On Certain False Dates in Shakespearian Quartos', *The Library*, 2nd series, 9 (1908), 113–31
Greg, 'Divisions'	W.W. Greg, 'Act-Divisions in Shakespeare', *RES* 4 (1928), 152–8
Greg, *Folio*	W.W. Greg, *The Shakespeare First Folio* (Oxford, 1955)
Greg, *Problem*	W.W. Greg, *The Editorial Problem in Shakespeare*, 3rd edn (Oxford, 1954)
Grey	Zachary Grey, *Critical, Historical and Explanatory Notes on Shakespeare*, 2 vols (1754)
Griffin	Alice V. Griffin (Venezky), *Pageantry on the Shakespearean Stage* (New Haven, CT, 1951)

Grim	*Grim the Collier of Croydon, 1662*, Tudor Facsimile Texts (1912)
Grote	David Grote, *The Best Actors in the World: Shakespeare and His Acting Company* (Westport, CT, 2002)
Grove	*The New Grove Dictionary of Opera*, ed. Stanley Sadie, 4 vols (1992)
Groves	Beatrice Groves, '"The Wittiest Partition": Bottom, Paul, and Comedic Resurrection', *N&Q* 54 (252, 2007), 277–82
Gryphius	Andreas Gryphius, *Herr Peter Squentz*, ed. Hugh Powell (Leicester, 1969)
Gurr, *Company*	Andrew Gurr, *The Shakespeare Company, 1594–1642* (Cambridge, 2004)
Gurr, 'Letter'	Andrew Gurr, 'Henry Carey's Peculiar Letter', *SQ* 56 (2005), 51–75
Gurr, 'Patronage'	Andrew Gurr, 'Patronage' in *The Oxford Handbook of Shakespeare*, ed. Arthur F. Kinney (Oxford, 2012), 390–403
Gurr, *Playing*	Andrew Gurr, *The Shakespearian Playing Companies* (Oxford, 1996)
Gurr, *Stage*	Andrew Gurr, *The Shakespearean Stage 1574–1642*, 4th edn (Cambridge, 2009)
Hackett, *Elizabeth*	Helen Hackett, *Shakespeare and Elizabeth* (Princeton, NJ, 2009)
Hackett, *MND*	Helen Hackett, *A Midsummer Night's Dream* (Plymouth, 1997)
Halasz	Alexandra Halasz, 'The Stationers' Shakespeare' in Straznicky, 17–27
Hale	David G. Hale, 'Bottom's Dream and Chaucer', *SQ* 36 (1985), 219–20
Halliwell, *Introduction*	James Orchard Halliwell[-Phillipps], *An Introduction to Shakespeare's Midsummer Night's Dream* (1841)
Halliwell-Phillipps, *Memoranda*	J.O. Halliwell-Phillipps, *Memoranda on the Midsummer Night's Dream* (Brighton, 1879)
Hamburger	Maik Hamburger, 'New Concepts of Staging *A Midsummer Night's Dream*', *SS 40* (1988), 51–61
Handful	*A Handful of Pleasant Delights*, ed. Hyder E. Rollins (Cambridge, MA, 1924)
Hankins	John Erskine Hankins, *Backgrounds of Shakespeare's Thought* (Hassocks, 1978)

Harris, 'Character'   V.C. Harris, '"Character Colonisation": Play(s)-within-the-play in *A Midsummer Night's Dream* and Its Recent Malayalam "Adaptation"' in *Shakespeare and the Art of Lying*, ed. Shormishtha Panja (Hyderabad, 2013), 178–86

Harris, 'Puck'   Jonathan Gil Harris, 'Puck/Robin Goodfellow' in *Fools and Jesters in Literature, Art, and History*, ed.Vicki K. Janik (Westport, CT, 1998), 351–62

Hattaway   Michael Hattaway, '"*Enter Cælia, the Fairy Queen, in her Night Attire*": Shakespeare and the Fairies', *SS 65* (2012), 26–41

Hawkes   Terence Hawkes, *Meaning by Shakespeare* (1992)

Heath   Benjamin Heath, *A Revisal of Shakespear's Text* (1765)

Hendriks   Margo Hendriks, '"Obscured by dreams": Race, Empire, and Shakespeare's *A Midsummer Night's Dream*', *SQ* 47 (1996), 37–60

Henslowe   *Henslowe's Diary*, ed. R.A. Foakes, 2nd edn (Cambridge, 2002)

Herbert, *Oberon*   T. Walter Herbert, *Oberon's Mazèd World* (Baton Rouge, LA, 1977)

Herbert, *Records*   *The Control and Censorship of Caroline Drama: The Records of Sir Henry Herbert*, ed. N.W. Bawcutt (Oxford, 1996)

Hinely   Jan Hinely, 'Expounding the Dream: Shaping Fantasies in *A Midsummer Night's Dream*' in *Psychoanalytic Approaches to Literature and Film*, ed. Maurice Charney and Joseph Reppen (1987), 120–38

Hinman   Charlton Hinman, *The Printing and Proof-Reading of the First Folio of Shakespeare*, 2 vols (Oxford, 1963)

Hirsh   James Hirsh, 'Act Divisions in the Shakespeare First Folio', *Papers of the Bibliographical Society of America*, 96 (2002), 219–56

Hodgdon, 'Gaining'   Barbara Hodgdon, 'Gaining a Father: The Role of Egeus in the Quarto and the Folio', *RES* ns 37 (1986), 534–42

Hodgdon, 'Looking'   Barbara Hodgdon, 'Looking for Mr Shakespeare after "The Revolution": Robert

	Lepage's Intercultural *Dream* Machine' in *Shakespeare, Theory, and Performance,* ed. James C. Bulman (1996), 68–91
Holland, 'Dream'	Norman N. Holland, 'Hermia's Dream' in *Shakespeare's Comedies*, ed. Gary Waller (1991), 75–92
Holland, *English*	Peter Holland, *English Shakespeares* (Cambridge, 1997)
Holland, 'Theseus'	Peter Holland, 'Theseus' Shadows in *Midsummer Night's Dream*', *SS 47* (1994), 139–51
Holloway	Julia Bolton Holloway, 'Apuleius and *A Midsummer Night's Dream*: Bottom's Metamorphoses' in *Tales within Tales: Apuleius through Time,* ed. Constance S. Wright and Julia Bolton Holloway (New York, 2000)
Honigmann	E.A.J. Honigmann, *Shakespeare: The Lost Years*, 2nd edn (Manchester, 1998)
Hope	Jonathan Hope, *Shakespeare's Grammar* (2003)
Hope and Witmore	Jonathan Hope and Michael Witmore, 'The Very Large Textual Object: A Prosthetic Reading of Shakespeare', *Early Modern Literary Studies*, 9 (2004), http://extra.shu.ac.uk/emls/09-3/hopewhit.htm, accessed 5 February 2015
Hoskins	W.G. Hoskins, 'Harvest Fluctuations and English Economic History, 1480–1619', *Agricultural History Review*, 12 (1964), 28–46
Hosley, 'Discovery'	Richard Hosley, 'The Discovery-Space in Shakespeare's Globe', *SS 12* (1959), 35–46
Hosley, 'Music-Room'	Richard Hosley, 'Was There a Music-Room in Shakespeare's Globe?', *SS 13* (1960), 113–23
Hotaling	Edward R. Hotaling, *Shakespeare and the Musical Stage* (Boston, MA, 1990)
Howard-Hill, 'Compositors'	T.H. Howard-Hill, 'The Compositors of Shakespeare's Folio Comedies', *SB* 26 (1973), 61–106
Howard-Hill, 'Printers'	T.H. Howard-Hill, 'Early Modern Printers and the Standardization of English Spelling', *MLR* 101 (2006), 16–29
Hulme	Hilda Hulme, *Explorations in Shakespeare's Language* (1962)

Hunter   Joseph Hunter, *New Illustrations of the Life, Studies, and Writings of Shakespeare*, 2 vols (1845)

Huon   *The Book of Duke Huon of Burdeux*, trans. John Bourchier, Lord Berners, ed. S.L. Lee, 2 vols, EETS extra ser. 40, 43 (1882–7)

Hutson   Lorna Hutson, 'The Shakespearean Unscene: Sexual Phantasies in *A Midsummer Night's Dream*', *Journal of the British Academy*, 4 (2016), 169–95, http://www.britac.ac.uk/publications/shakespearean-unscene-sexual-phantasies-midsummer-nights-dream. accessed 12 February 2017

Ichikawa   Mariko Ichikawa, '*Standing Aloof* on the Shakespearean Stage: What "*Enter*" and "*Exit*"/"*Exeunt*" could have meant', *SIY* 3 (2003), 209–27

Jackson, 'Pause'   MacD.P. Jackson, 'Pause Patterns in Shakespeare's Verse: Canon and Chronology', *Literary and Linguistic Computing*, 17 (2002), 37–46

Jackson, 'Producing'   Barry Jackson, 'Producing the Comedies', *SS 8* (1955), 74–80

James I   James I, *Daemonologie, in Forme of a Dialogve* (1603)

James IV   Robert Greene, *The Scottish History of James IV*, ed. Norman Sanders, Revels Plays (1970)

Johnson, 'Pavier'   Gerald D. Johnson, 'Thomas Pavier, Publisher, 1600–25', *Library*, 6th series, 14 (1992), 12–50

Jonson   *Ben Jonson*, ed. C.H. Herford, P. and E. Simpson, 11 vols (Oxford, 1925–52)

Juvenal   *Juvenal and Persius*, ed. Susanna Morton Braund, Loeb Classical Library (Cambridge, MA, 2004)

Kable   William S. Kable, 'Compositor B, the Pavier Quartos, and Copy Spellings', *SB* 21 (1968), 131–61

Kavanagh   James H. Kavanagh, 'Shakespeare in Ideology' in *Alternative Shakespeares*, ed. John Drakakis (1985), 144–65

Kennedy   Richard F. Kennedy, 'Speech Prefixes in Some Shakespearean Quartos', *Papers of the Bibliographical Society of America*, 92 (1998), 177–209

King
T.J. King, *Casting Shakespeare's Plays: London Actors and Their Roles, 1590–1642* (Cambridge, 1992)

Kittredge, *Witchcraft*
George Lyman Kittredge, *Witchcraft in Old and New England* (Cambridge, MA, 1928)

KnT
The Knight's Tale: see Chaucer

Kökeritz, 'Night-rule'
Helge Kökeritz, 'Shakespeare's *Night-rule*', *Language*, 18 (1942), 40–4

Kökeritz, *Pronunciation*
Helge Kökeritz, *Shakespeare's Pronunciation* (New Haven, CT, 1953)

Kott, *Shakespeare*
Jan Kott, *Shakespeare Our Contemporary*, trans. Boleslaw Taborski (1964)

Kott, *Translation*
Jan Kott, *The Bottom Translation*, trans. Daniela Miedzyrzecka and Lillian Vallee (Evanston, IL, 1987)

Krieger
Elliot Krieger, *A Marxist Study of Shakespeare's Comedies* (1979)

Kyd
Thomas Kyd, *The Spanish Tragedy*, ed. Clara Calvo and Jesús Tronch, Arden Early Modern Drama (2013)

Ladurie
Emmanuel le Roy Ladurie, *Times of Feast, Times of Famine: A History of Climate since the Year 1400*, trans. Barbara Bray (Garden City, NY, 1971)

Lal
Ananda Lal, '"We the globe can compass soon": Tim Supple's *Dream*', *SIY* 12 (2012), 65–81

Lamb, 'Fairies'
Mary Ellen Lamb, 'Taken by the Fairies: Fairy Practices and the Production of Popular Culture in *A Midsummer Night's Dream*', *SQ* 51 (2000), 277–312

Lamb, *Popular*
Mary Ellen Lamb, *The Popular Culture of Shakespeare, Spenser, and Jonson* (Abingdon, 2006)

Lander
Jesse M. Lander, 'Thinking with Fairies: *A Midsummer Night's Dream* and the Problem of Belief', *SS 65* (2012), 42–57

Laroque
François Laroque, *Shakespeare's Festive World*, trans. Janet Lloyd (Cambridge, 1991)

Latham
Minor White Latham, *The Elizabethan Fairies* (New York, 1930)

Leech and Shand
Clifford Leech and G.B. Shand, 'Chinks', *TLS* 25 December 1970, 1516 and 29 January 1971, 126

Leiter *Shakespeare around the Globe*, ed. Samuel L. Leiter et al. (New York, 1986)

Levine Laura Levine, 'Rape, Repetition, and the Politics of Closure in *A Midsummer Night's Dream*' in *Feminist Readings of Early Modern Culture*, ed. Valerie Traub et al. (Cambridge, 1996), 210–28

LGW *The Legend of Good Women*: see Chaucer

Linthicum M. Channing Linthicum, *Costume in the Drama of Shakespeare and His Contemporaries* (Oxford, 1936)

Long William B. Long, 'Perspective on Provenance: The Context of Varying Speech-heads' in *Speech-Headings*, 21–44

Loomba Ania Loomba, 'The Great Indian Vanishing Trick – Colonialism, Property, and the Family in *A Midsummer Night's Dream*' in *A Feminist Companion to Shakespeare*, ed. Dympna Callaghan, 2nd edn (Oxford, 2016), 181–205

Lydgate John Lydgate, *Reson and Sensuallyte*, ed. Ernst Sieper, 2 vols, EETS extra ser. 84, 89 (1901, 1903)

Lyly *The Complete Works of John Lyly*, ed. R. Warwick Bond, 3 vols (Oxford, 1902)

MacDonald Sara MacDonald, *Finding Freedom: Hegel's Philosophy and the Emancipation of Women* (Montreal, 2008)

McGuire, 'Egeus' Philip C. McGuire, 'Egeus and the Implications of Silence' in *Shakespeare and the Sense of Performance*, ed. Marvin Thompson and Ruth Thompson (Newark, DE, 1989), 103–15

McGuire, 'Intentions' Philip C. McGuire, 'Intentions, Options, and Greatness: An Example from *A Midsummer Night's Dream*' in *Shakespeare and the Triple Play*, ed. Sidney Homan (Lewisburg, PA, 1988), 177–86

Maguire Laurie Maguire, *Shakespeare's Names* (Oxford, 2007)

Maid's Met. *The Maid's Metamorphosis*, in Lyly, vol. 3, ed. Bond: see Lyly

Makaryk Irena R. Makaryk, *Shakespeare in the Undiscovered Bourn* (Toronto, 2004)

Mandel	Jerome Mandel, 'Dream and Imagination in Shakespeare', *SQ* 24 (1973), 61–8
Mangan	Michael Mangan, *A Preface to Shakespeare's Comedies: 1594–1603* (1996)
Map	Walter Map, *De Nugis Curialium*, ed. and trans. M.R. James, rev. C.N.L. Brooke and R.A.B. Mynors (Oxford, 1983)
Marienstras	Richard Marienstras, *New Perspectives on the Shakespearean World*, trans. Janet Lloyd (Cambridge, 1985)
Marlowe	*The Complete Works of Christopher Marlowe*, ed. Fredson Bowers, 2nd edn, 2 vols (Cambridge, 1981)
Marshall	David Marshall, 'Exchanging Visions: Reading *A Midsummer Night's Dream*', *ELH* 49 (1982), 543–75
Marvell	*The Prose Works of Andrew Marvell*, ed. Annabel Patterson et al., 2 vols (New Haven, CT, 2003)
Marx	Karl Marx and Friedrich Engels, *Collected Works*, trans. by various hands, 50 vols (1975–2004)
Massai	Sonia Massai, *Shakespeare and the Rise of the Editor* (Cambridge, 2007)
Massinger	*The Plays and Poems of Philip Massinger*, ed. Philip Edwards and Colin Gibson, 5 vols (Oxford, 1976)
Meagher	John C. Meagher, *Pursuing Shakespeare's Dramaturgy* (Madison, WI, 2003)
Mehl	Dieter Mehl, *The Elizabethan Dumb Show* (1965)
Merry Pranks	*The Mad Merry Prankes of Robbin Goodfellow* in *The Roxburghe Ballads*, ed. W.M. Chappell, 9 vols (Hertford, 1871–97), 2.81–5
Met.	Ovid, *Metamorphoses*, ed. and trans. Frank Justus Miller, rev. G.P. Goold, Loeb Classical Library, 2 vols (Cambridge, MA, 1984)
Miller	Ronald F. Miller, '*A Midsummer Night's Dream*: The Fairies, Bottom, and the Mystery of Things', *SQ* 26 (1975), 254–68
Milton	John Milton, *The Poems*, ed. John Carey and Alastair Fowler (1968)
MLR	*Modern Language Review*

Montemayor   See *Diana*

Montrose, 'Fantasies'   Louis Montrose, '*A Midsummer Night's Dream* and the Shaping Fantasies of Elizabethan Culture: Gender, Power, Form' in *New Historicism and Renaissance Drama*, ed. Richard Wilson and Richard Dutton (1992), 109–30

Montrose, *Purpose*   Louis Montrose, *The Purpose of Playing: Shakespeare and the Cultural Politics of the Elizabethan Theatre* (Chicago, IL, 1996)

Muir, 'Pyramus'   Kenneth Muir, 'Pyramus and Thisbe: A Study in Shakespeare's Method', *SQ* 5 (1954), 141–53

Muir, *Sources*   Kenneth Muir, *Shakespeare's Sources*, vol.1 (1957)

Munday   Anthony Munday, *John a Kent and John a Cumber*, ed. Arthur E. Pennell (New York, 1980)

Murphy   Andrew Murphy, *Shakespeare in Print* (Cambridge, 2003)

Murray   Margaret Alice Murray, *The Witch-Cult in Western Europe* (Oxford, 1921)

Nares   Robert Nares, *A Glossary [of] the Works of English Authors, Particularly Shakespeare and His Contemporaries*, new edn rev. James O. Halliwell and Thomas Wright, 2 vols (1888)

Nashe   *The Works of Thomas Nashe*, ed. R.B. McKerrow, suppl. ed. F.P. Wilson, 5 vols (Oxford, 1966)

Nemerov, 'Bottom'   Howard Nemerov, 'Bottom's Dream', *Virginia Quarterly Review*, 42 (1966), 555–73

Nemerov, 'Marriage'   Howard Nemerov, 'The Marriage of Theseus and Hippolyta', *Kenyon Review*, 18 (1956), 633–41

New Arcadia   Sir Philip Sidney, *The Countess of Pembroke's Arcadia (The New Arcadia)*, ed. Victor Skretkowicz (Oxford, 1987)

Nichols, *Illustrations*   John Nichols, *Illustrations of the Literary History of the Eighteenth Century*, 8 vols (1817–31)

Nichols, *Progresses*   John Nichols, *The Progresses and Public Processions of Queen Elizabeth I: A New Edition of the Early Modern Sources*, ed. Elizabeth Goldring et al., 5 vols (Oxford, 2014)

Noble	Richmond Noble, *Shakespeare's Use of Song* (1923)
North	*The Lives of the Noble Grecians and Romanes, compared together by* ... *Plutarke of Chæronea: Translated out of Greeke into French by Iames Amyot* ... *and out of French into Englishe, by Thomas North* (1579) See also Plutarch, *Lives*
Nosworthy	J.M. Nosworthy, 'Shakespeare's Pastoral Metamorphoses' in *The Elizabethan Theatre VIII*, ed. G.R. Hibbard (Port Credit, 1982)
N&Q	*Notes and Queries*
Nuttall	A.D. Nuttall, '*A Midsummer Night's Dream*: Comedy as *Apotrope* of Myth', *SS 53* (2000), 49–59
O'Connor	John O'Connor, 'Compositors D and F of the Shakespeare First Folio', *SB* 28 (1975), 81–117
Old Arcadia	Sir Philip Sidney, *The Countess of Pembroke's Arcadia (The Old Arcadia)*, ed. Jean Robertson (Oxford, 1973)
Olson	Paul A. Olson, '*A Midsummer Night's Dream* and the Meaning of Court Marriage', *ELH* 24 (1957), 95–119
Onions	C.T. Onions, *A Shakespeare Glossary*, enlarged and rev. Robert D. Eagleson (Oxford, 1986)
Oras	Ants Oras, *Pause Patterns in Elizabethan and Jacobean Drama* (Gainsville, FL, 1960)
Orgel	Stephen Orgel, *Imagining Shakespeare* (Basingstoke, 2003)
Ormerod	David Ormerod, '*A Midsummer Night's Dream*: The Monster in the Labyrinth', *SSt* 11 (1978), 39–52
Otten	Charlotte F. Otten, '"Dian's Bud" in *A Midsummer Night's Dream* IV.i.72', *N&Q* 35 (233, 1988), 466
Ovid, *Art*	*Ars Amatoria* in *The Art of Love and Other Poems*, ed. J.H. Mozley, 2nd edn rev. G.P. Goold, Loeb Classical Library (Cambridge, MA, 1979)
Ovid, *Heroides*	Ovid, *Heroides and Amores*, trans. and ed. Grant Showerman, 2nd edn, Loeb Classical Library (Cambridge, MA, 1977) See also *Met.*

Panofsky   Erwin Panofsky, *Studies in Iconology* (1939; New York, 1962)

Paracelsus   Theophrastus von Hohenheim (Paracelsus), *Liber de nymphis, sylphis, pygmaeis et salamandris (A Book on Nymphs, Sylphs, Pygmies and Salamanders), Four Treatises*, trans. C. Lilian Temkin et al. (Baltimore, MD, 1941)

Parker, *Margins*   Patricia Parker, *Shakespeare from the Margins: Language, Culture, Context* (Chicago, IL, 1996)

Parker, 'Murals'   Patricia Parker, 'Murals and Morals: *A Midsummer Night's Dream*' in *Editing Texts (Aporemata*, vol. 2), ed. Glenn W. Most (Göttingen, 1998), 190–218

Parker, 'Quince'   Patricia Parker, '(Peter) Quince: Love Potions, Carpenter's Coigns and Athenian Weddings', *SS 56* (2003), 39–54

Partridge, *Bawdy*   Eric Partridge, *Shakespeare's Bawdy*, 3rd edn (1968)

Partridge, *Orthography*   A.C. Partridge, *Orthography in Shakespeare and Elizabethan Drama* (1964)

Paster   Gail Kern Paster, *The Body Embarrassed* (Ithaca, 1993)

Patterson   Annabel Patterson, *Shakespeare and the Popular Voice* (Oxford, 1989)

Pearn   B.R. Pearn, 'Dumb-Show in Elizabethan Drama', *RES* 11 (1935), 385–405

Peele   *The Life and Works of George Peele*, gen. ed. Charles Tyler Prouty, 3 vols (New Haven, CT, 1952–70)

Pepys   Samuel Pepys, *Diary*, ed. Robert Latham and William Matthews, 11 vols (1970–83)

Pettitt   Tom Pettitt, '"Perchance you wonder at this show": Dramaturgical Machinery in *A Midsummer Night's Dream* and "Pyramus and Thisbe"' in *The Narrator, the Expositor, and the Prompter in European Medieval Theatre*, ed. Philip Butterworth (Turnhout, 2007), 211–34

Pliny   Pliny, *Natural History*, ed. W.H.S. Jones with A.C. Andrews, 10 vols, Loeb Classical Library (Cambridge, MA, 1938–63)

Plutarch, *Lives*   Plutarch, *Lives*, trans. Bernadotte Perrin, 11 vols, Loeb Classical Library (Cambridge,

	MA, 1914–18). All references to the *Life of Theseus* (vol. 1) unless otherwise indicated See also North
Plutarch, *Moralia*	Plutarch, *Moralia*, 16 vols, Loeb Classical Library (Cambridge, MA, 1927–2004). The dialogue on love is in vol. 9, trans. and ed. Edwin L. Minar, Jr. et al.
PMLA	*Publications of the Modern Language Association*
Pollard	Tanya Pollard, *Drugs and Theater in Early Modern England* (Oxford, 2005)
Portillo and Gómez-Lara	Rafael Portillo and Manuel J. Gómez-Lara, 'Shakespeare in the New Spain: or, What You Will' in *Shakespeare in the New Europe*, ed. Michael Hattaway et al. (Sheffield, 1994), 208–20
Potter	John Fletcher and William Shakespeare, *The Two Noble Kinsmen*, ed. Lois Potter, Arden Shakespeare, 3rd series, rev. edn (2015)
Potts	L.J. Potts, *Comedy* (1948)
Prawer	Siegbert Prawer, *Heine's Shakespeare* (Oxford, 1970)
Priestley	J.B. Priestley, *The English Comic Characters* (1925)
Promptbooks	*Shakespearean Prompt-Books of the Seventeenth Century*, ed. G. Blakemore Evans (Charlottesville): vol. 3, King's Company 'Nursery' promptbook (1964); vol. 7 part 1, Smock Alley *MND* promptbook (1989)
Purkiss	Diane Purkiss, *At the Bottom of the Garden: A Dark History of Fairies, Hobgoblins and Other Troublesome Things* (New York, 2003)
Quince	Rohan Quince, *Shakespeare in South Africa* (New York, 2000)
Rahter	Charles A. Rahter, 'Puck's Headless Bear – Revisited', *Susquehanna University Studies* 7 (1964), 127–32
Raman	Shankar Raman, *Framing 'India': The Colonial Imaginary in Early Modern Culture* (Stanford, CA, 2002)
Reportarie	*A Trve Reportarie of the . . . Babtisme of . . . Prince, Frederik Henry* [Edinburgh, 1594]

RES	*Review of English Studies*
Reynolds and Sawyer	Lou Agnes Reynolds and Paul Sawyer, 'Folk Medicine and the Four Fairies of *A Midsummer Night's Dream*', *SQ* 10 (1959), 513–21
Rickert	Edith Rickert, 'Political Propaganda and Satire in *A Midsummer Night's Dream*', *Modern Philology*, 21 (1923), 53–87, 133–54
Riffaterre	Michael Riffaterre, *Semiotics of Poetry* (Bloomington, IN, 1980)
Rimbaud	Arthur Rimbaud, *Illuminations*, trans. John Ashbery (Manchester, 2011)
Ringler	William A. Ringler, Jr., 'The Number of Actors in Shakespeare's Early Plays' in *The Seventeenth-Century Stage*, ed. Gerald Eades Bentley (Chicago, IL, 1968), 110–34
Ripa	Cesare Ripa, *Iconologia*, ed. Piero Buscaroli (Milan, 1992)
Roberts	Jeanne Addison Roberts, *The Shakespearean Wild* (Lincoln, NE, 1991)
Robin Good-Fellow	*Robin Good-Fellow, His Mad Prankes, and Merry Iests* (1628)
Roose-Evans	James Roose-Evans, *Experimental Theatre from Stanislavsky to Peter Brook*, 4th edn (1989)
Rothwell	Kenneth S. Rothwell, '*A Midsummer Night's Dream* on Screen' in *Shakespeare on Screen: A Midsummer Night's Dream*, ed. Sarah Hatchuel and Nathalie Vienne-Guerrin (Rouen, 2004), 13–36
RQ	*Renaissance Quarterly*
Rubinstein	Frankie Rubinstein, *A Dictionary of Shakespeare's Sexual Puns and Their Significance* (Basingstoke, 1989)
Rudd	Niall Rudd, 'Pyramus and Thisbe in Shakespeare and Ovid' in *Shakespeare's Ovid*, ed. A.B. Taylor (Cambridge, 2000), 113–25
Saenger	Michael Saenger, 'The Limits of Translation in *A Midsummer Night's Dream*', *SS* 65 (2012), 69–76
Sagar	Keith Sagar, '*A Midsummer Night's Dream*: A Marriage of Heaven and Hell', *Critical Survey*, 7 (1995), 34–43

Sanders	Julie Sanders, *Shakespeare and Music: Afterlives and Borrowings* (Cambridge, 2007)
SB	*Studies in Bibliography*
Schäfer	Jürgen Schäfer, 'The Orthography of Proper Names in Modern-spelling Editions of Shakespeare', *SB* 23 (1970), 1–19
Schandl	Veronika Schandl, *Socialist Shakespeare Productions in Kádár-Regime Hungary* (Lewiston, NY, 2008)
Schmidt	Alexander Schmidt, *Shakespeare Lexicon and Quotation Dictionary*, 3rd edn, rev. Gregor Sarrazin, 2 vols (1902; New York, 1971)
Schofield	Roger Schofield, 'Did the Mothers Really Die?' in *The World We Have Gained*, ed. Lloyd Bonfield et al. (Oxford, 1986), 231–60
Scot	Reginald Scot, *The Discouerie of Witchcraft* (1584)
Scragg	Leah Scragg, 'Shakespeare, Lyly and Ovid: The Influence of "Gallathea" on "A Midsummer Night's Dream"', *SS 30* (1977), 125–34
Selbourne	David Selbourne, *The Making of A Midsummer Night's Dream: An Eye-Witness Account of Peter Brook's Production* (1982)
Seneca	Seneca, *Tragedies*, ed. and trans. John G. Fitch, 2 vols, Loeb Classical Library (Cambridge, MA, 2002–4) See also *Ten Tragedies*
Seng	Peter J. Seng, *The Vocal Songs in the Plays of Shakespeare* (Cambridge, MA, 1967)
Shakespeare's England	*Shakespeare's England*, 2 vols (Oxford, 1916)
Shep. Cal.	*The Shepheardes Calender*: see Spenser
Sidney	See *New Arcadia*, *Old Arcadia*
Sidney, *Prose*	*Miscellaneous Prose of Sir Philip Sidney*, ed. Katherine Duncan-Jones and Jan van Dorsten (Oxford, 1973)
Sillars	Stuart Sillars, *Painting Shakespeare* (Cambridge, 2006)
Simpson	Percy Simpson, *Studies in Elizabethan Drama* (Oxford, 1955)
Sinfield	Alan Sinfield, 'Cultural Materialism and Intertextuality: The Limits of Queer Reading in *A Midsummer Night's Dream* and *The Two Noble Kinsmen*', *SS* 56 (2003), 67–78

Sisson, *India*   C.J. Sisson, *Shakespeare in India* (1926)

Sisson, *Readings*   C.J. Sisson, *New Readings in Shakespeare*, 2 vols (Cambridge, 1956)

Sitwell   Edith Sitwell, *A Notebook on William Shakespeare* (1948)

SIY   *The Shakespearean International Yearbook*

Skelton   John Skelton, *The Complete English Poems*, ed. John Scattergood (Harmondsworth, 1983)

Smidt   Kristian Smidt, *Unconformities in Shakespeare's Early Comedies* (Basingstoke, 1986)

Smith, 'Dove'   Hallett Smith, 'Bottom's Sucking Dove, "Midsummer Night's Dream", I.ii.82–3', *N&Q* 23 (221, 1976), 152–3

Smith, 'Dream'   Emma Smith, 'Dream, Illusion and Doubling in *A Midsummer Night's Dream*', British Library website, http://www.bl.uk/shakespeare/articles/dream-illusion-and-doubling-in-a-midsummer-nights-dream, accessed 20 April 2016

Smith, 'Forces'   Percy Smith, 'Imaginary Forces and the Ways of Comedy' in *Shakespeare in the New World: Stratford Papers 1968–69*, ed. B.A.W. Jackson (Hamilton, 1972), 1–20

Snodgrass   W.D. Snodgrass, *In Radical Pursuit: Critical Essays and Lectures* (New York, 1975)

Snyder   Susan Snyder, '*All's Well that Ends Well* and Shakespeare's Helens', *ELR* 18 (1988), 66–77

Sokol   B.J. Sokol and Mary Sokol, *Shakespeare, Law and Marriage* (Cambridge, 2003)

SP   *Studies in Philology*

Speech-Headings   *Shakespeare's Speech-Headings*, ed. George Walton Williams (Newark, DE, 1997)

Spenser   Edmund Spenser, *Poetical Works*, ed. J.C. Smith and E. De Selincourt (Oxford, 1912) See also *FQ*, *Shep. Cal.*

Spevack   Marvin Spevack, *A Complete and Systematic Concordance to the Works of Shakespeare*, 9 vols (Hildesheim, 1968–80)

Sprague   Arthur Colby Sprague, *Shakespeare and the Actors: The Stage Business in His Plays (1660–1905)* (Cambridge, MA, 1945)

Sprung	Guy Sprung, *Hot Ice: Shakespeare in Moscow* (Winnipeg, 1991)
SQ	*Shakespeare Quarterly*
SS	*Shakespeare Survey*
SSt	*Shakespeare Studies*
Stansbury	Joan Stansbury, 'Characterization of the Four Young Lovers in "A Midsummer Night's Dream"', *SS 35* (1982), 57–63
Statius	Statius, *Thebaid*, ed. D.R. Shackleton Bailey, 2 vols, Loeb Classical Library (Cambridge, MA, 2003)
Staton	Walter F. Staton Jr., 'Ovidian Elements in *A Midsummer Night's Dream*', *Huntington Library Quarterly*, 26 (1963), 165–78
Stern, *Making*	Tiffany Stern, *Making Shakespeare* (2004)
Stern, *Rehearsal*	Tiffany Stern, *Rehearsal from Shakespeare to Sheridan* (Oxford, 2000)
Stow	John Stow, *The Annales of England* (1600)
Straznicky	*Shakespeare's Stationers*, ed. Marta Straznicky (Philadelphia, PA, 2013)
Stroup	Thomas B. Stroup, 'Bottom's Name and His Epiphany', *SQ* 29 (1978), 79–82
Swann	Marjorie Swann, 'The Politics of Fairylore in Early Modern English Literature', *RQ* 53 (2000), 449–73
Talbert	Ernest William Talbert, *Elizabethan Drama and Shakespeare's Early Plays* (Chapel Hill, NC, 1963)
Tatlow	Antony Tatlow, *Shakespeare, Brecht, and the Intercultural Sign* (Durham, NC, 2001)
Taylor, 'Cobham'	Gary Taylor, 'William Shakespeare, Richard James and the House of Cobham', *RES* ns 38 (1987), 334–54
Taylor, 'Crux'	Gary Taylor, 'A Crux in *A Midsummer Night's Dream*', *N&Q* 32 (230, 1985), 47–9
Taylor, 'Gower'	A.B. Taylor, 'John Gower and "Pyramus and Thisbe"', *N&Q* 54 (252, 2007), 282–3
Taylor, 'Heart'	Anthony Brian Taylor, 'Bottom's "Hopping" Heart and Thomas Phaer', *N&Q* 42 (240, 1995), 309–15
Taylor, 'Ovid'	A.B. Taylor, 'Ovid's Myths and the Unsmooth Course of Love in *A Midsummer Night's Dream*' in *Shakespeare and the Classics*, ed.

	Charles Martindale and A.B. Taylor (Cambridge, 2004), 49–65
Taylor, 'Phaer'	Anthony Brian Taylor, 'Thomas Phaer and Nick Bottom's "Hopping" Heart', *N&Q* 34 (232, 1987), 207–8
Taylor, 'Quince'	A.B. Taylor, '"When everything seems double": Peter Quince, the Other Playwright in *A Midsummer Night's Dream*', *SS 56* (2003), 55–66
Taylor, Review	Gary Taylor, Review of *A Midsummer Night's Dream*, ed. Harold F. Brooks, *N&Q* 28 (226, 1981), 332–4
Taylor and Jowett	Gary Taylor and John Jowett, *Shakespeare Reshaped, 1606–1623* (Oxford, 1993)
Ten Tragedies	*Seneca His Tenne Tragedies, Translated into Englysh* (1581)
Tennenhouse	Leonard Tennenhouse, 'Strategies of State and Political Plays: *A Midsummer Night's Dream, Henry IV, Henry V, Henry VIII*' in *Political Shakespeare*, ed. Jonathan Dollimore and Alan Sinfield (Manchester, 1985)
Theobald, Letter	Lewis Theobald, Letter to William Warburton, 20 May 1729: Nichols, *Illustrations*, 2.230–5
Thirlby	Styan Thirlby, Letter to Lewis Theobald, 7 May 1729: Nichols, *Illustrations*, 2.222–30
Thiselton	Alfred Edward Thiselton, *Some Textual Notes on A Midsommer Nights Dreame* (1903)
Thomas, *Magic*	Keith Thomas, *Religion and the Decline of Magic* (1971; Harmondsworth, 1973)
Thomas, 'Weather'	Sidney Thomas, 'The Bad Weather in *A Midsummer-Night's Dream*', *Modern Language Notes*, 54 (1949), 319–22
Thompson	Ann Thompson, *Shakespeare and Chaucer* (Liverpool, 1978)
Thomson	Peter Thomson, *Shakespeare's Professional Career* (Cambridge, 1992)
Tilley	Morris Palmer Tilley, *A Dictionary of the Proverbs in England in the Sixteenth and Seventeenth Centuries* (Ann Arbor, MI, 1950)
Tradition	*A Midsummer Night's Dream: Shakespeare: The Critical Tradition*, ed. Judith M. Kennedy and Richard F. Kennedy (1999)

Trivedi	Poonam Trivedi, 'Shakespeare and the Indian Image(nary)' in *Re-playing Shakespeare in Asia*, ed. Poonam Trivedi and Minami Ryuta (New York, 2010), 54–75
Trnka	*Le Songe d'une nuit d'été*, illustrated with Jiří Trnka's puppets (Prague, 1960)
Turner, *Helix*	Henry S. Turner, *Shakespeare's Double Helix* (2007)
Turner, 'Printing'	Robert K. Turner Jr., 'Printing Methods and Textual Problems in *A Midsummer Night's Dream* Q1', *SB* 15 (1962), 33–55
TxC	Stanley Wells and Gary Taylor, with John Jowett and William Montgomery, *William Shakespeare: A Textual Companion* (Oxford, 1987)
Tyrrell	William Blake Tyrrell, *Amazons: A Study in Athenian Mythmaking* (Baltimore, MD, 1984)
Tyrwhitt	Thomas Tyrwhitt, *Observations and Conjectures upon Some Passages of Shakespeare* (Oxford, 1766)
Ulrici	Hermann Ulrici, *Shakespeare's Dramatic Art*, trans. L. Dora Schmitz, 2 vols (1876): as in *Tradition*, 153–6
Ungerer	Gustav Ungerer, *A Spaniard in Elizabethan England*, 2 vols (1974–6)
UTQ	*University of Toronto Quarterly*
Valeriano	Pierio Valeriano, *Hieroglyphica* (Basel, 1556)
van Emden	W.G. van Emden, 'Shakespeare and the French Pyramus and Thisbe Tradition', *Forum for Modern Language Studies*, 11 (1975), 193–204
Virgil	*Virgil*, trans. H. Rushton Fairclough, 2 vols, rev. edn, Loeb Classical Library (Cambridge, MA, 1999) See also *Aen.*
Walker	William Sidney Walker, *A Critical Examination of the Text of Shakespeare*, 3 vols (1860)
Wall	Wendy Wall, 'Why Does Puck Sweep?', *SQ* 52 (2001), 67–106
Warner	Marina Warner, 'Painted Devils and Aery Nothings: Metamorphoses and Magic Art' in *Shakespeare and the Mediterranean*, ed. Tom Clayton et al. (Newark, DE, 2004), 308–31

Watson   Robert N. Watson, 'The Ecology of Self in *Midsummer Night's Dream*' in *Ecocritical Shakespeare*, ed. Lynne Bruckner and Dan Brayton (Burlington, VT, 2011), 33–56

Weimann   Robert Weimann, *Shakespeare and the Popular Tradition in the Theater* (Baltimore, MD, 1978)

Weis   William Shakespeare, *Romeo and Juliet*, ed. René Weis, Arden Shakespeare, 3rd series (2012)

Wells, 'Revisited'   Stanley Wells, '*A Midsummer Night's Dream* Revisited', *Critical Survey*, 3 (1991), 14–29

Wells and Taylor, *Modernizing*   Stanley Wells and Gary Taylor, *Modernizing Shakespeare's Spelling* (Oxford, 1979)

Werstine, *Manuscripts*   Paul Werstine, *Early Modern Playhouse Manuscripts and the Editing of Shakespeare* (Cambridge, 2013)

Werstine, 'Narratives'   Paul Werstine, 'Narratives about Printed Shakespeare Texts: "Foul Papers" and "Bad" Quartos', *SQ* 41 (1990), 65–86

Werstine, 'Science'   Paul Werstine, 'The Science of Editing' in *A Concise Companion to Shakespeare and the Text*, ed. Andrew Murphy (Malden, MA, 2007), 109–27

Werstine, 'Suggestion'   Paul Werstine, 'McKerrow's "Suggestion" and W.W. Greg' in *Speech-Headings*, 11–16

Whiter   Walter Whiter, *A Specimen of a Commentary on Shakespeare*, ed. Alan Over and Mary Bell (1967)

Wiggins   Martin Wiggins, *British Drama 1533–1642: A Catalogue*, 7 vols (in progress: Oxford, 2012–)

Wilder   Lina Perkins Wilder, 'Changeling Bottom: Speech Prefixes, Acting, and Character in *A Midsummer Night's Dream*', *Shakespeare*, 4 (2008), 41–58

Wiles, *Almanac*   David Wiles, *Shakespeare's Almanac* (Cambridge, 1993)

Wiles, *Clown*   David Wiles, *Shakespeare's Clown* (Cambridge, 1987)

Williams   Gordon Williams, *A Dictionary of Sexual Language and Imagery in Shakespearean and Stuart Literature*, 3 vols (1994)

Williams, *Revels*   Gary Jay Williams, *Our Moonlight Revels:* A
                              Midsummer Night's Dream *in the Theatre*
                              (Iowa City, IA, 1997)
Williams, 'Tensions'   Penry Williams, 'Shakespeare's *A Midsummer
                              Night's Dream*: Social Tensions Contained' in
                              The Theatrical City, ed. David L. Smith et al.
                              (Cambridge, 1995), 55–66
Wilson, *Rule*   Thomas Wilson, *The Rule of Reason*, 3rd edn
                              (1580)
Wilson, 'Spellings'   J. Dover Wilson, 'The Spellings of the Three
                              Pages [of *Sir Thomas More*], with Parallels
                              from the Quartos', in Alfred W. Pollard et al.,
                              *Shakespeare's Hand in the Play of Sir Thomas
                              More* (Cambridge, 1923), 132–41
Wily   *Wily Beguiled, 1606*, ed. W.W. Greg, Malone
                              Society Reprints (Oxford, 1912)
Wind   Edgar Wind, *Pagan Mysteries in the
                              Renaissance*, rev. edn (Harmondsworth, 1967)
Wright, 'Amazons'   Celeste Turner Wright, 'The Amazons in
                              Elizabethan Literature', *SP* 37 (1940), 433–56
Yates   Frances A. Yates, *Astraea: The Imperial
                              Theme in the Sixteenth Century* (1975;
                              Harmondsworth, 1977)
Young   David P. Young, *Something of Great
                              Constancy: The Art of 'A Midsummer Night's
                              Dream'* (New Haven, CT, 1966)

INDEX

This index covers the Introduction, the commentary notes and the Appendices; it excludes the textual notes and references to the *OED*. The abbreviation 'n.' is used only for footnotes in the Introduction and Appendices; it is not used for commentary notes. Italic numbers refer to page numbers of the illustrations.

Index